Frommer's®

Nashville & Memphis

10th Edition

by Linda Romine

WILEY

John Wiley & Sons, Inc.

ABOUT THE AUTHOR

Linda Romine has been a professional writer for nearly 2 decades. With a background in music, she has worked on the editorial staffs of various newspapers and magazines as a reporter, music critic, travel editor, and restaurant reviewer.

Published by:

JOHN WILEY & SONS, INC.

111 River St.
Hoboken, NJ 07030-5774

ISBN 978-1-118-08603-2 (paper); ISBN 978-1-118-22332-1 (ebk); ISBN 978-1-118-23670-3 (ebk); ISBN 978-1-118-26164-4 (ebk)

Editor: Ian Skinnari
Production Editor: Katie Robinson
Cartographer: Guy Ruggiero
Photo Editor: Richard Fox
Production by Wiley Indianapolis Composition Services

Front Cover Photo: Elvis Presley memorial statue in Memphis ©Michael Ventura / Alamy Images
Back Cover Photo: Neon signs along Lower Broadway in Nashville ©Brian Jannsen / Alamy Images

For information on our other products and services or to obtain technical support, please contact our Customer Care Department within the U.S. at 877/762-2974, outside the U.S. at 317/572-3993 or fax 317/572-4002.

Wiley also publishes its books in a variety of electronic formats. Some content that appears in print may not be available in electronic formats.

Manufactured in the United States of America

5 4 3 2 1

CONTENTS

18 SIDE TRIPS FROM MEMPHIS 244

19 PLANNING YOUR TRIP TO NASHVILLE & MEMPHIS 251

Index 268

LIST OF MAPS

HOW TO CONTACT US

In researching this book, we discovered many wonderful places—hotels, restaurants, shops, and more. We're sure you'll find others. Please tell us about them, so we can share the information with your fellow travelers in upcoming editions. If you were disappointed with a recommendation, we'd love to know that, too. Please write to:

Frommer's Nashville & Memphis, 10th Edition
John Wiley & Sons, Inc. • 111 River St. • Hoboken, NJ 07030-5774
frommersfeedback@wiley.com

ADVISORY & DISCLAIMER

Travel information can change quickly and unexpectedly, and we strongly advise you to confirm important details locally before traveling, including information on visas, health and safety, traffic and transport, accommodations, shopping, and eating out. We also encourage you to stay alert while traveling and to remain aware of your surroundings. Avoid civil disturbances, and keep a close eye on cameras, purses, wallets, and other valuables.

While we have endeavored to ensure that the information contained within this guide is accurate and up-to-date at the time of publication, we make no representations or warranties with respect to the accuracy or completeness of the contents of this work and specifically disclaim all warranties, including without limitation warranties of fitness for a particular purpose. We accept no responsibility or liability for any inaccuracy or errors or omissions, or for any inconvenience, loss, damage, costs, or expenses of any nature whatsoever incurred or suffered by anyone as a result of any advice or information contained in this guide.

The inclusion of a company, organization, or website in this guide as a service provider and/or potential source of further information does not mean that we endorse them or the information they provide. Be aware that information provided through some websites may be unreliable and can change without notice. Neither the publisher nor author shall be liable for any damages arising herefrom.

FROMMER'S STAR RATINGS, ICONS & ABBREVIATIONS

Every hotel, restaurant, and attraction listing in this guide has been ranked for quality, value, service, amenities, and special features using a **star-rating system.** In country, state, and regional guides, we also rate towns and regions to help you narrow down your choices and budget your time accordingly. Hotels and restaurants are rated on a scale of zero (recommended) to three stars (exceptional). Attractions, shopping, nightlife, towns, and regions are rated according to the following scale: zero stars (recommended), one star (highly recommended), two stars (very highly recommended), and three stars (must-see).

In addition to the star-rating system, we also use **seven feature icons** that point you to the great deals, in-the-know advice, and unique experiences that separate travelers from tourists. Throughout the book, look for:

- Special finds—those places only insiders know about

- Fun facts—details that make travelers more informed and their trips more fun

- Best bets for kids and advice for the whole family

- Special moments—those experiences that memories are made of

- Places or experiences not worth your time or money

- Insider tips—great ways to save time and money

- Great values—where to get the best deals

The following **abbreviations** are used for credit cards:

AE	American Express	**DISC**	Discover	**V**	Visa
DC	Diners Club	**MC**	MasterCard		

TRAVEL RESOURCES AT FROMMERS.COM

Frommer's travel resources don't end with this guide. Frommer's website, **www.frommers. com,** has travel information on more than 4,000 destinations. We update features regularly, giving you access to the most current trip-planning information and the best airfare, lodging, and car-rental bargains. You can also listen to podcasts, connect with other Frommers.com members through our active-reader forums, share your travel photos, read blogs from guide-book editors and fellow travelers, and much more.

THE BEST OF NASHVILLE

Combining small-town warmth with an unexpected urban sophistication, Nashville is a friendly and prosperous Southern city with lots to love. In downtown's decades-old honky-tonks, where the air reeks of stale beer and cigarettes, live country music and bluegrass play day and night. Art museums, antebellum mansions, and a glittering new symphony hall offer cultural pursuits. Excellent restaurants, down-home diners, and chic cocktail lounges have earned national acclaim. Then there's the natural beauty of this place. Nashville's eye-catching skyline is ringed by lovely countryside with wooded hillsides, picturesque farms, and scenic rivers and lakes.

Things to Do Immerse yourself in the endlessly entertaining multimedia presentations at the **Country Music Hall of Fame and Museum.** Take your time, pausing to listen to scratchy, old recordings from Appalachian fiddlers, gaze at photo murals, and watch video performances by country music pioneers ranging from the Carter Family and Kitty Wells to George Strait and Taylor Swift. Then visit **Historic RCA Studio B** on nearby Music Row to see where Dolly Parton, Porter Wagoner, and the Everly Brothers cut 1960s hits that helped define the Nashville Sound, and where Elvis recorded "Are You Lonesome Tonight?"

Historic Sites Delve deep into Nashville's Old South heritage by visiting grand, 19th-century estates, including **Belle Meade Plantation,** whose wealthy owners bred some of the world's best thoroughbred horses; and former U.S. President Andrew Jackson's mansion and farm, **The Hermitage.** Brace yourself for a bone-chilling visit to Franklin's **Carnton Plantation,** where bloodstains are still visible from the Civil War battle that turned this stately home into a field hospital for wounded and dying soldiers.

Eating & Drinking Macaroni and cheese is considered a vegetable here, so loosen your belt to make room for satisfying "meat-and-three" meals at places like **Arnold's Country Kitchen** and **Monell's.** Sample some of the city's newest farm-to-fork restaurants specializing in locally sourced organic foods, including **The Silly Goose, tayst,** and **Burger Up.** Or hang with the hipsters over inventive cuisine and cocktails at former *Top Chef* contestant Arnold Myint's **ChaChah** and **Suzy Wong's House of Yum.**

Nightlife & Entertainment Be on the lookout for country music stars and recording industry insiders at locally owned restaurants and upscale watering holes such as **Sunset Grill** and **City House,** or go hear some live music: Jazz at **F. Scott's,** emerging singer-songwriters at listening rooms like **The Bluebird Café,** or rock and alternative country at venues including **The Basement** and **Exit/In.**

THE most unforgettable
NASHVILLE EXPERIENCES

- **Catching a Concert at the Ryman:** Worship at the altar of the "Mother Church of Country Music," the Ryman Auditorium, by attending a live performance in the 1890s tabernacle with the hard wooden pews and stained-glass windows. Whether it's Emmylou Harris or the Flaming Lips up there on the hallowed stage, try to imagine Ernest Tubb or Patsy Cline in their heyday, standing in the smoke-filled spotlight during the *Grand Ole Opry* radio broadcasts that originated here. See p. 97.

- **Goin' Honky-Tonkin':** Make like Hank Williams's 1947 hit song and do some honky-tonkin' along the legendary bars of Lower Broadway. Weathered dives like **Tootsie's Orchid Lounge** (p. 100) and **Robert's Western World** (p. 97) are seeping with old Nashville authenticity. Grab a bar stool or vie for standing room to hear the city's best singers and guitar slingers rock the house for tip money.

- **Searching for the Perfect Pair of Cowboy Boots:** You've arrived in Music City wearing flip-flops or flats, but you realize that any serious barhopping should take a back seat to boot shopping. Get your kicks trying on snakeskin, leather, buckled, and fringed styles with pointy, squared, or rounded toes as you search through shops like **Opry Originals** (p. 94) and **Betty Boots** (p. 93).

- **Getting Festive:** Wear something red and join the parade at the crazy **Tomato Art Festival** in East Nashville, or get tickets to the **Americana Music Festival and Conference Awards** to sit in on a televised show featuring performances by roots-music acts like the Avett Brothers, Alison Krauss, and the Civil Wars. Get up close and personal with your idols at meet-and-greet sessions held during the **Country Music Awards (CMA) Fest,** or better yet, bring your banjo and join a jam session at the **International Bluegrass Music Association**'s fall gathering. See "Calendar of Events," in chapter 2, for details.

- **Feasting on Southern Food:** You're no longer a visitor after your first meal at **Monell's,** an antiques-filled Victorian home. Once you belly up to the long, cloth-covered table loaded with bowls of mashed potatoes and green beans, baskets of hot cornbread, and platters of fried meats, the family-style Sunday supper experience makes it abundantly clear: You're home. See p. 68.

THE most unforgettable
FOOD & DRINK EXPERIENCES

- **Sopping Up Biscuits and Gravy:** Enjoy the inevitable wait for a table at the world-famous **Loveless Café,** a nostalgic country outpost that serves the best ham biscuits and red-eye gravy in town. Browse the barnyard gift shops for Loveless-brand fruit jams and cured hams and for distinctive souvenirs like "biscuit-love" bumper stickers and "bacon-strip" Band-Aids. See p. 73.

- **Sacrificing Comfort for Some Serious Soul Food:** You know that the spicy fried chicken's hot when the first bite makes you break out in a sweat. Mop your brow and power through it to experience the full-flavored, fiery deliciousness that has made a sojourn to **Prince's Hot Chicken Shack** a must for hard-core foodies. See p. 80.

o **Admiring the Views:** Whether dining on such dishes as shrimp bisque and bourbon-glazed quail at **Watermark** (p. 63) or feasting on plum pork or garlic-marinated beef tenderloin at **Germantown Café** (p. 68), you can savor spectacular views of the Nashville skyline. Book your table for dusk or after dark, when the distant city lights are especially stunning.

o **Sipping Craft Cocktails:** Slip into the clandestine **Patterson House** and bask in the vaguely Belle Epoque–ish ambience as dapper mixologists fuss over craft cocktails like the classic Pim's Cup, rose-infused Juliet & Romeo, and mysterious, absinthe-laced drinks. See p. 97.

o **Drinking Up the Atmosphere:** Order an expensive bottle of red wine—or a Bud Light and a glass. Either way, the indulgence will feel as tangible as you descend into the rich **Oak Bar** in the lower level of the historic, Beaux Arts **Hermitage Hotel.** You could be here for a power lunch or for a little deal-making at happy hour, or just relaxing over a cocktail. And whether you're male or female, you're encouraged to take a peek at one of the bar's top draws—its Art Deco men's room. See p. 112.

THE best ACTIVITIES FOR FAMILIES

o **Walkin' on the Wild Side:** Visit leopard cubs Rajasi, Yim, and Lisu at the 80-acre **Nashville Zoo at Grassmere,** and take the slow-moving, open-air train through the 80-acre attraction for behind-the-scenes glimpses of the zoo's elephants, giraffes, alligators, and pink flamingos. Top it all off with a carousel ride and a visit to the Jungle Gym playground. See p. 46.

o **Attending the Grand Ole Opry:** Take your kids, and maybe even your parents or grandparents, to a performance of *The Grand Ole Opry* out in Music Valley. Between short sets by country stars of yesterday and today, get into the act for audience participation bits as the radio announcers work the crowd, eliciting applause and laughter at the fast-paced, family-oriented, and often patriotic shows. See p. 101.

o **Scaling the Dragon:** When your car slows at the curb of **Fannie Mae Dees Park** and your kids eye the giant, serpentine sea dragon on the playground, let them run toward it and jump on. Climbing the colorful, mosaic sculpture has been a cherished childhood ritual for generations of Nashville residents. See p. 47.

o **Getting Crafty:** Be creative with paper, scissors, markers, and glue in the **Martin ArtQuest Gallery** at the **Frist Center for the Visual Arts.** Encourage your kids to explore a range of art experiences through more than 30 interactive multimedia stations, before walking with them through the Art Deco museum's multilevel galleries. See p. 43.

o **Going for Ice Cream:** Hot and tired after letting the kids romp in the park or explore museums and the zoo? It's time to treat the brood to ice cream at an old-fashioned parlor like **Elliston Place Soda Shop** (p. 74) or burger drive-in **Bobbie's Dairy Dip** (p. 74). At East Nashville's **Pied Piper Creamery** (p. 79) you can lick your ice-cream cones from the comfort of the turn-of-the-century house's big front porch. Or Mexican popsicles are another option, at wildly popular **Las Paletas** (p. 66) in 12South.

THE best FREE & DIRT CHEAP NASHVILLE

o **Guitar Shopping:** You don't have to be in the market for a 1953 Les Paul or a 1938 Martin D-28 to do a little cost-free daydreaming at **Gruhn Guitars.** Nashville's largest guitar dealer sells new and vintage fretted instruments including mandolins, dobros, and banjos. Pretend you're one of their VIP customers (let's say, Eric Clapton or Elvis Costello) as you admire Gruhn's world-renowned goods without spending a penny. See p. 93.

o **Picnicking in the Park:** Spread a blanket in the grass, open up your picnic basket, and relish the lush, natural beauty of **Percy Warner Park.** Stroll or bike your way around this crown jewel of Nashville green spaces, where wooded hills and grassy meadows encompass more than 2,000 acres. See p. 44.

o **Marveling at Masterpieces:** Walking through the **Fisk University** campus, founded in 1866 to educate freed slaves, you may be amazed at the cultural riches waiting inside the Carl Van Vechten Art Gallery: Masterpiece paintings by Renoir, Cézanne, Picasso, Toulouse-Lautrec, and O'Keeffe, part of the Alfred Stieglitz Collection. See p. 42.

o **Comparing Cool Record Stores:** As you're flipping through the cramped vinyl album stacks and CD racks for music by Cage the Elephant or the Louvin Brothers, you immediately understand why **Grimey's New & Preloved Music** (p. 92) is regarded as *the* best record store in town. That is, until later, when you're standing in Jack White's **Third Man Records** (p. 92) mulling the purchase of a turntable on which to play the latest Black Belles record or White Stripes reissue. Someone drops a quarter in the surreal "Monkey Machine" jukebox, and then you're torn.

o **Taking Advantage of Free Performances:** If you're visiting Nashville with champagne tastes and a beer budget, you're in luck. You can see big-name headliners perform, free, at many seasonal festivals and outdoor events. A couple of examples: Arena country-rock acts such as Keith Urban and Lady Antebellum headline star-studded performances at the Tennessee Titans' LP Field each June, and throughout the summer, Musicians Corner stages family-friendly live music and jam sessions on Saturdays at **Centennial Park.** See p. 44.

THE best LOCAL EXPERIENCES

o **Hanging Out in East Nashville:** Do brunch at casual **Margot Café** (p. 76) if you want to converse with locals while feasting on sumptuous, country-French dishes. (Make a reservation first.) Browse for one-of-a-kind gifts at **Art & Invention Gallery** (p. 85) just up the street, or go for dinner or drinks at quirky eateries like **The Wild Cow** (p. 80) and **Family Wash** (p. 105).

o **Patronizing the Arts:** Experience the excellent acoustics and architectural splendor of the **Schermerhorn Symphony Center,** a world-class, jewel-box of a concert hall where the Grammy Award-winning Nashville Symphony Orchestra performs. Hobnob with city philanthropists at one of the frequent benefit performances for local charities, when guest soloists might be Yo Yo Ma, Bela Fleck, or even Wynonna Judd. See p. 108.

- **Supporting Independent Bookstores:** Endear yourself to bestselling author and Nashville resident Anne Patchett by visiting **Parnassus,** her new bookstore in the Green Hills area. Chat up the literate, friendly staff to help you choose the perfect read, and then buy it in hardback, paperback, or electronic edition. See p. 86.

- **Rooting for the Home Team:** Thrill to the roar of the crowd as you're one among the tens of thousands of football fans inside LP Field during a home game by the NFL's **Tennessee Titans.** Feel the pride and camaraderie after a hard-won overtime victory, as downtown Nashville turns into one big block party. See p. 109.

- **Going Acoustic at The Station Inn:** It's Monday night, and that means the country-swing band the Time Jumpers is playing their weekly gig at **The Station Inn** (p. 100). The ugly cinder block building has become a Nashville institution where acoustic acts like the Grascals and Nashville Bluegrass Band entertain nightly. While the tourists are getting rowdy in the honky-tonks or line dancing at the **Wildhorse Saloon** (p. 100), you can relax with other musical purists in this comfortable, no-frills venue.

NASHVILLE IN DEPTH

Though Nashville's fortunes aren't exclusively those of the country music industry, the city is inextricably linked to its music. These days, country music is a $2-billion-a-year industry enjoying greater popularity than ever before. On any given night of the week downtown, you can hear live music in clubs and bars—and not all of the music is country music and bluegrass. There are clubs, cafes, and serious listening rooms for blues, rock, soul, jazz, hip-hop, and folk music, not to mention a bier hall for German polka tunes.

Nashville also has its share of shopping malls, stadiums, and arenas, but it is music that drives this city. Nashville delights not only fans of country music but just about anyone who enjoys a night on the town.

THE NASHVILLE SOUND

Music is everywhere in Nashville. You can hardly walk down a street here without hearing the strains of a country melody. In bars, in restaurants, in hotel lobbies, in the airport, and on the street corners, country musicians sing out in hopes that they, too, might be discovered and become the next big name. Nashville's reputation as Music City attracts thousands of hopeful musicians and songwriters every year, and though very few of them make it to the big time, they provide the music fan with myriad opportunities to hear the occasional great, undiscovered performer. Keep your ears tuned to the music that's the pulse of Nashville, and one day you just might be able to say, "I heard her when she was a no-name playing at a dive bar in Nashville, years ago."

As early as 1871, a Nashville musical group, the Fisk University Jubilee Singers, had traveled to Europe to sing African-American spirituals. By 1902, the city had its first music publisher, the Benson Company; and today, Nashville remains an important center for gospel music. Despite the fact that this musical tradition has long been overshadowed by country music, there are still numerous gospel-music festivals throughout the year in Nashville.

The history of Nashville in the 20th century is, for the most part and for most people, the history of country music. Though traditional fiddle music, often played at dances, had been a part of the Tennessee scene

ECLECTIC playlist FOR NASHVILLE/ TENNESSEE TRAVEL

"The Brand New Tennessee Waltz"	**Joan Baez**
"Pete the Best Coon Dog in Tennessee"	**Jimmy Martin**
"East Nashville Easter"	**Yonder Mountain String Band**
"Killing Time in Nashville"	**The Lost Cartographers**
"Nashville"	**Indigo Girls**
"Nashville"	**Liz Phair**
"Nashville Blues"	**The Louvin Brothers**
"Nashville Casualty & Life"	**Kinky Friedman**
"Nashville Cats"	**The Kingston Trio**
"Nashville Moon"	**Charlie Daniels Band**
"Nashville Parent"	**Lambchop**
"Nashville Pickin'"	**Doc Watson**
"The Nashville Scene"	**Hank Williams, Jr.**
"Nashville Shores"	**Jemima Pearl**
"Nashville Skyline"	**Dishwalla**
"Nashville Skyline Rag"	**Bob Dylan**
"Nashville Tears"	**John Anderson**
"Nashville Toupee"	**Southern Culture on the Skids**
"Nashville West"	**The Byrds**
"Nashville Woman's Blues"	**Bessie Smith**
"South Nashville Blues"	**Steve Earle**
"Tennessee"	**Arrested Development**
"Tennessee"	**BadMonkey**
"Tennessee"	**NRBQ**
"Tennessee"	**Carl Perkins**
"Tennessee"	**The Shakes**
"Tennessee"	**Shawn Colvin**
"Tennessee Blues"	**Clarence "Gatemouth" Brown**
"Tennessee Courage"	**Vern Gosdin**
"The Tennessee Jump"	**Chet Atkins**
"Tennessee Line"	**Daughtry**
"Tennessee Pusher"	**Old Crow Medicine Show**
"Tennessee Toddy"	**Marty Robbins**
"Tennessee Twister"	**Bob James and the Bob Cats**
"Tennessee Waltz"	**Les Paul and Mary Ford**
"Tennessee Waltz"	**Norah Jones**
"Tennessee Waltz"	**Otis Redding**
"Tennessee Waltz/Tennessee Mazurka"	**The Chieftains**
"Tennessee Whiskey"	**David Allan Coe**
"Tennessee Woman"	**Charlie Musselwhite**

Big Business

Nashville's economy is diversified. Scores of well-known corporations and associations have their headquarters and/or other major facilities in the area. These include BellSouth, Broadcast Music Inc. (BMI), Bridgestone/Firestone, Caterpillar Financial, Dell, Gibson Guitar Corp./Baldwin Pianos, Dollar General, Lifeway Christian Resources, National Federation of Independent Business, Nissan Motor Manufacturing USA, O'Charley's Inc., and Tractor Supply Co.

from the arrival of the very first settlers, it was not until the early 20th century that people outside the hills and mountains began to pay attention to this "hillbilly" music.

In 1925, radio station WSM-AM went on the air and began broadcasting a show called The *WSM Barn Dance,* which featured live performances of country music. Two years later, it renamed the show the *Grand Ole Opry,* a program that has been on the air ever since, and is the longest-running radio show in the country. The same year that the *Grand Ole Opry* began, Victor Records sent a recording engineer to Tennessee to record the traditional country music of the South. These recordings helped expose this music to a much wider audience than it had ever had, and interest in country music began to grow throughout the South and across the nation.

In 1942, Nashville's first country music publishing house opened, followed by the first recording studio in 1945. By the 1960s, there were more than 100 music publishers in Nashville and dozens of recording studios. The 1950s and early 1960s saw a rapid rise in the popularity of country music, and all the major record companies eventually opened offices here. Leading the industry at this time were brothers Owen and Harold Bradley, who opened the city's first recording studio not affiliated with the *Grand Ole Opry.* CBS and RCA soon followed suit. Many of the industry's biggest and most familiar names first recorded in Nashville at this time, including Patsy Cline, Hank Williams, Brenda Lee, Dottie West, Floyd Cramer, Porter Wagoner, Dolly Parton, Loretta Lynn, George Jones, Tammy Wynette, Elvis Presley, the Everly Brothers, Perry Como, and Connie Francis.

During this period, country music evolved from its "hillbilly music" origins. With growing competition from rock 'n' roll, record producers developed a cleaner, more urban sound for country music. Production values went up and the music took on a new sound, the "Nashville Sound." Today you can tour the old recording studio where many of those hits were recorded—Historic RCA Studio B.

In 1972, the country music–oriented Opryland USA theme park (now supplanted by a shopping mall) opened on the east side of Nashville. In 1974, the *Grand Ole Opry* moved from the downtown Ryman Auditorium, its home of more than 30 years, to the new Grand Ole Opry House just outside the gates of Opryland.

In more recent years, country music has once again adapted to maintain its listenership. While the overproduced, arena-pleasing acts like Brad Paisley, Taylor Swift, and Lady Antebellum thrill the masses, Americana music—a purer blend of rock, folk, and alternative country influences—is becoming increasingly pervasive in Nashville. Artists such as Emmylou Harris, the Avett Brothers, Justin Townes Earl, and the Civil Wars are at the forefront of this growing genre. The annual Americana Music Festival, which takes place in Nashville each October, draws musicians, writers, industry executives, and fans from all over the world.

LOOKING BACK AT NASHVILLE

Long before the first Europeans set foot in middle Tennessee, Native Americans populated this region of rolling hills, dense forests, and plentiful grasslands. Large herds of deer and buffalo made the region an excellent hunting ground. However, by the late 18th century, when the first settlers arrived, continuing warfare over access to the area's rich hunting grounds had forced the various battling tribes to move away. Though there were no native villages in the immediate area, this did not eliminate conflicts between Native Americans and settlers.

FRONTIER DAYS   The first Europeans to arrive in middle Tennessee were French fur trappers and traders: Charles Charleville, who established a trading post at a salt lick, and Timothy Demonbreun, who made his home in a cave on a bluff above the Cumberland River. By the middle part of the century, the area that is now Nashville came to be known as French Lick because of the salt lick.

Throughout the middle part of the century, the only other whites to explore the area were so-called long hunters. These hunters got their name from the extended hunting trips, often months long, that they would make over the Appalachian Mountains. They would bring back stacks of buckskins, which at the time sold for $1. Thus, a dollar came to be called a "buck." Among the most famous of the long hunters was Daniel Boone, who may have passed through French Lick in the 1760s.

The Indian Treaty of Lochaber in 1770 and the Transylvania Purchase in 1775 opened up much of the land west of the Appalachians to settlers. Several settlements had already sprung up on Cherokee land in the Appalachians, and these settlements had formed the Watauga Association, a sort of self-government. However, it was not until the late 1770s that the first settlers began to arrive in middle Tennessee. In 1778, James Robertson, a member of the Watauga Association, brought a scouting party to the area in his search for a place to found a new settlement.

The bluffs above the Cumberland River appealed to Robertson, and the following year he returned with a party of settlers. This first group, composed of men only, had traveled through Kentucky and arrived at French Lick on Christmas Eve 1779. The

DATELINE

9000 B.C.	Paleo-Indians inhabit area that is now Nashville.	1772	Watauga Association becomes first form of government west of the Appalachians.
A.D. 1000–1400	Mississippian-period Indians develop advanced society characterized by mound-building and farming.	1775	Transylvania Purchase stimulates settlement in middle Tennessee.
1710	French fur trader Charles Charleville establishes a trading post in the area.	1778	James Robertson scouts the area and decides to found a settlement.
1765	A group of long hunters camp at Mansker's Lick, north of present-day Nashville.	1779	Robertson's first party of settlers arrives on Christmas Eve.

continues

women and children, under the leadership of John Donelson, followed by flatboat, traveling 1,000 miles by river to reach the new settlement and arriving in April 1780. This new settlement of nearly 300 people was named Fort Nashborough, after North Carolinian General Francis Nash. As soon as both parties were assembled at Fort Nashborough, the settlers drew up a charter of government called the Cumberland Compact. This was the first form of government in middle Tennessee.

Fort Nashborough was founded while the Revolutionary War was raging, and these first settlers very soon found themselves battling Cherokee, Choctaw, and Chickasaw Indians—whose attacks were incited by the British. The worst confrontation was the Battle of the Bluffs, which took place in April 1781, when settlers were attacked by a band of Cherokees.

By 1784, the situation had grown quieter, and, in that year, the settlement changed its name from Nashborough to Nashville. Twelve years later, in 1796, Tennessee became the 16th state in the Union. Nashville at that time was still a tiny settlement in a vast wilderness, but in less than 20 years, the nation would know of Nashville through the heroic exploits of one of its citizens.

In 1814, at the close of the War of 1812, Andrew Jackson, a Nashville lawyer, led a contingent of Tennessee militiamen in the Battle of New Orleans. The British were soundly defeated and Jackson became a hero. A political career soon followed, and in 1829, Jackson was elected the seventh president of the United States.

In the early part of the 19th century, the state government bounced back and forth between eastern and middle Tennessee, and was twice seated in Knoxville, once in Murfreesboro, and had once before been located in Nashville before finally staying put on the Cumberland. By 1845, work had begun on constructing a capitol building, which would not be completed until 1859.

THE CIVIL WAR & RECONSTRUCTION   By 1860, when the first rumblings of secession began to be heard across the South, Nashville was a very prosperous city, made wealthy by its importance as a river port. Tennessee reluctantly sided with the Confederacy and became the last state to secede from the Union. This decision sealed Nashville's fate. The city's significance as a shipping port was not lost on either

1780 Second of Robertson's parties of settlers, led by Col. John Donelson, arrives by boat in April; in May, settlement of Nashborough founded.

1781 Battle of the Bluffs fought with Cherokee Indians.

1784 The small settlement's name changed from Nashborough to Nashville.

1796 Tennessee becomes the 16th state.

1814 Andrew Jackson, a Nashville resident, leads the Tennessee militia in the Battle of New Orleans and gains national stature.

1840 Belle Meade plantation home built.

1843 State capital moved from Murfreesboro to Nashville.

1850 Nashville is site of convention held by nine Southern states that jointly assert the right to secede.

1862 Nashville becomes first state capital in the South to fall to Union troops.

1864 Battle of Nashville, last major battle initiated by the Confederate army.

Epic Athena

In 1897, Nashville built a replica of the ancient Greek Parthenon in Centennial Park. Why? With more than a dozen colleges and universities, and a growing reputation as a center of learning and higher education, Nashville earned a reputation as the "Athens of the South." Inside the Nashville Parthenon is a statue of Athena. At 41 feet tall, she's the largest piece of indoor sculpture in the Western World.

the Union or the Confederate army, both of which coveted the city as a means of controlling important river and railroad transportation routes. In February 1862, the Union army occupied Nashville, razing many homes in the process. Thus, Nashville became the first state capital to fall to the Union troops.

Throughout the Civil War, the Confederates repeatedly attempted to reclaim Nashville, but to no avail. In December 1864, the Confederate army made its last stab at retaking Nashville, but during the Battle of Nashville they were roundly rebuffed.

Though the Civil War left Nashville severely damaged and in dire economic straits, the city quickly rebounded. Within a few years, the city had reclaimed its important shipping and trading position and also developed a solid manufacturing base. The post–Civil War years of the late 19th century brought a newfound prosperity to Nashville. These healthy economic times left the city with a legacy of grand classical-style buildings, which can still be seen around the downtown area.

Fisk University, one of the nation's first African-American universities, was founded in 1866. Vanderbilt University was founded in 1873, and in 1876, Meharry Medical College, the country's foremost African-American medical school, was founded. With this proliferation of schools of higher learning, Nashville came to be known as the "Athens of the South."

1866 Fisk University, one of the nation's first African-American universities, founded.	1943 *Grand Ole Opry* moves to Ryman Auditorium, in downtown Nashville.
1873 Vanderbilt University founded.	1944 Nashville's first recording studio begins operation at WSM-AM radio.
1897 The Parthenon built as part of the Nashville Centennial Exposition.	
1920 Nashville becomes center of nation's attention as Tennessee becomes 36th state to give women the vote, thus ratifying the 19th amendment to the U.S. Constitution.	1950s Numerous national record companies open offices and recording studios in Nashville.
	Late 1950s to early 1960s Record company competition and pressure from rock 'n' roll change the sound of country music, giving it a higher production value that comes to be known as the "Nashville Sound."
1925 WSM-AM radio station broadcasts first *Grand Ole Opry* program.	

continues

african-american HISTORY IN NASHVILLE

- Nashvillian **William Edmonson** was the first black artist to be honored with a one-man exhibit at New York's Museum of Modern Art, in 1937. (Today, visitors to Nashville can see his work in a permanent exhibit at Cheekwood Botanical Garden.)

- From the 1940s to the 1960s, **Jefferson Street** was known as the jazz, blues, and R & B district of Nashville. Legendary performers, ranging from Duke Ellington and Ella Fitzgerald to Ray Charles, Little Richard, and Ike and Tina Turner, played in nightclubs (now long gone) such as the Del Morocco and New Era.

- Civil Rights pioneer and lawmaker **John Lewis** was a seminary student in Nashville in February 1960. He helped organize sit-ins at segregated lunch counters across the city.

- **Wilma Rudolph,** a track star with Tennessee State's Tigerbelles, won three gold medals at the 1960 Summer Olympic Games in Rome. Known as the "fastest woman in the world," she was the first American woman to win three gold medals in one Olympics.

- Former Nashville resident **Oprah Winfrey** was a Tennessee State University sophomore when she became the first female and the first African American in Nashville to anchor a local newscast.

- The nation's oldest African American architectural firm, **McKissack & McKissack,** was founded in Nashville.

THE 20TH CENTURY   At the turn of the century, Nashville was firmly established as one of the South's most important cities. This newfound significance had culminated 3 years earlier with the ambitious Tennessee Centennial Exposition of 1897, which left as its legacy to the city Nashville's single-most-endearing structure: a

1972 Opryland USA theme park opens in Nashville.

1974 *Grand Ole Opry* moves to a new theater at the Opryland USA theme park.

1993 Ryman Auditorium closes for a renovation that will make the *Grand Ole Opry's* most famous home an active theater once again.

1994 With the opening of the Wildhorse Saloon and the Hard Rock Cafe, and the reopening of The Ryman Auditorium, Nashville becomes one of the liveliest cities in the South.

1996 Nashville Arena opens in downtown Nashville.

1997 Bicentennial Capitol Mall State Park opens north of state capitol building.

1999 NFL Tennessee Titans move into new Coliseum, and NHL Nashville Predators move into Gaylord Entertainment Center (now Bridgestone Arena) downtown.

2000 Titans take a trip to the Super Bowl as AFC champs. Opry Mills, a 1.2-million-square-foot entertainment and shopping

And the Rest Is History

In 1925, the *WSM Barn Dance* was a popular Saturday-night radio program that followed a broadcast of classical music from New York City. Preparing for the *Barn Dance* program one night, announcer George Hay joked, "For the last hour, we have been listening to music taken largely from grand opera and the classics. We now present our own 'Grand Ole Opry.'" And that's how the *Grand Ole Opry* got its name.

full-size reconstruction of the Parthenon. Though Nashville's Parthenon was meant to last only the duration of the exposition, it proved so popular that the city left it in place. Over the years, the building deteriorated until it was no longer safe to visit. At that point, the city was considering demolishing this last vestige of the Centennial Exposition, but public outcry brought about the reconstruction, with more permanent materials, of the Parthenon.

About the same time the Parthenon was built, trains began using the new Union Station, a Roman-Gothic train station. The station's grand waiting hall was roofed by a stained-glass ceiling, and, with its gilded plasterwork and bas-reliefs, was a symbol of the waning glory days of railroading in America. Today, Union Station has been restored and is one of Nashville's two historic hotels.

In 1920, Tennessee played a prominent role in the passing of the 19th Amendment to the U.S. Constitution, which gave women the right to vote in national elections. As the 36th state to ratify the 19th Amendment, the Tennessee vote became the most crucial battle in the fight for women's suffrage. Surprisingly, both the pro-suffrage and the antisuffrage organizations were headquartered in the Beaux Arts–style Hermitage Hotel. In 1994, this hotel was completely renovated; now known as the Hermitage, it is the city's premier historic hotel.

The 20th century also brought the emergence of country music as a popular musical style. The first recordings of country music came from Tennessee, and though it

complex, rises from the ashes of the demolished Opryland amusement park.

2001 Two new world-class venues open downtown: the Frist Center for the Visual Arts and the Country Music Hall of Fame and Museum. The Country Music Association (CMA) Fest (formerly known as Fan Fair) moves from its longtime home at the Tennessee State Fairgrounds to downtown Nashville.

2005 Centennial Park, a 132-acre green oasis and home to the Parthenon in Nashville's West End, becomes one of the first parks in the U.S. to get wireless Internet access.

2006 Nashville celebrates its bicentennial. The Schermerhorn Symphony Center, modeled after the ornate concert halls of Old Europe, opens downtown.

2009 Nashville's Gulch neighborhood is the first in the South to receive "LEED for Neighborhood Development" (LEED ND) certification.

continues

took a quarter of a century for "hillbilly" music to catch on, by 1945 Nashville found itself at the center of the country music industry. The city embraced this new industry and has not looked back since.

THE LAY OF THE LAND

Nashville has a striking skyline, with its mix of new high-rises and historic buildings. Incidentally, the skyscraper with the pointy-looking "ears" belongs to AT&T, but locals call it like they see it (the Batman Building). Although downtown Nashville was built around the Cumberland River, the city's sprawl extends for miles in all directions. Outlying areas include beautiful farmland, scenic parks and lakes, and rolling foothills that hint of the Appalachians in the eastern part of the state.

NASHVILLE IN FILM, TV & MUSIC

Music City's place in pop-culture history was forever sealed with television's long-running musical-comedy program *Hee Haw*. Hosted by country entertainers Buck Owens and Roy Clark, the corny weekly variety show was filmed in Nashville and featured all the greats of the 1960s and 1970s. If that was before your time, you can still check out DVDs of the popular program.

Kids' Play

The Nashville Children's Theatre, renowned for the high quality of its productions, is the oldest children's theater in the U.S.

Television retains a huge presence here, as The Nashville Network (TNN), Country Music Television (CMT), and Great American Country (GAC) continue to showcase the area's Southern charms. In addition, Nashville entertainer Bobby Jones hosts his self-titled gospel music show on BET (Black Entertainment Television). It has become the longest-running show at that network.

2010 Devastating spring floods leave much of Nashville underwater, destroying homes and businesses, including Opry Mills, and damaging the Grand Ole Opry House (which is restored and reopens the same year).

2011 The National Folk Festival, the longest-running annual music festival of its kind in the U.S., comes to Nashville. The free Labor Day Weekend event returns to Nashville in 2012 and 2013.

2012 Dolly Parton's Dollywood Company and Gaylord Entertainment announce a joint-venture to build a 114-acre family entertainment zone adjacent to the Gaylord Opryland Resort & Convention Center in Music Valley. The $50 million water and snow park is expected to break ground in early 2013 and open to the public in the summer of 2014.

Along with its myriad country artists, Nashville is also a burgeoning enclave for big-name talents in other musical genres, including pop, rock, bluegrass, jazz, and especially contemporary Christian music. Rock stars including Bon Jovi, Kid Rock, and R.E.M. have come here to write and record music. In addition to scores of country and bluegrass superstars, musicians as diverse as the Black Keys, Michael McDonald, Donna Summer, and Jack White have homes in Nashville.

With rags-to-riches stories around every corner, Nashville has been the inspiration behind some memorable movies. Over the past 4 decades, there have been several cinematic standouts, beginning with *Nashville* (1975). The late director Robert Altman's comic parody looks at the lives of assorted characters who converge in Music City during the early 1970s. In *Coal Miner's Daughter* (1980), Sissy Spacek earned an Academy Award for her portrayal of Loretta Lynn, a poor Kentucky girl who became one of country music's first female legends. One of my personal favorites, this film is especially appealing in the way it accurately portrays Nashville's heyday in the 1940s and 1950s, when such country pioneers as Hank Williams and others were in their prime.

Another unforgettable biopic is *Sweet Dreams* (1985). Jessica Lange plays music star Patsy Cline. The film follows the singer's tumultuous marriage and short-lived career. Cline was killed in a plane crash at the height of her fame.

Another, lesser-known country-music coming-of-age story that has held up pretty well over the years is *The Thing Called Love* (1993). Directed by Peter Bogdanovich and starring Samantha Mathis (and a then-unknown Sandra Bullock), it's perhaps best remembered as the last movie made by the promising young actor River Phoenix, who died shortly thereafter.

Sibling Joaquin Phoenix struck box office gold more than a decade later with another big-budget blockbuster, *Walk the Line*. In that Oscar-winning musical biography, Phoenix channels the "Man in Black," Johnny Cash, who was born in Arkansas, launched his career at Sun Records in Memphis, and became one of Nashville's most outspoken entertainers. Nashville native Reese Witherspoon portrays his wife, June Carter Cash, for which she won an Oscar.

In 2011, Gwyneth Paltrow threw herself into the sudsy melodrama about a country singer who drops out of rehab to pursue a comeback. The heavily promoted movie, *Country Strong*, co-starred Leighton Meester, Garrett Hedlund, and Nashville's Tim McGraw—who also earned acting accolades opposite Sandra Bullock in 2010's *The Blind Side*.

If you're looking for the real deal instead of actor portrayals and period pieces, I recommend *Down from the Mountain* (2000), an acclaimed documentary that showcases musicians featured in the soundtrack to the Coen Brothers' *O Brother, Where Art Thou?* starring Kentucky native George Clooney. Performances and interviews by Ralph Stanley, Emmylou Harris, and many others are featured.

Last, and perhaps least expected among the movies filmed in Nashville, is *The Green Mile* (1999), starring Tom Hanks. Novelist Stephen King's gripping story focuses on death row guards at a penitentiary in the 1930s.

EATING & DRINKING IN NASHVILLE

Although still known and loved for its Southern traditions, including sweet iced tea and plate-lunch specials known as the "meat-and-three" (an entree with sides),

Nashville has stretched its culinary wings in recent years. With noted up-and-coming chefs, nationally recognized restaurants, and an array of bistros, cafes, and ethnic eateries throughout the metro area, the dining scene is more sophisticated and diverse than you might expect.

Chain restaurants are everywhere these days, but Nashville has plenty of great, locally owned, independent eateries. With consistent food and service, they have been able to build loyal clientele while attracting tourists as well. For food lovers, Nashville is a tempting mix that could have you starting your day with biscuits and sausage gravy, sampling sushi at lunch, and feasting on German sauerbraten at supper.

Drinking in Nashville can be equally adventurous. The city boasts an eclectic blend of beer dives, microbreweries, trendy cocktail spots, and gourmet restaurants with extensive wine lists. The hard stuff is also a point of pride. After all, this is Jack Daniel's and George Dickel country (p. 134). Those two nearby historic whiskey distilleries draw their fair share of tourists, and their products are prominently featured on many restaurant and bar menus throughout the region and beyond.

WHEN TO GO

Summer is the peak tourist season in Nashville. Unless you're specifically visiting Nashville for the CMA Fest in June, you might want to avoid traveling during this time, when hotels sell out and prices go through the roof.

Summer is also when both Nashville and Memphis experience their worst weather. During July and August, and often in September, temperatures can hover around 100°F, with humidity at close to 100%. (Can you say "muggy"?) Spring and fall, however, last for several months and both are quite pleasant. Days are often warm and nights cool, though during these two seasons the weather changes, so bring a variety of clothes. Heavy rains can hit any time of year, and if you spend more than 3 or 4 days in town, you can almost bet on seeing some rain. Winters can be cold, with daytime temperatures staying below freezing, and snow is not unknown.

> ## Impressions
>
> *Take of London fog 30 parts; malaria 10 parts; gas leaks 20 parts; dewdrops gathered in a brickyard at sunrise 25 parts; odor of honeysuckle 15 parts. Mix. The mixture will give you an approximate conception of a Nashville drizzle.*
> —O. Henry, "A Municipal Report," in *Strictly Business,* 1910

Average Temperature & Rainfall in Nashville

	JAN	FEB	MAR	APR	MAY	JUNE	JULY	AUG	SEPT	OCT	NOV	DEC
Temp. (°F)	38	41	50	60	68	76	80	79	72	61	49	41
Temp. (°C)	3	5	10	16	20	24	27	26	22	16	9	5
Rainfall (in.)	4.3	4.2	5	4	4.6	3.8	3.8	3.3	3.4	2.7	3.9	4.6

Nashville Calendar of Events

For an exhaustive list of events beyond those listed here, check http://events.frommers.com, where you'll find a searchable, up-to-the-minute roster of what's happening in cities all over the world.

JANUARY

Nashville Auto Fest, Tennessee State Fairgrounds. This swap meet and car show includes a Sunday church service with the Christian Hot Rod Association (© **502/893-6731;** www.nashvilleautofest.com). Third weekend of January.

Stellar Gospel Music Awards, Grand Ole Opry House. Gospel's premier artists are recognized at this awards show (© **312/654-1100;** www.thestellarawards.com). Mid-January.

FEBRUARY

Antiques and Gardens Show of Nashville, Nashville Convention Center. Renowned experts exhibit antiques, decorative arts, and landscape designs (© **615/352-9064;** www.antiquesandgardenshow.com). Mid-February.

Heart of Country Antique Show, Gaylord Opryland Resort and Convention Center. Lectures, exhibitions, and free appraisals from more than 200 antiques dealers specializing in American art, furniture, porcelain, quilts, wood, and glass take place (© **314/962-8580;** www.heartofcountry.com). Early February.

Music City Soul Series, B.B. King's Blues Club. This Black History Month event showcases performances by Nashville's best musicians every Thursday night (© **615/256-2727;** www.bbkingclubs.com). All month.

MARCH

Nashville Lawn & Garden Show, Tennessee State Fairgrounds. An acre of live gardens and 250 exhibit booths are included (© **615/876-7680;** www.nashvillelawnandgardenshow.com). Early March.

"AWESOME APRIL"

The **Tin Pan South** songwriters' festival and the **Music City Walk of Fame Induction Ceremony** take place in this action-packed month, when Nashville weather is at its prettiest. Also on tap are the **Nashville Film Festival** and the **Country Music Marathon,** where 50 bands play on 27 entertainment stages throughout the course. For more detailed information on each of these events, and for tour packages and tickets,

contact the Nashville Convention and Visitors Bureau (© **800/657-6910;** www.visitmusiccity.com). All month.

MAY

Tennessee Renaissance Festival, in Triune (20 miles south of downtown Nashville). Maidens, knights, gypsies, jugglers, jousters, games, and food—think whole turkey legs that you can eat like a barbarian—are some of the diversions you'll find at this medieval fair held on the grounds of the **Castle Gwynn** (© 615/395-9950; www.tnrenfest. com). Weekends in May, including Memorial Day.

Tennessee Craft Fair, Centennial Park. With the largest display of Tennessee crafts, this fair opens the summer season. Food, demonstrations, and children's craft activities are part of the fun (© **615/385-1904;** www. tennesseecrafts.org). Early May.

Iroquois Steeplechase, Percy Warner Park. This horse race has been a Nashville ritual for more than 50 years. A benefit for Vanderbilt Children's Hospital, the event is accompanied by tailgate picnics (© **615/591-2991;** www.iroquoissteeplechase.org). Second Saturday in May.

JUNE

Bluegrass Nights at the Ryman, Ryman Auditorium. Thursday nights at the historic Ryman Auditorium play host to top-name bluegrass acts such as Alison Krauss and Ricky Skaggs (© **615/889-3060;** www. ryman.com). Thursdays June through July.

CMA (Country Music Association) Music Festival, Nashville Convention Center and other downtown locations. This is a chance for country artists and their fans to meet and greet each other in a weeklong music celebration. Glitzy stage shows and picture/autograph sessions with country music stars are all part of the action. Special events and sightseeing are included in the price of some tickets, along with bluegrass concerts and the Grand Masters Fiddling Championship. Contact the CMA Office (© **615/244-2840;** www.cmaworld.com) for tickets. Four days in mid-June.

Taste of Music City, on the Gateway Pedestrian Bridge. The festival features live jazz from local musicians, and food and wine from area restaurants (📞 **800/657-6910;** www.visitmusiccity.com). First Saturday in June.

JULY

Music City July 4th: Let Freedom Sing! Riverfront Park. This family-oriented, alcohol-free event attracts 100,000 people for entertainment, food, and fireworks. Top-name entertainers, such as Taylor Swift and Wynonna, have headlined the patriotic, televised extravaganza (📞 **800/657-6910;** www.musiccityjuly4th.com). July 4.

AUGUST

Tomato Art Fest, Five Points area, East Nashville. Food, friendly competitions, parades, and lots of tomato-themed arts and crafts are part of this annual event (no telephone; www.tomatoartfest.com). Second Saturday of August.

Fiddlin', Brewin', Bar-B-Q-'n Cook-off, Gaylord Opryland Resort and Convention Center. Barbecue, live music, kids' activities, dessert contests, and beer from Yazoo Brewing Co. converge for this entertainment event (📞 **800/657-6910;** www.visitmusiccity.com). Last weekend of August.

Music City BBQ Festival, Riverfront Park. More than 100 teams compete for honors in this statewide event (📞 **800/657-6910;** www.musiccitybbqfestival.com). Last weekend of August.

Music City Brewers Festival, at Walk of Fame Park. The event features more than 35 brewers from throughout the nation, live music, and food from local restaurants (📞 **800/657-6910;** www.visitmusiccity.com). Last weekend of August.

Tennessee Walking-Horse National Celebration, Celebration Grounds, Shelbyville (40 miles southeast of downtown Nashville). The World Grand Championship of the much-loved Tennessee walking horse; includes trade fairs and dog shows (📞 **931/684-5915;** www.twhnc.com). Late August.

SEPTEMBER

John Merritt Classic, LP Field. Tennessee State University's opening football game is celebrated with a charity golf tournament,

concerts, and special activities (📞 **615/963-5841;** www.merrittclassic.com). Labor Day weekend.

Belle Meade Fall Fest, Belle Meade Plantation. Antiques, crafts, children's festival, garage treasures, and food are for sale (📞 **800/270-3991** or 615/356-0501; www.bellemeadeplantation.com). Mid-September.

African Street Festival, Tennessee State University, main campus. Entertainment includes gospel, R & B, jazz, reggae music, and children's storytelling (📞 **615/251-0007;** www.aacanashville.org). Mid-September.

Soundland presented by Next Big Nashville, various locations. More than 100 of Nashville's best new bands perform at several venues throughout the city (📞 **800/657-6910;** www.nbnsoundland.com). Mid- to late September.

TACA Fall Craft Fair, Centennial Park. This upscale, fine-crafts market features artisans from throughout Tennessee (📞 **615/385-1904;** www.tennesseecrafts.org). Late September.

Wine on the River, on the downtown Shelby Street Pedestrian Bridge. Live jazz event features more than 300 international and domestic wines for tasting (📞 **615/664-2484;** www.wineontheriver.com). Late September.

OCTOBER

Americana Music Festival. More than 1,000 musicians, fans, and industry professionals attend this multiday event, which includes more than 50 showcases featuring established and emerging artists. It culminates with the televised Americana Music Awards show at The Ryman (📞 **615/386-6936;** www.americanamusic.org). Mid-October.

Southern Festival of Books, War Memorial Plaza. Sponsored by the National Endowment for the Humanities, the region's largest, free literary festival is a feast for book lovers. More than 200 authors gather for a variety of special events over 3 days (📞 **615/770-0006;** www.humanitiestennessee.org/programs). Second full weekend in October.

Oktoberfest, Historic Germantown, at the corner of Eighth Avenue North and Monroe Street. The festival includes tours of

Germantown, polka dancing, accordion players, and lots of authentic German food ((℡ **615/256-2729;** www.nashvilleoktober fest.com). Early to mid-October.

Jack Daniel's World Championship Invitational Barbecue, Lynchburg, Tennessee. More than 50 domestic and 18 international teams vie for the title of grand champion ((℡ **877-SPIRITS** (774-7487); www.jackdaniels barbecuemedia.com). Late October.

Native American Indian Association Pow Wow, Long Hunter State Park. Native Americans from the United States and Canada gather for this powwow, sponsored by the Native American Indian Association ((℡ **615/232-9179;** www.naiatn.org/ powwow). Mid-October.

World of Bluegrass: Bluegrass Fan Fest and IBMA Music Awards, Nashville Convention Center. The nation's premier bluegrass fan festival features big-name entertainers performing over 6 days, and includes exhibitions and jam sessions as well as the International Bluegrass Music Awards ((℡ **615/256-3222;** www.ibma.org). Late September or early October.

Grand Ole Opry **Birthday Bash,** Grand Ole Opry House. A 3-day party features performances, autographs, and picture sessions with *Opry* stars. In recent years, the all-star lineup has run the gamut from Ralph Stanley to Alan Jackson ((℡ **615/889-3060;** www. gaylordopryland.com). Mid-October.

Tailgate Antiques Show, Tennessee State Fairgrounds. Dealers selling furniture, folk art, linens, quilts, jewelry, and more are included ((℡ **615/862-8980;** www.music valleyantiquesmarket.com). Late October.

NOVEMBER

Longhorn World Championship Rodeo, Tennessee Miller Coliseum, outside Murfreesboro. Professional cowboys and cowgirls participate in this rodeo to win championship points (no telephone; www. longhornrodeo.com). Third weekend in November.

Christmas at Belmont, Belmont Mansion, Belmont University. The opulent antebellum mansion is decked out in Victorian Christmas finery, and the gift shop is a great place to nab Christmassy Victorian reproductions ((℡ **615/460-5459;** belmontmansion.com). Late November to late December.

A Country Christmas, Gaylord Opryland Resort and Convention Center. More than two million Christmas lights decorate the grounds of the hotel. Musical revues change every few years, with headliners ranging from Pam Tillis and Louise Mandrell to "Charlie Brown" and the Radio City Music Hall Rockettes ((℡ **888/777-OPRY** [6779] or 615/889-1000; www.gaylordhotels.com). November 1 to December 25.

DECEMBER

Franklin American Mortgage Music City Bowl, LP Field. This is an SEC versus ACC rival football game ((℡ **615/743-3130;** www.musiccitybowl.com). Late December.

Bash on Broadway, Lower Broadway. This New Year's Eve celebration includes an 80-foot guitar drop ((℡ **800/657-6910;** www.visit musiccity.com/newyearseve). December 31.

NASHVILLE NEIGHBORHOODS & SUGGESTED ITINERARIES

3

Nashville is spread out, with pockets of interesting neighborhoods, entertainment districts, and shopping areas scattered throughout the metro area, so having a car is important if you want to experience all the city has to offer. However, the downtown area is relatively compact, making it feasible to hit several of Music City's high points right off the bat on your first day in town—and without too much driving. As with any destination, your interests will dictate what you choose to do and see. The itineraries below focus primarily on country music, fine arts, history and culture, and shopping and entertainment. These suggestions can be experienced during any season and regardless of most weather conditions.

NASHVILLE ORIENTATION
Visitor Information

On the baggage-claim level of Nashville International Airport, you'll find the **Airport Welcome Center** (✆ **615/275-1675**), where you can pick up brochures, maps, and bus information, and get answers to any questions you may have about touring the city. This center is open daily from 6:30am to midnight. In downtown Nashville, you'll find the **Nashville Convention & Visitors Bureau Visitors Center,** Fifth Avenue and Broadway (✆ **800/657-6910** or 615/780-9401; www.visitmusiccity. com), the main source of information on the city and surrounding areas. The information center offers free Wi-Fi service and is located at the base of the radio tower of the **Bridgestone Arena,** 501 Broadway (✆ **615/259-4747**), and is open daily during daylight hours. Signs on interstate highways around the downtown area will direct you to the arena. Information is also available from the main office of the **Chamber of Commerce/ Nashville Convention & Visitors Bureau,** in the lower level of the US Bank building at the corner of Fourth Avenue North and Commerce (✆ **615/259-4730**). The office is open Monday to Friday 8am to 5pm.

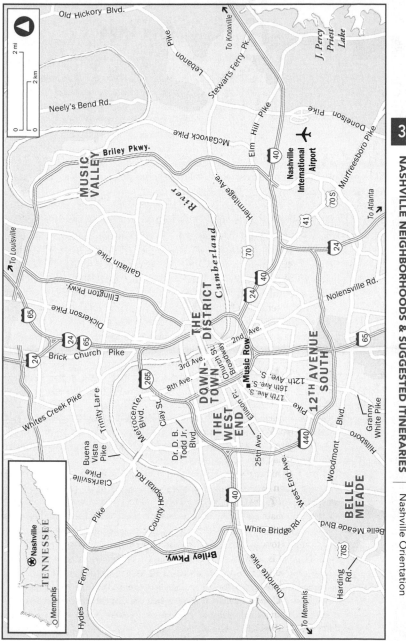

For information on the state of Tennessee, contact the **Tennessee Department of Tourism Development,** P.O. Box 23170, Nashville, TN 37202 (© **615/741-2158;** www.state.tn.us).

Did You Know?

Nashville has the largest U.S. population of Kurds. With 8,000 expatriates living in Music City, it has earned the nickname "Little Kurdistan."

City Layout

Nashville was built on a bend in the Cumberland River; this and other bends in the river have defined the city's expansion over the years. The area referred to as **downtown** is located on the west side of the Cumberland and is built in a grid pattern. Numbered avenues run parallel to the river on a northwest-southeast axis. Streets perpendicular to the river are named. Though the grid pattern is interrupted by I-40, it remains fairly regular until you get to Vanderbilt University, in the **West End** area.

For the most part, Nashville is a sprawling modern city. Though there are some areas of downtown that are frequented by pedestrians, the city is primarily oriented toward automobiles. With fairly rapid growth in recent years, the city's streets and highways have been approaching their carrying capacity, and rush hours see plenty of long backups all around the city. The most important things to watch out for when driving around Nashville are the numerous divisions of the interstate highways that encircle the city. If you don't pay very close attention to which lane you're supposed to be in, you can easily wind up heading in the wrong direction.

MAIN ARTERIES & STREETS   The main arteries in Nashville radiate from downtown, like spokes on a wheel. **Broadway** is the main artery through downtown Nashville and leads southwest from the river. Just after crossing I-40, Broadway forks, with the right fork becoming **West End Avenue.** West End Avenue eventually becomes **Harding Road** out in the Belle Meade area. If you stay on Broadway (the left fork), the road curves around to the south, becoming **21st Avenue** and then **Hillsboro Pike.**

Eighth Avenue is downtown's other main artery and runs roughly north-south. To the north, Eighth Avenue becomes **Rosa Parks Boulevard;** to the south, it forks, with the right fork becoming **Franklin Pike** and the left fork becoming **Lafayette Road** and then **Murfreesboro Pike.**

War-Torn Cathedral Still Stands

Interesting architecture and history make the gentrified Germantown neighborhood just north of downtown a nice place for an afternoon stroll. Alongside expensive new condos and professional office buildings are 19th-century mansions, shotgun houses, and such unexpected gems as the **Church of the**

Assumption of the Blessed Virgin Mary (1227 Seventh Ave. N.). The cathedral was only a few years old when, in 1864, it was pillaged by soldiers during the Civil War. Beautifully restored, the Catholic church remains an active parish today.

There are also several roads that you should become familiar with out in the suburbs. **Briley Parkway** describes a large loop that begins just south of the airport, runs up the east side of the city through the area known as Music Valley, and then curves around to the west, passing well north of downtown. On the south side of the city, **Harding Place** connects I-24 on the east with Belle Meade on the west. Don't confuse Harding Place with Harding Road.

FINDING AN ADDRESS Nashville's address-numbering system begins downtown, at Broadway and the Cumberland River, and increases as you move away from this point. In the downtown area, and out as far as there are numbered avenues, avenues include either a north or a south designation. The dividing line between north and south is the Broadway and West End Avenue corridor.

STREET MAPS You can get a map of the city (as well as scads of brochures) from the **Nashville Convention & Visitors Bureau Visitors Center,** Fifth Avenue and Broadway (☎ **615/780-9401**), which is located below the glass tower of the Bridgestone Arena. Maps can also be obtained in many hotel lobbies and at the **Airport Welcome Center** (☎ **615/275-1675**), on the baggage-claim level at the Nashville International Airport.

If you happen to be a member of **AAA,** you can get free maps of Nashville and Tennessee from your local AAA office or from the Nashville office at 2501 Hillsboro Rd., Ste. 1 (☎ **615/297-7700**). They're open Monday to Friday 8:30am to 5:30pm and Saturday 9am to 1pm.

Neighborhoods in Brief

While there are plenty of neighborhoods throughout the city, few are of real interest to most visitors. There are, however, named areas of the city that you'll want to be familiar with. There are also several outlying bedroom communities that may be of interest.

Downtown With the state capitol, the Tennessee State Museum, the Tennessee Center for the Performing Arts, the Tennessee Convention Center, and The Ryman Auditorium, downtown Nashville is a vibrant and growing Southern city. However, this is still almost exclusively a business and government district, and after dark the streets empty out, with the exception of the area known as the District.

The District With restored buildings housing interesting shops, restaurants, nightclubs, and bars, this downtown historic district (along Second Ave. and Broadway) is the center of Nashville's nightlife scene. With each passing year, it becomes a livelier spot; pickup trucks and limousines jockey for space at night along Second Avenue. On Friday and Saturday nights, the sidewalks are packed with partiers who roam from dive bar to retro-disco to line-dance hootenanny.

Germantown A few blocks northwest of downtown lies the charming historic community of Germantown. Named for the European immigrants who first started settling here in the mid–19th century, the 18 square blocks are bounded by Jefferson Street to the north, Rosa Parks Boulevard on the west and Third Avenue North on the east. On the National Register of Historic Places, the once-blighted area has become a benchmark for urban redevelopment in recent years, with new loft condos, cafes, shops, and professional offices.

Jefferson Street and Fisk University Next to Germantown, stretching west along Jefferson Street, is an area known for some of the city's best soul food spots and African-American–owned businesses. This section of Nashville is home to historic Fisk University as well as Tennessee State University. Frontyard tailgating before college football games is a popular pastime here.

The Gulch Just south of downtown lies this once-abandoned industrial area that's become the hottest real estate in Nashville. Old warehouses are being razed and revamped, and gleaming high-rise condos and lofts are being developed, as upscale new hotels, restaurants, and clubs compete for space here.

Eighth Avenue South Just south of downtown and the Gulch, Eighth Avenue is an emerging district lined with antiques shops, corner cafes, and family-friendly eateries. If you're into leisurely bargain shopping or are on a hunt for a one-of-a-kind antique, this no-frills, nontouristy area is great for browsing.

12th Avenue South (12South) This laid-back community south of the Gulch is enjoying a renaissance. Idealists, entrepreneurs, and young adults with dreams have been buying up and restoring old houses to set up shop. As a result, an interesting, off-the-beaten-path array of quirky boutiques and happening restaurants and nightspots now dot the area roughly bordered by Linden and Kirkwood avenues.

Berry Hill A few miles west of 12South lies the Berry Hill neighborhood, a middle-class residential area with a few interesting boutiques and recording studios, as well as a couple of restaurants.

Music Row Recording studios and record companies make this neighborhood, located around the corner from 16th Avenue South and Demonbreun Street (pronounced "Demon-bree-in"), the center of the country music recording industry. Driving down the tree-lined boulevards, you'll see stately homes converted into the offices of country music publishers, public relations agents, and the occasional gated recording studio. Although Music Row is a distinct district, the general area between the edge of downtown and the West End is also sometimes referred to as Midtown.

The West End While tourists and barflies congregate in the District, the moneymakers and musicians of the Nashville scene gather in the West End, referred to by locals as the intellectual side of town. Located adjacent to Vanderbilt and Belmont universities, this upscale neighborhood is home to many small shops, lots of excellent restaurants, and several dozen hotels. Also known as **Hillsboro Village,** the area has a lively late-night dining scene fueled by the college crowd and well-heeled locals looking to see and be seen. At the edge of the West End is the affluent **Belle Meade** community. Mansions abound in Belle Meade, and country stars own many of them. Two such historic mansions—Belle Meade Plantation and Cheekwood—are open to the public.

East Nashville Across the Cumberland River from downtown is this enclave of bars, coffee shops, and funky boutiques that one travel magazine called "Nashville's version of Manhattan's East Village." Many homes in the area, which date back to the early 1900s, are being preserved and renovated by young families attracted to the area. Increasingly, culturally diverse East Nashville is also home to some of the locals' best-loved restaurants, such as Marché Artisan Foods (p. 78h).

Music Valley This area on the far-northeast side of the Nashville metro area is where you'll find the Gaylord Opryland Resort and Convention Center, the Grand Ole Opry House, Opry Mills shopping center, and numerous other country-themed tourist attractions. There are few exceptional

Love Can Build a Bridge

Or at least it can restore it. The **Shelby Street Bridge** is a case in point. Dating back to 1909, the unique, multispan truss bridge is one of several over the Cumberland River connecting downtown Nashville with East Nashville. Closed to vehicles in 1998, the bridge was to be demolished, but historians and architects fought for its conversion to a pedestrian bridge. Refurbished at a cost of $15 million, the bridge is now a National Historic Landmark. In addition to its extensive use as a pedestrian and bike route, the Shelby Street Bridge has become a favorite backdrop for country music videos shot in Nashville, including Big & Rich's "Save a Horse (Ride a Cowboy)."

restaurants in the area (except within the Gaylord Opryland Resort itself).

Green Hills Upscale shopping, chain restaurants, and wealthy residential areas define the suburban sprawl of Green Hills. Among Nashvillians, Green Hills is considered to be a lively, desirable neighborhood. Tourists might visit the Mall at Green Hills, the go-to, shop-'til-you-drop spot that anchors the area. The famed Bluebird Cafe (p. 102), home to up-and-coming songwriters, is also out in this neck of the woods.

THE BEST OF NASHVILLE IN 1 DAY

The day begins with a crash course in the origins of American popular music. It's a history lesson most pop-culture enthusiasts will love. The Country Music Hall of Fame and Museum is an endlessly entertaining and informative experience that will help you grasp Nashville's importance as a songwriting and recording mecca. A few blocks away is the hallowed hall where it all began: The Ryman Auditorium. Soak up the spirits of Hank Williams and Patsy Cline, and then stroll the lively honky-tonk strip along Broadway. Your afternoon continues with a visit to Nashville's best art museum, the Frist Center for the Visual Arts. The evening is yours to barhop or bootscoot at the Wildhorse Saloon, Tootsie's Orchid Lounge, B.B. King's Blues Club, or any other nightspot that strikes your fancy. *Start: Country Music Hall of Fame and Museum.*

1 Country Music Hall of Fame and Museum ★★

Start your day downtown at the acclaimed Country Music Hall of Fame and Museum. It's chock-full of colorful exhibits and music, and seeing this will help you get your bearings for later exploration. See p. 35.

Walk north 4 blocks until, on your right, you see:

2 Ryman Auditorium ★★★

This sacred concert hall was a magnet for the so-called hillbilly and country music boom back in the 1940s and 1950s. And because you're going to attend a performance of the *Grand Ole Opry* while you're here, it will be nice to see the modest venue where it all began. See p. 38.

Suggested Nashville Itineraries

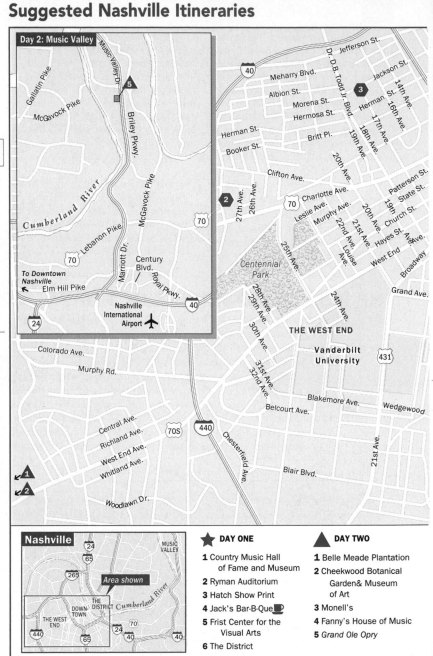

Day 2: Music Valley

Music Valley Dr.

Gallatin Pike

McGavock Pike

Briley Pkwy.

5

Cumberland River

McGavock Pike

Lebanon Pike

Marriott Dr.

70

Century Blvd.

Royal Pkwy.

To Downtown Nashville
Elm Hill Pike

Nashville International Airport

24

70

40

Jefferson St.

40

Meharry Blvd.

Albion St.

Dr. D.B. Todd Jr. Blvd.

Jackson St.

3

14th Ave.

16th Ave.

Herman St.

Morena St.

Hermosa St.

17th Ave.

18th Ave.

19th Ave.

Herman St.

Britt Pl.

Booker St.

Clifton Ave.

20th Ave.

Patterson St.

State St.

2

Charlotte Ave.

70

Leslie Ave.

Murphy Ave.

19th Ave.

Church St.

27th Ave.

26th Ave.

22nd Ave.

21st Ave.

20th Ave.

Louise Ave.

Hayes St.

West End Ave.

Broadway

25th Ave.

Centennial Park

24th Ave.

Grand Ave.

28th Ave.

29th Ave.

30th Ave.

THE WEST END

Vanderbilt University

431

Colorado Ave.

Murphy Rd.

31st Ave.

32nd Ave.

Blakemore Ave.

Wedgewood

Belcourt Ave.

Central Ave.

Richland Ave.

70S

440

Chesterfield Ave.

West End Ave.

Whitland Ave.

Blair Blvd.

21st Ave.

1

2

Woodlawn Dr.

Nashville

24

65

MUSIC VALLEY

265

Area shown

THE DISTRICT

Cumberland River

DOWNTOWN

THE WEST END

440

65

24

70

40

40

⭐ **DAY ONE**

1 Country Music Hall of Fame and Museum

2 Ryman Auditorium

3 Hatch Show Print

4 Jack's Bar-B-Que

5 Frist Center for the Visual Arts

6 The District

🔺 **DAY TWO**

1 Belle Meade Plantation

2 Cheekwood Botanical Garden& Museum of Art

3 Monell's

4 Fanny's House of Music

5 *Grand Ole Opry*

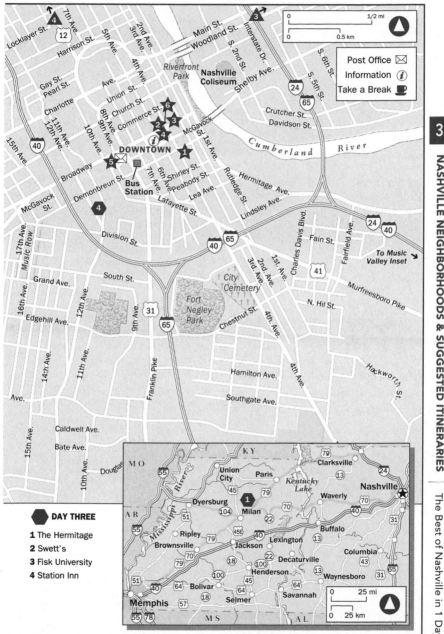

DAY THREE

1 The Hermitage
2 Swett's
3 Fisk University
4 Station Inn

Walk south back to Broadway, and then turn left and continue past the honky-tonks almost to Third Avenue. On your left, you'll see:

3 Hatch Show Print ★★

Take a trip back in time and get lost in the nostalgic aura of this longtime print shop, where posters of live concerts by virtually all of country music's greatest stars were created. See p. 85.

4 Jack's Bar-B-Que 🍽

Slip in here and grab a Coke or a shredded-pork sandwich and some greasy fries. Jack's is a basic, no-frills dive. Make yourself at home. 416 Broadway. 𝒞 615/254-5715. www.jacks barbque.com. See p. 80.

5 Frist Center for the Visual Arts ★★★

Drive a few blocks west on Broadway to this outstanding museum, housed in a historic post-office building. First-rate exhibitions from throughout the world are shown here. The permanent ArtQuest Gallery is a wondrous, hands-on creativity center where children and adults alike can experiment with their own artwork. See p. 43.

6 Barhopping in the District

After a bit of rest and a bite to eat, browse the bars and colorful nightlife along Broadway and the surrounding area. You can hear live music most anywhere, from Tootsie's Orchid Lounge to B.B. King's Blues Club. See chapter 7, "Nashville Entertainment & Nightlife."

THE BEST OF NASHVILLE IN 2 DAYS

On your first day in town, follow the itinerary outlined above. Today you're enjoying an antebellum plantation and a botanical garden before heading out to Music Valley for a performance of the *Grand Ole Opry.* **Start:** *Belle Meade Plantation.*

1 Belle Meade Plantation ★★

Take a tour of this elegant Greek Revival home, built in 1853 on 30 tree-shaded acres. After you've traipsed through the antiques-laden formal house, saunter the grounds of this former horse farm to find the log cabin, creamery, and carriage house. See p. 39.

2 Cheekwood Botanical Garden & Museum of Art ★★

A bit farther toward the western outskirts of town, near Percy Warner Park, you'll find this mansion and museum set amid a lush, 55-acre park. Enjoy exploring the wooded walking trails, landscaped gardens, and outstanding collections of American art and decorative furnishings from around the world. See p. 42.

3 Monell's 🍽 ★★★

High-tail it downtown, and head north to historic Germantown for a family-style meal of Southern cooking at Monell's. 1235 Sixth Ave. N. 𝒞 615/248-4747. www.monellstn.com. See p. 68.

4 East Nashville

Cross the Woodland Street Bridge from downtown to get to East Nashville. Park your car and stroll the shops and galleries, but be sure to stop in at Fanny's House of Music—and, if you're not too full from the feed at Monell's, grab an ice-cream cone across the street at Pied Piper Creamery. See p. 79.

5 *Grand Ole Opry* ★★★

This is the ultimate for country music fans. Be prepared for a patriotic, toe-tappin' time and plenty of corny jokes. It's all part of the tradition here, where big-name acts share the stage with fading stars of yesteryear and new up-and-coming talents. See p. 101.

THE BEST OF NASHVILLE IN 3 DAYS

For days 1 and 2, follow the itineraries above. History, African-American heritage, and old-time bluegrass music make today's itinerary sort of a multicultural sightseeing stew. You'll start with a tour of President Andrew Jackson's plantation home, just east of town, before heading back to the city. Grab some soul food at Swett's before spending the afternoon touring the impressive campus of Fisk University. In the evening, head to the West End for dinner at one of the great restaurants here; there are plenty of options for all tastes and budgets. Tonight it's a performance of live bluegrass music in the Gulch landmark known as the Station Inn. ***Start:*** *From downtown, take Interstate 40 east to exit 221A (The Hermitage exit).*

1 The Hermitage ★

Andrew Jackson's stately Southern plantation home offers a fascinating glimpse into the former U.S. President's life here in Tennessee. Originally built in the Federal style in 1821, it was expanded and remodeled in 1831, and acquired its current appearance in 1836. Tours include all areas of the main house, as well as the kitchen, the smokehouse, the garden, Jackson's tomb, an original log cabin, the spring house (a cool storage house built over a spring), and, nearby, the Old Hermitage Church and Tulip Grove mansion. See p. 112.

2 Swett's 🍽 ★★★

This cafeteria, specializing in Southern soul food, is the city's oldest African-American-owned restaurant, in business since 1954. Try the fried chicken, collard greens, sweet potatoes, and cornbread. Trust me: Choose the banana pudding for dessert. 2725 Clifton Ave. ✆ 615/329-4418. www.swettsrestaurant.com. See p. 67.

3 Fisk University ★★

Founded in 1866 as a liberal arts institution committed to educating newly freed slaves, Fisk University is still a vibrant university in the heart of Nashville. Stroll the lovely campus to admire the Victorian Gothic architecture and to learn about the world-renowned Fisk Jubilee Singers. In a neo-Romanesque former church that dates back to 1888, the Carl Van Vechten Gallery showcases masterworks of art by Picasso and Cezanne. See p. 42.

4 Station Inn ★

This battered-looking, unpretentious little music hall has been around for many years. Aside from The Ryman (and its summer bluegrass series), this is the year-round venue of choice for top-tier bluegrass acts. Local country swing favorites The Time Jumpers are currently the hottest ticket in town, but don't be surprised if other local stars, such as Vince Gill, show up to exercise their mandolin-playing chops. See p. 100.

EXPLORING NASHVILLE

Nashville, Music City, the Country Music Capital of the World. There's no question why people visit Nashville. But you may be surprised to find that there's more to see and do here than just chase country stars. Sure, you can attend the *Grand Ole Opry,* linger over displays at the **Country Music Hall of Fame and Museum,** take a tour past the homes of the country legends, and hear the stars of the future at any number of clubs. However, the state capital of Tennessee also has enough history, culture, professional sports, and outdoor recreation opportunities to please a wide cross section of travelers.

So even if you could care less about Toby Keith and Taylor Swift, you'll find something to keep you busy while you're in town. However, if you can't wait for the next Brad Paisley or Miranda Lambert release, you'll be in hog heaven on a visit to Nashville.

ON THE MUSIC TRAIL

For information on the *Grand Ole Opry* and other country music performance halls, theaters, and clubs, see chapter 7, "Nashville Entertainment & Nightlife." For information on country music gift shops, see chapter 6, "Nashville Shopping." If you want to drive by some houses of the country stars, pick up a copy of the "Homes of the Stars" map, sold at the **Ernest Tubb Record Shop,** 417 Broadway (© **615/255-7503**), and at other country music souvenir shops around town. But consider yourself forewarned: The reality is that most of today's superstars live in ultraexclusive, gated enclaves, so your chances of driving by a mansion to catch Tim McGraw mowing his grass are slim to none.

At the **Visitors Center** in the **Bridgestone Arena,** you can also get a booklet with more information on the homes of the stars.

Cooter's Place   "Breaker! Breaker!" Actor Ben Jones, who starred as Cooter in the late-1970s TV show *The Dukes of Hazzard,* owns this "good-ol'-boys" hangout, where you can buy Confederate flags and other Southern knickknacks. A museum dedicated to the cult TV hit displays props, records, costumes, posters, and scripts related to the show and its stars. Allow 20 to 30 minutes to tour the museum and have your picture taken in front of the General Lee—a bright orange 1969 Dodge Charger.

2613 McGavock Pike. © **615/872-8358.** www.cootersplace.com. Free admission. Daily 9am–7pm. Take McGavock Pkwy. to Music Valley Dr.

Nashville Attractions: Downtown Area & Music Row

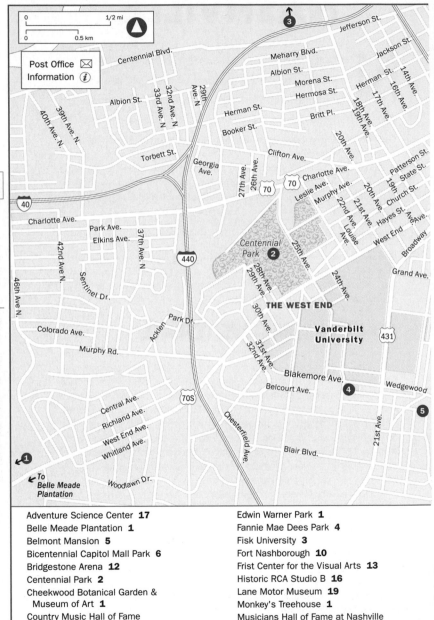

Adventure Science Center **17**

Belle Meade Plantation **1**

Belmont Mansion **5**

Bicentennial Capitol Mall Park **6**

Bridgestone Arena **12**

Centennial Park **2**

Cheekwood Botanical Garden & Museum of Art **1**

Country Music Hall of Fame and Museum **14**

Edwin Warner Park **1**

Fannie Mae Dees Park **4**

Fisk University **3**

Fort Nashborough **10**

Frist Center for the Visual Arts **13**

Historic RCA Studio B **16**

Lane Motor Museum **19**

Monkey's Treehouse **1**

Musicians Hall of Fame at Nashville Municipal Auditorium **8**

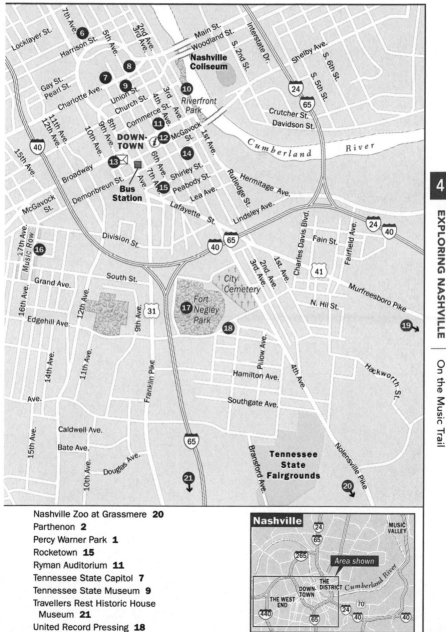

Nashville Zoo at Grassmere **20**
Parthenon **2**
Percy Warner Park **1**
Rocketown **15**
Ryman Auditorium **11**
Tennessee State Capitol **7**
Tennessee State Museum **9**
Travellers Rest Historic House
   Museum **21**
United Record Pressing **18**

Nashville Attractions: Music Valley

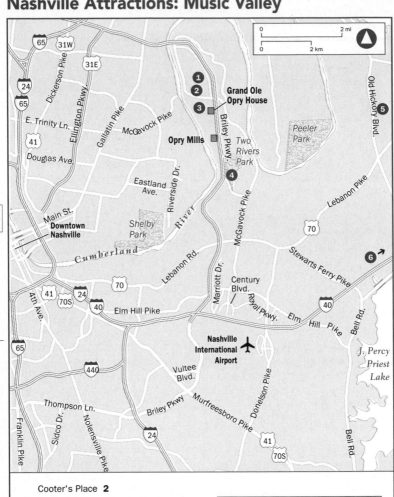

Cooter's Place **2**
General Jackson Showboat at
  Opryland Resort **3**
Grand Old Golf & Games **1**
Grand Ole Opry Museum **3**
The Hermitage **5**
Nashville Shores **6**
Opryland Resort **3**
Wave Country and Skatepark **4**
Willie Nelson & Friends Museum &
  General Store **2**

Country Music Hall of Fame and Museum ★★   Country music fans should not miss this wonderfully entertaining museum. Here you can immerse yourself in the deep roots of country music. Savvy exhibits let visitors absorb bluegrass, country swing, rockabilly, Cajun, honky-tonk, and contemporary country music through what seems like miles of individual CD listening posts, interactive jukeboxes, and eye-catching multimedia displays.

Elvis's gold-leafed Cadillac (a gift from Priscilla) is a top draw, but on my many return visits here, I always relish revisiting these artifacts: a crude banjo made of hand-split oak and groundhog hide; black-and-white film footage of comic Stan Laurel mugging with the Cumberland Ramblers in 1935; Jimmie Rodgers's guitar and trademark railroad brakeman's cap; and Bill Monroe's walking cane, his personal Bible (with a joker playing-card bookmark tucked inside), and his beloved 1923 Gibson F-5 mandolin. And, as if all of this weren't more than a visitor could stand, the museum also showcases such down-home objets d'art as the kitschy cornfield from TV's *Hee Haw*—complete with Junior Samples's denim overalls and Lulu Roman's plus-size gingham dress. Because of its vast repository of materials, the museum's core exhibit, "Sing Me Back Home: A Journey Through Country Music," is continually refreshed with new artifacts and audio/video. So chances are, if you've been here before, you'll find something new on a return trip.

If you want to arrange a visit to the old RCA recording studio (see "Historic RCA Studio B," below), where Elvis and other greats laid down a few hits, you'll need to sign up here at the Hall of Fame. The studio itself is located in the Music Row area of Nashville. Allow 2 to 3 hours.

Note: In July 2011, the museum leadership launched a capital campaign designed to double the attraction's size by spring 2014. New buildings will include an 800-seat theater, additional exhibit galleries, and a children's education gallery, as well as classrooms and a recording studio. The museum will be integrated into the new Music City Center and Omni Hotel (currently under construction adjacent to the museum).

222 Fifth Ave. S. (at Demonbreun). Ⓒ **800/852-6437** or 615/416-2001. www.countrymusichallof fame.com. Admission $20 adults, $18 seniors, $12 children 6–17, free for children 5 and under. Platinum Package tickets, which include the Historic RCA Studio B Tour (p. 36), are a bargain at $31 for adults and $23 for children 6–17. Daily 9am–5pm. Closed major holidays and Tues Jan–Feb.

Gaylord Opryland Resort and Convention Center ★ 📷   Hotels aren't usually tourist attractions, but this one is an exception. With 2,881 rooms, the place is beyond big, but what makes it worth a visit are the three massive atria that form the hotel's three main courtyards. Together these atria are covered by more than 8 acres of glass to form vast greenhouses full of tropical plants. There are gently

---

💬 **Symbolism in the Architecture of the Country Music Hall of Fame and Museum**

Architecture	Symbol
Dark windows	Piano keys
Upward arch of roof	Fin of a 1950s Cadillac
Spire	Country's WSM radio tower
Tiered rotunda	Vinyl 78s, 45s, and CDs
From overhead	Museum resembles a bass clef

NOTABLE SONGS & ALBUMS recorded IN MUSIC CITY

YEAR	ARTIST	SONG/ALBUM
1956	Elvis Presley	"Heartbreak Hotel"
1957	The Everly Brothers	"Bye Bye Love"
1958	Brenda Lee	"Rockin' Around the Christmas Tree"
1964	Roy Orbison	"Oh, Pretty Woman"
1966	Bob Dylan	*Blonde on Blonde*
1967	Robert Night	"Everlasting Love"
1971	Joan Baez	"The Night They Drove Old Dixie Down"
1978	Kansas	"Dust in the Wind"
1987	R.E.M.	*Document*
1992	Vanessa Williams	"Save the Best for Last"
2000	Matchbox Twenty	*Mad Season*
2001	India.Arie	*Acoustic Soul*
2004	Jimmy Buffett	*License to Chill*
2006	The Raconteurs	*Consolers of the Lonely*
2007	Alison Krauss and Robert Plant	*Raising Sand*
2007	Bon Jovi	*Lost Highway*
2007	Kid Rock	*Rock n Roll Jesus*
2007	White Stripes	*Icky Thump*
2008	Kings of Leon	*Only By the Night*
2009	Elvis Costello	*Secret, Profane & Sugarcane*
2009	Reba McEntire	*Keep On Loving You*
2009	Chevelle	*Sci-Fi Crimes*
2010	Lady Antebellum	*Need You Now*
2010	Sugarland	*The Incredible Machine*
2010	Keith Urban	*Get Closer*
2010	Alan Jackson	*Freight Train*
2011	The Civil Wars	*Barton Hollow*
2011	The Black Keys	*El Camino*
2011	Vince Gill	*Guitar Slinger*

gurgling streams, splashing waterfalls, bridges, pathways, ponds, and fountains. There are also plenty of places grab a drink or a meal.

The largest of the three atria here is the Delta, which covers 4½ acres and has a quarter-mile-long "river," a 110-foot-wide waterfall, an 85-foot-tall fountain, and an island modeled after the French Quarter in New Orleans. On this island are numerous shops and restaurants, which give the hotel the air of an elaborate shopping mall: You can take boat rides on the river and, at night, catch live music in a nightclub on the island. Allow 1 to 2 hours.

2800 Opryland Dr. ✆ **615/889-1000.** www.gaylordopryland.com. Free admission. Daily 24 hr. Parking $10. Take I-40 to exit 215 and take Briley Pkwy. (155 N.) to exit 12; turn left at the second traffic light into the Gaylord Opryland complex.

Historic RCA Studio B ★   Dubbed "Home of 1,000 Hits," this humble building on Music Row was a hotbed of recording activity from the time it opened in 1957 until the early 1970s (it closed in 1977). Guided tours include vintage film footage, photo displays, and a lingering look inside the legendary studio where Elvis recorded his immortal "Are You Lonesome Tonight?" Other hits cut here include The Everly Brothers' "All I Have to Do Is Dream," Roy Orbison's "Only the Lonely," and Dolly Parton's "I Will Always Love You." Tours are available only through the Country Music Hall of Fame and Museum (see above), which shuttles visitors between the downtown museum and the Music Row recording studio. Allow about an hour and a half.

Music Row (departures from Country Music Hall of Fame and Museum, 222 Fifth Ave. S.). ⓒ **800/852-6437** or 615/416-2001. www.countrymusichalloffame.com. Admission available only through Country Music Hall of Fame and Museum "Platinum Tour" package.

Musicians Hall of Fame and Museum at Nashville Municipal Center 🎵

Ever wonder who was behind the haunting steel-guitar hook on Bob Dylan's "Lay Lady Lay"? Nashville's newest music museum answers that mystery and many others, as it pays tribute to the backup musicians behind the stars. Its displays are more old-school than those of the nearby Country Music Hall of Fame. No sensory overload here—just low-tech exhibit cases chock-full of fascinating music trivia. It's fun to see candid pics of Paul and the late Linda McCartney living on a Nashville farm with their young children in the early 1970s. Or to ogle the autographed snare drum used on the Red Hot Chili Peppers' *Mothers' Milk* and *Blood Sugar Sex Magik*. **Note:** In 2011, the museum that had previously been at 301 Sixth Ave. N. was displaced by construction of the city's new convention center. The museum has temporarily moved into the Nashville Municipal Auditorium.

417 4th Ave. N. ⓒ **615/862-6390.** www.musicianshalloffame.com. (Prices and hours were current before relocation.) Admission $15 adults; $12 seniors, students, and military; $9.95 children 7–12; free for children 6 and under. Mon–Thurs 10am–6pm; Fri–Sat 10am–5pm. Closed major holidays.

United Record Pressing ★★

In business since 1949, this vinyl record pressing plant in downtown Nashville is one of only four such manufacturers in the country. United, which pressed the Beatles' records (before they signed with Capitol), is still going gangbusters, making albums for everyone from Jay-Z and Eminem to Lady Gaga and Kings of Leon. Over the years, United has pressed millions of albums for nearly everyone you can think of: James Brown, Elvis, Bob Dylan, the Rolling Stones, U2, Michael Jackson, Jennifer Lopez, and Kanye West. United has begun offering tours, which provide fascinating, behind-the-scenes glimpses of the record-making process: In storage areas are barrels of tiny lacquer pellets used to form the shiny discs we know as albums; on a table display are samples of the hard, plastic blobs known as "biscuits," which get melted and pressed within the albums; and you'll tour the factory floor as the noisy, heavy machinery cranks out tens of thousands of albums each day—pushing out one album at a time to drop onto a spindle (not unlike the method employed by vintage hi-fidelity stereos). The plant is full of other eye-popping discoveries as well, including sheets of colorful album labels by all of your favorite artists. You'll almost certainly leave here with a sense of awe over the history of this place, as well as a greater appreciation for the craft and precision required to make quality record albums.

> ### 💬 Music Row
>
> Nashville's Music Row has lots of high-profile recording studios and music publishing offices representing big-name country artists as well as others. Music Row clients have run the gamut from Harry Connick, Jr., and Sheryl Crow to Matchbox Twenty and Yo-Yo Ma.

453 Chestnut St. ℅ **615/259-9396** or 866/407-3165. www.urpressing.com. Tours offered at 2pm Tues and 11am Fri. $5 adults. Call for reservations.

Willie Nelson and Friends Museum & General Store 👆 Less a museum than a souvenir shop with a few dusty exhibits in a big back room, this tourist site for die-hard Willie fans features many of his old guitars, gold and platinum records, movie posters, and even his pool table. It's a hodgepodge that includes areas devoted to fellow Outlaws Waylon Jennings, Johnny Cash, and Kris Kristofferson, as well as an extensive collection of B-movie Western star Audie Murphy's memorabilia. Unexpected finds, such as a ticket stub from Elvis Presley's final concert, can be jarring. The museum displays are tucked behind saloonlike doors of a gift shop that hawks everything from shot glasses, T-shirts, and swizzle sticks to feathery dream catchers and dolphin figurines. Allow 20 to 30 minutes.

2613A McGavock Pike. ℅ **615/885-1515.** www.willienelsongeneralstore.com. Admission $8 adults, free for children 12 and under. Daily 8:30am to 9pm (last entry at 8:30pm). Closed Dec 25 and Jan 1. Take McGavock Pkwy. to Music Valley Dr.

4 | Downtown Area

All downtown attractions are accessible from the downtown trolley.

Ryman Auditorium ★★★ If you're as enamored of music history as I am, you could devote several hours to a self-guided tour of this National Historic Landmark, where you're free to stand onstage—even belt out a few bars if the spirit moves you—or sit in the hardwood "pews," and wander the halls upstairs and down, looking at memorabilia in glass showcases. However, the typical tourist may be satisfied with a quick walk through the stately red-brick building. In either case, the best way to experience The Ryman is to attend a performance here. The site of the *Grand Ole Opry* from 1943 to 1974, the Ryman Auditorium is known as the "Mother Church of Country Music," the single-most-historic site in the world of country music. Originally built in 1892 as the Union Gospel Tabernacle by riverboat captain Tom Ryman, this building, with its arched stained-glass windows, served as a place of worship. The place evolved into a concert venue where, over the years, singers such as Enrico Caruso, Hank Williams, and Elvis Presley performed. The *Grand Ole Opry* broadcast here from 1943 to 1974. Since the hall's renovation in 1994, The Ryman has regained its prominence as a temple of bluegrass and country music. Its peerless acoustics make it a favored venue of rock's best singer-songwriters and classical musicians, as well. Acts as diverse as Coldplay, Keith Urban, and Grace Potter and the Nocturnals have performed here. In 2005, director Jonathan Demme filmed Neil Young's Ryman

---

Traveling Between Downtown and Music Valley

A cab ride from downtown to the Gaylord Opryland Resort and Convention Center costs about $25. A trolley serves Music Valley attractions, but a car is really the best way to get around. If you're staying as a guest at the Opryland in Music Valley, you may purchase round-trip shuttle service to downtown tourist sites, including the Wildhorse Saloon and the Ryman Auditorium. These buses run continuously throughout the day and until late at night, with the last downtown pickup around 11pm weeknights and at 1:30am on Saturday nights.

performance for the concert film *Prairie Wind*. Allow at least an hour for a self-guided tour.

116 Fifth Ave. N. (btw. Commerce and Broadway). *(C)* **615/458-8700** or 615/889-3060. www.ryman.com. Self-guided tours admission $13 adults, $6.25 children 4–11, free for children 3 and under. Daytime tour plus guided backstage tour tickets $16 adults, $10 children 4–11. ***Note:*** Backstage tours are subject to cancellation due to concerts and special events. Daily 9am–4pm. Closed Thanksgiving, Dec 25, and Jan 1.

MORE ATTRACTIONS

Historic Buildings

Belle Meade Plantation ★★   Belle Meade was built in 1853 after this plantation had become famous as a stud farm that produced some of the best racehorses in the South. Today, the Greek Revival mansion is the centerpiece of the affluent Belle Meade region of Nashville and is surrounded by 30 acres of manicured lawns and shade trees. A long driveway leads uphill to the mansion, which is fronted by six columns and a wide veranda. Inside, the restored building has been furnished with 19th-century antiques that hint at the elegance and wealth that the Southern gentility enjoyed in the late 1800s.

Tours led by costumed guides follow a theme (for example, holidays, aspects of plantation life, and so on) that changes every 3 months. These themed tours provide fascinating glimpses into the lives of the people who once lived at Belle Meade. Also on the grounds are a large carriage house and a stable that were built in 1890 and that now house a collection of antique carriages. During your visit, you can also have a look inside a log cabin, a smokehouse, and a creamery. Belle Meade's parklike grounds make it a popular site for festivals throughout the year.

5025 Harding Rd.*(C)* **800/270-3991** or 615/356-0501. www.bellemeadeplantation.com. Admission $16 adults, $14 seniors, $10 children 6–12, free for children 5 and under. Mon–Sat 9am–5pm; Sun 11am–5pm. (Last tour starts at 4pm.) Closed Thanksgiving, Dec 25, Jan 1, and Easter. Take 70 S. to Belle Meade Blvd. to Deer Park Dr., and follow the signs.

Belmont Mansion ★   Built in the 1850s by Adelicia Acklen, then one of the wealthiest women in the country, this Italianate villa is the city's most elegant historic home open to the public, and its grand salon is one of the most elaborately decorated rooms in any antebellum home in Tennessee. Belmont Mansion was originally built as a summer home, yet no expense was spared in its construction. On your tour of the mansion, you'll see rooms filled with period antiques, artwork, and marble statues. This museum also has an excellent gift shop full of reproduction period pieces. Allow at least 90 minutes to tour the mansion.

1900 Belmont Blvd. ⓒ **615/460-5459.** www.belmontmansion.com. Admission $10 adults, $9 seniors, $3 children 6–12, free for children 5 and under. Mon–Sat 10am–4pm; Sun 1–4pm. (Last tour starts at 3:15pm.) Closed all major holidays. Take Wedgewood Ave. off 21st Ave. S. (an extension of Broadway), turn right on Magnolia Ave., left on 18th Ave. S., then left on Acklen.

Fort Nashborough Though it's much smaller than the original, this reconstruction of Nashville's first settlement includes several buildings that faithfully reproduce what life in this frontier outpost was like in the late 18th century. The current fort looks oddly out of place in modern downtown Nashville, but if you're interested in Tennessee's early settlers, this site is worth a brief look. Allow 30 minutes or more if you've got kids who want to play here.

170 First Ave. N. (btw. Church and Commerce). No phone. Free admission. Daily 9am–4pm. At the edge of Riverfront Park, on the banks of the Cumberland River.

The Hermitage ★ You may not know it, but you probably see an image of one of Nashville's most famous citizens dozens of times every week. It's Andrew Jackson's. His visage appears on the $20 bill, and he's the man who built The Hermitage, a stately Southern plantation home. Jackson moved to Tennessee in 1788 and became a prosecuting attorney. He served as the state's first congressman and later as a senator and judge. However, it was during the War of 1812 that he gained his greatest public acclaim as the general who led American troops in the Battle of New Orleans. His role in that battle helped Jackson win the presidency in 1828 and again in 1832. Though the Hermitage now displays a classic Greek Revival facade, this is its third incarnation. Originally built in the Federal style in 1821, it was expanded and remodeled in 1831, and acquired its current appearance in 1836. Recordings that describe each room and section of the grounds accompany tours through the mansion and around it. In addition to the main house, you'll also visit the kitchen, the smokehouse, the garden, Jackson's tomb, an original log cabin, the springhouse (a cool storage house built over a spring), and, nearby, the Old Hermitage Church and Tulip Grove mansion. You can tour the museum and grounds in a few hours—or linger here for an entire day.

Old Hickory Blvd., Nashville. ⓒ **615/889-2941.** www.thehermitage.com. Admission $18 adults, $15 seniors, $12 students 13–18; $8 children 6–12, free for children 5 and under. The family rate, for 2 adults and 2 children, is $45. Apr–Oct 15 daily 8:30am–5pm; Oct 16–Mar 9am–4:30pm. Closed Thanksgiving, Dec 25, and 3rd week of Jan. Take I-40 east to exit 221, then head north 4 miles.

The Parthenon Centennial Park, as the name implies, was built for the Tennessee Centennial Exposition of 1897, and this full-size replica of the Athens Parthenon was the exposition's centerpiece. The original structure was only meant to be temporary, however, and, by 1921, the building, which had become a Nashville landmark, was in an advanced state of deterioration. In that year, the city undertook reconstruction of its Parthenon, and, by 1931, a new, permanent building stood in Centennial Park. The building now duplicates the floor plan of the original Parthenon in Greece. Inside stands the 42-foot-tall statue of Athena Parthenos, the goddess of wisdom, prudent warfare, and the arts. Newly gilded with 8 pounds of gold leaf, she is the tallest indoor sculpture in the country.

In addition to this impressive statue, there are original plaster castings of the famous Elgin marbles—bas-reliefs that once decorated the pediment of the Parthenon. Inside the air-conditioned galleries, you'll find an excellent collection of 19th- and 20th-century American art. The Parthenon's two pairs of bronze doors, which weigh in at 7½ tons per door, are considered the largest matching bronze doors in the world. Allow about 30 minutes.

Centennial Park, West End Ave. (at West End and 25th aves.). © **615/862-8431.** www.nashville. gov/parthenon. Admission $6 adults, $4 seniors and children 4–17, free for children 3 and under. Tues–Sat 9am–4:30pm (Apr–Sept also Sun 12:30–4:30pm, except Sun after Labor Day).

Tennessee State Capitol   The Tennessee State Capitol, completed in 1859, is a classically proportioned Greek Revival building that sits on a hill on the north side of downtown Nashville. The capitol is constructed of local Tennessee limestone and marble that slaves and convict laborers quarried and cut. Other notable features include the 19th-century style and furnishings of several rooms in the building, a handful of ceiling frescoes, and many ornate details. President and Mrs. James K. Polk are both buried on the capitol's east lawn. You can pick up a guide to the capitol at the Tennessee State Museum. It won't take long to admire it from the outside.

Charlotte Ave. (btw. Sixth and Seventh aves.). © **615/741-2692.** Free admission. Tues–Fri 10am– 5pm; Sun 1–5pm. Closed Mon and all state holidays.

Travellers Rest Historic House Museum   Built in 1799, Travellers Rest, as its name suggests, once offered gracious Southern hospitality to travelers passing through a land that had only recently been settled. Judge John Overton (who, along with Andrew Jackson and General James Winchester, founded the city of Memphis) built Travellers Rest. Overton also served as a political advisor to Jackson when he ran for president. Among the period furnishings you'll see in this restored Federal-style farmhouse is the state's largest public collection of pre-1840 Tennessee-made furniture. Allow an hour to tour the museum, more if you want to wander the grounds and outbuildings.

636 Farrell Pkwy. © **615/832-8197.** www.travellersrestplantation.org. Admission $10 adults, $9 seniors, $5 students 13–18, $3 children 6–12, free for children 5 and under. Mon–Sat 10am–4pm; Sun 1–4pm. Closed Sun in Mar and Easter, Thanksgiving, Dec 24–25, and Dec 31. Take I-65 to exit 78B (Harding Place West), go west to Franklin Pike, turn left, and then follow the signs.

Museums

Adventure Science Center ☺   It's hard to say which exhibit kids like the most at the Center. There are just so many fun interactive displays to choose from in this

---

Going to Church

With more than 700 churches, dozens of seminaries, and numerous Christian-music-publishing companies based in Nashville, it's easy to see how Music City got its other best-known nicknames: "The Buckle of the Bible Belt" and "The Protestant Vatican." Among the organizations with headquarters here are the Southern Baptist Convention, the United Methodist Church, the National Baptist Convention, the National Association of Free Will Baptists, the Gideons International, the Gospel Music Association, and Thomas Nelson, the world's largest producer of Bibles.

modern, hands-on museum. Though the museum is primarily meant to be an entertaining way to introduce children to science, it can also be fun for adults. Kids of all ages can learn about technology, the environment, physics, and health as they roam the museum pushing buttons and turning knobs. The latest craze is the BLUE MAX, a flight-simulator thrill ride that lets riders perform daring aerial maneuvers from the safety of a cockpit. In the **Sudekum Planetarium,** there are regular shows that take you exploring through the universe. Allow 2 hours.

800 Ft. Negley Blvd. ✆ **615/862-5160.** www.adventuresci.com. Admission $12 adults, $10 seniors and children 3–12, free for children 2 and under. BLUE MAX rides cost an additional $5. Planetarium admission costs an additional $6. IMAX admission is an additional $8. Mon–Sat 10am–5pm (till 7pm Fri–Sat Memorial Day to Labor Day); Sun 12:30–5:30pm. Closed Thanksgiving, Dec 25, and Jan 1. Fourth Ave. S. to Oak St., to Bass St. to Fort Negley.

Cheekwood Botanical Garden & Museum of Art ★★ ☺   Once a private estate, Cheekwood is situated in a 55-acre park that's divided into several formal gardens and naturally landscaped areas. The museum itself is housed in a Georgian-style mansion, with such features as a lapis lazuli fireplace mantel. Within the building are collections of 19th- and 20th-century American art, Worcester porcelains, antique silver serving pieces, Asian snuff bottles, and a good deal of period furniture. The grounds are designed for strolling, and there are numerous gardens, including Japanese, herb, and perennial, as well as greenhouses full of orchids. Kids will enjoy romping around the grassy meadows on the grounds. Don't miss the glass bridge that rewards hikers along the wooded sculpture trail. You'll also find a gift shop and good restaurant, The Pineapple Room, on the grounds. Allow a couple of hours to tour the museum, or up to a full day if you plan to explore the grounds and garden.

1200 Forrest Park Dr. (8 miles southwest of downtown). ✆ **615/356-8000.** www.cheekwood.org. Admission $12 adults, $10 seniors, $5 college students and children 6–17, free for children 5 and under; household ticket $30. Tues–Sat 9:30am–4:30pm (also Memorial Day and Labor Day Mon); Sun 11am–4:30pm. Closed Thanksgiving, Dec 25, Jan 1, and 2nd Sat in June. Take West End Ave. to Belle Meade Blvd. and turn left; then left at Page Rd. and left on Forrest Park Dr.

Fisk University ★★   Fisk University was founded in 1866 as a liberal arts institution committed to educating newly freed slaves. Prominent 20th-century cultural figures, such as educator W. E. B. DuBois, artist Aaron Douglas, and poet Nikki Giovanni, attended the school. Fisk is perhaps best known for its Jubilee Singers, an African-American singing group that preserved spirituals, or slave songs, from extinction. The choir's 1873 tour of the U.S. and Europe helped finance the construction of Fisk University. Jubilee Hall, one of the oldest structures on the campus, is a Victorian Gothic gem listed on the register of National Historic Landmarks. Now used as a dormitory, the building houses a floor-to-ceiling portrait of the original Jubilee Singers, commissioned by Queen Victoria of England as a gift to Fisk. In another building, a neo-Romanesque former church that dates back to 1888, is the Carl Van Vechten Gallery, which includes the prestigious Alfred Stieglitz Collection of modern American and European art. Works by Picasso, Cézanne, Renoir, Toulouse-Lautrec, and O'Keeffe are among the unexpected treasures here. The museum is generally open every day (closed Sun and school holidays), but call ahead to be sure. For more information, contact Fisk University Galleries, 1000 17th Ave. N. (✆ 615/329-8720; galleries@fisk.edu).

1000 17th Ave. N. ✆ **615/329-8720.** www.fisk.edu. Free admission; donations encouraged. Tues–Sat 10am–5pm. Closed holidays and during college breaks.

Frist Center for the Visual Arts ★★★ ☺   Opened in 2001, the Frist Center for the Visual Arts brings world-class art exhibits to the historic downtown post office building. The nonprofit center does not maintain a permanent collection but rather presents exhibitions from around the globe. Upcoming exhibits include "Creation Story: Gees Bend Quilts and the Art of Thornton Dial" (May 25–Sept 13, 2012), and "Constable Oil: Sketches from the Albert and Victoria Museum" (June 22–Sept 30, 2012). Upstairs, the **Martin ArtQuest Gallery** encourages visitors to explore a range of art experiences through more than 30 interactive multimedia stations. Creative kids and like-minded adults could spend hours here. The Frist is free to visitors 18 and under, making it an excellent value. Seniors get half-price admission the third Monday of each month, when musical activities such as singalongs are held. And on Thursday and Friday nights, college students are admitted free.

919 Broadway. ✆ **615/244-3340.** www.fristcenter.org. Admission $10 adults, $7 seniors, free for children 18 and under. (Admission prices may change for special exhibitions.) Mon–Wed 10am–5:30pm; Thurs–Fri 10am–9pm; Sat 10am–5:30pm; Sun 1–5:30pm. Closed Thanksgiving, Dec 25, and Jan 1. Btw. Ninth and 10th aves. next to the Union Station Hotel.

Lane Motor Museum   Housed in a former large bakery building, this unexpected find features about 150 unusual cars, including amphibious, alternative-fuel, and military vehicles, minicars, and motorcycles. Most are European vehicles from the 1950s through the 1970s. Cars are arranged by country (Austria, Germany, Great Britain, Italy, Japan, and Sweden, among others). The museum boasts the largest collection of Czechoslovakian cars outside of Europe. Whatever the vehicles' country of origin, mechanics and car buffs alike will enjoy ogling the candy-colored Citroëns and one-of-a-kind prototypes, such as a 1928 Martin Aerodynamic Car, and a 1946 Hewson Rocket. More than just pretty to look at, the Lane also has a practical mission: to keep all the cars in its collection, from Fiats to Lamborghinis, in good running order. Give yourself about an hour and a half here.

702 Murfreesboro Pike. ✆ **615/742-7445.** www.lanemotormuseum.com. Admission $7 adults, $5 seniors, $2 children 6–17, free for children 5 and under. Thurs–Mon 10am–5pm. Closed Thanksgiving, Dec 25, and Jan 1.

Tennessee State Museum ☺   Kids always rush to find the 3,000-year-old Egyptian mummy on display, but along the way maybe they will gain a better understanding of Tennessee history during a visit to this museum beneath the Tennessee Performing Arts Center. The museum showcases Native American artifacts as well as

---

Planes, Trains & Automobiles

Constructed during the Depression, Nashville's main post office is home to the Frist Center for the Visual Arts. Classical and Art Deco architectural styles are prominent within the marble and gray-pink granite building, which is on the National Register of Historic Places. Intricate grillwork celebrates icons of American progress: an airplane, a locomotive, a ship, and an automobile.

Among other achievements represented in the icons: scientific research (microscope, test tube, and flask), harvesting (sheaf of wheat and sickle), industry (cogwheels), publishing (book press), sowing (hand plow), metalwork (hammer and anvil), the pursuit of knowledge (lamp of learning resting on books), and nautical endeavors (dolphin and propeller).

objects from 18th-century century pioneer life. You'll see Daniel Boone's rifle and a powder horn that once belonged to Davy Crockett, along with exhibits on presidents Andrew Jackson and James K. Polk.

Visitors may view pre–Civil War artifacts, including full-scale replicas of old buildings and period rooms, a log cabin, a water-driven mill, a woodworking shop, an 18th-century print shop, and an 1855 parlor. Although the lower level of the museum is devoted mostly to the Civil War and Reconstruction, exhibits change; visitors are advised to call ahead to see what is currently on display. One block west, on Union Street, you'll find the museum's Military Museum, which houses displays on Tennessee's military activity from the Spanish-American through Vietnam wars. Allow 2 to 3 hours.

Fifth Ave. (btw. Union and Deaderick sts.). ℂ **800/407-4324** or 615/741-2692. www.tnmuseum. org. Free admission; donations encouraged. Tues–Sat 10am–5pm; Sun 1–5pm (except Military Museum). Closed Easter, Thanksgiving, Dec 25, and Jan 1.

Parks, Plazas & Botanical Gardens

To celebrate the 200th anniversary of Tennessee statehood, Nashville constructed the impressive **Bicentennial Capitol Mall State Park** (ℂ **615/741-5280**), north of the state capitol. The mall, which begins just north of James Robertson Parkway and extends (again, north) to Jefferson Street between Sixth and Seventh avenues, is a beautifully landscaped open space that conjures up the countryside with its limestone outcroppings and landscaped, native plants. It's a very pleasant place for a leisurely stroll.

However, this mall is far more than just a park. It is also a 19-acre open-air exhibition of Tennessee history and geography and a frame for the capitol, which sits atop the hill at the south end of the mall. Also at the south end of the mall is a 200-foot-long granite map of the state, and behind this are a gift shop/visitor center, a Tennessee rivers fountain, and an amphitheater used for summer concerts. Along Sixth Avenue, you'll find a walkway of Tennessee counties, with information on each county (beneath the plaques, believe it or not, are time capsules). Along Seventh Avenue is the Pathway of History, a wall outlining the state's 200-year history. Within the mall, there are also several memorials.

Known together as "The Warner Parks" (ℂ **615/370-8051;** www.nashville.gov), Edwin Warner Park and Percy Warner Park offer beautiful scenery, miles of hiking and equestrian trails, picnic areas, and outdoor recreation sites. **Percy Warner Park** (2500 Old Hickory Blvd.) is the crown jewel of Nashville green spaces. Named for Percy Warner, a local businessman and avid outdoorsman, the wooded hills and rolling meadows extend for more than 2,000 acres. Though popular with bicyclists, be aware that they must share the winding, paved roads with vehicular traffic. Perfect for picnics and other outdoor pursuits, the park offers clean shelters, restrooms, and even a 27-hole golf course. **Edwin Warner Park,** 50 Vaughn Rd. (on Old Hickory Blvd., near Hwy. 100), also has lovely picnic areas, scenic overlooks, and a dog park.

After visiting this park, it seems appropriate to take a stroll around **Centennial Park,** located on West End Avenue at 25th Avenue. This park, built for the 1896 centennial celebration, is best known as the site of the Parthenon, but also has many acres of lawns, colorful playground equipment, 100-year-old shade trees, and a small lake.

New in 2011 is a live-music series at Centennial Park, called **Musicians Corner.** Free live-music performances are held from 3 to 6pm every Saturday from early May to early July, and again from early July to early November. Inspired by "Speakers Corner" in London, England, Musicians Corner is a free-spirited community series that includes local food, eco-friendly vendors, and charity outreach efforts. The "Kidsville" component of the series includes child-friendly weekly arts and crafts, music education activities, games, entertainment, bubbles, balloons, and occasional prizes. For more information, visit **www.musicianscornernashville.com**.

See also the entry for Cheekwood Botanical Garden & Museum of Art on p. 42.

Neighborhoods
THE DISTRICT

The District, encompassing several streets of restored downtown warehouses and other old buildings, is ground zero for the Nashville nightlife scene. It's divided into three areas. Second Avenue between Broadway and Union Street, the heart of the District, was originally Nashville's warehouse area and served riverboats on the Cumberland River. Today, most of the old warehouses have been renovated and now house a variety of restaurants, nightclubs, souvenir shops, and other stores. Anchoring Second Avenue at the corner of Broadway is the **Hard Rock Cafe,** and a few doors up the street is the **Wildhorse Saloon,** a massive country music dance hall. Along Broadway between the Cumberland River and Fifth Avenue, you'll find several of country music's most important sites, including the **Ryman Auditorium** (home of the *Grand Ole Opry* for many years), **Tootsie's Orchid Lounge** (where *Opry* performers often dropped by for a drink), **Gruhn Guitars,** and the **Ernest Tubb Record Shop.** Along this stretch of Broadway, you'll also find **Robert's Western World,** the entrance to the **Bridgestone Arena,** and the **Nashville Convention & Visitors Bureau Visitors Center.** The third area of the District is Printer's Alley, which is off Church Street between Third and Fourth avenues. Though not as lively as it once was during the days of Prohibition and speak-easies, the alley is an interesting place for an afternoon or early-evening stroll. At night, a few clubs still offer live music. For more information, visit **www.thedistrictnashville.org**.

MUSIC ROW

Located along 16th and 17th avenues (between Demonbreun St. and Grand Ave.), Music Row is the very heart of the country music recording industry and is home to dozens of recording studios and record-company offices. The neighborhood is a mix of old restored homes and modern buildings that hint at the vast amounts of money generated by the country music industry. This is one of the best areas in town for spotting country music stars, so keep your eyes peeled. Anchoring the Music Row "turnaround" (a circular roadway at the entrance to the area) is *Musica.* The 40-foottall bronze sculpture of nine nude figures was considered a bit shocking when it was unveiled in the fall of 2003. After all, Nashville is considered "the buckle of the Bible Belt."

THE GULCH

The Gulch is a rapidly growing area just south of downtown that's being developed at a furious pace. Upscale eateries including **Watermark Restaurant** (p. 63) stand in stark contrast to weathered landmarks like the bluegrass venue **The Station Inn** (p. 100). Newly constructed condominiums, loft towers, and other mixed-use highrises tower over the area. Retail has followed, with the kind of new restaurants, nightclubs, clothing stores, and nightspots that have fueled the Gulch's urban appeal.

EIGHTH AVENUE SOUTH & 12TH AVENUE SOUTH

While Eighth Avenue boasts the biggest cluster of antiques shops and consignment stores in the area just south of downtown, a few blocks away lies another unique neighborhood that's off the beaten tourist track. Known as 12th Avenue South (12South), the area has undergone a refurbishment over the past decade, as homeowners have moved in and spruced up their cute bungalows and established a real community presence here. The area, roughly bounded by Linden and Kirkwood avenues, is also home to several commendable restaurants and boutiques. There are a couple of clothing stores, including **Katy K's Designs.** Start your sojourn into 12South with a bite to eat at **Burger Up** (p. 63) or **Corrieri's Formaggeria** (p. 81), browse the boutiques, and end the trip with a gourmet Popsicle from **Las Paletas** (p. 66).

BERRY HILL

A few miles away lies Berry Hill, one of the most quaint neighborhoods in metropolitan Nashville. A middle-class residential area that sprang up after World War II, it today features many small, locally owned shops, galleries, and boutiques, such as **Curious Heart Emporium** (p. 85) and **The Yellow Porch** restaurant (p. 74), as well as more than 40 record studios and music publishing offices housed in old homes. To reach Berry Hill from downtown Nashville, take 8th Avenue South, which becomes Franklin Pike. Cross Bradford Avenue to enter the Melrose area of Berry Hill. Turn left onto Berry Road and right onto Bransford to reach the shopping area.

EAST NASHVILLE

If you're looking for an antidote to the West End's pricey restaurants, college crowds, and frenetic social scene, look east. Across the Cumberland River from downtown Nashville lies the endearing community of East Nashville. A bit more affordable and a lot more laid back, East Nashville is a friendly and diverse neighborhood beloved for its bistros and bars, including **Margot Café & Bar, Family Wash,** and **Lipstick Lounge.** From downtown, take the Woodland Street Bridge east and follow it a mile or so to reach the area.

MUSIC VALLEY

The Gaylord Opryland Resort and Convention Center is a destination unto itself. Book a stay here, and you might never venture beyond the acres of parking lots surrounding the massive hotel complex. Opryland and the adjacent Opry Mills mall are the anchors for this entire geographic area, collectively known as Music Valley. (Damage from severe floods in May 2010 forced Opry Mills to close for more than two years. The mall is tentatively set to reopen in spring of 2012.) In any event, aside from the massive mall and the Opry resort, there is not much variety in this part of town. A few country music souvenir shops and a couple of live-music venues are interspersed among chain hotels and restaurants. Increasingly, Music Valley seems to be attracting an older clientele—including escorted tour-bus groups. The area caters to this demographic. Music Valley has its advantages if you want to shop and to wander the vast corridors of the Gaylord Opryland Resort. Plus, if the urge strikes, from here you can book tours to other Nashville attractions, including the Wildhorse Saloon and Ryman Auditorium downtown, and the *General Jackson* Showboat.

A Day at the Zoo

Nashville Zoo at Grassmere ☺   This 80-acre zoo just south of downtown has it all, from giraffes, elephants, and alligators to meerkats, rainbow-colored lorikeets, and African wild hogs. In the naturalistic habitats, you'll see river otters, bison, elk, black bear, gray wolves, bald eagles, and cougars, as well as other smaller animals. In the past 2 years, the zoo has added Eurasian lynx, African-crested porcupines, and giant anteaters. A new flamingo exhibit is also in the works, and in March 2011, the zoo welcomed the births of three new leopard cubs, Rajasi, Yim, and Lisu. In the park's aviary, you can walk among many of the state's songbirds, and at the Cumberland River exhibit expect to see fish, reptiles, and amphibians. Kids can ride wood-carved cougars and other critters on the zoo's colorful new carousel, and frolic under a water feature in the Jungle Gym playground. Allow 3 to 4 hours. *Tip:* To beat the crowds, try visiting the zoo during off-peak times of the day. Best bets are any weekday around 1pm, or Sunday morning at 9am.

3777 Nolensville Pike. ℂ **615/833-1534.** www.nashvillezoo.org. Admission $14 adults, $12 seniors, $9 children 3–12, free for children 2 and under. Parking $5. Mar 15–Oct 15 daily 9am–6pm; Oct 16–Mar 14 daily 9am–4pm. Closed Thanksgiving, Dec 25, and Jan 1. Follow Fourth Ave. south to Nolensville Pike to U.S. 11 and turn on Zoo Rd.

ESPECIALLY FOR KIDS

Even if your child is not a little Tim McGraw or Faith Hill in training, Nashville is full of things for kids to see and do. In addition to the attractions listed below, see also the listings in this chapter for Cheekwood Botanical Garden & Museum of Art (p. 42), Adventure Science Center (p. 41), the Frist Center for the Visual Arts (p. 43), the Nashville Zoo at Grassmere (above), and the Tennessee State Museum (p. 41).

Fannie Mae Dees Park   Better known to local families as "Dragon Park," this city park near Vanderbilt University in the West End gets its name from the colorful, mosaic sea-dragon art sculpture created by artist Pedro Silva. The dragon has become a local landmark for children, who can't resist crawling all over the tall, spiny-backed creature. The park, which includes tall shade trees as well as grassy, open areas, also includes a lovely garden and playground, as well as picnic tables and shelters.

2400 Blakemore Ave. ℂ **615/862-8400.** www.nashville.gov/parks. Free.

Grand Old Golf & Games/Valley Park GoKarts   With three miniature-golf courses, a go-kart track, and family game room, this place, located near the Gaylord Opryland Resort, is sure to be a hit with your kids. You can easily spend the whole day here.

2444 Music Valley Dr. ℂ **615/871-4701.** www.grandoldgolf.net. Fees 1 course $7.50, 2 courses $8.50, 3 courses $9.50; rates for children 10 and under $3.50, $4, and $4.50. Fees for go-karts $7 for single seat, $8 for double seat. May–Sept Mon–Thurs 10am–10pm, Fri–Sat 10am–11pm, Sun noon–11pm; Oct–Nov daily noon–9pm; Dec–Feb daily noon–5pm; Mar–Apr daily 11am–10pm. All open hours are weather-permitting. Closed Thanksgiving, Dec 25, and Jan 1. Take Briley Pkwy. to McGavock Pike to Music Valley Dr.

The Monkey's Treehouse   Looking for a fun, creative diversion for your toddlers and young children? This indoor playground has a huge "tree" for climbing, a dollhouse, and a variety of other creative and physical activities to engage the little ones. A pretend grocery store and giant sandbox fuel kids' imaginations, while a soft area for tumbling and playing allows for more energetic pursuits. There's even a play area just for babies.

8074 Highway 100. ℂ **615/646-5002.** www.themonkeystreehouse.com. Day passes $7 per child ages 12 months to 11 years. Babies 11 months and under are free with a paid child's admission. Open play and semiprivate parties Mon–Fri 9am–5pm; Sun 9am–noon. Closed major holidays.

Sand-Castle Nirvana

Not only does Nashville Shores boast what it dubs the world's largest free-style slide—it's four stories (170 ft.) high—but the outdoor recreation attraction also has an 8,000-square-foot beach-style sandbox. The critical issue of sand wetness is constantly monitored, ensuring the best possible texture and consistency for building sand castles.

Nashville Shores Tucked on the pristine shores of Percy Priest Lake, about 10 miles outside Nashville, this massive water park and family recreation destination offers white-sand beaches, jet-ski and boat rentals, eight water slides, and even kayaking areas. In the summer, Dive-In Movies are a popular way to stay cool; you float in a lagoonlike pool while watching action on a 40-foot inflatable screen. Other activities include lake cruises, miniature golf, volleyball, basketball, and horseshoes. Allow 3 to 4 hours here. Or, if you want to extend your stay, the venue offers lakeside cabin rentals and RV camping.

4001 Bell Rd. ⓒ **615/889-7050.** www.nashvilleshores.com. Admission $25 adults 48 in. and taller; $18 for 47 in. and shorter, seniors 55 and over, and military; free for children 2 and under. After 3pm, general admission is half-price. Mon–Sat 10am–6pm; Sun 11am–6pm. Parking $5.

Rocketown A combination indoor skate park, skate shop, live-music venue, and coffee bar, this Christian outreach ministry for teenagers was founded by Grammy-winning singer-songwriter Michael W. Smith and endorsed by NFL greats including Indianapolis Colts' former head coach Tony Dungy. Simply put, it offers kids a safe place to hang out and have fun. Nashville has one of the largest and most vibrant evangelical Christian communities in the country, with Rocketown's "Skate Church" a prime example of that movement. It's held on Wednesdays and Thursdays, from 7:30 to 9pm. Hours of operation vary according to what events are booked here, so call ahead before you visit.

601 4th Ave. S. ⓒ **615/843-4006.** www.rocketown.com. Mon 3–9pm; Tues 3–7:30pm; Wed–Thurs 3–9pm; Fri 3pm–midnight; Sat 9am–midnight; Sun 1–7pm.

Wave Country and Skatepark Skate, bike, or speed-slide in the water. It's your choice at these two parks, operated by the Nashville Parks and Recreation Department. Located just off Briley Parkway at Two Rivers Park and Golf Course, Wave Country has a huge freshwater wave pool, as well as a wave-free pool, three water flumes, and two speed slides. The Skatepark allows skateboards, in-line skates, and pegged BMX bikes; helmets are required, and protective kneepads are recommended. So pick your park, pack a picnic, and make an afternoon of it.

2320 Two Rivers Pkwy. (off Briley Pkwy.). ⓒ **615/885-1052.** www.nashville.gov. $12 adults, $10 children 5–12, free for children 4 and under; half price for children after 4pm. Mon–Thurs 10am–5pm (till 6pm Memorial Day to Labor Day); Fri–Sat 10am–6pm; Sun 11am–6pm.

Picnic It

To reserve a picnic shelter in any of Nashville's city parks, call ⓒ **615/862-8408.**

Walking Tour: Downtown Nashville

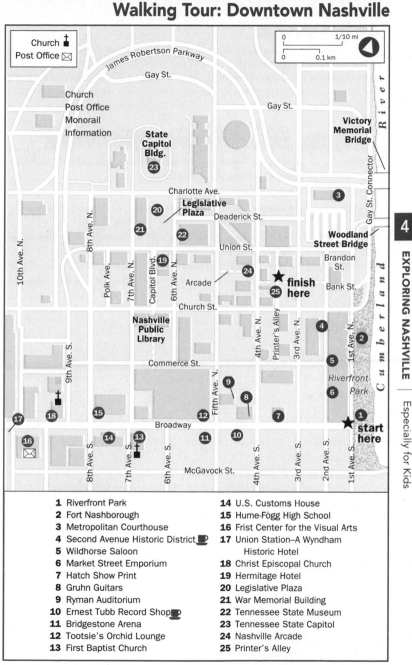

1 Riverfront Park
2 Fort Nashborough
3 Metropolitan Courthouse
4 Second Avenue Historic District
5 Wildhorse Saloon
6 Market Street Emporium
7 Hatch Show Print
8 Gruhn Guitars
9 Ryman Auditorium
10 Ernest Tubb Record Shop
11 Bridgestone Arena
12 Tootsie's Orchid Lounge
13 First Baptist Church

14 U.S. Customs House
15 Hume-Fogg High School
16 Frist Center for the Visual Arts
17 Union Station–A Wyndham
       Historic Hotel
18 Christ Episcopal Church
19 Hermitage Hotel
20 Legislative Plaza
21 War Memorial Building
22 Tennessee State Museum
23 Tennessee State Capitol
24 Nashville Arcade
25 Printer's Alley

STROLLING AROUND NASHVILLE

If you'd like a bit more information on some of these sites or would like to do a slightly different downtown walk, pick up a copy of the *Nashville City Walk* brochure at the Visitors Center in the Bridgestone Arena. This brochure outlines a walk marked with a green line painted on downtown sidewalks. Along the route are informational plaques and green metal silhouettes of various characters from history.

WALKING TOUR: DOWNTOWN NASHVILLE

START:	**Riverfront Park at the intersection of Broadway and First Avenue. (There's a public parking lot here.)**
FINISH:	**Printer's Alley.**
TIME:	**Anywhere from 3 to 8 hours, depending on how much time you spend in the museums, shopping, or dining.**
BEST TIMES:	**Tuesday through Friday, when both the Tennessee State Museum and the Tennessee State Capitol are open to the public.**
WORST TIMES:	**Sunday, Monday, and holidays, when a number of places are closed. Or anytime the Titans have a home football game, which makes traffic and parking a mess.**

Though Nashville is a city of the New South and sprawls in all directions with suburbs full of office parks and shopping malls, it still has a downtown where you can do a bit of exploring on foot. Within the downtown area are the three distinct areas that make up the District, a historic area containing many late-19th-century commercial buildings that have been preserved and now house restaurants, clubs, and interesting shops. Because Nashville is the state capital, the downtown area also has many impressive government office buildings.

Start your tour at the intersection of Broadway and First Avenue, on the banks of the Cumberland River, at:

1 Riverfront Park

The park was built as part of Nashville's bicentennial celebration, and it's where the Nashville trolleys start their circuits around downtown and out to Music Row. If you grow tired of walking at any time during your walk, just look for a trolley stop and ride the free trolley back to the park.

Walk north along the river to:

2 Fort Nashborough

This is a reconstruction of the 1780 fort that served as the first white settlement in this area.

Continue up First Avenue to Union Street and turn left. Across the street is the:

3 Metropolitan Courthouse

This imposing building, which also houses the Nashville City Hall, was built in 1937. It incorporates many classic Greek architectural details. Of particular interest are the bronze doors, the etched-glass panels above the doors, and the lobby murals. At the information booth in the lobby, you can pick up a brochure detailing the building's many design elements.

If you now head back down Second Avenue, you'll find yourself in the:

4 Second Avenue Historic District

Between Union Avenue and Broadway are numerous Victorian commercial buildings, most of which have now been restored. Much of the architectural detail is near the tops of the buildings, so keep your eyes trained upward.

5 Take a Break ☕

Second Avenue has several excellent restaurants where you can stop for lunch or a drink. The Old Spaghetti Factory, 160 Second Ave. N. (© **615/254-9010**), is a cavernous place filled with Victorian antiques. There's even a trolley car parked in the middle of the main dining room. A couple of doors down is B.B. King's Blues Club, at 152 Second Ave. N. (© **615/256-2727**), a bluesy bar with a juke-joint atmosphere where you can sample Southern food or grab a burger.

A few doors down from The Old Spaghetti Factory you'll find:

6 Wildhorse Saloon

This is Nashville's hottest country nightspot. In the daylight hours, you can snap a picture of the comical, cowboy-booted horse statue near the front entrance.

Also along this stretch of the street is the:

7 Market Street Emporium

The emporium holds a collection of specialty shops.

At the corner of Second Avenue and Broadway, turn right. Between Third and Fourth avenues, watch for:

8 Hatch Show Print

The oldest poster shop in the United States still prints its posters on an old-fashioned letterpress printer. The most popular posters are those advertising the *Grand Ole Opry.*

Cross Fourth Avenue and you'll come to:

9 Gruhn Guitars

This is the most famous guitar shop in Nashville; it specializes in used and vintage guitars.

Walk up Fourth Avenue less than a block and you will come to the new main entrance of:

10 Ryman Auditorium

The *Grand Ole Opry* was held here from 1943 to 1974. The building was originally built as a tabernacle to host evangelical revival meetings, but because of its good acoustics and large seating capacity, it became a popular setting for theater and music performances.

After leaving the Ryman Auditorium, walk back down to the corner of Broadway and Fourth Avenue.

11 Take a Break ☕

If you didn't stop for lunch on Second Avenue, now would be a good time. On the opposite side of the street from The Ryman, at Fourth and Broadway, is The Merchants restaurant, at 401 Broadway (© 615/254-1892), a favorite Nashville power-lunch spot. The atmosphere is sophisticated and the cuisine is American Southern.

In the same block as The Merchants, you'll find the:

12 Ernest Tubb Record Shop

This store was once the home of the *Midnite Jamboree,* a country music radio show that took place after the *Grand Ole Opry* was over on Saturday nights.

Continue up the block to the corner of Fifth Avenue and you'll come to the main entrance of the new:

13 Bridgestone Arena

The Bridgestone Arena is a sports and entertainment venue that also houses one of two downtown Nashville Convention & Visitors Bureau Visitors Centers. If you haven't already stopped in for information or to check out the gift shop or pick up a map, now would be a good time.

Back across Broadway, you'll find:

14 Tootsie's Orchid Lounge

Grand Ole Opry musicians used to duck in here after their shows at The Ryman. One of the more famous bars in Nashville, it offers live country music all day long.

From this corner, head up Broadway, and at the corner of Seventh Avenue, you'll find the:

15 First Baptist Church

This modern building incorporates a Victorian Gothic church tower built between 1884 and 1886. The church's congregation wanted a new church but didn't want to give up the beautiful old tower. This is the compromise that was reached.

Across Seventh Avenue is the:

16 U.S. Customs House

Now leased as private office space, this Victorian Gothic building was built in 1877 and displays fine stonework and friezes. The imposing structure, with its soaring tower and arched windows, could be in any European city.

Directly across the street is:

17 Hume-Fogg High School

Built between 1912 and 1916, the building incorporates elements of English Tudor and Gothic design.

Two blocks farther up Broadway, you'll see a decidedly different style of architecture, the:

18 Frist Center for the Visual Arts

This breathtaking art museum is housed in the historic U.S. Post Office building, designed with elements of both neoclassical and Art Deco architectural styling.

The post office shares a parking lot with:

19 Union Station Hotel

This Victorian Romanesque Revival building was built in 1900 as Nashville's main passenger railroad station, but, in 1986, it was renovated and reopened as a luxury hotel. The stone exterior walls incorporate many fine carvings, and the lobby is one of the most elegant historic spaces in Nashville.

Head back the way you came and cross over to the opposite side of Broadway at Ninth Avenue. Here you'll find:

20 Christ Episcopal Church

Constructed between 1887 and 1892, the building is in the Victorian Gothic style and is complete with gargoyles. This church also has Tiffany stained-glass windows.

Continue back down Broadway and, at Seventh Avenue, turn left and walk up to Union Street and turn right. In 1 block, you'll come to the:

21 Hermitage Hotel

This is Nashville's last grand old hotel. The lobby exudes Beaux Arts extravagance, with a stained-glass skylight and marble columns and floor.

Across Union Street from the Hermitage Hotel is:

22 Legislative Plaza

This large public plaza is a popular lunch spot for downtown office workers.

Fronting this plaza is the:

23 War Memorial Building

This neoclassical building was built in 1925 to honor soldiers who died in World War I. The centerpiece is an atrium holding a large statue titled *Victory.* This building also houses the Tennessee State Museum Military Branch.

On the opposite side of the plaza is the:

24 Tennessee State Museum

In the basement of the same building that houses the Tennessee Performing Arts Center, this museum contains an extensive and well-displayed collection of artifacts pertaining to Tennessee history.

Returning to the Legislative Plaza and continuing to the north across Charlotte Street will bring you to the:

25 Tennessee State Capitol

This Greek Revival building was built between 1845 and 1859. Be sure to take a look inside, where you'll find many beautiful architectural details and works of art.

If you walk back across the Legislative Plaza and take a left on Union Street and then a right on Fifth Avenue (cross to the far side of the street), you'll come to the west entrance of the:

26 Nashville Arcade

This covered shopping arcade was built in 1903 and is modeled after an arcade in Italy. Only a few such arcades remain in the United States, and, unfortunately, no one has yet breathed new life into this one. Still, you can mail a letter here or buy a bag of fresh-roasted peanuts.

Walk through the arcade and continue across Fourth Avenue. The alley in front of you leads to:

27 Printer's Alley

For more than a century, this has been a center for evening entertainment. Today, things are much tamer than they once were, but you can still find several nightclubs featuring live music.

ORGANIZED TOURS

City & Homes-of-the-Stars Tours

Gray Line Nashville, 2416 Music Valley Dr. (© 800/251-1864 or 615/883-5555; www.graylinenashville.com), offers more than half a dozen tours ranging in length from 3½ hours to a full day. On the popular 3½-hour tour of the stars' homes, you'll ride past the current or former houses and mansions of such chart toppers as Hank Williams, Dolly Parton, Trisha Yearwood, Martina McBride, and Alan Jackson. Other themed tours focus exclusively on historical sites, honky-tonks, and nightlife. Adult tour prices range from $41 for the "Homes of the Country Stars" bus tour to $90 for a dinner cruise on the *General Jackson* Showboat.

For a fun and campy tour of Nashville aboard a gaudy pink bus, try **Nash-Trash Tours** (© 800/342-2132 or 615/226-7300; www.nashtrash.com), narrated by the spandex-clad "Jugg" sisters. Sheri Lynn and Brenda Kay dish the dirt on all your favorite country stars. Throw in a few risqué jokes, plenty of music, and a policy that allows passengers to bring aboard coolers (with alcohol, if desired), and it all makes for a trashy good time in Music City. Because the 90-minute tours can become rowdy, they're not advised for young children (those 12 and under are not allowed). Hours vary, but generally speaking, tours are offered Tuesday through Saturday. Call in advance for current times and to make reservations, which are required. Tickets, which cost $32 for adults, $30 for seniors and ages 13 to 18, include tip for the bus driver but not 9.25% sales tax. (Rates are discounted in Jan.) Bring plenty of extra cash if you want to buy any of the commemorative souvenirs the sisters hawk. *Note:* The bus is not wheelchair-accessible.

For groups such as family reunions, churches, and students who would like to learn more about the African-American history of Nashville, contact Bill Daniel at **Nashville Black Heritage Tours,** in nearby Smyrna, Tennessee (© 615/890-8173).

Riverboat Tours

The Gaylord Opryland Resort and Convention Center, 2800 Opryland Dr. (© 615/883-2211; www.generaljackson.com), operates a paddle-wheeler—the *General Jackson* **Showboat** and **Music City Queen** (© 615/458-3900)—on the Cumberland River. Tours depart from a dock near the Gaylord Opryland Resort. At 300 feet long, the *General Jackson* Showboat recalls the days when riverboats were the most sophisticated way to travel. You go on this cruise for the paddle-wheeler experience, not necessarily for the food (not so great) and entertainment that go along with it. Choose entertainment from comedy-variety acts to those with live country music. During the summer, the Southern Nights Cruise offers a three-course dinner and dancing under the stars to live bands. Fares for this trip fall into two categories, depending on how and where the meal is served. For the entertainment plus table seating at dinner served by waitstaff, the costs range from $89 to $96 for adults. Less expensive tickets ($61) are available if you opt for the buffet served on the outdoor decks. Midday cruises are also available mid-April to mid-October, with prices ranging from $47 to $62 for adults. Further discounted rates are available for cruise only, or cruise and buffet only, without entertainment. In addition, special-event cruises with such themes as Valentine's Day, Mardi Gras, Tennessee Titans tailgating, and the holidays are offered year-round. Prices vary. Call for details.

NASHVILLE name GAME

Can you identify these country stars and legends by their real first/last names?

Birth Name	Stage Name
Audrey Faith Perry	Faith Hill
Alvis Edgar	Buck Owens
Virginia Pugh	Tammy Wynette
Eileen Regina Edwards	Shania Twain
Floyd Elliot Wray	Collin Raye
Waylon Albright	Shooter Jennings
Sarah Ophelia Colley Cannon	Minnie Pearl
Patricia Lynn	Trisha Yearwood
Maurice Woodward	Tex Ritter
Ernest Jennings Ford	Tennessee Ernie Ford
William Neal Browder	T. G. Sheppard
Anthony Graham	T. Graham Brown
Randy Bruce Traywick	Randy Travis
Patricia Lee Ramey	Patty Loveless
Ruby Blevins	Patsy Montana
Lonnie Melvin	Mel Tillis
Loretta Webb	Loretta Lynn
Loretta Lynn Morgan	Lorrie Morgan
James Cecil Dickens	Little Jimmy Dickens
Eileen Muriel Deason	Kitty Wells
Kathleen Alice	Kathy Mattea
Louis Marshall	Grandpa Jones
Troyal Brooks	Garth Brooks
Virginia Patterson Hensley	Patsy Cline
Brenda Gail Webb Gatzimos	Crystal Gayle

Bonus question: Which country star's middle name is also his wife's maiden name? **Answer:** Vince Grant Gill, who married Amy Grant.

Double bonus question: Which singer-songwriter named one of her daughters after Minnie Pearl? **Answer:** Amy Grant, who named her daughter Sarah Cannon Chapman.

OUTDOOR ACTIVITIES

BOAT RENTALS   In the summer, pontoon boats can be rented at **Four Corners Marina,** on Percy Priest Lake, 4027 Lavergne Couchville Pike, Antioch (© **615/641-9523**). The gorgeous lake, only a few miles east of downtown, is surrounded by a series of parks, trees, and natural beauty.

At Kingston Springs, about 20 miles west of Nashville off I-40, you can rent canoes from **Tip-a-Canoe,** 1279 U.S. 70, at Harpeth River Bridge (© **800/550-5810** or 615/254-0836; www.tip-a-canoe.com), or bring your own. Canoe trips of varying lengths, from a couple of hours up to 5 days, can be arranged. Rates, which include paddles, life jackets, cushions, and the shuttle upriver to your chosen put-in point,

THE "man in black" IS BACK

Johnny Cash, a Sun Studio pioneer with Elvis in the 1950s who became one of country music's most enduring stars, is poised for a posthumous comeback in 2012, with the launch of two major tourist sites dedicated to the American icon.

On Feb. 26, 2012, on what would have been the singer-songwriter's 80th birthday, family members including daughter Rosanne Cash gathered at his boyhood home in the tiny farming community of Dyess, Arkansas, 45 miles north of Memphis, to break ground on the **Johnny Cash Boyhood Home Project.**

Restoration of the modest home where he grew up is being undertaken with Arkansas State University in Jonesboro, and with fundraising help from Cash's friends and fellow country-music legends George Jones and Kris Kristofferson.

The museum is being planned as a permanent tribute to Cash's early life and to "reflect an historical slice of American life during the 1930s Great Depression," according to published reports.

Dyess has a rich cultural heritage, having benefitted from the government's New Deal economic program to help the poor. In 1935, Johnny's parents, Ray and Carrie Cash, were among the families who received a new house, acres of farmland, and a mule. The Cash clan lived in Dyess from 1935 to 1954. Growing up, Johnny—then known as J.R.—worked in the area's cotton fields and sang in the church choir, before graduating from high school in 1950.

For updates on the Dyess project, visit Arkansas State's heritage sites website: http://arkansasheritagesites.astate.edu.

The other major initiative honoring the so-called Man in Black is the **Johnny Cash Museum,** which at press time had just been announced for downtown Nashville and is expected to open by the summer of 2012. The museum is at 119 Third Avenue South at the intersection of Lower Broadway, near the Country Music Hall of Fame and historic Ryman Auditorium.

The 18,000-square-foot space includes interactive exhibits and a 250-seat auditorium for live musical performances. Bill Miller, the star's lifelong confidante, has spearheaded the $7-million museum that includes memorabilia from family and friends.

Also on display are items from the House of Cash (a former museum in nearby Hendersonville, TN, where Johnny and June Carter Cash lived in their later years) and the "Walk the Line" singer's famed Gibson guitar, on loan from the Rock and Roll Hall of Fame Museum.

start at $25 per canoe and go up to $125 for a 5-day trip. Double-decker pontoon boats are also available at a cost of $350 per 8 hours, plus gas and tax. The Harpeth River is a meandering, scenic river of mostly Class I water with some Class II—and a few spots where you'll have to carry the canoe.

GOLF   For many golfing visitors, Opryland's **Gaylord Springs Golf Links,** 18 Springhouse Lane (✆ 615/458-1730; www.gaylordsprings.com), is a highlight. This par-72, 18-hole course is set on the bank of the Cumberland River. The course boasts not only challenging links, but also an antebellum-style clubhouse that would have made Rhett Butler feel right at home. Greens fees range from $40 to $75 for 18 holes. For the most serious enthusiasts, the Golf Institute at Gaylord Springs offers high-tech analysis of golfers' swings, two indoor hitting bays for year-round instruction, and on-site customized club fittings and repair workshop.

HORSEBACK RIDING   If you want to go for a ride through the Tennessee hills, there are a couple of nearby places where you can rent a horse. **A Cowboy Town,** 3665 Knight Rd., Whites Creek, 7 miles north of downtown Nashville, is a Western-style family theme park. Admission, which is $38 per day for adults, includes stage shows, such as gunfights, hiking, hayrides, and horseback riding. The park is open only on weekends from May 1 to October 31. To make reservations by phone on weekdays, call ✆ **615/242-6201;** on weekends, call ✆ **615/876-1029.** Also visit www.acowboytown.com.

   JuRo Stables, 735 Carver Lane, Mt. Juliet (✆ **615/773-7433;** www.jurostables. com), is located about 15 minutes from Nashville on I-40 east, at the Mt. Juliet exit, with charges starting at $27 an hour for adults and $22 for children. Ninety-minute rides are also available, as are sunset and evening rides. In business for more than 2 decades, JuRo Stables is open daily, year-round.

SWIMMING, SKATING & TENNIS   The Thomas F. Frist Centennial **Sportsplex,** 222 25th Ave. N. (✆ **615/862-8490;** www.sportsplextennis.com), is a year-round recreation center at Centennial Park offering everything from ice skating and swimming to tennis, with both indoor and outdoor courts. Lap lanes for indoor swimming are available Monday through Saturday. There is also a small indoor children's pool. Day passes for tourists vary according to activities.

   If you're visiting in warm weather and want to go jump in a lake, head for **Percy Priest Lake.** You'll find this large man-made reservoir just east of downtown Nashville, at exit 219 off I-40. Stop by the information center to get a map showing the three designated swimming areas.

WHERE TO EAT IN NASHVILLE

The rest of the country may make fun of Southern cooking, with its fatback and chitlins, collard greens, and fried everything, but there is much more to Southern food than these tired stereotypes. Yes, you can find excellent French, German, Italian, Japanese, and Mediterranean fare, but as long as you're below the Mason-Dixon line, you owe it to yourself to try country cooking. Barbecue and fried catfish are two inexpensive staples, as are the old-fashioned American "meat-and-three's." These are mom-and-pop places where you get an entree (fried chicken, meatloaf, pork chop, and so on) and your choice of three vegetables. Corn bread and biscuits are usually included. The restaurants recommended here are almost entirely those that are locally owned and operated. For more independently owned restaurant suggestions, visit www.nashvilleoriginals.com.

BEST RESTAURANT BETS

o **Best Meat-and-Three: Arnold's Country Kitchen,** 605 Eighth Ave. S. (© **615/256-4455**), is a modest downtown hole-in-the-wall kind of place, but crowds congregate here every weekday at lunchtime for good reason: Simply prepared, delicious plate lunches, brimming with "meats" such as fried chicken and sides including buttery mashed potatoes and collard greens, personify Southern, home-style cooking. See p. 65.

o **Best Spot for a Romantic Dinner:** Something of a well-kept secret among locals and the college crowd, **Tin Angel,** 3201 West End, is a cozy and intimate West End bistro with loads of charm: twinkling lights in the picture window, pressed-tin ceilings, comfy booths, and a crackling fireplace. This is a place to linger with your loved one over a few glasses of wine and dinner. See p. 74.

o **Best Farm-to-Fork Restaurant: The Silly Goose** is a silly name for an insanely good casual eatery in East Nashville, where farm-fresh salads and excellent sandwiches include artisanal cheeses, locally sourced fruits and vegetables, and sustainably raised meats and poultry from Tennessee farms. See p. 79.

o **Best Spot for a Business Lunch: The Merchants,** 401 Broadway (© **615/254-1892**), is a locally owned, business-casual restaurant in the heart of downtown. The upstairs dining room is a relatively quiet, semisecluded space for signing that record deal or discussing other pressing matters over a martini and pecan-crusted trout or pork tenderloin. See p. 62.

PRICE CATEGORIES

Expensive	$41 and up
Moderate	$20–$40
Inexpensive	Under $20

- **Best for Kids:** It's not everywhere that you get to eat in a restaurant next to a full-size trolley car, and anyway, isn't spaghetti one of the major food groups? For less than most restaurants charge for a round of drinks, the whole family can eat at **The Old Spaghetti Factory,** 160 Second Ave. N. (© **615/254-9010**) in the heart of the District. See p. 66.

- **Best for Big Families:** You'll think it's Sunday dinner at Grandma's when you enter the cozy Victorian home that houses **Monell's,** 1235 Sixth Ave. N. (© **615/248-4747**) downtown. You'll share a big table with family and fellow travelers, passing dishes of old-fashioned Southern staples such as fried chicken, mashed potatoes, and greens. See p. 68.

- **Best Splurge:** With live jazz, an award-winning wine list boasting more than 300 selections, and expertly cooked seasonal specialties ranging from pan-seared red snapper to grilled wild boar, **F. Scott's,** 2210 Crestmoor Rd. (© **615/269-5861**), is a sophisticated culinary destination just right for pulling out all the stops on a special night out. See p. 69.

- **Best Views:** The **Germantown Café,** 1200 Fifth Ave. N. (© **615/242-3226**), overlooks downtown Nashville's gleaming skyline as seen from the northern edge of the city. And sister eatery **Germantown Café East,** 501 Main St. (© **615/242-3522**) in East Nashville, has equally compelling, westward-facing views of the same skyline. See p. 68.

- **Best Service:** Everything about The Hermitage Hotel is extraordinary, and that includes the service. Well-trained waitstaff are intuitively attentive to the dining needs of customers enjoying Southern-influenced, farm-fresh dishes at the hotel's top-notch restaurant, the **Capitol Grille,** 231 Sixth Ave. N. (© **615/345-7116**). See p. 59.

- **Best Southern Soul Food:** One of Nashville's oldest African-American–owned restaurants, **Swett's,** 2725 Clifton Ave. (© **615/329-4418**), is still the benchmark for home-style comfort foods such as pork chops, slow-simmered green beans, corn bread, and macaroni and cheese. That first bite of banana pudding may bring tears to your eyes. See p. 67.

- **Best Bang for Your Buck:** The **Nashville Farmers Market,** 900 Eighth Ave. N. (© **615/880-2001**), has it all: The gorgeous, farm-fresh produce is a feast for the eyes, and quick-service restaurants inside the concessions area offer a cornucopia of cuisines, as well as prices that are easy on the wallet. See p. 66.

DOWNTOWN, THE GULCH & 12SOUTH

Expensive

Capitol Grille ★★★ AMERICAN/SOUTHERN   Chef Tyler Brown maintains the high standards at the Hermitage Hotel's flagship restaurant, a lower-level dining

Nashville Restaurants: Downtown Area, the West End & Green Hills

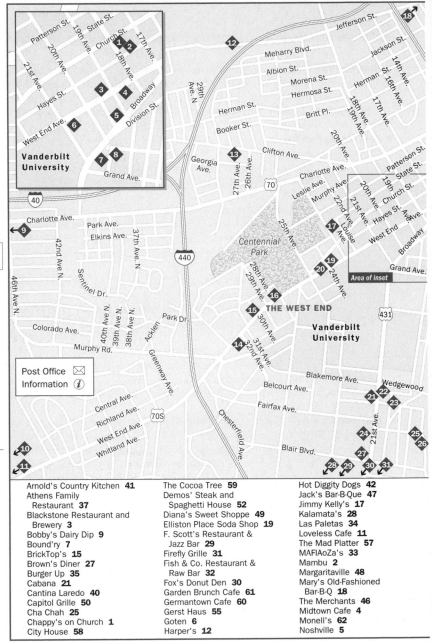

Post Office ✉
Information ⓘ

Arnold's Country Kitchen **41**
Athens Family
  Restaurant **37**
Blackstone Restaurant and
  Brewery **3**
Bobby's Dairy Dip **9**
Bound'ry **7**
BrickTop's **15**
Brown's Diner **27**
Burger Up **35**
Cabana **21**
Cantina Laredo **40**
Capitol Grille **50**
Cha Chah **25**
Chappy's on Church **1**
City House **58**

The Cocoa Tree **59**
Demos' Steak and
  Spaghetti House **52**
Diana's Sweet Shoppe **49**
Elliston Place Soda Shop **19**
F. Scott's Restaurant &
  Jazz Bar **29**
Firefly Grille **31**
Fish & Co. Restaurant &
  Raw Bar **32**
Fox's Donut Den **30**
Garden Brunch Cafe **61**
Germantown Cafe **60**
Gerst Haus **55**
Goten **6**
Harper's **12**

Hot Diggity Dogs **42**
Jack's Bar-B-Que **47**
Jimmy Kelly's **17**
Kalamata's **28**
Las Paletas **34**
Loveless Cafe **11**
The Mad Platter **57**
MAFIAoZa's **33**
Mambu **2**
Margaritaville **48**
Mary's Old-Fashioned
  Bar-B-Q **18**
The Merchants **46**
Midtown Cafe **4**
Monell's **62**
Noshville **5**

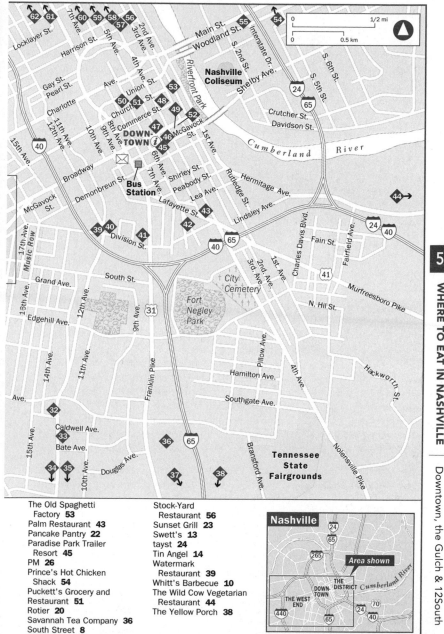

The Old Spaghetti
  Factory **53**
Palm Restaurant **43**
Pancake Pantry **22**
Paradise Park Trailer
  Resort **45**
PM **26**
Prince's Hot Chicken
  Shack **54**
Puckett's Grocery and
  Restaurant **51**
Rotier **20**
Savannah Tea Company **36**
South Street **8**

Stock-Yard
  Restaurant **56**
Sunset Grill **23**
Swett's **13**
tayst **24**
Tin Angel **14**
Watermark
  Restaurant **39**
Whitt's Barbecue **10**
The Wild Cow Vegetarian
  Restaurant **44**
The Yellow Porch **38**

room brimming with politicians and power-lunchers, but he does much more. No longer the fussy bastion of gourmet meals it once was, the Capitol Grille now showcases sustainably grown produce, such as heirloom tomatoes, squash, pumpkins, watermelons, and potatoes, that the chef and his team tend themselves on the hotel's 66-acre Glen Leven Farm, on the outskirts of Nashville. Entrees including grilled grouper, Niman Ranch pork chops, and Kobe beef short ribs are cooked to perfection. Starters include crab cakes, salads, and pâtés. Best of these is the sweet onion bisque with bacon and chives and a crouton-sized grilled cheese cube made with brie. Befitting such a prestigious hotel, service is expectedly polished yet unpretentious—a nice combination for well-traveled diners with high expectations.

In the Hermitage Hotel, 231 Sixth Ave. N. ⓒ **615/345-7116.** www.thehermitagehotel.com. Reservations recommended. Main courses $24–$36. AE, DC, DISC, MC, V. Daily 6:30–11am, 11:30am–2pm, and 5:30–10pm.

Chappy's on Church ★★ CAJUN/CREOLE/BRUNCH
Mississippi Gulf Coast restaurateur John Chapman lost his 20-year-old restaurant, Chappy's, during Hurricane Katrina. Relocating to Nashville, he set up shop in this yellow-brick corner building on Church Street in 2006. An old New Orleans vibe, with French street lamps and stained glass, pervades the romantic, two-tiered restaurant and bar. Creole soups, seafood, grits, and bread pudding are among Chef Chapman's signature dishes. Elevate your spirits with the Sunday-morning champagne brunch, which features live music.

1721 Church St. ⓒ **615/322-9932.** www.chappys.com. Reservations recommended. Main courses $19–$32. AE, DISC, MC, V. Mon–Fri 11am–2pm and 5–10pm; Sat–Sun 11am–10pm (brunch until 3pm).

Fish & Co. Restaurant and Raw Bar SEAFOOD/BRUNCH
Chalkboard specials invite diners to dive into oysters done in a variety of ways, as well as platters of grilled or fried salmon, grouper, and bacon-wrapped trout. Meals include heavenly warm bread and sides such as fried okra and potato-shrimp hash. Bustling and lively, Fish & Co. draws a younger, outgoing clientele—the kind of crowd that doesn't shy away from ordering desserts. Tempting choices include cinnamon-roll beignets and a chocolate-and-marshmallow crème brûlée. Southern-inspired Sunday brunch boasts Low Country shrimp and grits, and Charleston she-crab soup, as well as vanilla-bourbon bread pudding garnished with bananas, pecans, and sorghum butter.

2317 12th Ave. S. ⓒ **615/320-1119.** www.fishco-nashville.com. Reservations recommended. Entrees $18–$34. MC, V. Sun–Thurs 11am–9pm; Fri 11am–10pm; Sat noon–10pm.

The Merchants ★ AMERICAN
Housed in a restored brick building amid the rowdy bars of lower Broadway, this classy restaurant is another favorite power-lunch spot and after-work hangout for the young executive set. The restaurant's first floor is a cafe and bar (The Grille menu includes a smattering of burgers, salads, and sandwiches in the $10–$14 price range), while the upstairs is a more formal dining room. Lunch or dinner here might begin with shrimp-and-lobster fondue. From there, you could move on to pan-seared, pecan-crusted trout with chive butter, or perhaps a pork tenderloin with smoked cheddar and chorizo polenta. The Merchants also boasts an extensive wine list.

401 Broadway. ⓒ **615/254-1892.** www.merchantsrestaurant.com. Reservations recommended. Main courses $13–$21. AE, DC, DISC, MC, V. Sun–Wed 11am–midnight; Thurs–Sat 11am–2am.

The Palm Restaurant STEAKS
The "in" place to see and be seen, the Palm is an upscale enclave, located within the cushy confines of the Hilton Suites downtown.

Conspicuous consumption is a hallmark here, where a 36-ounce New York strip for two comes with a $94 price tag. Chops include thick cuts of lamb, pork, and veal, while beefeaters may opt for everything from prime rib to aged porterhouse. Salads, pasta, chicken, and fish dishes should appease diners who don't do beef. String beans, creamed spinach, mashed potatoes, and other sides are served family style. Celebs favor the private dining rooms, though if you keep your eyes peeled, you may see a Tennessee Titan or two, or the occasional country music star.

1140 Fifth Ave. S. ⓒ **615/742-7256.** www.thepalm.com. Reservations recommended. Main courses $15 lunch, $24–$49 dinner. AE, DC, DISC, MC, V. Mon–Fri 11am–11pm; Sat 5–11pm; Sun 5–10pm.

Stock-Yard Restaurant STEAKS   If The Palm seems too pompous, head a few blocks uptown to the old Nashville Union Stockyard building, where local old-money types have gathered to slice slabs of beef for decades. It's where Dad comes for Father's Day, or Son on his graduation. Prime rib, porterhouse, rib-eyes, and surf-and-turf combos are available in small, medium, and large portions. If you're not a steak eater but still would like to visit this Nashville tradition, you'll find several seafood, pork, and chicken dishes, as well as a few pasta plates. Although there's plenty of free parking on-site, the restaurant offers a free shuttle to hotels within a 15-mile radius. Call ahead for a space on the buses, which seat between 14 and 45 people.

901 Second Ave. N. ⓒ **615/255-6464.** www.stock-yardrestaurant.com. Reservations highly recommended. Main courses $30–$40. AE, DC, DISC, MC, V. Mon–Thurs 5–10pm; Fri–Sat 5–11pm; Sun 5–9pm.

Watermark Restaurant ★★★ AMERICAN/SOUTHERN   When Executive Chef Joe Shaw, a protégé of Birmingham's renowned Frank Stitt, opened this fine-dining spot in the Gulch in late 2005, Nashvillians had high expectations. Shaw delivered, but his departure 2 years later did little to dampen Watermark's immense appeal. The sophisticated urban dining room and bar is a sleek, modern space, done in blacks and whites. Exquisite preparations of Southern-influenced delicacies include Low Country oyster stew with roasted leeks, bacon, and sherry; and wood-grilled quail, swordfish, and lamb-loin entrees. Local and regional products, such as artisanal cheeses and farm-fresh produce, enliven the flavors brought to the table by experienced waitstaff. Be sure to save room for a dessert wine or the fancy s'mores—a marshmallow-y Jack Daniel's soufflé with graham streusel and chocolate ganache.

507 12th Ave. S. ⓒ **615/254-2000.** www.watermark-restaurant.com. Reservations recommended. Main courses $26–$45. AE, DISC, MC, V. Mon–Thurs 5:30–9:30pm; Fri–Sat 5:30–10pm.

Moderate

Burger Up BURGERS   The 12South area's newest burger joint isn't your typical greasy spoon. Burger Up has staked its claim as the go-to place for steaklike, high-quality hamburgers in Nashville. Beef, bison, turkey, and even quinoa-and-black-bean burgers are served on homemade buns, with fries and Jack Daniel's maple-bourbon ketchup (optional). For something different, try the fried pickle chips and, if you dare, the Krispy Kreme bread pudding for dessert.

2901 12th Ave. S. ⓒ **615/279-3767.** www.burger-up.com. $9–$13. AE, D, MC, V. Sun–Thurs 11am–10pm; Fri–Sat 11am–11pm.

Cantina Laredo MEXICAN   A spacious, upscale dining room done in warm woods and metals sets the stage for the newest eatery in the Gulch. The restaurant specializes in plentiful portions of gourmet Mexican food. Everything from the

Elliston Place Soda Shop (p. 74) Fried baloney sandwiches, meat-and-three's, milkshakes, and pies please adults and kids alike at this authentic diner that's been in business since 1939.

Monell's (p. 68) Southern comfort foods are served family style in this lovely Victorian home in the historic Germantown neighborhood north of downtown. Kids can pick and choose what they want from the bowls and platters of food that are passed around.

Pied Piper Creamery (p. 79) An informal children's play area with toys and books fills the front parlor of this 100-year-old home-turned-ice-cream-shop in East Nashville. Kid-pleasing ice-cream cones include Smurf-berry and Birthday Cake flavors, and there's a big

front porch where you can linger while licking away.

The Old Spaghetti Factory (p. 66) A winning combination of simplicity and novelty makes this downtown pasta place a fun, affordable option for families. What kid wouldn't want to eat spaghetti and meatballs in an antique trolley car?

I Dream of Weenie (p. 78) Who needs a trolley when there's a 1960s-era, mustard-yellow Volkswagen bus doing hot dogs in dozens of crazy ways? The weird little "weenerie," a cash-only, walk-up eatery in East Nashville, also offers its dogs plain, for picky little eaters. In nice weather, take a picnic blanket and spread out in the grassy area by the big magnolia tree.

enchiladas, chiles rellenos, and carnitas to the fajitas and tacos is fresh and first rate. The guacamole that's made tableside may be gimmicky, but it tastes great. Creamy flan or chocolate cake might seem like good dessert options, but consider the crepes instead.

592 12th Ave. S. ✆ **615/259-9282.** www.cantinalaredo.com. Reservations recommended. Main courses $12–$27. AE, DISC, MC, V. Mon–Thurs 11am–10pm; Fri–Sat 11am–11pm; Sun 11am–9pm.

Demos' Steak & Spaghetti House 🍴 STEAKS/AMERICAN This fourth-generation family business is a downtown fixture. Popular as a lunch spot for locals who work in the area, Demos' also does a brisk business with tourists. The reasons are obvious: An eclectic menu offers something for everyone, from fork-tender steaks to baked chicken; the portions are generous; and the staff is focused on keeping customers happy. Weekday lunch specials include salad or chicken soup, as well as fresh-baked bread, and are a steal at under $6, with entree choices like red beans and rice, seafood fettuccine, and lasagna.

300 Commerce St. ✆ **615/824-9097.** www.demosrestaurants.com. Dinner $10–$15; lunch $6–$8. AE, MC, V. Mon–Thurs 11am–10:30pm; Fri–Sat 11am–11pm.

Gerst Haus ★★ GERMAN Since 1955, this beloved Nashville landmark has been best known for its beer-hall atmosphere and classic German food. From its plum perch across the street from LP Field (home of the NFL's Tennessee Titans), chances are the Gerst Haus will be endearing new fans of hearty Bavarian fare for generations to come. Platters include the crowd-pleasing Wiener schnitzel (breaded-and-fried veal) and the tender and tangy sauerbraten (wine-braised lean beef). Sausages and brats also abound on the menu. Red cabbage, rye bread, and handmade spaetzle are savory sides.

301 Woodland St. ☏ **615/244-8886.** www.gersthaus.com. Main courses $13–$19. AE, MC, V. Daily 11am–11pm.

Margaritaville BURGERS   Cleverly named menu items like the Cheeseburger in Paradise and all manner of "frozen concoctions" play to parrot-heads (fans) of Jimmy Buffett, the enduringly popular singer-songwriter who's best known for his hit song "Margaritaville." Merchandising of retail items like hats and T-shirts are as prominent as the food/drink aspect of this visually impressive place: A piano staircase leading to the second-floor bar plays ascending music notes when you step on the keys/stairs. Some say Margaritaville is touristy and overpriced. In any case, its theme park polish seems jarring alongside Broadway's authentic, timeworn honky-tonks.

322 Broadway. ☏ **866/250-5480.** www.margaritavillenashville.com. Prices $8–$25. AE, DISC, MC, V. Daily 11am–2am (retail sales open at 10am).

Puckett's Grocery ★ SOUTHERN/BREAKFAST   From the moment in 2011 when the owners of the popular Franklin, Tennessee, Puckett's opened this downtown Nashville location at 5th and Church, it was an instant hit. Old-timey kitsch— think oversized black-and-white photos of fishin' poles, weathered barns, and Granddaddy's beloved pickup truck—celebrates the original Puckett's, which was a gas station and grocery where food was served back in the 1950s. Beer, burgers, chicken-fried steak, and big breakfasts whet appetites and slake the thirsts of the laid-back customers who linger here in booths or at barstools. Happy hour specials and live music are frequently on tap. And should you need a box of Ziploc bags or a roll of paper towels, you can get those here, too. They're part of that faux-grocery decor.

500 Church. ☏ **615/770-2772.** www.puckettsgrocery.com. Plate lunches $7–$10; dinner entrees $12–$25. MC, V. Tues–Thurs 6am–10pm; Fri–Sat 6am–11pm.

Inexpensive

Arnold's Country Kitchen ★★ SOUTHERN   Plan to arrive early to grab a parking spot in the cracked and busted lot next to Arnold's, a soul food landmark for more than 2 decades. Be prepared to stand in line and to share a table with strangers too, if you plan to eat your buffet meal on the premises. But don't worry; over fried green tomatoes, barbecued pork, fried chicken, and knee-weakening mashed potatoes, you're always among friends.

605 Eighth Ave. S. ☏ **615/256-4455.** Main courses $6.50. Cash only. Mon–Fri 10:30am–2:30pm.

Diana's Sweet Shoppe ★★ ICE CREAM/SANDWICHES   To step inside this old-fashioned soda shop is like going back in time. The beautiful, burled walnut and glass fixtures and antique Violano Virtuoso (a player piano/violin) aren't reproductions but the real thing. Nashville-based Gibson Guitars purchased the furnishings from the 1926 Port Huron, Michigan, landmark and reopened Diana's here in Music City. (Gibson was founded in Kalamazoo.) A glass candy counter displays gorgeous candies and squares of glistening fudge. A quaint yet elegant full-service cafe is in the back part of the room, where patrons sit in intimate, polished wood booths. The cafe's specialties are salads, soups, and especially sandwiches, which come cold, toasted, or steamed. Try the roast beef with cheddar and horseradish, or the gooey grilled-cheese and pesto panini. Sides, including homemade potato salad, are rich and creamy. For dessert, savor a silver dish of milk chocolate ice cream, a peanut butter milkshake, or a root beer float.

318 Broadway. ℂ **615/242-5397.** www.dianasnashville.com. Prices $7–$10. AE, DISC, MC, V. Sun–Thurs 10:30am–8pm; Fri–Sat 10:30am–9pm.

Hot Diggity Dogs 🍴 HOT DOGS   Hot dogs and bratwursts come dressed with sauerkraut, coleslaw, mustard, pickles, or dozens of other combinations at this rick-ety-looking house just south of downtown. It's a small, cramped diner where you order the minute you open the door. Snag a stool by the window or venture to the outdoor deck to enjoy a beer, a dog, and a side of fries. And in your wildest weenie dreams, I'll bet you couldn't have guessed that they also offer vegetarian dogs. But they do.

614 Ewing Ave. ℂ **615/255-3717.** www.hotdiggitydogstn.com. Hot dogs $2.45, bratwursts $4.85. MC, V. Mon–Fri 10:30am–4:30pm; Sat 11am–4:30pm.

Las Paletas ★ ICE CREAM/MEXICAN   Sweet indulgences such as these *pale-tas* (traditional Mexican popsicles) are sublime when they're both delicious *and* wholesome—made fresh daily without preservatives or syrupy artificial additives. The small, unmarked storefront at the edge of the 12th Avenue South corridor offers several dozen flavors on any given day: Rose-petal, hibiscus, tamarind, watermelon, and prune are delicate tastes, while jalapeño and chili-cucumber are bright and bold on the palate. At only $2.50 a pop, you can afford to try more than one.

2907 12th Ave. S. ℂ **615/386-2101.** Popsicles $2.50. Cash only. Tues–Sat noon–6pm. Hours are seasonal; call ahead.

Mafiaoza's PIZZA   With a toasty fire crackling in the pizza ovens and the dim roar of a lively cocktail crowd, this pizzeria in the trendy 12th Avenue South district has built a loyal following. An outdoor patio gives patrons a great place to hang while throwing back a few beers or bottles of vino. Skip the soggy, tomato-laden bruschetta, but try the meaty pasta dishes and thin-crust pizzas, sold by the slice or whole pie.

2400 12th Ave. S. ℂ **615/269-4646.** www.mafiaozas.com. Main courses $6.75–$25. AE, DISC, MC, V. Tues–Fri 4pm–3am; Sat–Sun 11am–3am.

Nashville Farmers' Market ★★ 🍴 AMERICAN   A food lover's delight, this extensive farmers' market is a feast for the eyes and a temptation for appetites. Strol-ling through the open-air stalls past pickup trucks loaded with turnips, corn on the cob, and tomatoes, you'll come to an enclosed concession area with scads of great quick-service restaurants, including **AM@FM** (noted local chef Arnold Myint's new eatery; no phone); **Jamaicaway** (ℂ 615/255-5920); **Swajruha Indian Restau-rant** (ℂ 615/736-7001); **Louisiana Seafood Co.** (ℂ 615/499-6865); the **Original Nooleys (New Orleans)** (ℂ 615/259-9818); **Green Asia** (ℂ 615/732-0839); and **El Burrito Mexicano** (ℂ 615/255-0136); plus coffee shops and pastries and barbecue.

900 Eighth Ave. N. ℂ **615/880-2001.** www.nashvillefarmersmarket.org. Main courses under $10. MC, V. Daily from 10am.

The Old Spaghetti Factory ★ ☺ ITALIAN   With its ornate Victorian decor, you'd never guess that this restaurant was once a warehouse. Where boxes and bags were stacked, diners now sit surrounded by burnished wood. There's stained and beveled glass all around, antiques everywhere, and plush seating in the waiting area. The front of the restaurant is a large and very elegant bar. Now if they'd just do some-thing about that trolley car someone parked in the middle of the dining room. A complete meal—including a salad, bread, spumoni ice cream, and a beverage—will cost you less than a cocktail in many restaurants. Where else can you opt for gluten-free pasta dishes and order an Oreo milkshake for dessert? A great spot to bring the family, this is one of the cheapest places to get a good meal downtown.

160 Second Ave. N. ℂ **615/254-9010.** www.osf.com. Main courses $9–$12. AE, DISC, MC, V. Mon–Fri 11:30am–2pm; Mon–Thurs 5–9:30pm; Fri 5–10pm; Sat noon–10:30pm; Sun noon–9:30pm.

Paradise Park Trailer Resort AMERICAN   Funny how fried bologna and Spam-and-cheese sandwiches taste so mighty good with Guns N' Roses blaring in the background. But they do at this cheap, 24-hour diner that looks and feels like a trailer park in the wrong part of town. The could-care-less staff wear T-shirts reading "Best Mullet in Town," a thought for you to ponder as you sink back into your plastic lawn chair and decide whether to cap off your paper-plate meal with the Twinkie or the Moon Pie, both of which are on the menu. Paradise Park also serves bacon and eggs and pancakes for breakfast.

411 Broadway. ℂ **615/251-1515.** www.paradiseparkonline.com. Main courses $6–$9. MC, V. Daily 24 hr.

Swett's ★★★ SOUTHERN   Southern soul food is doled out, cafeteria style, in the city's oldest minority-owned restaurant, which has been in business since 1954. Fresh-cooked collard greens, sweet potatoes, buttered corn, pork-laden green beans, and crumbly corn bread keep the place packed from lunchtime until after supper. Entrees include juicy fried chicken as well as beef, pork, and fish dishes, but I can make a meal of the wicked macaroni and cheese. Wash it down with sweet iced tea—and save room for banana pudding or peach pie.

2725 Clifton Ave. ℂ **615/329-4418.** www.swettsrestaurant.com. Main courses $7.85 AE, DISC, MC, V. Daily 11am–8pm.

GERMANTOWN & JEFFERSON STREET

For restaurants in this section, see the "Nashville Restaurants: Downtown Area, the West End & Green Hills" map, on p. 60.

Expensive

The Mad Platter AMERICAN   Located in an old brick corner store in a historic neighborhood of restored Victorian houses, the Mad Platter feels like a cozy upscale library, with bookshelves crammed with knickknacks and old copies of *National Geographic*. The ambience is reserved, not pretentious, and service is personable, if a bit slow at times. The menu, including vegetarian options, changes daily. Appetizers might include a Gorgonzola-and-asparagus napoleon, as well as a prosciutto roulade stuffed with truffle mousse. Recent entrees have included grilled duck breast basted with a pomegranate molasses, and a rack-of-lamb *moutarde*. Don't leave without trying the best-named dessert in all of Nashville: The Chocolate Elvis is an obscenely rich, fudgy cake that is worthy of The King.

1239 Sixth Ave. N. ℂ **615/242-2563.** www.themadplatterrestaurant.com. Reservations recommended. Main courses $18–$29. AE, DC, DISC, MC, V. Mon–Fri 11am–2pm; Tues–Sat 5:30–11pm; Sun 5–10pm.

Moderate

City House ★★ ITALIAN/PIZZA   Antipasto, pizza, and pasta are plentiful at this new rustic Italian restaurant in the Germantown neighborhood. But City House's hallmark is its charcuterie, including house-cured meats, salami, terrines, and meat-balls. Menus change frequently to reflect the whims and creative pursuits of the restaurant's young chefs. House-made sausages with cabbage, cannellini beans, and horseradish will stick to your ribs, while cornmeal-crusted catfish is a tad lighter, served with baby butter beans, lemon, parsley, and chilies. An extensive wine collection includes a variety of dessert wines, and the restaurant's screened-in wood porch makes a great place to linger in nice weather.

1222 Fourth Ave. N. © **615/736-5838.** www.cityhousenashville.com. Main courses $9–$24. AE, DISC, MC, V. Mon 5–10pm; Wed–Sat 5–10pm; Sun 5–9pm.

Garden Brunch Café ★★ BRUNCH   In a tidy bungalow on Jefferson Street, not far from the Fisk University campus, is this little weekends-only brunch spot, where service is especially warm and gracious. Jazz standards and mellow reggae softly playing in the background provide an artsy aural backdrop within the intimate dining room, where portraits of Malcolm X and the Beatles adorn the walls and polished wood tables are set with fresh flowers and flatware. The concise menu showcases health-conscious dishes such as grilled salmon on mixed greens with honey-Dijon vinaigrette, seared or blackened fish and grits, and "Mom's" creamy oatmeal, served with a side of fresh fruit and whole-wheat toast. Delicious, simply prepared classics including eggs Benedict, omelets, ham and biscuits, and steak and eggs are a bit more indulgent, but worth every scrumptious calorie. Feeling decadent? Go for their signature, stuffed French toast or Bananas Foster pancakes.

924 Jefferson St. © **615/891-1217.** www.gardenbrunchcafe.com. Main courses $9–$17. MC, V. Fri–Sun 9am–2pm.

Germantown Café ★ AMERICAN/BRUNCH   For a stunning view of the Nashville skyline at sunset, stake out a dinner table at this pristine bistro in the Germantown neighborhood, just north of downtown. Sip a cocktail and pore over the eclectic menu, which includes artful interpretations of crab cakes, French onion soup, and even fried green tomatoes with goat cheese. Grilled fish entrees, such as the herb-crusted skate, are excellent, as are the tasso-stuffed chicken and the substantial mustard-marinated pork tenderloin served with a savory plum sauce. As for side dishes, the garlic mashed potatoes are out of this world. There is a second location in East Nashville (501 Main St.; © **615/242-3522**).

1200 Fifth Ave. N. © **615/242-3226.** www.germantowncafe.com. Reservations recommended. Main courses $12–$28 dinner, $8–$15 lunch. AE, DC, DISC, MC, V. Mon–Sat 11am–2pm and 5–11pm; Sun brunch 10:30am–2pm.

Monell's ★★★ ☺ BRUNCH/SOUTHERN   Dining out doesn't usually involve sitting at the same table with total strangers, but be prepared for just such a community experience at Monell's. Housed in a restored brick Victorian home dating back to 1905, this traditional boardinghouse-style lunch spot feels as if it has been around for ages, which is just what the proprietors want you to think. A meal at Monell's is meant to conjure up family dinners at Grandma's house, so remember to say "please" when you ask for the mashed potatoes or peas. The food is good, old-fashioned home cookin' most of the year, and everything is all-you-can-eat. Feast on fried chicken, meatloaf, and sliced beef roast with gravy. Kids eat for about half-price, and ages 4 and under eat free.

1235 Sixth Ave. N. © **615/248-4747.** www.monellstn.com. Reservations not accepted. Main courses $13 lunch, $15–$18 dinner. MC, V. Mon–Fri 10:30am–2pm; Tues–Fri 5–8:30pm; Sat 8:30am–1pm; Sun 8:30am–4pm.

Inexpensive

Harper's 🍴 SOUTHERN   If the thought of slow-simmered turnip greens, crispy fried chicken, tender sweet potatoes, and fluffy yeast rolls makes your mouth water, wipe off your chin and immediately head to the Jefferson Street district for some of Nashville's best soul food. Be sure to save room for a slice of pie or a heaping bowl of banana pudding. Popular with white-collar professionals and blue-collar laborers alike, Harper's attracts a friendly, diverse clientele.

2610 Jefferson St. ⓒ **615/329-1909.** Main courses $5–$11. AE, DISC, MC, V. Mon–Fri 10am–8pm; Sat–Sun 11am–6pm.

MUSIC ROW, THE WEST END & GREEN HILLS

For restaurants in this section, see the "Nashville Restaurants: Downtown Area, the West End & Green Hills" map, on p. 60.

Expensive

Bound'ry FUSION/TAPAS   With its colorful murals and whimsical decor, this Music Row eatery is popular with young adults and the cocktail crowd. The eclectic menu features tapas such as pork egg rolls with chipotle-juniper barbecue sauce, and fried calamari served with anchovy aioli. Bound'ry's signature salad combines endive and radish relish with crispy ham, tomatoes, and black-eyed peas. Large platter entrees include vegetarian dishes such as polenta stacked with eggplant, portobello mushrooms, and cheeses, as well as meaty pork chops and steaks, including the 16-ounce porterhouse. Wine and beer choices are quite extensive here.

911 20th Ave. S. ⓒ **615/321-3043.** www.pansouth.net. Reservations recommended; not accepted Fri–Sat after 6:30pm. Tapas $4.75–$11; main courses $22–$31. AE, DC, DISC, MC, V. Sun–Thurs 5–10pm; Fri–Sat 5–11pm. Bar Sun–Thurs 4–11:30pm; Fri–Sat 4pm–12:30am.

F. Scott's Restaurant & Jazz Bar ★★★ 🍴 AMERICAN   Chic and urbane, F. Scott's is an unexpected gem tucked amid the shopping center hinterlands surrounding the Green Hills area. The classic movie-palace marquee out front announces, in no uncertain terms, that this place is different. Inside, everything is tastefully sophisticated yet comfortable and cozy. The restaurant's seasonally inspired menu is among the most creative in the city. Although the menu changes frequently, you might start with an appetizer of squash blossoms stuffed with duck confit, Camembert, and Marconi almonds, or a savory lobster and corn chowder. Whether you're in the mood for something safe (linguine Bolognese), healthy (pan-seared red snapper), or more adventurous (grilled wild boar spareribs), you can be sure it will be exquisitely prepared and artfully plated. Live nightly jazz in the lounge provides another incentive to keep sophisticates coming back. F. Scott's has an award-winning wine list that includes more than 300 selections.

2210 Crestmoor Rd. ⓒ **615/269-5861.** www.fscotts.com. Reservations recommended. Main courses $23–$32. AE, DC, DISC, MC, V. Mon–Thurs 5:30–10pm; Fri–Sat 5:30–11pm; Sun (Dec only) 5:30–9pm.

Jimmy Kelly's ★ STEAKS   Tradition is the name of the game at Jimmy Kelly's, so if you long for the good old days of gracious Southern hospitality, be sure to schedule a dinner here. The restaurant is in a grand old home with neatly trimmed lawns and a valet parking attendant (it's free) waiting out front. Inside you'll almost always find the dining rooms and bar bustling with activity as waiters in white jackets navigate from the kitchen to the tables and back. Though folks tend to dress up for dinner here, the several small dining rooms are surprisingly casual. The kitchen turns out well-prepared traditional dishes such as chateaubriand in a burgundy-and-mushroom sauce and blackened catfish (not too spicy, to accommodate the tastes of middle Tennessee). Whatever you have for dinner, don't miss the corn bread—it's the best in the city.

217 Louise Ave. ⓒ **615/329-4349.** www.jimmykellys.com. Reservations recommended. Main courses $15–$40. AE, DC, MC, V. Mon–Sat 5–10pm.

Mambu FUSION   Chefs Corey Griffith and Anita Hartel co-own this quirky restaurant that's like a secluded hideaway, located in an old blue house behind the Hutton Hotel. Each dining room in the cluttered Victorian is chock-full of kitschy decor, from fake flowers to found-object folk art. The menu is a mishmash too, blending Asian influences and Mediterranean flavors with plain-old American fare. For instance, you could begin a meal with the spinach-and-watermelon salad or the arugula with mango, walnuts, and goat cheese; or nibble on crab cakes, hummus, or pot stickers while deciding what entree to order. The herb-crusted rack of lamb is a sure bet. However, tasting a bit less inspired than its name might imply, the pan-seared garam masala salmon over red potatoes with curry-drizzled veggies and tzatziki sauce is slightly ho-hum.

1806 Hayes St. ⓒ **615/329-1293.** www.mamburestaurant.com. Reservations recommended. Main courses $19–$35. AE, DC, MC, V. Mon–Thurs 4–9pm; Fri–Sat 4–10pm.

Midtown Cafe ★★ AMERICAN   Located just off West End Avenue, this small, upscale restaurant conjures up a very romantic atmosphere with indirect lighting and bold displays of art. The chic, understated design and sumptuous food have been pulling in Nashvillians for years. Rich and flavorful sauces are the rule here, with influences from all over the world. The dinner tasting menu is a good way to sample the fare. Be sure to start a meal with the lemon-artichoke soup, which is as good as its reputation around town. From there, consider moving on to crab cakes served with cayenne hollandaise, and available as either an appetizer or an entree. Lunches here are much simpler than dinners, with lots of sandwiches on the menu. However, a few of the same dishes from the dinner menu are available, including the crab cakes.

102 19th Ave. S. ⓒ **615/320-7176.** www.midtowncafe.com. Dinner reservations recommended. Main courses $16–$32; lunch $10–$20. AE, DC, DISC, MC, V. Mon–Fri 11am–2:30pm; daily 4:30–10pm.

Sunset Grill ★★ AMERICAN   In the West End neighborhood of Hillsboro Village, the Sunset Grill is that rare breed of restaurant that's both critically acclaimed in the national press and an enduring favorite with the locals. The decor is minimalist and monochromatic, with original paintings to liven things up a bit. The menu changes daily, with an emphasis on seafood preparations. After all these years, I still can't resist the Sonoma Salad, a scrumptious combination of mixed field baby greens, tart apples, almonds, and blue cheese in a pink wine-garlic vinaigrette. Others may prefer the ostrich carpaccio, spicy voodoo pasta, or Szechuan duck. Desserts, such as coconut sushi or butterscotch-habanero bread pudding, show creative panache. On Sundays, Sunset offers half-price wine specials. With more than 300 varieties by the bottle and more than 100 by the glass, you have plenty of choices.

2001 Belcourt Ave. ✆ **615/386-FOOD** (3663). www.sunsetgrill.com. Reservations recommended. Main courses $11–$33. AE, DC, DISC, MC, V. Tues–Fri 11am–3pm; Mon–Thurs 5pm–midnight; Fri–Sat 5pm–1:30am; Sun 5–10pm.

Moderate

Athens Family Restaurant ★★ 🎁 BREAKFAST/GREEKBeloved by locals for their omelets, kid-friendly Mickey Mouse pancakes, and other breakfast specialties, this 24-hour, family-run diner is just as popular for lunch, dinner, and late-night fare. Athens makes a mouthwatering spanakopita (flaky phyllo crust stuffed with spinach and feta cheese), and an array of other Greek dishes, including gyros, chicken and lamb entrees, and rice. Pita bread is served warm and supple, perfect for dipping into creamy hummus and tangy tzatziki sauce. Featured on Food Network's *Diners, Drive-Ins and Dives,* the casual eatery also serves substantial burgers, including a bacon-and-lamb version.

2526 Franklin Pike. ✆ **615/383-2848.** www.athensfamilyrestaurant.com. Entrees $12–$15. MC, V. Daily 24 hr.

Blackstone Restaurant & Brewery BURGERS   At this glitzy brewpub, brewing tanks in the front window silently crank out half a dozen different beers ranging from a pale ale to a dark porter. Whether you're looking for a quick bite of pub grub (pizzas, soups, burgers) or a more formal dinner (a meaty pork loin well complemented by apple chutney and a smidgen of rosemary, garlic, and juniper berries), you'll be satisfied with the food here, especially if you're into good microbrews. Fish and chips can't be beat, especially when washed down by a St. Charles Porter ale. This place is big, and you'll have the option of dining amid a pub atmosphere or in one of the sparsely elegant dining areas.

1918 West End Ave. ✆ **615/327-9969.** www.blackstonebrewpub.com. Sandwiches, pizza, and main courses $13–$22. AE, DC, DISC, MC, V. Mon–Thurs 11am–midnight; Fri–Sat 11am–1am; Sun 11am–10pm.

BrickTops ★★ AMERICAN   The rich, chunky guacamole and gargantuan veggie burger keep me returning time and again to one of Nashville's West End favorites. Contemporary decor, with warm woods and amber lighting, lend a casual sophistication to the large dining room, which tends to attract energetic young working professionals and college kids with their well-heeled, visiting parents. Appetizers and sides are especially noteworthy. Try the deviled eggs, homemade potato chips with blue cheese dip, and grilled artichokes with rémoulade. Elsewhere on the menu, take your pick from flat breads, salads, and entrees such as Atlantic salmon, baby back ribs, or steak frites. In nice weather, the patio is a great place to enjoy a prickly pear margarita or pitcher of beer with friends.

3000 West End Ave. ✆ **615/298-1000.** www.bricktops.com. Reservations recommended. Entrees $15–$27. MC, V. Mon–Thurs 11am–10pm; Fri 11am–11pm; Sat 10am–4pm; Sun 10am–10pm; brunch Sat–Sun 10am–3pm.

Cabana ★ AMERICAN   Ultracool Cabana boasts one of the liveliest after-dark scenes of all the West End's restaurant/lounges. Co-owned by restaurateur Randy Rayburn (Midtown Cafe, Sunset Grill), Cabana has a sprawling, 2,900-square-foot outdoor patio that's in use year-round. Gorgeous young people hover at the bar or mingle in chic private cabanas equipped with flatscreen TVs. Food here is affordable and, above all, fun. Nosh on homemade potato chips with Gorgonzola dipping sauce. Then dive into top-notch interpretations on Tennessee sliders (miniature fried-ham sandwiches) or the childlike chicken-wing lollipops, and frosty root beer floats with freshly baked cookies on the side.

1910 Belcourt Ave. © **615/577-2262.** www.cabananashville.com. Reservations accepted. Main courses $10–$21. AE, DISC, MC, V. Mon–Sat 4pm–3am; Sun 4pm–midnight.

ChaChah ★★ TAPAS   Young entrepreneur Arnold Myint was a local culinary star long before he was a seventh-season competitor on Bravo TV's *Top Chef*. Along with Suzy Wong's House of Yum and the Farmer's Market eatery AM@FM, he runs ChaChah. It's an upscale tapas bar and nightspot that's two doors down from PM, Myint's global bar and grill that's been a favorite of Belmont University college students for several years. ChaChah's cool, minimalist decor sets the tone for a sophisticated menu that includes small plates, a variety of teas, and cocktails like the Hibiscus Kiss. The falafel wrap is delicious and artfully plated, while the carrot soup has a piquant, gingery zing and the consistency of a rich pudding.

2013 Belmont. © **615/298-1430.** www.chachahnashville.com. Reservations recommended. Tapas $4–$9; main courses $14–$24. AE, DISC, MC, V. Mon–Fri 11am–2:30pm; daily 5–10pm; Sun brunch 10:30am–2:30pm; Sat 4pm–3am; Sun 4pm–midnight.

Firefly Grille AMERICAN   In a funky old house buried behind the sprawling commerce of the Green Hills shopping area, the Firefly Grille is a local favorite. Christmas lights, tinsel, black-and-white publicity stills of country music stars, and assorted toys and doodads hang from the ceiling and plaster the red walls inside the two small dining rooms. The place always seems to be packed, as patrons vie for one of the small, closely spaced tables. A handful of salads, sandwiches, and entree choices keep the menu simple and focused. At 10 ounces, the beef burgers topped with crispy bacon and white cheddar are perfectly cooked to order. Prices double at dinner, with more sophisticated offerings like pumpkin-seed-roasted pork tenderloin with ravioli, and grilled rack of Australian lamb served with crème fraîche mashed potatoes.

2201 Bandywood Dr. © **615/383-0042.** www.fireflygrillenashville.com. Reservations recommended. Lunch entrees $9.50–$14; dinner entrees $16–$24. MC, V. Mon–Sat 11am–2pm; Mon–Thurs 5–9pm; Fri 5–10pm.

Goten ★ JAPANESE   Glass-brick walls and a high-tech Zen-like elegance set the mood at this West End Japanese restaurant, across the street from Vanderbilt University. The valet parking is a clue that this restaurant is slightly more formal than other Japanese restaurants in Nashville. Don't come here expecting watery bowls of miso soup and a few noodles. Hibachi dinners are the specialty, with the menu leaning heavily toward steaks, which are just about as popular in Japan as they are in Texas. However, if you prefer sushi, don't despair; the sushi bar here is Nashville's best, and you can get slices of the freshest fish in town.

1719 West End Ave. © **615/321-4537.** www.gotennashville.com. Reservations recommended. Main courses $11–$30. AE, DC, DISC, MC, V. Mon–Fri 11:30am–2:30pm; Sun–Thurs 5–9:30pm; Fri–Sat 4:30–10:30pm.

La Hacienda Taqueria ★★ MEXICAN   Ethnic eateries and Mexican restaurants have flooded the outskirts of Nashville in recent years, but this former taco stand rises above the rest. Now a family-friendly, full-service restaurant, it's adorned with rustic handmade wood tables and oversized chairs, as well as colorful wall murals. Crisp, hot tortilla chips, potent salsa, and chunky guacamole are exceptional, as are the enchiladas, flautas, rice, and refried beans. The menu includes tasty little crisp tacos with a long list of fillings, including chorizo and beef tongue. There are also fajitas with chicken, beef, or shrimp. You can get Salvadoran *pupusas* (corn tortillas), and just about everything comes with fresh house-made tortillas. Wash it all down with a glass of *tamarindo*.

2615 Nolensville Rd. © **615/256-6142.** www.lahaciendainc.com. Main courses $7–$20. AE, DISC, MC, V. Mon–Thurs 10am–9pm; Fri–Sat 10am–10pm; Sun 10am–10pm.

Loveless Cafe ★ ⊡ BREAKFAST/SOUTHERN

For some of the best country cooking in the Nashville area, take a trip out past the city's western suburbs to this old-fashioned roadhouse and popular Nashville institution. People rave about the cooking here—and with good reason. The country ham with red-eye gravy, Southern fried chicken, and homemade biscuits with homemade fruit jams are made just the way Granny used to make them back when the Loveless opened nearly 40 years ago. This restaurant may be a little out of the way, but it's well worth it if you like down-home cookin'—and if you're prepared to endure a long wait to get one of the few available tables inside.

8400 Tenn. 100, about 7½ miles south of Belle Meade and the turnoff from U.S. 70 S. © **615/646-9700.** www.lovelesscafe.com. Reservations recommended. Main courses $7–$17. AE, DISC, MC, V. Daily 7am–9pm.

PM BURGERS/FUSION

You might not expect this, but noted Thai-American chef Arnold Myint's casual East-meets-West bistro serves up one of the best burgers in Nashville. It's true; just ask the locals, who consistently vote it tops in various polls. The hefty, juicy hamburgers are nothing fancy—just perfectly cooked and simply delicious. PM's wildly eclectic menu reflects international cuisines, including Latin American and Asian. Try the rice bowls, sushi, chicken skewers, or wraps. Service has slipped in recent years, but the food at this spacious old Belmont University hangout is consistent.

2017 Belmont Blvd. © **615/297-2070.** pmnashville.com. Reservations not necessary. Main courses $14–$24; burgers $9. MC, V. Mon–Sat 11am–1am; Sun 4pm–1am.

South Street SEAFOOD/SOUTHERN

The flashing neon sign proclaiming AUTHENTIC DIVE BAR, a blue-spotted pink cement pig, and an old tire swing out front should clue you in that this place doesn't take itself too seriously. In fact, this little wedge-shaped eatery is as tacky as an episode of *Hee Haw,* but with Harleys often parked out front. On the menu, you'll find everything from fried pickles to handmade nutty buddies (candy bars). However, the mainstays are crispy catfish, pulled pork barbecue, smoked chicken, ribs, and steaks with biscuits. If you're feeling flush, you can opt for the $55 crab-and-slab dinner for two (two kinds of crab and a "slab" of ribs).

907 20th Ave. S. © **615/320-5555.** www.pansouth.net. Main courses $10–$26. AE, DC, DISC, MC, V. Sun–Thurs 11am–midnight; Fri–Sat 11am–2am.

tayst Restaurant & Wine Bar ★★★ AMERICAN

Nashville's first green-certified restaurant is also a destination for foodies. The menu is organized into three sections, or first, second, and third "tastes." A handful of choices in each category manage to cover all the culinary bases, from meats, game, and poultry to pastas, salads, and vegetarian options. Each course is paired with a recommended wine selection, but budget-conscious connoisseurs are free to order without the wine pairings. Inventive preparations of common dishes are a delight, from the trout with stone-ground grits and pickled ramps, to the roasted lamb with garlic bread pudding, mint, and peas.

2100 21st Ave. ⓒ **615/383-1953.** www.taysrestaurant.com. Reservations recommended. Main courses $17–$34. AE, DC, MC, V. Tues–Thurs 5–10pm; Fri–Sat 5–11pm.

Tin Angel ★ AMERICAN/BRUNCH   A mainstay in the West End, Tin Angel is a well-kept secret among locals and college students. The pressed-tin ceiling, dark wood paneling, and crackling fireplace lend romance and warmth to the bistro that's known for its soups, fresh salads, and pasta dishes. If you're looking to avoid (other) tourists, it's also a pleasant place to enjoy a leisurely Sunday brunch, with service that's unfrenzied and friendly.

3201 West End Ave. ⓒ **615/298-3444.** www.tinangel.net. Reservations recommended. Main courses $12–$23. AE, DISC, MC, V. Mon–Fri 11am–10pm; Sat 5–10pm; Sun 11am–3pm.

The Yellow Porch ★★ AMERICAN   In the cute Berry Hill neighborhood south of Nashville, next to a gas station and just across a busy, multilane highway, lies this irresistible little bistro. Look for the rocking chair garden planter out front. Everything here is excellent, but salads are exceptional. Try the port-poached, sun-dried cherry salad with baby greens, spiced walnuts, and balsamic vinaigrette. Also tempting is the antipasti plate with Genoa salami, Tennessee prosciutto, cheeses, hummus, sun-dried tomato pesto, and Greek olives. Steaks include a tequila-marinated porterhouse with poblano skillet corn, tomatillo salsa, and mole sauce, while myriad vegetarian options include Mediterranean vegetarian lasagna.

734 Thompson Lane. ⓒ **615/386-0260.** www.theyellowporch.com. Main courses $13–$27. AE, DISC, MC, V. Mon–Sat 11am–3pm and 5–10pm.

Inexpensive

Bobbie's Dairy Dip ★ BURGERS/ICE CREAM   Scrumptious black-bean veggie burgers with guacamole and salsa may be the most unexpected find at this nostalgic, pink-and-green neon, drive-in ice-cream stand that's been around for decades. Beefy burgers, sloppy chili dogs, and greasy, fresh-cut fries are also preferred preludes to creamy, hand-dipped milkshakes, hot-fudge sundaes, and other cool treats.

5301 Charlotte Pike. ⓒ **615/463-8088.** Main courses $7–$9. AE, DISC, MC, V. Daily 11am–10pm (open seasonally; call ahead).

Brown's Diner BURGERS   Character. That's the lure of this ugly little landmark. That, and mouthwatering cheeseburgers. Inside the grubby gray trailer, it's dark and smoky, with wood-paneled walls and a dive-bar vibe that's as authentic as the food. Fried-fish platters with coleslaw and hush puppies, greasy cheeseburgers and crispy French fries, and an all-time white-trash favorite—Frito chili pie—are as flavorful and unpretentious as it gets. Beer is the beverage of choice, but Brown's devotees also brag about the politically incorrect joys of whole milk, served in frosted beer mugs.

2102 Blair Blvd. ⓒ **615/269-5509.** No website. Burgers $4; catfish dinner $7. DISC, MC, V. Daily 11am–10pm.

Elliston Place Soda Shop ★ ☺ AMERICAN/ICE CREAM   One of the oldest eateries in Nashville, the Elliston Place Soda Shop has been around since 1939, and it looks it. The lunch counter, black-topped stools, and signs advertising malted milks and banana splits all seem to have been here since the original opening. It's a treat to visit this time capsule of Americana, with its red-and-white tiled walls, old beat-up Formica tables, and individual booth jukeboxes. The soda shop serves plate lunches of an entree and veggies, with four different specials of the day. Sandwiches, including clubs and fried baloney, as well as hamburgers are on the menu. Elliston's also has the best chocolate milkshakes in town.

2111 Elliston Place. © **615/327-1090.** Main courses $2–$10. MC, V. Mon–Fri 7am–6pm; Sat 7am–5pm.

Kalamatas ★ MEDITERRANEAN   Risk the road rage that usually comes with a traffic-choked drive out to the Green Hills neighborhood for this oasis of sumptuous Mediterranean cuisine. Its setting may be a nondescript suburban shopping center, but the food is consistently fresh and flavorful. Leafy green salads are flecked with feta cheese and olives, and the falafel is crisp and flavorful. The creamy hummus—laced with a drizzle of olive oil—is out of this world when dipped with soft wedges of warm pita bread.

3764 Hillsboro Rd. © **615/383-8700.** www.eatatkalamatas.com. Main courses $5–$19. AE, DISC, MC, V. Mon–Thurs 11am–8pm; Fri–Sat 11am–9pm.

Noshville ★★ BREAKFAST/DELICATESSEN   There's only so much fried chicken and barbecue you can eat before you just have to have a thick, juicy Reuben or a bagel with hand-sliced lox. When the deli craving strikes in Nashville, head for Noshville. The deli cases in this big, bright, and antiseptic place are filled to overflowing with everything from beef tongue and pickled herring to corned beef and chopped liver. Make mama happy: Start your meal with some good matzo-ball soup. Then satisfy the kid inside you by splurging on a hefty, two-fisted chocolate-and-vanilla-iced shortbread cookie. There's another location at 4014 Hillsboro Circle (© **615/269-3535**).

1918 Broadway. © **615/329-NOSH** (6674). www.noshville.com. Main courses $7–$18. AE, DC, DISC, MC, V. Mon 6:30am–2:30pm; Tues–Thurs 6:30am–8:30pm; Fri 6:30am–9:30pm; Sat 7:30am–9:30pm; Sun 7:30am–8pm.

Pancake Pantry ♨AMERICAN/BREAKFAST   The *New York Times, Bon Appé-tit,* and long lines (even in all kinds of foul weather) attest to the immense popularity of this satisfying but otherwise unextraordinary eatery in Nashville's West End. College students, country music stars, NFL players, tourists, and locals alike queue up outside the red-brick building for the chance to sit inside and sip a cup of coffee and cut into a stack of steamy flapjacks. With such varied wait times, it's worth noting that the Pancake Pantry also includes lunch items among its extensive breakfast menu.

1796 21st Ave. S. © **615/383-9333.** www.thepancakepantry.com. Main courses $6–$15. AE, DC, DISC, MC, V. Mon–Fri 6am–3pm; Sat–Sun 6am–4pm.

Rotier's Restaurant BURGERS   If you're a fan of old-fashioned diners, don't miss Rotier's. This little stone cottage is surrounded by newer buildings but has managed to remain a world unto itself. Sure, it looks like a dive from the outside, and the

---

Tired of Waiting?

The Pancake Pantry may be a breakfast lover's first choice, but the daunting lines can aggravate appetites as well as patience. Across the street, the brew-pub **Boscos** (p. 106) and bakery **Provence** (p. 81) both do a delectable brunch. Next door, barflies looking for hangover relief flock to laid-back **Jackson's in the Village** (1800 21st Ave. S., at Belcourt Ave.; © **615/385-9968**) for Bloody Marys and fried eggs.

interior doesn't seem to have been upgraded in 40 years, but the food is good and the prices are great. The cheeseburger here is said to be the best in the city, and the milkshakes are pretty good, too. For bigger appetites, there is that staple of Southern cooking—the "meat-and-three." You get a portion of meat (minute steak, pork chops, fried chicken, whatever) and three vegetables of your choice. They also do daily blue-plate specials and cheap breakfasts.

2413 Elliston Place. © **615/327-9892.** Sandwiches/main courses $4.25–$16. MC, V. Mon–Fri 10:30am–10pm; Sat 9am–10pm.

MUSIC VALLEY & EAST NASHVILLE

Music Valley includes the Gaylord Opryland Resort (and Opry Mills mall, scheduled to reopen in spring 2012), which offers a plethora of eateries—from food court buffets to sit-down restaurants. While the airport area is mostly devoid of recommendable places to grab more than a quick bite, the flourishing East Nashville neighborhood has excellent bars, bistros, and cafes.

Expensive

Margot Café & Bar ★★★ FRENCH/ITALIAN/BRUNCH Chef-owner Margot McCormack's cozy brick cafe in East Nashville is a romantic charmer, a 1930s-era building chock-full of flower boxes and exposed brick walls adorned with copper pots. The menu changes daily but might include pan-roasted chicken breast with butternut squash polenta, Swiss chard, and walnuts; braised rabbit; or house-made spaghetti with spinach-Alfredo sauce. The bar offers French and Italian wines by the glass, sangria and limoncello, and other cocktails and cordials. Sunday brunch is the best in Nashville: Sip a mimosa and enjoy your coffee served in individual French-press carafes. Mouthwatering breads, pastries, and breakfast dishes such as the creamy chicken-artichoke casserole are sublime. Service is exceedingly friendly and efficient.

1017 Woodland St. © **615/227-4668.** www.margotcafe.com. Reservations highly recommended. Main courses $18–$26. AE, MC, V. Tues–Sat 6–10pm; Sun 11am–2pm.

Old Hickory Steakhouse ★★★ STEAKS Of all of the resort hotel's many restaurants, the Old Hickory Steakhouse is the property's best. Its antebellum mansion decor, replete with a library lounge serving single-malt whiskeys and rare cognacs, reflects Old South grandeur. The menu is much more cosmopolitan than the setting implies, however. Delicious steaks, including certified Angus beef and lean bison cuts, are grilled perfectly to diners' specifications. Succulent Atlantic salmon with bacon ravioli is the best nonsteak entree. A tantalizing array of sheep, cow, and goat cheese from throughout the U.S. and Western Europe is served tableside, from a glass-encased cart, along with plump fresh fruits. Service is impeccable, making Old Hickory worth the drive to Music Valley from wherever you might be.

2800 Opryland Dr. © **615/871-6848.** www.gaylordopryland.com. Reservations recommended. Main courses $36–$56. AE, DISC, MC, V. Daily 5–10pm.

Moderate

Caney Fork Fish Camp SEAFOOD Two-fisted fried catfish sandwiches, barbecued pork ribs, and comfort food favorites such as meatloaf and mashed potatoes fill

Nashville Restaurants: Music Valley & East Nashville

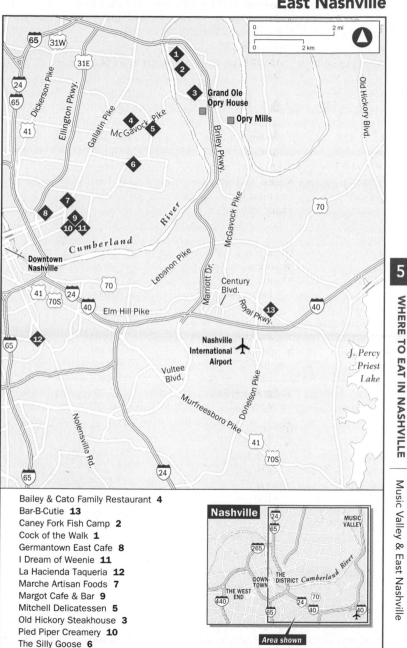

Bailey & Cato Family Restaurant **4**
Bar-B-Cutie **13**
Caney Fork Fish Camp **2**
Cock of the Walk **1**
Germantown East Cafe **8**
I Dream of Weenie **11**
La Hacienda Taqueria **12**
Marche Artisan Foods **7**
Margot Cafe & Bar **9**
Mitchell Delicatessen **5**
Old Hickory Steakhouse **3**
Pied Piper Creamery **10**
The Silly Goose **6**

the bill at this cavernous, log cabin/lodgelike restaurant near Opryland. Fireplaces, a waterfall and small pond, and big-screen TVs augment the outdoorsy camp decor, with fishing nets, rods, lures, and an old 1939 pickup truck adding visual interest.

2400 Music Valley Dr. ⓒ **615/724-1200.** www.caneyforkfishcamp.com. Main courses $8–$23. AE, DISC, MC, V. Mon–Thurs 4–10pm; Fri–Sat 11am–11pm; Sun 11am–9pm.

Cock of the Walk SEAFOOD/SOUTHERN   No, roosters aren't on the menu. The restaurant takes its unusual name from an old flatboatman's term for the top boatman. This big, barnlike eatery is well known around Nashville for having some of the best seafood in town. Like the catfish filets and dill pickles on the menu, the shrimp and chicken are also fried in peanut oil. Rounding out the hearty platters are such sides as beans and turnip greens, brought to the table in big pots.

2624 Music Valley Dr. ⓒ **615/889-1930.** www.cockofthewalkrestaurant.com. Reservations accepted for groups of 20 or more. Main courses $11–$21. AE, DISC, MC, V. Mon–Fri 5–9pm; Sat 4–9pm; Sun 11am–9pm.

Marché Artisan Foods ★★★ BRUNCH/FRENCH   Part market, part bistro and deli, this vegetarian-friendly restaurant serves breakfast, lunch, and dinner. A sunny spot with big picture windows for people-watching, the cafe is owned by Margot McCormack, of Margot Café (see above), right around the corner. McCormack's attention to detail and freshness is evident in every aspect of the meals served here, from the fresh-cut summer zinnias in glass jars on the marble tables, to artisanal breads and crisp biscotti, fluffy omelets, luscious salads, and creamy quiches. Before you feast, sip coffee or champagne as you browse the edible goods that abound: Imported olive oils, pestos, and pastas are artfully displayed around wooden farmhouse tables.

1000 Main St. ⓒ **615/262-1111.** www.marcheartisanfoods.com. Reservations not accepted for lunch. Main courses $11–$16. AE, DISC, MC, V. Tues–Fri 8am–9pm; Sat 8am–4pm and 5–9pm; Sun 9am–4pm.

Inexpensive

Bailey & Cato Family Restaurant ★ SOUTHERN   The weathered-looking, faded pink cottage in the Inglewood section of East Nashville might not look like much from the street, but trust me: You want to go inside. This family-owned soul food restaurant opened in 2009, and the buzz spread quickly that it was the real deal. Bailey & Cato serves up such mouthwatering comfort food as barbecued ribs, oxtails in a brown gravy, meatloaf and mashed potatoes, and crispy fried chicken like Grandma used to make. Southern sides include turnip greens, cooked cabbage, sweet potatoes, and golden corn bread. A list of the day's homemade cakes, pies, and puddings are posted near the steam table. Order it for takeout, or try to nab one of the few tables inside.

1307 McGavock Pike. ⓒ **615/227-4694.** Main courses under $10. MC, V. Tues–Wed 11am–9pm; Thurs–Sat 11am–10pm; Sun noon–9pm.

I Dream of Weenie HOT DOGS   In a cool yellow Volkswagen bus near Fanny's House of Music and the Pied Piper Creamery in East Nashville sits this stationery food truck that does hot dogs. If you like yours hot, get the Flamin' Frank, with jalapeños, onions, mustard, hot chili, and salsa. Along with ketchup and relish, other hot dog toppings include coleslaw, chowchow, cheese, and sauerkraut. If you're in luck, maybe your visit will coincide with the occasional dessert treat: Weenie sometimes serves fresh-baked chocolate espresso buzz cookies. Make sure you arrive with cash, because the Weenie doesn't do plastic.

113 S. 11th St. ⓒ **615/226-2622.** www.facebook.com/IDreamofWeenie. Hot dogs $3.75. Cash only. Mon–Thurs 11am–midnight; Fri 11am–3am; Sat 10am–3am.

Mitchell Delicatessen ★ DELICATESSEN   This New York–style delicatessen does a brisk weekend business from opening to closing, as East Nashville residents filter in to choose bagels, lox, freshly made salads, box lunches, and hot and cold sandwiches. An unassuming storefront anchoring an older residential neighborhood that may be a bit off the beaten path for most tourists, Mitchell's is most definitely worth Google-ing for directions. All of the sandwiches, including the French dip, the turkey with bacon and avocado, and the sopressato-stuffed muffalatta, are hefty and inexpensive. Hot bar items include stick-to-your-ribs fare like beef brisket, chicken stew, and meatloaf with butter-smashed potatoes.

1402 McGavock Pike. ⓒ **615/262-9862.** www.mitchelldeli.com. Sandwiches $5–$7. DISC, MC, V. Mon–Sat 7am–8pm; Sun 7am–4pm.

Pied Piper Creamery ★ ICE CREAM   This unassuming ice-cream shop housed in a pretty Victorian home in a residential area of East Nashville has been garnering national attention in the food press. Run by a young mother who has a passion for rich, creamy ice-cream flavors, the Pied Piper features kid-pleasing choices like birthday cake with rainbow sprinkles and blue (or pink) icing, and dozens more. Traditional flavors include chocolate, toffee, blueberry cheesecake, and peppermint, but the top seller is Trailer Trash: vanilla ice cream with Twix, M&M's, Reese's pieces, and assorted other crushed candy bars. Trailer Trash 2.0? Same thing, only in chocolate. The Lady Goo Goo boasts bits of Nashville's famous Goo Goo clusters. Kids' games, books, a front room play area, and even ABC refrigerator magnets on the ice-cream freezer make kids feel at home, while the home's wide, shady front porch invites families to sit and enjoy the frozen treats.

114 S. 11th St. ⓒ **615/227-4114.** www.thepiedpipercreamery.com. Under $10. MC, V. Mon–Thurs noon–9pm; Fri–Sat noon–10pm; Sun 1–9pm.

The Silly Goose ★★★ AMERICAN/SANDWICHES   Farm-fresh produce and locally sourced cheeses, meats, and other ingredients are the focus of this informal and insanely good restaurant. Iced teas and rosemary lemonade are served in jelly jars, and napkins are red bandana cloths. Seating is at artisan-crafted wood picnic tables and a small bar positioned directly in front of the open kitchen. (Go ahead, chat up the tattooed hipster chopping herbs while you peruse the clipboard-clamped menu at your place setting.) Sandwiches and wraps are hearty, artfully plated delights. The Zipper layers smoked salmon with honeyed-black-pepper goat cheese, caramelized onion, and baby arugula on toasted marble rye. Turkey, ham, chicken, roast beef, and vegetarian options are equally tempting, as are salads and several couscous variations: The King Kong features sesame couscous with curried shrimp, mint, ginger, and cashews. Sides such as roasted beets are healthy—less so are the homemade ice creams and chocolate mousse desserts. At meal's end, your check will be presented via iPad, for you to sign your name with your finger.

1888 Eastland Ave. ⓒ **615/915-0757.** www.sillygoosenashville.com. Sandwiches $5–$7. DISC, MC, V. Tues–Thurs 11am–9pm; Fri–Sat 11am–10pm.

The Wild Cow ★★ VEGETARIAN   With its spring-green walls, photos of free-grazing bovines, and fresh, organic food, the Wild Cow would be my favorite vegetarian restaurant even if it wasn't one of only two in all of Nashville. The cozy neighborhood cafe has caught on with customers, who patiently wait their turn for a booth or one of the few tables inside, where vegan, vegetarian, and gluten-free foods, as well as hormone- and rennet-free dairy products, are incorporated into delicious dishes. An array of veggie burgers (try yours Muppet Style, with sauerkraut and Green Goddess dressing), inventive stews, tacos, and salads make choosing difficult. The tasty and texturally interesting green-chile root salad tops green leaf lettuce with seasoned jicama, toasted pumpkin seeds, fresh-roasted beets, and grilled tofu, all tossed with a green-chile dressing. Chilled beer, natural sodas, kombucha, and energy drinks are available, as are Naked Juices and smoothies.

1896 Eastland Ave. ✆ **615/262-2717.** www.thewildcow.com. Entrees $8.50–$8.75. DISC, MC, V. Sun–Mon 11am–9pm; Wed–Thurs 11am–9pm; Fri–Sat 11am–10pm.

BARBECUE & HOT CHICKEN

Inexpensive

Bar-B-Cutie ★ BARBECUE   If you're out by the airport and have an intense craving for barbecue, head to Bar-B-Cutie. Just watch for the sign with the bar-b-doll cowgirl in short shorts. Bar-B-Cutie has been in business since 1948 and, while there is mesquite-grilled chicken available, you'd be remiss if you didn't order the pork shoulder or baby back ribs. There's another Bar-B-Cutie at 5221 Nolensville Rd. (✆ **615/834-6556**), on the south side of town.

501 Donelson Pike. ✆ **888/WE-BAR-B-Q** (932-2727) or 615/872-0207. www.bar-b-cutie.com. Full meals $5–$10. AE, DC, MC, V. Sun–Thurs 10am–9pm; Fri–Sat 10am–10pm.

Jack's Bar-B-Que BARBECUE   When the barbecue urge strikes you downtown, don't settle for cheap imitations; head to Jack's, where you can get pork shoulder, Texas beef brisket, St. Louis ribs, and smoked turkey, sausage, and chicken. There's another Jack's, at 334 W. Trinity Lane (✆ **615/228-9888**), in north Nashville.

416 Broadway. ✆ **615/254-5715.** www.jacksbarbque.com. Main courses $4–$23. AE, DISC, MC, V. Summer Mon–Sat 10:30am–10pm; winter Mon–Wed 10:30am–3pm, Thurs–Sat 10:30am–10pm, Sun during Tennessee Titans home games.

Mary's Old-Fashioned Bar-B-Q ★ BARBECUE   Succulent pork short ribs and cornmeal-dusted fried fish sandwiches are served on white bread at this Jefferson Street landmark. Ask for hot sauce, onions, and pickles, if you like.

1108 Jefferson St. ✆ **615/256-7696.** Meals $9–$15. MC, V. Mon–Thurs 8am–midnight; Fri–Sat 8am–2am.

Prince's Hot Chicken Shack ★ SOUTHERN   Grease will soak through the brown paper bag in which your fiery, deep-fried chicken is unceremoniously served. That's to be expected here at this proud but run-down joint in a dicey part of town. Line up at the counter with the diverse local clientele to pick your poison—mild, medium, or extrahot sauce? If you need a cool-down, pray you've got enough change for the Coke machine.

123 Ewing Dr. ✆ **615/226-9442.** Meals $6.50–$9. Cash only. Tues–Thurs noon–9pm; Fri–Sat noon–4am.

Whitt's Barbecue BARBECUE   Walk in, drive up, or get it delivered. Whitt's serves some of the best barbecue in Nashville. There's no seating here, so take it back to your hotel or plan a picnic. You can buy barbecue pork and turkey by the pound, or order sandwiches and plates with the extra fixin's. The pork barbecue sandwiches are topped with zesty coleslaw. Among the many other locations are those at 2535 Lebanon Rd. (© **615/883-6907**), and at 114 Old Hickory Blvd. E. (© **615/868-1369**).

5310 Harding Rd. © **615/356-3435.** www.whittsbarbecue.com. Meals $3–$8; barbecue $7.65 per lb. AE, DC, DISC, MC, V. Mon–Sat 10:30am–8pm.

CAFES, DELIS, BAKERIES & PASTRY SHOPS

When you just need a quick pick-me-up, a rich pastry, or some good rustic bread for a picnic, there are several good cafes, coffeehouses, and bakeries scattered around the city. The stretch of 12th Avenue South is where you'll find the funky **Frothy Monkey,** 2509 12th Ave. S. (© **615/292-1808;** www.frothymonkeynashville.com), a bungalow with hardwood floors, a skylight, and free Wi-Fi. If a picnic lunch is on your agenda, head to nearby **Corrieri's Formaggeria,** 1110 Caruthers Ave. (© **615/385-9272;** www.cfcheese.com), a friendly little Italian grocery, deli, and cheese shop where you can buy freshly prepared soups, sandwiches, and panini, as well as artisan meats, cheeses, and gourmet foods to go.

Several trendy teahouses and upscale bakeries and candy shops have opened in recent years. The **DrinkHaus Espresso + Tea,** 500 Madison St. (© **615/255-5200;** www.drinkhaus.com), serves fresh-squeezed lemonade and quiche, sandwiches, and sweets. Truffles, toffee, cakes, and other confections are the specialty of **The Cocoa Tree,** 1200 Fifth Ave. N., Ste. 104 (© **615/255-5060;** www.thecocoatree.com).

English Earl Grey, orange-blossom oolong, and rosebud-and-petals herb teas are among the delightful choices at the **Savannah Tea Company,** 707 Monroe St. (© **615/383-1832;** www.savannahteacompany.com). This Germantown teahouse has more than 100 types of loose-leaf teas, including more than two dozen flavors of black tea alone. Wedding cakes are also sold at the cute shop, which doubles as a dainty cafe serving afternoon tea replete with fresh scones and clotted cream and jam. (Advance reservations are required.)

Bongo Java, 2007 Belmont Blvd. (© **615/385-JAVA** [5282]; www.bongojava. com), located near Belmont University, is located in an old house on a tree-lined street. It has good collegiate atmosphere, but parking during peak hours can pose a challenge. Nearby in the West End, where coffee shops and cafes are ubiquitous, two of my favorites are **Grins** (pronounced "greens") **Vegetarian Café,** at 25th Avenue and Vanderbilt Place (© **615/322-8571**); and **Fido,** 1812 21st Ave. S. (© **615/777-FIDO** [3436]), an arty former pet shop and current musicians' hangout that is one of the friendliest Wi-Fi spots in the neighborhood. You can link to both places through Bongo Java's website, listed above.

Across the street from Fido you'll find **Provence Breads & Café ★**, 1705 21st Ave. S. (© **615/386-0363;** www.provencebreads.com), a European-style coffee-house that bakes crusty French baguettes along with the most delectable tarts and cookies in town. Gourmet sandwiches and salads, along with brunch items, are on the extensive menu. Provence also has a stylish bistro in the downtown library, 601

Church St. (© 615/644-1150). Also in this area is the new, New York City–style Italian deli, **Savarino's Cucina;** it's at 2121 Belcourt Ave. (© **615/460-9878**).

Cupcakes are all the rage these days in cities across the country. Nashville gets its due with **Gigi's Cupcakes,** 1816 Broadway (© **615/342-0140;** www.gigiscupcakes usa.com), where you can choose from more than two dozen flavors of cake beneath a hefty blob of buttercream frosting.

Sweet 16th—A Bakery, 311 N. 16th St. (© **615/226-8367;** www.sweet16th. com), is a charming bakery anchoring a trendy residential neighborhood in East Nashville. Heavenly aromas fill the cheerful, immaculate shop, which has a few window seats for those who like to savor their pastries over coffee. From fresh scones and iced éclairs to festive cookies and decadent brownies, this sweet spot has it all.

With a less extensive menu but a bit more longevity, **Fox's Donut Den,** 3900 Hillsboro Rd. (© **615/385-1021;** www.foxsdonutden.com), has been making donuts and muffins in the Green Hills area for 3 decades. Sugar-glazed or iced with vanilla frosting or chocolate ganache, the sweets here are decidedly old school.

And, finally, **Calypso Cafe,** 2424 Elliston Place (© **615/321-3878;** www.calypso cafe.com), is an inexpensive local chain with multiple locations that features Caribbean-inspired salads and sandwiches, including good vegetarian options such as Boca burgers.

PRACTICAL INFORMATION

RESERVATIONS   At restaurants that take reservations, it's always a good idea to make them, particularly for dinner. To make reservations at any hour, visit **www. opentable.com**, which handles many local restaurants. If you strike out, consider eating at the bar. It won't be as comfortable as the dining room, but the food and service tend to be roughly comparable.

WHEN TO DINE   Nashville area restaurants are far less busy early in the week than they are Friday through Sunday. If you're flexible about when you indulge in fine cuisine and when you go for pizza and a movie, choose the low-budget option on the weekend and pamper yourself on a weeknight. Note that many chefs have Sunday or Monday (or both) off.

BARGAINS   Lunch is an excellent, economical way to check out a fancy restaurant. At higher-end restaurants that offer it (many don't), you can get a sense of the dinner menu without breaking the bank. To get a bargain at dinner, investigate **group-buying sites** such as Groupon (www.groupon.com) and Living Social (www. livingsocial.com). Sign up for Nashville alerts when you start planning your trip, and you may land a great deal.

DRESS CODES   Few fine-dining establishments in Nashville adhere to strict dress codes. At pricier places, you can dress up without feeling out of place, but business casual is usually the norm. Being the Country Music Capital of the World, Nashville movers and shakers (and those who aspire to be) love to get dolled up in flashy suits and sequined dresses, expensive cowboy boots, Stetsons, and lots of bling. (They don't call this NashVegas for nothing.) However, the vast majority of Nashville restaurants are much more laid back. Nice jeans and business-casual attire are the norm at most moderately priced and expensive restaurants.

BEST tennessee-based EATERIES

All three of these homegrown Tennessee chains have multiple locations throughout the state and beyond.

Back Yard Burgers: More prevalent in Memphis than in Nashville, this fast-food chain specializes in home-style grilled burgers, spicy seasoned fries, and hand-dipped milkshakes. Founded in Cleveland, Mississippi, in 1987, today it's a publicly traded, Nashville-based company with more than 120 locations nationwide. Burgers are big, juicy, and meaty (they also serve substantial hot dogs), but my favorite drive-through indulgence is the savory grilled chicken sandwich, and an extra-thick chocolate milkshake. If you're staying in the Nashville airport area, there's a convenient location at 2744 Elm Hill Pike (© **615/391-3555;** www.backyardburgers.com).

Cracker Barrel Old Country Store: A sure bet on any road trip through Tennessee, Cracker Barrels are ubiquitous along interstates. You'll recognize them by the rows of wooden rocking chairs on the brown buildings' wide porches. The restaurant chain, based in Lebanon, Tennessee, is the real McCoy, serving hearty portions of consistently good, home-style food at breakfast, lunch, and dinner. Chock-full of old farm equipment, kitchen gadgets, and other antiques, the eateries all have crackling stone fireplaces that are especially welcoming in cold winter weather. You can also browse for old-fashioned candy in the gift stores, and even rent audiobooks for your travels.

There are more than 603 restaurants throughout the country, including multiple locations in Memphis and Nashville. In the Music Valley area of Nashville, there's a location at 2406 Music Valley Dr. (© **615/883-5440**). Best breakfast bet: fried ham, biscuits and gravy, scrambled eggs, and Southern-style grits swimming in butter. For more locations: © **800/333-9566;** www.crackerbarrel.com.

J. Alexander's: Based in Nashville, J. Alexander's operates contemporary, full-service American restaurants in more than a dozen central U.S. states, with two locations in Nashville and one in Memphis. Unlike Back Yard Burgers and Cracker Barrel, J. Alexander's has a relaxing yet upscale atmosphere and offers a full bar with wines available by the glass or bottle. Signature dishes: baby back ribs, prime beef, and cilantro shrimp. My choice: rattlesnake pasta. In Nashville: 2609 West End Ave. (© **615/340-9901**), and 3401 West End Ave. (© **615/269-1900**). In Memphis: 2670 N. Germantown Pkwy., Cordova (in the suburbs, near Wolfchase Galleria mall; © **901/381-9670;** www.jalexanders.com).

INGREDIENTS Nashville's most enduring dining tradition is the "meat-and-three." Southern home cooking begins with fresh meat and vegetables enhanced with rich ingredients: Butter, cream, bacon fat, and lard are used with liberal abandon in comfort foods like biscuits and gravy, pork-seasoned turnip greens, green beans, and mashed potatoes. Main dishes like catfish, chicken, pork chops, and steak cutlets are often dredged in flour and then fried in hot fat. Fried green tomatoes are done this way too, with nothing more than salt and pepper added to make them taste absolutely sublime. A dash of bottled hot sauce is added to almost everything. Wash it down with iced tea, and you're eating like a local.

6

NASHVILLE SHOPPING

Nashville is a great shopping city, so be sure to bring your credit cards. Whether you're looking for handmade stage outfits costing thousands of dollars or a good deal on a pair of shoes at a factory-outlet store, you'll find plenty of spending opportunities in Music City.

THE NASHVILLE SHOPPING SCENE

As in most cities of the South, the shopping scene in Nashville is spread out around the city. In downtown Nashville, you'll find scads of gift and souvenir shops, plus a few musical instrument and record stores that cater to country music fans. Most of the big, national retailers, big-box stores, and department stores are concentrated in the suburban malls that ring the city, but for locally owned boutiques, galleries, and one-of-a-kind shops, look to Nashville's neighborhoods: The high-end Hillsboro Village/West End area beyond Vanderbilt University; the burgeoning 12South neighborhood south of the city center; and bohemian East Nashville, just across the Cumberland River from downtown.

Country music buffs will appreciate plenty of opportunities to shop for Western wear. There are dozens of shops specializing in the de rigueur attire of country music. For young women, that means feminine, above-the-knee dresses paired with kickin' cowboy boots, a big off-the-shoulder handbag, and perhaps a stylish cowboy hat. For guys, it means cool boots, cuffed jeans, plaid snap shirts, and leather jackets. You probably can't find a better selection of cowboy boots anywhere outside Texas, and if your tastes run to sequined denim shirts or skirts, you can find those here, too.

Store hours vary, but most businesses in Nashville are open daily, with some exceptions on Sunday. It's best to call ahead.

NASHVILLE SHOPPING A TO Z

Antiques

For the best antiques browsing, drive just south of downtown to the corner of Eighth Avenue South and Douglas Street, where several large antiques shops are clustered.

Art & Home Furnishings

Art & Invention Gallery ★★ Beautiful handmade necklaces, bracelets, earrings, and brooches; flannel folk-art dolls; and cherrywood spoons and kitchen utensils are just a few of the items displayed in this gorgeous East Nashville gallery. Exquisitely crafted furniture, colorful letterpress wall prints, glass bowls and vases, handmade journals, and even locally penned graphic novels also fill the vibrant space. This boutique is also the unofficial home of the annual Tomato Art Festival, held in East Nashville the second week of August. 1106 Woodland St. ℂ **615/226-2070.** www.artandinvention.com.

The Arts Company Many of Nashville's most promising artists, working divergent media such as painting, sculpture, and photography, display and sell their pieces at this prominent downtown gallery. It's also home base for the monthly trolley hop that takes customers to several downtown galleries. 415 Fifth Ave. N. ℂ **615/254-2040.** www.theartscompany.com.

Cumberland Art Gallery With an emphasis on regional artists, this well-regarded West End gallery deals in sculptures, paintings, photographs, and works on paper in a wide variety of styles. 4107 Hillsboro Circle. ℂ **615/297-0296.** www.cumberlandgallery.com.

Curious Heart Emporium ★ Quirky gifts such as offbeat refrigerator magnets, photography books, stuffed animals, children's toys, whimsical folk art, and artsy home decor create an eclectic mix at this unusual shop. Always interesting, Curious Heart store has two locations, including one near the Loveless Cafe southwest of town at 8414 Hwy. 100. Berry Hill, 2832 Bransford Ave. ℂ **615/298-7756.** www.curiousheartemporium.com.

Hatch Show Print ★★ If you buy only one souvenir while you're in Nashville, consider doing it here. A historic landmark, this is the oldest letterpress poster print shop in the country, and not only does it still design and print posters for shows, but it also sells posters to the public. Reprints of old circus, vaudeville, and *Grand Ole Opry* posters are the most popular. 316 Broadway. ℂ **615/256-2805.** www.hatchshowprint.com.

Local Color Gallery Tennessee artists—mostly watercolorists and other painters—are showcased in this aptly named downtown gallery owned by Brooke Robinson. Landscapes, still lifes, and portraits are among the most common genres represented. 1912 Broadway. ℂ **615/321-3141.** www.localcolornashville.com.

The Rymer Gallery With its prominent downtown location close to several upscale hotels, the high-end Rymer Gallery has an extensive roster of artists working in an array of different media, from bronze sculpture and oil paintings to abstract inkjet prints mounted on aluminum. Regarded as one of the top galleries in the area, this one is definitely worth a look. 233 Fifth Ave. N. ℂ **615/752-6030.** www.therymergallery.com.

Bicycles

Halcyon Bike Shop Laid-back and friendly, the crew at this locally owned bike shop in the 12South neighborhood has built a loyal following by helping cyclists fix up and repair their bicycles. 1118 Halcyon Ave. ℂ **615/730-9344.** www.halcyonbike.com.

Nashville Bicycle Lounge New and used bicycles and repairs are offered at this community-minded establishment, which has the atmosphere of a coffee shop or lounge more than it does a retail venture. If you're looking to join in a community bike ride while you're in the area, come hang here for a while to find out what's happening. 961 Woodland St. ℂ **615/227-2772.** www.nashvillebicyclelounge.com.

Books

BookMan/BookWoman   Widely regarded (and rightfully so) as Nashville's best used-book bookstore, this Vandy-area favorite has tens of thousands of books, including hardcover and collectors' editions. Their inexpensive paperbacks encompass nearly every genre, including mysteries, science fiction, photography, and children's books. 1713 21st Ave. S.© **615/383-6555.** www.bookmanbookwoman.com.

Elder's Bookstore ★   This dusty little shop looks as if some of the antiquarian books on sale were stocked back when they were new. In business since 1930, Edler's proclaims itself the oldest and finest bookstore in Tennessee. Every square inch of shelf space is jammed full of books, and there are more stacks of books seemingly everywhere you turn. This place is a book collector's dream come true. And who needs a fancy, in-store Starbucks cafe when you've got the retro Elliston Soda Shop right next door? 2115 Elliston Place.© **615/327-1867.** www.eldersbookstore.com.

Fairytales Bookstore & More   Children's books are only part of the mix at this beloved East Nashville store, where you can find educational toys, arts and crafts kits, children's dress-up costumes, and other creative pursuits. Read-aloud story times featuring beloved children's book characters like Clifford the Big Red Dog, and others by authors such as Richard Scarry and Eric Carle, are offered frequently. In 2012, the store relocated within the same, cozy old house as the popular ice-cream shop, the Pied Piper Creamery, in the Five Points neighborhood. It's an ideal setting for a fun family outing. 114 S. 11th St.© **615/915-1960.** www.fairytalesbookstore.com.

Parnassus Books   With the recent demise of so many bookstores, including the Borders chain, Nashville's own bestselling author Anne Patchett is going against the grain with the November 2011 opening of a new, independent bookstore in the Green Hills area. Fiction, nonfiction, and children's books, in both printed and digital forms, have been attracting appreciative crowds and national media attention. In the months leading up to the grand opening, Patchett began cultivating a loyal clientele by blogging about her hopes and dreams for the bookstore. Community activism promises to be another important component of Parnassus, which gets its name from the Greek mountain where music, literature, and poetry were born. Greenbriar Village.© **615/953-2243.** www.parnassusbooks.net.

Crafts

Pangaea ★   From hand-carved soaps and South American textiles to one-of-a-kind Elvis icons, this eclectic boutique in Nashville's trendy Hillsboro Village area has interesting gifts to suit a variety of tastes, if not budgets. (They also sell cool clothes.) Items are on the pricey side, but for a unique shopping experience adjacent to scores of hip coffee shops and galleries, even window-shopping at Pangaea is time well spent. 1721 21st Ave. S.© **615/269-9665.** www.pangaeanashville.com.

Ten Thousand Villages   Fair-trade gift items, including jewelry, crafts, home decor, and more, fill this colorful store, located in Greenbriar Village, right around the corner from where Anne Patchett's new bookstore is being built. 3900 Hillsboro Pike.© **615/385-5814.** www.nashville.tenthousandvillages.com.

Department Stores

Dillard's   Dillard's is recognized as one of the nation's leading department stores. They carry many leading brands and have stores at several malls around Nashville:

Mall at Green Hills, 2126 Abbott Martin Rd. (© 615/297-0971); RiverGate Mall, 1000 RiverGate Pkwy., Goodlettsville (© 615/859-2811); and Cool Springs Galleria, 1800 Galleria Blvd. (© 615/771-7101).

Macy's   Anchoring many of the major shopping malls in Nashville is this well-known national chain, noted for its wide selection of fine lines. **Cool Springs Galleria,** 1800 Galleria Blvd., in Franklin (© 615/771-2100); **Mall at Green Hills,** 2126 Abbott Martin Rd. (© 615/383-3300); **Hickory Hollow Mall,** 917 Bell Rd. (© 615/731-5050); and **RiverGate Mall,** 1000 RiverGate Pkwy., Goodlettsville (© 615/859-5251).

Nordstrom   The highly anticipated opening of Tennessee's first (and only) Nordstrom occurred with much fanfare September 2011 at the **Mall at Green Hills,** 2126 Abbott Martin Rd. (© 615/850-6700). The high-end U.S. retailer is known for its upscale apparel for men, women, and children, as well as cosmetics, fragrances, and other merchandise.

Discount Shopping

French's Shoes and Boots   Dingo, Durango, Justin, Tony Lama, and Timberland are among the well-known boot brands sold at this downtown Nashville discounter. Men's, women's, and kids' selections are available. Whether you're looking for pigskin, cowhide, or lizard cowboy boots, this place probably has them. They also sell casual shoes and boots, including Uggs and Skechers. One side of the store is devoted to bargain racks that offer an unbeatable discount: Buy one pair at full price and get two more pairs of equal or lesser value free. Founded in Crossville, Tennessee, French's now has several locations throughout the state. 126B 2nd Ave. N. © 615/736-2934. www.frenchsbootsandshoes.com.

Lebanon Premium Outlets   Well worth the hour-long drive from Nashville, the Prime Outlets, in Lebanon, Tennessee, are the mother lode of brand-name merchandise at bargain prices. The massive orange-and-yellow outdoor mall is clean and well-maintained, and offers substantial discounts on Ann Taylor, Coach, Banana Republic, Tommy Hilfiger, and dozens of other well-known brands. From downtown Nashville, take I-40 east to exit 238. One Outlet Village Blvd., Lebanon, TN. © 615/444-0433. www.premiumoutlets.com.

RCC Western Stores ★   Whether you're looking for a bargain on a rhinestone-studded handbag, Harley Davidson black motorcycle boots, or a pair of high-end Lucchese barnwood-burnished ostrich cowboy boots, this place delivers. The suburban Goodlettsville store also sells work clothing and casual apparel and accessories, including shirts, leather jackets, skirts, belts, buckles, bandanas, and wallets. It's located in an old shopping center about a 20-minute drive north of downtown Nashville. On Interstate 65, take exit 97 and look for the Kmart; RCC Western Stores is next door. 240 Long Hollow Pike, Goodlettsville. © 615/859-4600. www.rccwesternstores.com.

Fashions

See also "Western Wear," below.

Boutique Bella   If you're looking for a Splendid T or Kooba handbag, this West End shop will fit the bill. Although its men's apparel shop closed in late 2009, ladies can find dozens of denim brands including 7 for All Mankind and Humanity. It's located in the Park Place Shopping Center. 2817 West End Ave. © 615/467-1471. www.boutiquebella.com.

Coco A longtime local favorite for women with expensive tastes, this ladies' boutique sells designer sportswear, dresses, and accessories, and features such lines as Ellen Tracy and Emmanuel. Both the fashions and the clientele tend to be upscale. 4239 Harding Rd. ✆ **615/292-0362.**

The Cotton Mill Discriminating fashionistas looking for the latest from Marc Jacobs, See by Chloe, Milly, Alice & Olivia, and Badgley Mischka look to this Green Hills–area boutique. The Cotton Mill prides itself on its "beautiful people" clientele, and if you fit the bill, expect to be pampered here. 4009 Hillsboro Circle. ✆ **615/298-2188.** www.thecottonmillnashville.com.

Diamond Star Halo Vintage ★ Veteran vintage enthusiast and former *New York Post* fashion critic and *Glamour* magazine style columnist Libby Callaway returned to her native Nashville a few years ago to begin selling her unique clothing and accessories. You'll find her distinctive fashions inside the same old Victorian-era house as Fanny's House of Music in East Nashville (p. 93). Celebrities including Taylor Swift rave about DSHV's decades-old fashion finds, which include dresses, blouses, jackets, scarves, and accessories. The shop also carries stylish vintage men's clothing. 1101 Holly St. ✆ **615/750-5746.** www.libbycalloway.com.

Flavour A go-to spot for the coolest jeans and fresh looks for both men and women, this boutique is your best shopping bet if you want to stay in the downtown/midtown area. Brands ranging from True Religion and Morphine Generation to Da-Nang, Cha Cha, and Alice & Trixie are just a few of those offered at this Music Row retailer. 1522-B Demonbreun. ✆ **615/254-2064.** www.flavourclothing.com.

Imogene + Willie ★ Dubbed "a denim junkie's paradise" by *GQ* Magazine, which named it one of the Top 10 independent men's stores in America, Imogene + Willie creates heritage-style jeans, cotton button-down shirts and tees, and hand-crafted neckties, vests, and other fashion items, in a restored gas station/garage in the 12South neighborhood. Open since 2009, Carrie and Matt Eddmenson have clothed and styled Nashville's own Black Keys (for a *Spin* cover story), and local music super-stars Kings of Leon, Matt Kearney, and Brooks & Dunn are also satisfied customers. 2601 12th Ave. S. ✆ **615/292-5005.** www.imogeneandwillie.com.

Jamie One of Nashville's most elite women's boutiques, Jamie exudes luxury. Deep-pocketed shoppers looking for just the right look from Prada or Versace, Donna Karan, or Vera Wang will likely find it here, along with the jewelry and shoes to match. 4317 Harding Rd. ✆ **615/292-4188.** www.jamie-nashville.com.

Local Honey In a cute Belmont University–area bungalow wedged between ChaChah tapas bar and Bongo Java coffee shop is this vintage boutique catering to a young, hip, mostly female clientele. Affordably priced dresses, blouses, jackets, and accessories, as well as women's apparel by local designers, are focal points. Tidwell and Perryman pants, shirts, jackets, and ties are also sold here. 2009 Belmont Blvd. ✆ **615/915-1354.** www.localhoneynashville.blogspot.com.

Posh Boutique Trendy clothes and footwear by the likes of Prophetik (a Nashville-based sustainable clothing line getting big buzz), Diesel, Boyfriend, J Brand Jeans, and MM Couture attract a young, affluent clientele. That's not to say you can't scour the place for occasional bargains. There's a second location at the Hill Center, 4027 Hillsboro Pike, Ste. 705 (✆ **615/269-6250**). 1801 21st Ave. S. ✆ **615/383-9840.** www.poshonline.com.

Scarlett Begonia   Ethnic fashions, jewelry, and fine crafts from around the world prove that there is life beyond country Nashville. The emphasis here is on South American clothing, and the quality is much higher than you'll find in the average import store. 2805 West End Ave. (C) **615/329-1272.** www.scarlettbegonia.com.

Urban Outfitters   With the opening of this stylish store in the Gulch, downtown dwellers finally have hope that other desirable retail chains will follow. Although the store also sells a bit of contemporary furniture, wall art, and pop-culture collectibles, Urban Outfitters' core merchandise is casual clothing for both men and women. Graphic T-shirts and tank tops, jackets, jumpers, shirts, shoes, and accessories are part of the mix. 405 12th Ave. S. (C) **615/254-3339.** www.urbanoutfitters.com.

Fine Gifts/Souvenirs

Nashville abounds in shops purveying every manner of country-themed souvenirs. The greatest concentrations of these shops are in the Music Row and Music Valley (Opryland Resort) areas, where several of the stores specialize in particular country music performers. Several of the gift shops, including Cooter's and the Willie Nelson Museum on McGavock Pike (Music Valley), also have backroom museums where you can see music memorabilia. But these museums are really just an excuse to get you into the big souvenir shop out front, though if you're a fan, you'll enjoy touring the exhibits and maybe picking up a souvenir. See "On the Music Trail," p. 31, for further information.

Fire Finch ★   Eclectic, primitive-style artwork and other interesting, upscale gift items are sold in this atmospheric store. Bracelets, brooches, clutches, and candles are among the varied inventory. And, yes, you might see a finch or two. A second location is located downtown, at 305 Church St. ((C) **615/942-5271**). 1818 21st Ave. S. (C) **615/829-3533.** www.firefinch.net.

Social Graces   Designer stationery sets, invitations, handmade paper, and an assortment of luxurious writing gifts and accessories are lavishly displayed here. As part of a full day of shopping, the relatively quiet, contemplative atmosphere at this store makes a nice change of pace from some of the West End's livelier shops. 1704 21st Ave. S. (C) **615/383-1911.** www.socialgracesonline.com.

This Oktipus Printing Co.   Opened in late 2011, this irresistible print shop in the Five Points area of East Nashville specializes in old-fashioned printed materials, using wood blocks and letterpressing. Stationery, cards, invitations, and posters are done inside the tiny shop, on an antique-looking printing press. Gifts such as handmade paper journals, tiny pots of ink, and vintage printed materials like old cards and black-and-white photographs make fun, affordable mementoes. 1108 Woodland St. (C) **615/713-0241.**

A Thousand Faces ★★   Beautifully crafted one-of-a-kind gifts including jewelry, artwork, and home decor are packed inside every square inch of this vibrant West End boutique that's perfect for leisurely browsing. Their motto boasts "a plethora of neat stuff," and that about sums it up. Creatively merchandised and chock-full of interesting finds, this is one of the West End's most popular shops. 1720 21st Ave. S. (C) **615/298-3304.** www.athousandfaces.com.

Flea Markets

Nashville Farmers' Market   In addition to the scores of outdoor farm stalls selling fresh produce, and the indoor restaurants and concessions, the Nashville

Farmers' Market includes about 100 flea market vendors selling everything from leather goods and wool blankets to dishes and baby clothes. Open 7 days a week, the market is adjacent to the Bicentennial Capital Mall State Park. 900 Eighth Ave. N. © **615/880-2001.** www.nashvillefarmersmarket.org.

Tennessee State Fairgrounds Flea Market   This huge flea market is held the fourth weekend of every month (except Dec, when it's the third weekend), attracting more than 1,000 vendors selling everything from cheap jeans to handmade crafts to antiques and collectibles. You'll find the fairgrounds just a few minutes south of downtown. Tennessee State Fairgrounds, Fourth Ave. © **615/862-5016.** www.nashvilleexpo center.org.

Food

International Market and Restaurant ★   Open daily until 9pm, this one-of-a-kind find in the Belmont University neighborhood offers lots of Asian imports on items ranging from chopsticks and rice to specialty culinary ingredients and fine teas. A buffet line at one end of the market brims with freshly prepared, hot Thai dishes, including satays and noodles. 2010 Belmont Blvd. © **615/297-4453.**

Lazzaroli Pasta   Fresh pastas, including homemade ravioli and sauces, and take-and-bake meals are mainstays at this new Germantown market. Whether you want traditional egg noodles or hand-cut pappardelle, you'll find it here, along with gourmet pantry items, cheeses, and classic Italian desserts such as tiramisu and fresh-filled cannoli. 1314 Fifth Ave. N. © **615/291-9922.** www.lazzaroli.com.

Olive & Sinclair Chocolate Co.   Scott Witherow trained at London's Le Cordon Bleu before coming home to Tennessee to start this "bean-to-bar" chocolate-making company. Carefully handcrafted in small batches from single-origin cacao beans (the Dominican Republic and Ghana), the intensely rich chocolate bars come in a variety of chocolate flavors: Dark, Buttermilk White, Sea Salt, Cinnamon, and Coffee. Beautifully packaged and hand wrapped in gold foil, the bars retail for $6 on the company's website. You can also find them in stores, coffee shops, and hotel gift stores throughout Nashville and beyond. Although Olive & Sinclair doesn't have its own retail outlet yet, they offer tours of their small factory in the Riverside Village area of East Nashville, with products available for purchase afterward. Tours are usually at 9am and 10:30am Saturdays, but times and dates often vary: If you're on Twitter, follow them (@olivesinclair) for updates. 1404 McGavock Pike. © **615/262-3007.** www. oliveandsinclair.com.

The Peanut Shop   If you've been trudging around downtown Nashville all day and need a quick snack, consider a bag of fresh-roasted peanuts. This tiny shop in the Arcade (connecting Fourth Ave. N. and Fifth Ave. N.) has been in business since 1927 and still roasts its own peanuts. In fact, there are more styles of peanuts sold here than you've probably ever seen in one place. A true Nashville institution. *Tip:* The Arcade alleyway is shuttered on Saturdays and Sundays. 19 Arcade. © **615/256-3394.** www.nashvillenut.com.

The Turnip Truck Natural Market   Baskets of apples, pumpkins, squash, and other seasonal produce fill the entry of this local whole-foods grocery story in East Nashville. Celebrating a decade in business, The Turnip Truck has a focus on fresh, locally farmed produce and everyday essentials, including dairy and frozen foods and self-dispensing bins with oats, nuts, and beans. And here's good news for urban condo dwellers: A second location, **The Turnip Truck Urban Fare,** opened in 2011 at

321 12th Ave. S. in the Gulch (② **615/248-2000**). 970 Woodland Ave. ② **615/650-3600.** www.theturniptruck.com.

Malls/Shopping Centers

Cool Springs Galleria   A 15-minute drive south of Nashville off I-65 (at the Moore's Lane exit) is the city's newest shopping mall. Although it is more convenient to affluent locals and tourists in the Brentwood suburb than it is for most tourists to downtown Nashville, this is a top-tier mall that has it all. 1800 Galleria Blvd. ② **615/771-2128.** www.coolspringsgalleria.com.

Hickory Hollow Mall   Familiar mall stores such as Aeropostale, Claire's, Payless Shoes, and Lane Bryant are among the scores of specialty shops at this retail venue west of the Nashville area, in Antioch. There's also a food court and two major department stores, Macy's and Sears. You'll find the mall southwest of downtown off I-24 east, at exit 60. 5252 Hickory Hollow Pkwy., Antioch. ② **615/731-3500.** www.hickoryhollowmall.com.

Hill Center Green Hills   Celebrities and everyday fashion mavens love the upscale shops and boutiques within this collection of storefronts in the shadow of The Mall at Green Hills. Open for about 5 years, it remains one of the city's premier retail-therapy destinations. Clothing, jewelry, and home-decor stores offer an eclectic mix that includes Anthropologie, Snap Kids, and the cutting-edge H. Audrey (owned by Holly Williams, daughter of Hank Jr.). Restaurants such as California Pizza Kitchen and grocery chain Whole Foods Market are among the many other top draws here. 4015-4031 Hillsboro Pike. ② **615/252-8101.** www.hillcentergreenhills.com.

The Mall at Green Hills   Now that the Nordstrom department store is finally a reality, locals love The Mall at Green Hills even more than ever, ensuring its reign as Nashville's most popular place to shop. In this congested area surrounded by other good shopping centers, the Mall caters to customers with discriminating tastes. Here, you'll find Sephora, Crabtree & Evelyn, Tiffany & Co., Brooks Brothers, Ann Taylor Loft, Chico's, and Pottery Barn, along with Nordstrom co-anchor stores Macy's and Dillard's. 2126 Abbott Martin Rd. ② **615/298-5478.** www.themallatgreenhills.com.

Opry Mills   Tentatively scheduled to reopen in spring 2012 after being shuttered by severe flooding that hit the Nashville area in May 2010, Opry Mills previously offered an array of department stores, specialty boutiques, restaurants, and entertainment venues. Among Opry Mills' 200 (pre-flood) tenants, anchor Bass Pro Shops Outdoor World has remained open throughout the mall's closure. 433 Opry Mills Dr. ② **615/514-1000.** www.oprymills.com.

RiverGate Mall   If you're looking for shopping in northern Nashville, head up I-65 North to exit 95 or 96. The RiverGate Mall includes four department stores and scores of boutiques and specialty shops. 1000 RiverGate Pkwy., Goodlettsville ② **615/859-3456.** www.rivergate-mall.com.

Music

Ernest Tubb Record Shop ★★ 📷   The creaking hardwood floor and narrow rows of record bins recall the 1950s heyday of this historic record shop that's been in business since 1947, when country star Ernest Tubb founded the *Midnite Jamboree* live-music event held here, following the *Grand Ole Opry* performance at the nearby Ryman. Whether you're looking for a reissue of an early Johnny Cash album, an

"Walkin' the Floor Over You"

Ernest Tubb was one of Nashville's earliest country recording stars. This native Texan, known to friends as "E.T.," scored a big hit with "Walkin' the Floor Over You" in 1941. The beloved entertainer, who in gratitude to his audiences had the word "Thanks" emblazoned on the back of his guitar, earned a slew of industry awards, played Carnegie Hall, and was inducted into the Country Music Hall of Fame. After a long and successful career as one of the pioneers in country music, he died in Nashville in 1984.

obscure bluegrass band's CD, or the latest hit from Lady Antebellum, you'll find it at Ernest Tubb. There's another, larger shopping mall location out near Opryland, at 2416 Music Valley Dr. (© **615/889-2474**); this is where the *Midnite Jamboree* is held each Saturday night at midnight. Ernest Tubb's shiny green and cream-colored tour bus sits inside the modern retail shop. 417 Broadway. © **615/255-7503.** www.ernest tubb.com.

The Great Escape   This old store adjacent to the Vanderbilt campus caters to the record and comic book needs of college students and other collectors and bargain seekers. The used-records section has a distinct country bent, but you can find other types of music as well. This is a big place with a great selection, including records, CDs, comic books, video games, and so on. 5400 Charlotte Ave. © **615/385-2116.** www. thegreatescapeonline.com.

Grimey's New & Preloved Music ★   New and "preloved" (don't call them used) CDs are bought and sold at Grimey's, this independently owned record store and community clearinghouse for all things related to the local music scene. You can buy T-shirts, posters, concert memorabilia, and other cool stuff, and get a leg up on everything that's going on around town. Downstairs you'll find The Basement, a popular venue for record-release parties, live performances, and other events. 1604 Eighth Ave. S. © **615/254-4801.** www.grimeys.com.

Third Man Records ★★   Rock fans shouldn't miss this unique record shop that's the brainchild of former White Stripes frontman Jack White, the musician, independent record producer, and vinyl enthusiast who moved to Nashville a few years ago from Detroit. Posters, pins, collectibles, turntables, and vinyl albums, 45s, and CDs by the White Stripes, The Raconteurs, the Dead Weather, the Black Belles, and others are for sale. Purists can snap up LPs by country music queen Loretta Lynn and rockabilly legend Wanda Jackson, both of whom had recent comeback albums produced by White. The cramped room is full of kitsch, including an old wooden telephone booth and the comical, coin-operated "Monkey Band" machine that unleashes hard rock songs as toy monkeys inside a glass case dance and play cymbals and drums. Behind the scenes, Third Man is also a one-stop production house where musicians can rehearse and record before having their albums pressed in Nashville. 623 7th Ave. S. © **615/891-4393.** www.thirdmanrecords.com.

Musical Instruments

Cotten Music Center   High-end acoustic stringed instruments have kept this West End music store in business since 1961. Acoustic guitars and mandolins, new and vintage electric guitars, and accessories, including strings, straps, cases, and gig bags, are sold here. Check the Backroom Bargains for great deals. The shop offers lessons, repair service, and special orders too. 1815 21st Ave. S. ℂ **615/383-8947.** www. cottenmusic.com.

Fanny's House of Music ★   Pink ukuleles, electric guitars, drum sets, and a stringed, antique psaltery or two are typically for sale in this women-owned boutique in East Nashville. Located in a charming Victorian house, the shop also sells music stands, recorders, sheet music, amplifiers, guitar strings, and other instrumental accessories. There are plenty of hard-backed chairs scattered about the rooms; sit a spell and pick out a tune or two on one of the guitars you're thinking about buying. Fanny's also offers private music lessons for kids through adults. Friendly and informal, Fanny's is a fun place to browse, even if you're not in the market for a new or used instrument. 1101 Holly St. ℂ **615/750-5746.** www.fannyshouseofmusic.com.

> ### Kids' Stuff
>
> Don't overlook music attractions as shopping sources. For instance, in addition to an extensive selection of books and CDs, the **Country Music Hall of Fame and Museum** (p. 35) features a wondrous kids' corner, with hundreds of goodies, from kazoos and coin purses to rooster-headed pencil sharpeners and cowboy-hatted rubber duckies.

Fork's Drum Closet   Drums and other percussion instruments fill this large shop near the far end of 12th Avenue South. Billed as the largest drum shop in the Southeastern U.S., Fork's sells Yamaha, Pearl, Ludwig, Tama, Vic Firth, and Gretsch brands, as well as supplies and accessories for beginners through pros. 2701 12th Ave. S. ℂ **615/383-8343.** www.forksdrumcloset.com.

Gruhn Guitars ★★   Johnny Cash, Neil Young, Elvis Costello, and Eric Clapton are clients, and you can be too. Nashville's biggest guitar dealer (and one of the largest in the world) stocks classic used and collectible guitars, as well as reissues of musicians' favorite instruments. Fretted instruments of all kinds can be found here. If you're in the market for a 1953 Les Paul or a 1938 Martin D-28, this is the place to hit. 400 Broadway. ℂ **615/256-2033.** www.gruhn.com.

Western Wear

In addition to the places listed below, you can pick up clothing at the Wildhorse Saloon and other shops in the District. There are also clothing stores in Music Valley and on Music Row.

Betty Boots   Looking for the perfect pair of cowgirl boots or a sexy Stetson? One of downtown's newest Western-wear shops caters to the ladies. In addition to Nashville-inspired gear, you'll find flip-flops, purses, and a few souvenirs. Service is superfriendly. 321 Broadway. ℂ **615/736-7698.**

Boot Country   Cowboy boots, more cowboy boots, and still more cowboy boots. That's what you'll find at this boot store. Whether you want a basic pair of work boots or some fancy python-skin showstoppers, you'll find them here. 304 Broadway. ℂ **615/259-1691.** www.facebook.com/bootcountrynashville.

Katy K's Designs ★★ 🎁   Patsy Cline would look right at home at this 12South landmark that's been a trendsetter for more than a decade now. Specializing in 1950s-era Western wear, the boutique sells everything from spangled gowns by Nudie's of

Hollywood to corsets and crinoline petticoats. Browse the designer boots, belts, buckles, snap shirts, sexy vintage dresses, and cute baby clothes. It's a kick. 2407 12th Ave. S. ☎ **615/297-4242.** www.katyk.com.

Nashville Cowboy   You can smell the leather a block away from this downtown store. A staggering collection of boots, belts, hats, and buckles are on display. Coats come in all sizes and styles, from the simple to the fringed-suede and lambskin-lined varieties. 132 Second Ave. N. ☎ **615/259-8922.** www.nashvillecowboy.com.

Opry Originals ★   In 2009, Manuel, Nashville's legendary clothier to the country music stars for more than 4 decades, launched a line of spangled duds for everyday dudes in this expansive new retail store in the heart of downtown Nashville's. One of the nicest and newest stores in the District, shopping here is interesting and fun. With something for everyone, from drumsticks and guitar picks to Opry-brand jackets, shirts, jeans, and boots, this is a one-stop souvenir destination that also sells home furnishings, retro kitchen decor, and cookbooks. 300 Broadway. ☎ **615/259-9777.** www.opry.com.

Trail West   Not quite the draw it once was, this Western-wear store has a large inventory and steeper prices than those of some of their competitors. They handle the Brooks & Dunn Collection plus all the usual brands of hats, boots, and denim. There are other locations at 2416 Music Valley Dr., across from the Gaylord Opryland Resort and Convention Center (☎ **615/883-5933**), and at 219 Broadway (☎ **615/255-7030**). 214 Broadway. ☎ **615/255-7030.**

NASHVILLE ENTERTAINMENT & NIGHTLIFE

L ive music surrounds you in Nashville. Country, bluegrass, rock, and Americana music styles are the most prevalent, but you'll also hear jazz, blues, soul, and classical music in every part of the city.

Boozy bars such as **Tootsie's Orchid Lounge** contrast with quiet listening-room showcases like **The Bluebird Cafe,** and Nashville has what the New York Times recently noted is the best live-music scene in the country.

Some of this music can be found in unexpected places: street corners, parks, hotel lounges, parking lots, and museums. Like Memphis, the city overflows with talented musicians who play where they can, much to the benefit of visitors to Nashville.

And, of course, there's the granddaddy of them all, the long-running country music radio broadcast, the *Grand Ole Opry.*

Performing arts groups, too, are thriving in Music City. Nashville boasts a dynamic, Grammy-winning symphony orchestra and a world-class concert hall, as well as opera and ballet companies, and the state's largest professional theater troupe as well as its oldest children's theater group.

Check the websites of *The Nashville Scene,* the city's arts-and-entertainment weekly, and *The Tennessean,* the daily newspaper, for up-to-the-minute club listings, music festivals, and other concert events. Hard copies of the paper are available around town, but you can quickly access content at www.nashvillescene.com and www.tennessean.com.

Nashville nightlife happens all around town but predominates in two main downtown areas: the **District,** which includes the notorious strip of honky-tonks along Broadway, and the **Gulch,** a former rail yard on the southern edge of downtown that now teems with high-rise condos, retail shops, and some of the city's trendiest nightclubs and restaurants.

In these two areas, you'll find the venerable **Wildhorse Saloon,** bluegrass landmark **The Station Inn,** and a few dozen other clubs showcasing bands on any given weekend night. On the sidewalks, people are shoulder to shoulder as they parade from one club to the next, and in the streets, stretch limos vie for space with tricked-out pickup trucks.

Within the District, Broadway and Second Avenue are currently the main drags—where you'll find the most impressive of the area's clubs. Downtown also includes **Printer's Alley,** once the epicenter of Nashville nightlife. The gritty alley still has a few late-night haunts, but the whole area is a bit on the seedy side.

Within a few blocks of the District, you'll also find the **Tennessee Performing Arts Center** as well as the **Bridgestone Arena,** where big-name concerts, televised awards shows, and National Hockey League (with hometown team the **Nashville Predators**) games are held.

About 10 miles northeast of downtown lies **Music Valley,** which, on the whole, offers a more family-oriented, sedate nightlife scene. Here you'll find the Grand Ole Opry House, Nashville Palace, and Texas Troubadour Theatre, as well as the Gaylord Opryland Resort, which has a few nightclubs.

And, finally, the low-key **East Nashville** neighborhood, which lies between downtown and Music Valley, has a growing number of hip cafes, coffeehouses, and bars showcasing the best local and regional new singers, songwriters, poets, and artists.

Tickets to major concerts and sporting events can be purchased through **Ticketmaster** (© 800/745-3000; www.ticketmaster.com), which maintains a desk at the Tennessee Performing Arts Center box office. A service charge is added to all ticket sales. Finally, for a comprehensive list of live music, performing arts, and sports events, visit **www.nowplayingnashville.com**.

THE COUNTRY MUSIC SCENE
In the District, Music Row & the Gulch

In addition to the clubs mentioned here, you'll find several small bars along lower Broadway, in an area long known as **Honky-Tonk Row** or **Honky-Tonk Highway** The teeming, 2-block strip between Fourth and Fifth avenues is a nostalgic neon hootenanny of country music sights, sounds, and occasionally some good old-fashioned rabble-rousing. Best of all, there's never a cover charge.

Douglas Corner Cafe   Though it has the look and feel of a neighborhood bar, this is one of Nashville's top places for songwriters trying to break into the big time—it's the city's main competition for The Bluebird Cafe. The club also has occasional shows by established performers. It's located a few minutes south of downtown, near all the antiques shops. 2106 Eighth Ave. S. © **615/298-1688.** www.douglascorner.com. Cover up to $7.

Layla's Bluegrass Inn   Pure hillbilly—and proud of it—Layla's is a stalwart of the strip here in downtown Nashville. In addition to hosting hillbilly and rockabilly acts, the cozy venue hosts country, Americana, and, of course, bluegrass and even progressive "newgrass" musicians. Its vintage cowgirl/cowboy decor and "howdy pardner" appeal hark back to Nashville's first big heyday in the 1940s and 1950s. 418 Broadway. © **615/726-2799.** www.laylasbluegrassinn.com. No cover.

Legends Corner   Today's starving artists are tomorrow's country music superstars, and this beloved dive in the District sets the stage for such happily-ever-after scenarios. Die-hard barhoppers insist that Legends Corner has downtown's best live local music and one of the friendliest staffs in all of Music City. Nostalgic memorabilia on the walls adds a quaint, down-home charm. And you can't beat the price: The tip jar gets passed around the room like a collection plate, enabling the rowdy crowds to help support the struggling pickers and grinners who've put Nashville on the map. Ages 21 and older only after 6pm. 428 Broadway. © **615/248-6334.** www.legendscorner.com. No cover.

absinthe, ANYONE?

A place like no other in Nashville, **The Patterson House,** 1711 Division St. (© **615/636-7724;** www.thepatterson nashville.com), sets a new standard for sophisticated cocktails, served in sumptuous surroundings. Beyond the doors of this gray, unmarked house at the edge of Music Row is a dimly lit lounge where the sparkle of stemware and glass liquor bottles is reflected in the muted-silver wallpaper and the golden glow of low-hanging chandeliers. The intimate room is a classy, modern-day speak-easy of sorts, recalling the secretive, backroom indulgences of the American Prohibition era.

Patrons, seated on stools surrounding the square bar in the center of the room or in rich brown booths lining the perimeter of the space, focus their sights on the rock-star mixologists—young bartenders who work their magic with gin, vodka, whiskey, tequila, brandy, and other liquid refreshments. All eyes are on these dapper hosts, as they shake, muddle, stir, and pour with precision and aplomb.

Cocktail choices, written in calligraphy on handmade paper booklets, list drink choices by the type of alcohol, and further subcategorize them with the weakest drinks at the top and the most potent at the bottom of each page. The refreshing Juliet & Romeo, an alluring blend of Plymouth gin, lime, mint, cucumber, and rose water, is one of the milder choices. On the opposite end of the spectrum is the Bacon Old Fashioned, an ingeniously bold drink that boasts bacon-infused 4 Roses bourbon with maple syrup and coffee-pecan bitters. In between these two extremes are variations on the Pim's Cup, several complex margaritas, and mysterious drinks that include absinthe, that notorious vice of such tragic historic figures as French artist Toulouse-Lautrec.

The Patterson House is open 5pm to 3am Tuesday through Sunday. They don't take reservations, but for the best chance at getting a seat inside, visit early in the evening on a weeknight. Incidentally, the nightspot also serves good food, including Margherita pizza and fried goat-cheese balls (there's even an Elvis panini), although food is of secondary significance to the drinks. If you hunger for more, plan months in advance to nab a reservation for the ultra-exclusive **Catbird's Seat Restaurant,** a new (opened late Oct 2011) 32-seat, gourmet restaurant located upstairs, where diners gather around a U-shaped table, surrounding two chefs as they prepare a seven-course tasting menu while conversing with guests. The restaurant is open for dinner Wednesday through Saturday. Reservations are taken online only. For more information, visit www.thecat birdseatrestaurant.com.

Robert's Western World ★★   A few doors down from Tootsie's, this former Western-wear store is the best of the strip's honky-tonks for cutting a rug on the cramped dance floor. Live bands, including Brazilbilly, rock the house most Friday and Saturday nights. Cowboy boots and other kitsch line the walls of this venerable club. They're for sale, and they come in all sizes, shapes, and styles. 416 Broadway. © **615/244-9552.** www.robertswesternworld.com. No cover.

Ryman Auditorium ★★★ 📷   Take in a live performance at "The Mother Church of Country Music" to absorb the rich musical and cultural heritage of today's modern Music City. Once the home of the *Grand Ole Opry* radio broadcast, the venue, built as a house of worship in the late 1800s, introduced the world to legends like Hank Williams, Sr., Kitty Wells, Bill Monroe, and Patsy Cline in the 1940s and

Nashville After Dark

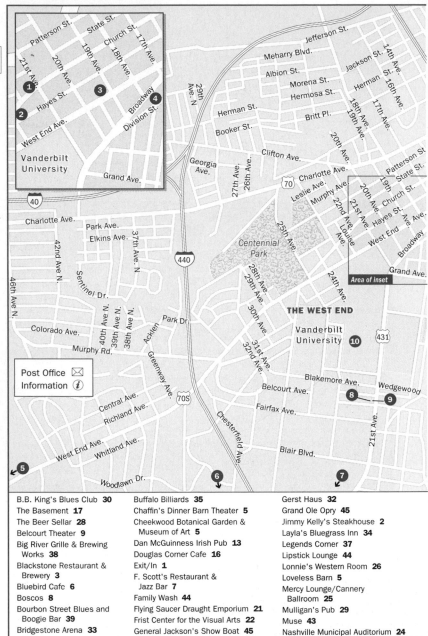

B.B. King's Blues Club **30**	Buffalo Billiards **35**	Gerst Haus **32**
The Basement **17**	Chaffin's Dinner Barn Theater **5**	Grand Ole Opry **45**
The Beer Sellar **28**	Cheekwood Botanical Garden &	Jimmy Kelly's Steakhouse **2**
Belcourt Theater **9**	Museum of Art **5**	Layla's Bluegrass Inn **34**
Big River Grille & Brewing	Dan McGuinness Irish Pub **13**	Legends Corner **37**
Works **38**	Douglas Corner Cafe **16**	Lipstick Lounge **44**
Blackstone Restaurant &	Exit/In **1**	Lonnie's Western Room **26**
Brewery **3**	F. Scott's Restaurant &	Loveless Barn **5**
Bluebird Cafe **6**	Jazz Bar **7**	Mercy Lounge/Cannery
Boscos **8**	Family Wash **44**	Ballroom **25**
Bourbon Street Blues and	Flying Saucer Draught Emporium **21**	Mulligan's Pub **29**
Boogie Bar **39**	Frist Center for the Visual Arts **22**	Muse **43**
Bridgestone Arena **33**	General Jackson's Show Boat **45**	Nashville Municipal Auditorium **24**

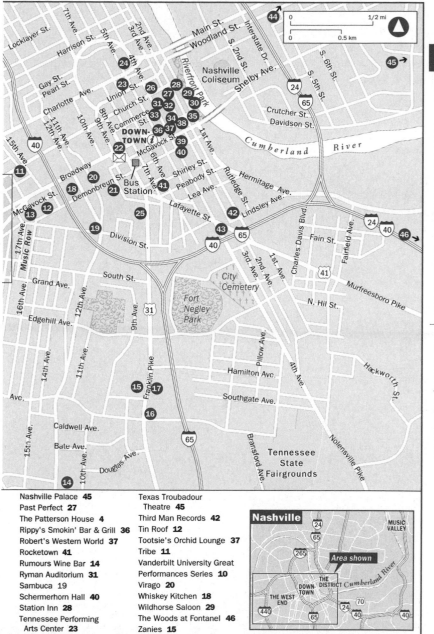

1950s. With acoustics that are said to be better than Carnegie Hall's, the intimate auditorium has become the venue of choice for music's top touring acts. In recent years, musicians from all genres, including Jack White, Neil Young, Yo-Yo Ma, Vince Gill, Aretha Franklin, Ricky Skaggs, and Elvis Costello have played to packed houses at the National Historic Landmark. 116 Fifth Ave. N. © **615/254-1445** or 615/889-6611. www.ryman.com. Tickets $18–$43.

The Station Inn ★ For decades widely regarded as one of the best bluegrass venues around, this humble little dive still thrives in the shadow of the rapidly developing Gulch district south of Broadway in downtown. Live music is on tap 7 nights a week. Seating is first-come, first-served, so plan to arrive early, especially for such favorites as the Time Jumpers or the Grascals. A relatively more laid-back antidote to the boozy bars on Broadway, the Station Inn has a strict no-smoking policy. 402 12th Ave. S. © **615/255-3307.** www.stationinn.com. Cover $7 Tues–Sat, free Sun.

Tootsie's Orchid Lounge ★ 🍸 This rowdy country dive has been a Nashville tradition since the days when the *Grand Ole Opry* was still performing in The Ryman Auditorium around the corner. Back then, *Opry* stars used to duck into Tootsie's for a drink. Today, you can see signed photos of the many stars who have downed a few here. Free live country music spills out onto the sidewalks daily 10am to 3am, and celebrities still occasionally make the scene. 422 Broadway. © **615/726-0463.** www.tootsies.net. No cover.

Wildhorse Saloon Run by the same company that gave Nashville the Opryland Resort and stages the *Grand Ole Opry*, this massive, three-story dance hall attracts everyone from country music stars to line-dancing senior citizens groups. In recent years, the saloon has tried to reach beyond its outdated, boot-scootin' roots to attract more mainstream crowds by booking nostalgia acts such as the B-52s, Hanson, and Sister Hazel. Because the club closes for private parties from time to time, be sure to

📎 KNOW BEFORE YOU GO

Opry bound? Be aware that not all country stars are members of the grand ol' gang. So if you're hoping to see, say, George Strait, Wynonna, or the Dixie Chicks, look elsewhere. Many fans might not realize that *Opry* members are invited performers who must agree to a certain number of *Opry* appearances per year. Consequently, due to scheduling conflicts or other concerns, not every country singer who's a household name is represented.

But plenty of them are. The *Opry's* stellar roster includes Trace Adkins, Dierks Bentley, Clint Black, Garth Brooks, Jim Ed Brown, Roy Clark, John Conlee, Skeeter Davis, Diamond Rio, Little Jimmy Dickens, Joe Diffie, Holly Dunn, The Gatlin Brothers, Vince Gill, Billy Grammer, Tom T. Hall, Emmylou Harris, Jan Howard, Stonewall Jackson, Alan Jackson, George Jones, Hal Ketchum, Alison Krauss, Patty Loveless, Loretta Lynn, Martina McBride, Del McCoury, Reba McEntire, Montgomery Gentry, Lorrie Morgan, The Osborne Brothers, Brad Paisley, Dolly Parton, Charley Pride, Jeanne Pruett, Del Reeves, Riders In The Sky, Ricky Van Shelton, Jean Shepard, Rascal Flatts, Ricky Skaggs, Ralph Stanley, Marty Stuart, Pam Tillis, Randy Travis, Travis Tritt, Carrie Underwood, Ricky Van Shelton, Steve Wariner, The Whites, and Trisha Yearwood.

call first before you head out. 120 Second Ave. N. ℂ **615/251-1000.** www.wildhorsesaloon. com. Cover varies.

In Music Valley

General Jackson Showboat ★   If you'd like to combine some evening entertainment with a cruise on the Cumberland River, try the *General Jackson*. This huge reproduction paddle-wheeler brings back the glory days of river travel. Comedy and country music with a strong patriotic undercurrent keep the predominately bus-tour clientele happy. During the summer, the Southern Nights Cruise offers dancing under the stars to live bands; dinner is optional. 2812 Opryland Dr. ℂ **615/889-6611**, ext. 1000. Tickets $20 night cruises, $52 dinner cruises. Louise Mandrell Christmastime dinner shows $67.

> ### A Rave Review from GOOP
>
> *Never have I met such warm people, heard such good music, eaten so much fried chicken. . . . It's pretty damn great.*
> —Actress Gwyneth Paltrow, who wrote this on her influential blog, GOOP, after filming her movie *Country Strong* in Nashville.

Grand Ole Opry ★★★ 📷   The show that made Nashville famous, the *Grand Ole Opry* is the country's longest continuously running radio show and airs every weekend from a theater adjacent to the Gaylord Opryland Resort. Over the years, the *Opry* has had several homes, including The Ryman Auditorium in downtown Nashville. In late 2003, the 4,400-seat Grand Ole Opry House got its first major refurbishment since 1974, when the program was moved from The Ryman to its current home in the Music Valley. Through it all, the *Opry* remains a comforting mix of country music and gentle humor that has endured for nearly three-quarters of a century. Over the decades, the program has featured nearly all the greats of country music. There is an *Opry* show on Tuesday and Friday (at 7pm), and two performances on Saturday (7 and 9:30pm). Additionally, a new Opry Country Classics performance (weeknights vary) shines the spotlight on classic country songs that have defined country music for generations of fans. 2804 Opryland Dr. ℂ **800/SEE-OPRY** (733-6779) or 615/871-OPRY (6779). www.opry.com. Tickets $28–$53.

Nashville Palace   Especially popular with the tour-bus crowd, the Nashville Palace is easy to find, located directly opposite the Gaylord Opryland Resort. Open nightly from 5pm to 1:30am, the venue offers live country and western music and line dancing. A more laid-back alternative to The Bluebird Cafe (p. 102), the New Writers' Night (Mon 6–11pm) features up-and-coming songwriters. Occasionally, the Palace features tributes to country legends, such as Waylon Jennings. 2400 Music Valley Dr. ℂ **615/889-1540.** www.nashvillepalace.net. Cover $5.

Texas Troubadour Theatre   Although the original jamboree started at Ernest Tubb's downtown record shop on Broadway, the Music Valley location now hosts the weekly **Ernest Tubb *Midnite Jamboree*.** Recent headliners have included Bill Anderson, the Osborne Brothers, and Connie Smith; to find out who's scheduled during your visit, log on to the Ernest Tubb Record Shop's website at www.etrecordshop.com. If you're looking for a down-home dose of gospel music ministry the morning after, make it to the **Cowboy Church** on time: The old-timey, nondenominational services kick off Sundays at 10am sharp (ℂ **615/859-1001;** www.nashvillecowboychurch.org).

Come as you are or don your best Stetson and bolo tie. Either way, you'll fit right in with the eclectic, all-ages congregation of locals and tourists alike who pack the pews every week for a patriotic praise-and-worship service. Music Valley Village, 2416 Music Valley Dr. ✆ **615/889-2474.**

Green Hills Area

The Bluebird Cafe ★★ 📷   For a quintessential Nashville experience, visit this unassuming 100-seat club that remains one of the nation's premier venues for up-and-coming as well as established songwriters. Surprisingly, you'll find the Bluebird not in the District or on Music Row but in a suburban shopping plaza across the road from the Mall at Green Hills. There are usually two shows a night. Between 6 and 7pm, there is frequently music in the round, during which four singer-songwriters play some of their latest works. After 9pm, when more-established acts take the stage, there's a cover charge. This is the place in Nashville to catch the music of people you'll be hearing from in coming years. Because the club is so small, reservations (taken noon–5pm) are recommended. 4104 Hillsboro Rd. ✆ **615/383-1461.** www.bluebird-cafe.com. No cover for early shows, but there is a minimum $7 order per person at tables. Cover fees vary ($8–$20) for late shows after 9pm.

ROCK, BLUES, JAZZ & MORE

The Basement   This eclectic, live-music venue hosts an array of alternative, rock, and indie artists. Look for it in the same unassuming little building that houses Grimey's New and Preloved Music, one of the best record stores in town. Like the Station Inn in the Gulch, this club has gone smoke free (except for the outdoor patio). 1604 Eighth Ave. S. ✆ **615/254-8006.** www.thebasementnashville.com.

Exit/In   Mercifully free of the glitz of the bigger nightspots in the District, this battered old building has long been a local favorite of alternative rock and even the fast-growing alternative-country genre. Music ranges from rock to blues to reggae and a little country; there's usually live music 6 nights a week. And guess what? Jimmy Buffett got his start here. 2208 Elliston Place. ✆ **615/321-3340.** www.exitin.com. Cover varies.

Loveless Barn ★★   You can get more than your ham and biscuit on at the Loveless Cafe, thanks to a new barn that's been built behind the landmark diner on the outskirts of town. Every Wednesday night, *Live from the Loveless Cafe* radio show takes place here, airing on WSM. Announcers such as renowned WSM radio personality Eddie Stubbs and local musician/actor and all-around good guy Jim Lauderdale sometimes serve as announcers for the programs, which feature bluegrass, country,

---

💬 **Music City Loves Jack White**

Nashville's "cool quotient" has gone up considerably since the enigmatic musician/indie record producer Jack White started calling it home. The multitalented Detroit native recorded the top-selling *Icky Thump* album here with his former band the White Stripes. White's downtown Nashville recording studio is home to his **Third Man Records** imprint, retail store, and recording studio (p. 92).

rockabilly, folk, and alternative bands. The roster of past performers includes Marty Stuart and His Fabulous Superlatives, Abigail Washburn, Nanci Griffith, Cherryholmes, Doyle Lawson and Quicksilver, and The Civil Wars. Shows start at 7pm and last about 2 hours. Don't worry, you can buy beer and good grub here. It's a laid-back, come-as-you-are kind of gathering. 8400 Tenn. 100. ✆ **615/646-9700.** www.musiccityroots. com. Tickets $10; $5 with a student ID. Directions from Nashville: Take I-40 W. toward Memphis to exit 192 (McCrory Lane). Turn left and go 4 miles to Hwy. 100. Turn left; the Loveless Cafe is ahead on the left.

Mercy Lounge/Cannery Ballroom
A century after its beginnings as an 1883 flour mill, the multilevel warehouse began life as a live-music venue, hosting acts such as Jane's Addiction and Midnight Oil. Today the ground floor Cannery Ballroom can hold up to 1,000 people. Upstairs, the Mercy Lounge can hold 500 people. A rowdy crowd usually dominates the scene, drawn in for cheap drinks and headliners like Beirut, Third Eye Blind, the Jayhawks, and others. *Tip:* This place can be a bit tricky to find. From downtown, head south on Eighth Avenue, and you'll see it, up on a paved hill. Be prepared to pay for parking on one of the surface lots in the area. One Cannery Row. ✆ **615/251-3020.** www.mercylounge.com. Cover varies.

The Muse
If you're looking for an edgier underground scene, take a dive into The Muse, Nashville's most cutting-edge performance space. Here, on any given night, you can catch punk and rap acts such as Unstoppable Death Machine, Sisters Grimm, K-Will, and The Screemin' Boweevils. 835 Fourth Ave. S. ✆ **615/251-0190.** www. themusenashville.com. Cover $6–$8.

The Woods Amphitheater at Fontanel
Retired country music superstar Barbara Mandrell built the over-the-top log mansion at the height of her fame, raised her family here, and then sold it a few years ago. Since then, it's been turned into a tourist attraction that boasts a farmhouse-style restaurant, mansion tours, and an open-air concert venue that booked acts including Gretchen Wilson, Chicago, Steely Dan, and Steve Martin and the Canyon Rangers in its 2011–12 inaugural season. And, just in case you're wondering, "fontanel" is the word for that soft spot on a newborn baby's head. 4225 Whites Creek Pike. ✆ **800/820-8687** or 615/624-1600. www.woods amphitheater.com. Directions: I-24 W. to exit 88B/Clarksville, to exit 40 for TN-45 N. (Old Hickory Blvd.), left for 2 miles, then left on U.S. 431 (Whites Creek Pike). Fontanel will be half a mile to the left.

Jazz & Blues

The **Tennessee Jazz & Blues Society** publishes a free monthly newsletter featuring news and event listings of interest to music buffs of these genres (www.jazzblues. org). If you're here in the summer, check to see who's playing at the society's concert series at Belle Meade Plantation (✆ **615/356-0501**).

B.B. King's Blues Club ★★
Nashville can consider itself lucky to have landed one of the legendary blues guitarist's few clubs. The original, launched in Memphis in 1991, has become Beale Street's crown jewel (satellite locations have since sprouted up in a few other U.S. cities). B.B. himself inaugurated the Music City spot with a sold-out, standing-room-only show in September 2003. Since then, locals and tourists craving another alternative to Nashville's pervasive country music bars have ensured this authentic blues bar has a solid future in the District. 152 Second Ave. ✆ **615/256-2727.** http://nashville.bbkingclubs.com. Cover $5–$7 (usually $50–$200 for B.B.'s increasingly infrequent, but always sold-out, concerts).

Sour Note

Gibson Guitar, one of the oldest guitar makers in the country, has a strong Tennessee presence, with its international headquarters and warehouses in Nashville and a guitar-making factory in Memphis. Controversy erupted in August 2011, when the FBI seized these locations. The Feds allege that Gibson intentionally mislabeled pallets of Indian rosewood and ebony, which are used to adorn some of Gibson's high-end guitars, to sidestep laws banning the import of these raw materials. In countries such as Madagascar, laws ban the export of certain woods and other natural resources. Within a few days of the gun-toting raids, which made front-page news in Tennessee and beyond, Gibson's business operations returned to normal, and the Memphis plant reopened for tours. Gibson immediately and vigorously denied the charges and hired Washington D.C. lobbyists to address the issue of these imports.

Bourbon Street Blues and Boogie Bar If you're wandering around in the District wishing you could hear some wailing blues guitar, head over to Printer's Alley and check out the action at this club tucked within downtown's historic Printers Alley district. Live blues and a Cajun-American menu are on tap 7 nights a week. 220 Printers Alley. © **615/242-5837.** www.bourbonstreetblues.com. Cover $5–$10.

F. Scott's Restaurant & Jazz Bar Live jazz is presented 6 nights a week at this classy restaurant/lounge that has been a standard-bearer for Nashville sophisticates since its opening in 1986. It offers a selection of more than 300 wines, an upscale dinner menu, and an intimate bar. Arrive early if you want a seat at the 40-seat bar area for the jazz sets. Valet parking is an added perk at F. Scott's, located a stone's throw from The Mall at Green Hills. 2210 Crestmoor Rd. © **615/269-5861.** www.fscotts. com. No cover.

3rd & Lindsley Bar and Grill Eight blocks south of Broadway, in a new office complex surrounded by old warehouses, you'll find Nashville's premier bar and grill. The atmosphere may lack the rough edges and smoke that you'd expect of a blues club, but the live music encompasses everything from Americana and soul to rock. Recent acts have included the Subdudes, Edwin McCain, and Jenny Gill with her dad, Vince. Good pub grub is available for lunch, dinner, and take-out. 818 Third Ave. S. © **615/259-9891.** www.3rdandlindsley.com. Cover up to $20.

Celtic

Dan McGuinness Irish Pub A lively pub atmosphere pervades this Music Row watering hole, where you can hear live music and succumb to cheap eats like the hearty "Pie and Pint" combo, a bowl of traditional shepherd's pie and a 20-ounce draft for $3. And, as expected, that includes Guinness. 1538 Demonbreun. © **615/252-1991.** www.danmcguinnesspub.com. No cover.

Mulligan's Pub This small pub in the heart of the District is always packed at night and definitely has the feel of an Irish pub. There's good Irish food, cold pints, and live Irish and American folk music Thursday to Saturday nights. 117 Second Ave. N. © **615/242-8010.** www.mulliganspubandrestaurant.com. No cover.

THE BAR & PUB SCENE

The Nashville bar scene, for the most part, is synonymous with the Nashville restaurant scene; an establishment has to serve food in order to serve liquor. So, in addition to the places listed below, if you want a cocktail, step into almost any moderately priced or expensive restaurant. The first thing you're likely to see is a bar.

Bars

Beer Sellar As the name implies, this downtown mainstay is all about the brew. By the bottle or on tap, there's a vast selection of beers that draws a rambunctious throng of fun-loving types. The dark but homey basement bar has a kickin' jukebox too. 107 Church St. © **615/254-9464.** www.beersellar.net.

Buffalo Billiards You might not dance by the light of the moon, but you can shoot pool, drink, and throw a few darts at this grungy warehouse located smack-dab in the middle of the District. 154 Second Ave. N. © **615/313-7665.** www.buffalobilliards.com/nashville.

A Comedy Club

Nashville's oldest, if not only, comedy club, **Zanies Comedy Club** has shows Wednesday through Sunday nights. All the big names have played here, including Jay Leno and Jerry Seinfeld. Zanies is at 2025 Eighth Ave. S. (© **615/269-0221;** www.zanies.com). Cover $20 (cover slightly higher for big-name comedians; minimum of two drink or food orders in addition to cover charge).

Family Wash A cozy former East Nashville laundromat has become a landmark beer joint known for having the best pub grub in town. While chilling to the live nightly music, sample some hearty shepherd's pie or roasted chicken with mashed potatoes and gravy. 2038 Greenwood Ave. © **615/226-6070.** www.familywash.com.

Gerst Haus Though ostensibly a German restaurant, this place is more like a lively beer hall than anything else. They serve their own amber lager, and on weekends there is a live polka band in the evenings. 228 Woodland St. © **615/244-8886.** www.gersthaus.com.

Jimmy Kelly's Steakhouse Sip a sherry, smoke a cigar, and revel in the Old South splendor that pervades this decades-old local favorite. Jimmy Kelly's is primarily a steakhouse, and the bar isn't very large, but you'll feel as though you're part of a Nashville tradition when you have a drink here. The place is always lively, and the clientele tends to be older and well-to-do. 217 Louise Ave. © **615/329-4349.** www.jimmykellys.com.

Lonnie's Western Room Formerly known as the "Voodoo Room" in the 1960s and 1970s, Lonnie's is a timeworn piano bar that's evolved into the college crowd's cult favorite for late-night karaoke. One of the liveliest nightspots in downtown's historic Printers Alley, Lonnie's also offers nightly open-mic sessions. 208 Printers Alley. © **615/251-1122.** www.lonnieswesternroom.com.

Past Perfect ★ An antidote to the country carousing of Broadway's bars, Past Perfect is an unassuming little pub around the corner, just up the street from the Schermerhorn Symphony Center. Blue Moon, Yuengling, and Bud Light are on draft, or if you prefer, the narrow, shotgun-style bar also offers wine and infused vodkas. Monday night is old-fashioned cocktail night, where a five-spot will get you a Sazerac, Singapore Sling, or Harvey Wallbanger. Pass the time at Past Perfect with its indoor putting green, Wii games, Wednesday-night trivia, and excellent eats: Quarter-pound bison burgers (the triple-decker Hindenberger), bratwurst, pasta, and wraps are popular. Past Perfect even does brunch, serving steak and eggs, French toast, and biscuits and gravy. 122 3rd Ave. S. © **615/736-7727.** www.pastperfectnashville.com.

Rippy's Smokin' Bar & Grill   With its expansive, open-air patio, this barbecue-and-beer joint at Fifth and Broadway offers a rowdy good time—and the best people-watching within spitting distance of the honky-tonks across the street. Especially in good weather, this is a prime indoor/outdoor party spot. 429 Broadway. © **615/244-7477.**

Tin Roof   American pub fare, a casual atmosphere, and a thriving happy hour scene make this Music Row bar a refreshing antidote to the crowded dives along Broadway downtown. Music-industry execs, session musicians, and college kids frequent this club, where there always seems to be a party. 1516 Demonbreun St. © **615/313-7103.** www.tinroofbars.com.

Whiskey Kitchen   Opened in the fall 2009, this fancified tavern at 12th Avenue South specializes in whiskeys, from single-malt, Scotch blends, and bourbons to American, rye, and wheat varieties. Beer, wine, and cocktails share the menu with burgers, pizzas, and oysters on the half shell, which come with shots of bloody marys. You'll either love or hate the decor, which includes crocodile-leather wall coverings. The patio has a cozy brick fire pit. 118 12th Ave. S. © **615/254-3029.** www.whiskeykitchen.com.

Brewpubs

Big River Grille & Brewing Works   With a weird, retro-contemporary atmosphere that harks back to a friendly '70s fern bar, this vast pub, part of a small Chattanooga-based chain, does a brisk food business. Handcrafted "boutique" beers include lagers, Pilseners, and stouts, along with a seasonal brew that changes throughout the year. On weekends, this place stays packed. 111 Broadway. © **615/251-4677.** www.bigrivergrille.com.

Blackstone Restaurant & Brewery   Nashville's most upscale brewpub draws a lot of business travelers who are staying in nearby hotels. Casual comfort is the setting here, with cushioned chairs, a fireplace, and a marbled bar. The food, including wood-fired pizzas and pretzels, is consistently good. But the beer is the main focus. Choose from a variety of brews, including several that change with the seasons. There's also a six-pack sampler. 1918 West End Ave. © **615/327-9969.** www.blackstonebrewery.com.

Boscos ★   With locations in Memphis and Nashville, Tennessee-based Boscos has built a reputation as the best brewpub around. Here in Music City, Boscos occupies a cavernous but congenial space in Hillsboro Village. Either inside the vivacious brewpub or outside on the lovely teakwood deck, patrons can wash down fresh fish dishes, gourmet pizzas, and stuffed mushrooms with a choice of more than half a dozen beers on tap. The bar sometimes serves cask-conditioned ales. 1805 21st Ave. S. © **615/385-0050.** www.boscosbeer.com.

more NIGHTLIFE

An ever-increasing array of nightspots keeps Nashville jumping after dark. Redevelopment is bustling in the Gulch. Across the street from the venerable bluegrass venue the Station Inn is **Sambuca,** 601 12th Ave. S. (© **615/248-2888;** www.sambucarestaurant.com), a Dallas-based nightspot with an eclectic menu and live music—with an emphasis on jazz. The upper-deck outdoor patio, with its cushy sofa seats and dazzling views of the Nashville skyline, make it a popular spot for a romantic date. Next door is another hipster hangout, **Ru San's,** 505 12th Ave. S. (© **615/252-8787;** www.ru-sans.com), a vibrant, ultramodern sushi bar.

A few blocks west of downtown, **Suzy Wong's House of Yum,** 1517 Church St. (© **615/329-2913;** www.suzywongs nashville.com), is adjacent to **Tribe,** Nashville's best gay bar (see listing, above). At Suzy Wong's, designer cocktails along the lines of the ginger-flecked "Lolita's Kiss" are all the rage, as is the late-night Orient-inspired dining menu created by noted chef/restaurateur Arnold Myint. The hot spot also has a smoke-free outdoor courtyard.

Farther south of downtown, **Rumours Wine Bar,** 2304 12th Ave. S. (© **615/292-9400;** www.rumourswinebar.com), is a cozy house converted into a trendy bar that offers more than 50 by-the-glass wines along with tasty tapas, flatbreads, and fish specialties. The arty patio, with its whimsical metal sculptures, is an unexpected delight.

Meanwhile, **Virago** has relocated from the Music Row area to newer digs in the ever-expanding Gulch area, at 1126 McGavock (© **615/254-1902**), next door to the **Whiskey Kitchen** (above). The supertrendy nightspot and sushi restaurant is known as much for its dramatic decor and its reputation as a magnet for beautiful people as it is for its upscale food.

Flying Saucer Draught Emporium Beers from all over the world, as well as 75 beers on tap, make this a top pick for hops connoisseurs. In the shadow of the nearby Frist Center for the Visual Arts, the Flying Saucer is housed in a rambling old building that used to be the baggage-claim area for the historic Union train station. The bar's big, open-air porch is just made for socializing over soft pretzels and loaded brats. 1010 Demonbreun St. © **615/259-7468.** www.beerknurd.com.

Gay & Lesbian Dance Clubs & Bars

The Lipstick Lounge ★ The periwinkle and cherry-red corner house in an East Nashville residential area entertains patrons with karaoke, trivia contests, Wii Wednesdays, and frequent live music. Along with a full breakfast menu, inventive cocktails, and an upstairs pool table, this is a beloved lesbian lounge where everyone can feel at home. 1400 Woodland St. © **615/226-6343.** www.thelipsticklounge.com. Cover $3–$5.

Tribe A cosmopolitan gay bar, Tribe attracts fashionable men and women. Music videos and a pool table provide diversions away from the dance floor, but the energetic crowds don't usually disperse until late into the night and early morning. Sunday evenings are dedicated to show tunes. 1517A Church St. © **615/329-2912.** www.triben ashville.com. No cover.

THE PERFORMING ARTS
The Tennessee Performing Arts Center

A major renovation completed in fall 2003 gave the drab, utilitarian **Tennessee Performing Arts Center (TPAC),** 505 Deaderick St. (✆ **615/782-4000;** www.tpac. org), a much-needed makeover. Glass walls and an electronic marquee now illuminate the formerly nondescript, concrete exterior of Nashville's premier performance facility. The center houses three theaters: the Andrew Johnson, the James K. Polk, and the Andrew Jackson, whose expanded lobby now dazzles patrons with a 30-foot waterfall and other aesthetic touches. The three spaces can accommodate large and small productions (ticket prices $10–$45). Resident companies based here include the **Nashville Ballet** (✆ **615/297-2966;** www.nashvilleballet.com), which each year stages two full-length ballets and two programs of selected pieces; and the **Nashville Opera** (✆ **615/832-5242;** www.nashvilleopera.org), which mounts four lavish productions annually.

TPAC, as locals know it, is also home to two theater companies. The **Tennessee Repertory Theatre** (✆ **615/244-4878;** www.tennesseerep.org) is the state's largest professional theater company. Its five seasonal productions run from September to May and include dramas, musicals, and comedies. TPAC's other resident theater company is **Circle Players** (✆ **615/332-PLAY** [7529]; www.circleplayers.net), Nashville's oldest nonprofit volunteer arts group. This company does six productions per season and seems to take more chances on lesser-known works than the Rep does.

In addition to productions by Nashville's main performing arts companies, TPAC also hosts various acts and an annual **"Broadway Series"** (✆ **615/782-4000**) that brings first-rate touring productions such as *The Addams Family, Monty Python's Spamalot, and Mary Poppins* to Nashville between October and June. Tickets to TPAC performances are available either at the TPAC box office or through **Ticketmaster** (✆ **615/255-9600;** www.ticketmaster.com).

The **Nashville Symphony** (✆ **615/783-1200;** www.nashvillesymphony.org), which presents a mix of classical and pops concerts, as well as a children's series, has a stunning new home in the **Schermerhorn Hall** (corner of Fourth Ave. S. at Demonbreun). The acoustically superior 1,872-seat venue features 30 soundproof overhead windows, making it the only major concert hall in the world featuring natural light.

Other Venues & Series Around the City & Beyond

Looking beyond TPAC, you'll find a wide array of performances in the **Great Performances at Vanderbilt** series (✆ **615/322-2471;** www.vanderbilt.edu), which is staged at Vanderbilt University's Ingram Hall, Blair School of Music, 24th Avenue South at Children's Way (tickets $10–$26). Each year, this series includes more than a dozen internationally acclaimed performing arts companies from around the world. Recent acts have included Compañia Flamenco with José Porcel; pianist Alfredo Rodriguez with Trio; and Spirit of Uganda dance company. The emphasis is on chamber music and modern dance, but touring theater productions are also scheduled.

The **Nashville Municipal Auditorium,** 417 Fourth Ave. N. (✆ **615/862-6390;** www.nashvilleauditorium.com), for many years was the site of everything from circuses to revivals. Today the aging, dome-roofed venue plays host to everyone from Bob Dylan to Bob the Builder. Plus, there's always the occasional rodeo, boxing match, or monster-truck mash. A stone's throw away, the **Bridgestone Arena,** 501 Broadway (© **615/770-2000**), is now the venue of choice for major rock and country music concerts, ice shows, the Arena Football League's Kats, and NHL hockey, courtesy of the Nashville Predators.

The **Frist Center for the Visual Arts** offers Frist Fridays on the last Friday of every month (May–Sept). Free admission includes live music and appetizers outside in the courtyard, along with entry into the Frist's galleries (5:30–9pm). For more information, call © **615/244-3340.**

Farther away, the verdant grounds of **Cheekwood Botanical Garden & Museum of Art,** 1200 Forrest Park Dr. (© **615/356-8000;** www.cheekwood.org), are the site of annual summer concerts by the Nashville Symphony each June.

In addition, I highly recommend the **Belcourt Theatre,** 2102 Belcourt Ave. (© **615/383-9140;** www.belcourt.org), where you can catch the latest art-house film releases and other cinematic fare that's all but ignored by today's modern multiplexes. From October to December, the theater stages a weekend classics matinee series called "The Best Old Movies for Families." Live entertainment, including musical events and occasional lectures/discussions, are also staged occasionally at the Belcourt—fitting, as the venue was one of the early homes of the *Grand Ole Opry.*

If you enjoy dinner theater, you may want to check out **Chaffin's Barn Dinner Theatre,** 8204 Tenn. 100 (© **800/282-BARN** [2276] or 615/646-9977; www. dinnertheatre.com), housed in a big old Dutch-colonial barn 20 minutes outside Nashville (dinner and show $40 adults, $20 children 12 and under; show only $33 adults, $25 children). The dinner is an all-you-can-eat country buffet (think fried catfish, ham, green beans, and fruit cobblers and berry shortcakes). Recent stage shows have run the gamut from *I'll Be Seeing You* and *'Til Death Do Us Part,* to *Annie* and *Southern Fried Funeral.* Performances are Tuesday through Saturday. Reservations are required and must be paid for 24 hours in advance. To reach Chaffin's Barn, take I-40 west to exit 199 (Old Hickory Blvd.) and head south to Old Harding Road (Tenn. 100), turn right, and continue for 4 miles.

SPECTATOR SPORTS

AUTO RACING The **Music City Raceway,** 3302 Ivy Point Rd., Goodlettsville (© **615/876-0981;** www.musiccityraceway.com), is the place to catch National Hot Rod Association (NHRA) drag-racing action. The drag strip, known as Nashville's "Playground of Power," has races on Tuesdays, Fridays, Saturdays, and some Sundays between March and October. Admission ranges from $5 to $10.

BASEBALL The **Nashville Sounds** (© **615/242-4371;** www.nashvillesounds. com), a Triple-A team affiliate of the Milwaukee Brewers, play at Greer Stadium, 534 Chestnut St., off Eighth Avenue South. Admission ranges from $6 to $12 (advance-purchase tickets $10 reserved seats, $6 for general admission; day-of-game tickets $12 reserved seats, $8 general admission). *Note:* There are no children's prices, and all kids need to have a ticket.

FOOTBALL Having made numerous play-off appearances, the **Tennessee Titans** draw loyal crowds to the 68,000-seat LP Field on the banks of the Cumberland River. The stadium is at 1 Titans Way, Nashville, TN 37213 (© **615/565-4200;** www. titansonline.com).

GOLF TOURNAMENTS   **Vanderbilt Legends Club** (© 615/791-8100) hosts an annual LPGA event each spring. Call for prices and dates.

HOCKEY   Nashville's own NHL hockey team, the **Nashville Predators** (© 615/770-PUCK** [7825]; http://predators.nhl.com), plays at the Sommet Center on lower Broadway in downtown Nashville—or "Smashville," as the sport's brawny fans like to brag. Ticket prices range from $10 to $95.

HORSE SHOWS   Horse shows are important events on the Nashville area's calendar. The biggest and most important horse show of the year is the annual **Tennessee Walking Horse National Celebration** (© 931/684-5915; www.twhnc.com). This show takes place 40 miles southeast of Nashville in the town of Shelbyville and is held each year in late August. Advance reserved ticket prices range from $7 to $60, while general admission tickets are $5 to $12.

The city's other big horse event is the annual running of the **Iroquois Steeplechase** (© 615/591-2991; www.iroquoissteeplechase.org), on the second Saturday in May. This is one of the oldest steeplechase races in the country and is held in Percy Warner Park in the Belle Meade area. Proceeds from the race benefit the Vanderbilt Children's Hospital. General admission tickets are $12 at the gate or $10 in advance.

WHERE TO STAY IN NASHVILLE

B
ecause Nashville caters to tens of thousands of music fans each year, the city has an abundance of hotels for all budgets. Downtown has the best selection of historic and unique properties, most of them very expensive and expensive, and a few that are moderately priced. Stay here, or at one of the Music Row motels, if your plans include attending a concert at The Ryman, a day at the Country Music Hall of Fame and Museum, or a night of barhopping in the honky-tonks along lower Broadway.

8

A large selection of excellent chain hotels dominates the West End area, which is convenient for travelers who need close proximity to Vanderbilt University, its renowned medical center, or Belmont University. But if the *Grand Ole Opry* is the main focus of your stay, try to stay in Music Valley, either at the Gaylord Opryland Resort and Convention Center or in one of the less expensive chain hotels that surround it.

THE BEST HOTEL BETS

- **Best Hotel:** The posh **Hermitage Hotel,** 231 Sixth Ave. N., offers impeccable service and attention to detail. With its beautiful stained-glass ceiling in the Beaux Arts lobby, gourmet dining options, and extra large, sumptuously furnished rooms with marble bathrooms and big soaking tubs, everything about this iconic grand hotel personifies perfection. See p. 112.
- **Best for Families:** At the West End's large **Embassy Suites,** 1811 Broadway, tastefully appointed suites offering bedrooms and separate sitting rooms with comfy pullout sofas, as well as in-room fridges and microwaves, make it easy for traveling families to spread out and make themselves at home. Teddy bear welcome kits make kids feel special. See p. 116.
- **Best Splurge:** The modern, Vanderbilt University–area **Loews Hotel,** 2100 West End Ave., offers a touch more sophistication than others in this area. Splurge on one of the spacious, upper-level rooms with views of the Nashville skyline. Pamper yourself with concierge-level services that include perks like complimentary breakfast and evening hors d'oeuvres in a swank lounge. See p. 113.
- **Best Bang for Your Buck:** You get a lot for the money at the **Hyatt Place Opryland,** 220 Rudy's Circle, where the rooms include comfy beds as well as soft, sectional-style furniture with pullout sofas. Rooms have wet bars, fridges, and 42-inch-screen plasma TVs with

PRICE CATEGORIES

Very expensive	More than $200	**Moderate**	$100 to $150
Expensive	$150 to $200	**Inexpensive**	Under $100

plug-and-play capability. Free in-room Wi-Fi, breakfast (in the lobby area kitchen), and freshly brewed Starbucks coffee are other budgetary incentives. See p. 126.

o **Most Romantic:** It may not be the most luxurious downtown hotel, but the pristine **Indigo,** 301 Union Ave., a fresh new boutique property, offers an intimate setting in a historic former bank building. Its inconspicuous location at the quieter north edge of downtown also gives it a slightly clandestine charm. See p. 117.

o **Best Service:** Just because it's the biggest hotel in Tennessee doesn't mean it has to be impersonal. In fact, the 2,881-room **Gaylord Opryland Resort and Convention Center,** 2800 Opryland Dr., impresses for going the extra mile to provide excellent customer service at every turn. From the hardworking valets, shuttle-bus drivers, and personable housekeeping staff to helpful registration clerks, the focus seems to be squarely on providing total guest satisfaction. See p. 122.

o **Best Green Hotel:** The modern **Hutton Hotel,** 1808 West End Ave., sets a new standard of excellence for sustainability, from the decor, which features reclaimed wood and bamboo furnishings, to its use of biodegradable cleaning products and energy-saving lighting, plumbing, and elevators. Even the hotel's two luxury courtesy vehicles are hybrid SUVs. See p. 118.

o **Best Airport-Area Hotel:** With its huge indoor/outdoor pool, spacious and immaculate public spaces, and better-than-average casual restaurant, a stay at the **Marriott Nashville Airport,** 600 Marriott Dr., feels like a more expensive extravagance than it actually is. This top-notch high-rise has maintained consistently high standards for more than a decade now. See p. 122.

o **Best Historic Hotel for Train Buffs:** Few hotels can match the rich architectural history of stately **Union Station,** 1001 Broadway, set within a stunning Romanesque Gothic train station that dates back to 1910. Although all furnishings and public spaces are chic and modern, architectural elements such as the railway station's vaulted, Tiffany stained-glass ceiling (not to mention the cargo trains that still pass by the hotel) may have you swooning with nostalgia. See p. 119.

o **Best Chain Hotel in Music Valley:** You'll have your pick of properties in this hotel-cluttered area off the interstate, but the **Holiday Inn Express Opryland,** 2461 McGavock Pike, is a newer hotel next to a wooded area and a bit farther away from the traffic noise of the others. Roomy accommodations and a lovely, sun-filled indoor pool are other special pleasures. See p. 125.

DOWNTOWN AREA, MUSIC ROW & THE WEST END

Very Expensive

The Hermitage Hotel ★★★ 📷 This historic downtown hotel, built in 1910 in the classic Beaux Arts style, is Nashville's grand hotel. This is the city's top choice if you crave space, grandeur, and exceptional customer service. The lobby, with its marble columns, gilded plasterwork, and stained-glass ceiling, is the most magnificent in the city. Afternoon tea is served here Thursday through Saturday. The large guest rooms are plush, with down-filled duvets and pillows on the beds. All rooms feature large windows and marble-floored bathrooms with double vanities, wall-mounted TVs, and luxurious soaking bathtubs. (Ask the staff to draw you a warm bath with a sprinkling of rose petals.) Silky bathrobes and slippers, as well as fine soaps and other bath amenities, further enhance the experience. Northside rooms have stunning views of the state capitol. In the hotel's lower level, the renowned **Capitol Grille** (p. 59) and the clubby **Oak Bar** offer excellent service and fine food and drink in stylish settings.

231 Sixth Ave. N., Nashville, TN 37219. www.thehermitagehotel.com. ✆ **888/888-9414** or 615/244-3121. Fax 615/254-6909. 122 units. $269–$369 suite; $1,500–$2,500 and up Presidential Suite. AE, DC, DISC, MC, V. Valet parking $26, plus tax; no self-parking. Pets allowed ($50 daily fee). **Amenities:** Restaurant and lounge; babysitting; concierge; room service. *In room:* A/C, TV/DVD, CD player, hair dryer, MP3 docking station, umbrella, Wi-Fi (free).

Hilton Nashville Downtown ★★

One of Nashville's newer hotels boasts a bustling downtown location, with a palm-lined and Wi-Fi–equipped atrium lobby. Booking a room here is a good bet if you plan to spend time at LP Field (where the Tennessee Titans play) or the Country Music Hall of Fame and Museum, both of which are within walking distance of the Hilton. Each suite comes equipped with a pullout sofa and two TVs, making the Hilton a comfy-but-sophisticated place to hang your hat while in Music City. Rooms include pillowtop mattresses, Egyptian cotton sheets, and curved shower curtains.

121 Fourth Ave. S., Nashville, TN 37201. www.nashvillehilton.com. ✆ **800/HILTONS** (445-8667) or 615/620-1000. Fax 615/620-2050. 330 units (all suites). $219–$459 suite. AE, DC, DISC, MC, V. Valet parking $22; no self-parking. **Amenities:** 3 restaurants; 2 lounges; health club; indoor pool; valet service. *In room:* A/C, TV w/pay movies, fridge, hair dryer, microwave, Wi-Fi ($12 per 24 hr.).

Loews Vanderbilt Hotel ★★★

This high-rise across the street from Vanderbilt University maintains an air of quiet sophistication, which makes it the most *luxe* of all the West End hotels. European tapestries and original works of art adorn the travertine-floored lobby. The hotel also houses the upscale Kraus commercial art gallery. The lower guest rooms, with angled walls that slope inward, are among the hotel's most charming, with a wall of curtains lending a romantic coziness. Service is gracious and attentive. Concierge-level rooms are more spacious and upscale and include complimentary breakfast and evening hors d'oeuvres in an elegant lounge with a view of the city. One level below the lobby, you'll find a Ruth's Chris Steakhouse.

2100 West End Ave., Nashville, TN 37203. www.loewsvanderbilt.com. ✆ **800/23-LOEWS** (235-6397) or 615/320-1700. Fax 615/320-5019. 340 units. $199–$349 double; $800–$1,600 suite. AE, DC, DISC, MC, V. Valet parking $25; self-parking $22. Pets allowed; no deposit required if paying by credit card, although guests are liable for damage caused by pets. **Amenities:** 2 restaurants; babysitting; concierge; concierge-level rooms; exercise room and spa; room service; shoe-shine service; valet service; Wi-Fi (free, in lobby and restaurant). *In room:* A/C, TV, CD player, hair dryer, Internet ($9.95 per 24 hr.), minibar, umbrella.

Sheraton Nashville Downtown ★

For years, this drab, ho-hum hotel was an also-ran, but an impressive renovation has refreshed its look and appeal. Offering easy access to The Ryman, the State Capitol, and other sites, the smoke-free hotel has recently hosted several major, national music festivals—perhaps exciting if you're a music fan but an annoyance if you dislike crowds and late-night noise. Rooms are

Nashville Hotels: Downtown Area, Music Row & the West End

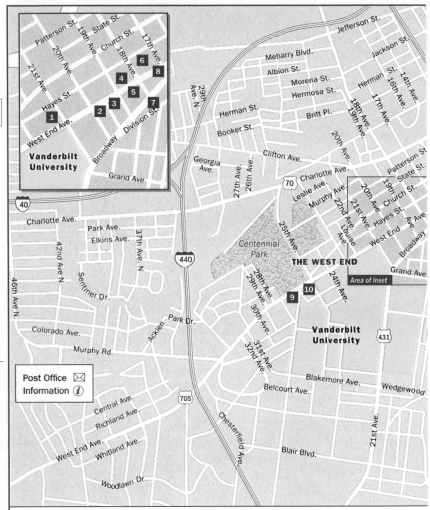

Best Western Music Row **12**

Comfort Inn Downtown-Music Row **13**

Courtyard Marriott Vanderbilt **2**

Courtyard Nashville Downtown **20**

Days Inn Vanderbilt/Music Row **4**

Doubltree Hotel Nashville **22**

Embassy Suites Nashville at
  Vanderbilt **7**

Hampton Inn and Suites Downtown **18**

Hampton Inn and Suites Green Hills **11**

Hampton Inn Vanderbilt **3**

Hermitage Hotel **24**

Hilton Garden Inn Nashville Vanderbilt **8**

Hilton Nashville Downtown **17**

Holiday Inn Select Vanderbilt **9**

Holiday Inn Express Nashville
  Downtown **16**

Homewood Suites Hilton Downtown **15**

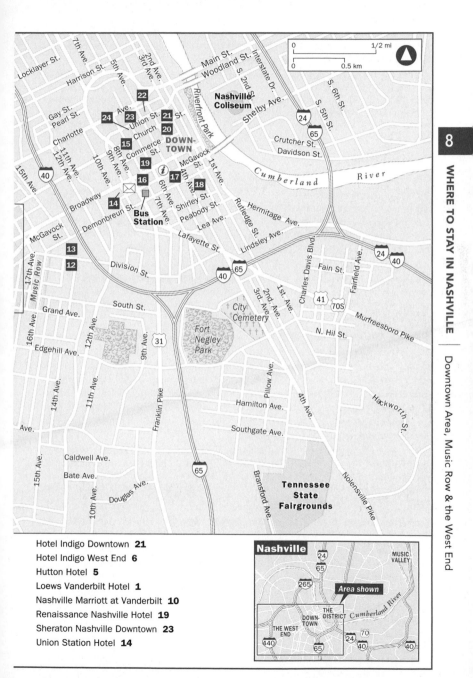

Hotel Indigo Downtown **21**
Hotel Indigo West End **6**
Hutton Hotel **5**
Loews Vanderbilt Hotel **1**
Nashville Marriott at Vanderbilt **10**
Renaissance Nashville Hotel **19**
Sheraton Nashville Downtown **23**
Union Station Hotel **14**

nicely appointed, with comfortable beds and 37-inch flatscreen TVs. Upper floors in this 25-story high-rise have the best views. Fitness buffs should note the hotel's impressively large, 24-hour fitness center, equipped with dozens of top-of-the-line cardio machines. The adjoining, indoor pool is windowless and very small, however. Like many hotels, the Sheraton offers free Wi-Fi in the lobby and on the club-level floors. In-room wireless access is available in standard rooms for $9.95 per day.

623 Union St., Nashville, TN 37219. www.sheratonnashvilledowntown.com. © **800/325-3535** or 615/259-2000. Fax 615/742-6096. 472 units. $199–$209 double; $269 and up for suites. AE, DC, DISC, MC, V. Valet parking $24; self-parking $20. Dogs up to 50 lb. accepted (no fee, but must sign nuisance waiver). **Amenities:** Restaurant/lounge; concierge; fitness center; indoor pool; room service. *In room:* A/C, TV with pay movies, hair dryer, Wi-Fi ($9.95 in standard rooms; free in club levels).

Expensive

Courtyard Nashville Downtown ★
This clean, inviting, and smoke-free hotel is within easy walking distance of The Ryman and other downtown attractions, yet far enough away from the rowdy night life of Broadway to offer a more peaceful environment. Rooms and public spaces are done in cheerful bright blues and pale yellows. The staff goes out of its way to offer friendly service. All guest rooms have new bedding, free high-speed Internet access, spacious work desks and task chairs, and multiline telephones.

170 Fourth Ave. N., Nashville, TN 37219. www.marriott.com. © **888/687-9377** or 615/256-0900. Fax 615/256-0901. 192 units. $169–$209 double; $224 and up for suites. AE, DC, DISC, MC, V. Valet parking $22; no self-parking. **Amenities:** Restaurant. *In room:* A/C, TV w/pay movies, fridge, hair dryer, Internet (free, in standard rooms), microwave, Wi-Fi (free, in King Suites).

Doubletree Hotel Nashville ★★
Of the high-rise hotels in downtown Nashville, this is one of the best choices if you're here on vacation. Although convenient for business travelers, it offers a less hectic atmosphere than the Renaissance, which can be overrun with conventiongoers. Warm, contemporary decor features maple-colored wood paneling and comfy seating in the elegant, second-floor lobby, where there's a full-service Starbucks cafe. Perks include fresh-baked cookies upon your check-in. Corner rooms, with their sharply angled walls of glass, are the most appealing units in the hotel.

315 Fourth Ave. N., Nashville, TN 37219. www.nashvilledoubletree.com. © **800/222-TREE** (8733) or 615/244-8200. Fax 615/747-4894. 338 units. $109–$189 double; from $199 suite. AE, DC, DISC, MC, V. Valet parking $24; off-site self-parking $18. **Amenities:** Restaurant; lounge; concierge; exercise room; indoor pool; room service, Wi-Fi (free, in lobby). *In room:* A/C, TV w/pay movies, hair dryer, Wi-Fi ($9.95 per 24 hr.).

Embassy Suites Nashville at Vanderbilt ★★ ☺
In the city's fashionable West End/Vanderbilt University district, this property combines gracious service and impeccable decor. A sunny garden atrium features lush plants and cascading waterfalls, while the spacious, tastefully appointed suites have comfy pullout sofas, easy chairs, work desks, and lamps. Families with young children should ask for the Build-A-Bear Explorer kit, which includes a teddy bear, hat, and passport. With other value-added touches including free, cooked-to-order breakfast, nightly manager's reception, and shuttle service within a 2-mile radius of the hotel, this is a good choice for those who want to feel pampered without paying an arm and a leg. Downstairs is an Omaha Steak House.

1811 Broadway, Nashville, TN 37203. www.embassysuites.com. © **800/362-2779** or 615/320-8899. Fax 615/320-8881. 208 units (all suites). $149–$239 suite. Rates include cooked-to-order breakfast. AE, DC, DISC, MC, V. Valet parking $19; self-parking $15. **Amenities:** Restaurant; lounge; exercise room; room service; sauna. *In room:* A/C, TV w/pay movies, hair dryer, kitchenette (microwave, minibar, and sink), Wi-Fi ($6 per 24 hr.).

Hampton Inn and Suites Downtown ★ ✔

Built in 2007 and bridging the gap between the nearby honky-tonks of Broadway and the emerging Gulch area, this well-run hotel is just a block south of the Country Music Hall of Fame and Museum. Appealing to independent travelers who want convenience and style, the six-story red-brick inn offers continental breakfast in a spacious, contemporary lobby, where there's plenty of natural sunlight and free Wi-Fi. Clean, modern rooms are equipped with comfy beds and crisp linens, as well as flat-panel TVs and wet bars. Budget-minded travelers will recognize the free parking (within a secure, gated area) as a real deal, given the $20-plus-per-night parking rates charged by most other downtown hotels.

310 Fourth Ave. S., Nashville, TN 37201. www.hamptoninn.com. © **800/HAMPTON** (426-7866) or 615/277-5000. Fax 615/564-1700. 154 units. $189–$359 double; $259 and up suite. AE, DC, DISC, MC, V. Free self-parking. **Amenities:** Fitness room; indoor pool; whirlpool. *In room:* A/C, TV w/pay movies, fridge, hair dryer, microwave, Wi-Fi (free).

Holiday Inn Express Nashville Downtown ★

With an inviting, spacious lobby and simple yet elegant furnishings, this above-ordinary property offers a slightly less expensive alternative to the historic Union Station Hotel across the street. In fact, rooms with westward views of the Union Station's Gothic beauty are an added plus—and though you'll still be able to see and hear the trains rumbling down the railroad tracks, they're not right outside your window as they are at Union Station. This hotel sits across the street from the Frist Center for the Visual Arts, but it's a bit of a hike (about 5 blocks down Broadway) to the bars and nightclubs in the District. The distance is something to consider if you're thinking about hoofing it in the sweltering summer heat. Thankfully, the hotel boasts downtown's only outdoor swimming pool, a premium perk for sure.

920 Broadway, Nashville, TN 37203. www.holiday-inn.com. © **800/258-2466** or 615/244-0150. Fax 615/244-0445. 287 units. $149–$179 double; $244–$319 suite. Rates include continental breakfast. AE, DISC, MC, V. Self parking $15. **Amenities:** Exercise room; outdoor pool. *In room:* A/C, TV, fridge and microwave (in suites and in all rooms on the 6th and 7th floors), hair dryer, Wi-Fi (free).

Homewood Suites Hilton Downtown ★★

Staying here may make you feel as if you have your own downtown apartment. Tucked inside a historic building, it has become increasingly popular with business travelers and those planning extended stays. Spacious studios and suites with one or two bedrooms have furnished kitchens with full-sized refrigerators, stoves, and dishwashers. Large work desks, two TVs, and two phones are included. You can even bring your pet; the hotel offers cat and dog beds, treats, and other accessories.

706 Church St., Nashville, TN 37203. www.nashvilledowntown.homewoodsuites.com. © **800/445-8667** or 615/742-5550. Fax 615/742-9949. 113 units. $149–$189 double. AE, DISC, MC, V. Valet parking $20; self-parking (off-site) $9. Pets allowed ($100 nonrefundable fee). **Amenities:** Exercise room. *In-room:* Hair dryer kitchenette, Wi-Fi (free).

Hotel Indigo Downtown ★★ 🛍

Opened in 2010, this 15-story boutique hotel occupies two lovely bank buildings dating back to 1909 and 1926. With 96 smoke-free rooms, this intimate gem has a clean, contemporary look and coffeehouse vibe, with its two-story Starbucks and art gallery. The immaculate, average-sized rooms feature terrazzo floors, marble bathroom vanities, and modern interior design elements that pair white furnishings and glass lamps with dark woods. Flatscreen TVs, narrow work desks, Keurig coffeemakers, and Aveda bath products are other in-room flourishes. The hotel's perch, around the corner from pricier Hermitage Hotel and within strolling distance of LP Field and all of downtown's major tourist attractions, is another reason to book a stay here.

301 Union, Nashville, TN 37201. www.musiccityhotel.com. © **877/8-INDIGO** (846-3446) or 615/891-6000. Fax 615/891-6010. 99 units. $159–$189 double. AE, DC, DISC, MC, V. Self-parking $20. Pets under 75 lb. allowed ($75 deposit). **Amenities:** Restaurant/lounge; fitness center; valet service. *In room:* A/C, TV, hair dryer, MP3 docking station, Wi-Fi (free).

Hotel Indigo West End ★

Nashville's other Hotel Indigo property (not affiliated with the downtown location) occupies an angular 11-story—and, as its name implies, deep blue—building with an accessible location about halfway between downtown and the West End. East-facing upper rooms and the eighth-floor outdoor patio have great views of the Nashville skyline. Indigo's Zen-like theme of promising guests "peace and serenity" is highlighted in framed leaf and seashell prints, chartreuse and plum-colored walls, and black-and-white photo murals. Rooms feature plush bedding and are surprisingly spacious, with polished wood-laminated floors, throw rugs, and comfy chairs and work desks.

1719 West End Ave., Nashville, TN 37303. www.hotelindigo.com. © **877/270-1396** or 615/329-4200. Fax 615/3294205. 139 units. $159–$229 double. AE, DISC, MC, V. Valet parking $23; self-parking $19. Pets accepted ($25 flat rate). **Amenities:** Lounge; fitness center. *In room:* A/C, TV, hair dryer, Wi-Fi (free).

Hutton Hotel ★★★

Unpretentious yet stylish, this independent boutique hotel set a new standard in sustainable luxury when it opened in 2009. Architecturally stunning, the contemporary property touts many green initiatives, including biodegradable cleaning products, decor made from reclaimed wood, and bamboo flooring and furnishings. Rooms are well appointed with sumptuous bedding and bathrobes. The marble bathrooms include environmentally friendly fixtures, including walk-in showers with programmable temperature controls. Each suite has a large work desk, sofa, chair, and a 42-inch high-definition TV. Seven of the suites are equipped with in-room cardio equipment.

1808 West End Ave., Nashville, TN 37203. www.huttonhotel.com. © **615/340-9333.** Fax 615/340-0010. 248 units. $189–$199 double; $249 suite. AE, DC, DISC, MC, V. Valet parking $24; self-parking $20. Pets allowed with $50 deposit. **Amenities:** Restaurant; concierge; exercise room; room service. *In room:* A/C, TV, hair dryer, minibar, Wi-Fi (free).

Nashville Marriott at Vanderbilt ★★

This rose-colored high-rise hotel rivals the nearby Loews for elegance and sophistication. Upper rooms at the 11-story property offer bird's-eye views of both the Vanderbilt football stadium and the Parthenon in nearby Centennial Park. The location is ideal for those who want to be in the thick of things. It's within a corner of an upscale shopping complex and close to all the West End action. (The downside is that during peak dinner hours and weekends, the hotel parking lot and garage can become a tangled traffic jam.) Guests visiting here on business will appreciate the spacious rooms, decorated in soothing cream colors, with well-lighted work desks and multiline phones.

2555 West End Ave., Nashville, TN 37203. www.marriott.com. © **800/228-9290** or 615/321-1300. Fax 615/321-1400. 307 units. $149–$359 double; $350–$459 suite. AE, DC, DISC, MC, V. Valet parking $22; self-parking $19. **Amenities:** Restaurant; lounge; concierge; health club; indoor pool; room service; valet service. *In room:* A/C, TV w/pay movies, hair dryer, Wi-Fi ($9.95 per 24 hr.).

Renaissance Nashville Hotel ★   Because it's connected to the Nashville Convention Center, this large, modern hotel is usually filled with conventiongoers and consequently can feel crowded and chaotic. However, it does offer all the expected luxuries. The king rooms (especially the corner ones) have large bathrooms and are a better choice than rooms with two beds, which are a bit cramped. Whichever style room you choose, you'll have a comfortable chair in which to relax, and walls of glass let in plenty of light. The upper floors (24th and 25th) offer additional amenities, including a concierge, a private lounge, bathrobes, express checkout, complimentary continental breakfast and evening hors d'oeuvres, and evening turndown service. There's a Starbucks in the lobby, as well as several lounges and restaurants. Although the hotel is smoke free, you'll likely have to walk through a gauntlet of smokers once you step outside the front lobby.

611 Commerce St., Nashville, TN 37203. www.renaissancehotels.com. ⓒ **800/327-6618** or 615/255-8400. Fax 615/255-8202. 673 units. $169–$229 double; $300–$500 suite. AE, DC, DISC, MC, V. Valet parking $29; self-parking $6. **Amenities:** 2 restaurants; 2 bars; concierge; exercise room; indoor pool and whirlpool; room service; sauna; sundeck; valet service. *In room:* A/C, TV w/ pay movies, hair dryer, Wi-Fi ($14 per 24 hr.).

Union Station Hotel ★★ 🖻   Built in 1900 and housed in the Romanesque Gothic former Union Station railway terminal, this hotel is a grandly restored National Historic Landmark. Following a $10-million renovation, completed in 2007, all guest rooms and public spaces have been updated. The lobby is the former main hall of the railway station and has a vaulted ceiling of Tiffany stained glass. In contrast to the historic atmosphere, decor in the public spaces such as the lobby is contemporary. Although guest rooms offer exterior views, some also have the disadvantage of overlooking the railroad tracks, a plus for railroad buffs but perhaps less endearing to those who can't sleep with the clang-and-roar that continues day and night. Be sure to take advantage of the hotel's valet parking; self-parking is inconvenient and down several flights of outdoor stairs (and it's more expensive).

1001 Broadway, Nashville, TN 37203. www.unionstationhotelnashville.com. ⓒ **800/996-3426** or 615/726-1001. Fax 615/248-3554. 125 units. $169–$239 double; $349–$499 suite. AE, DC, DISC, MC, V. Valet parking $20; self-parking $22. **Amenities:** Restaurant and lounge; exercise room; limited room service. *In room:* A/C, TV w/pay movies, hair dryer, Wi-Fi ($12 per 24 hr.).

Moderate

Courtyard Marriott Vanderbilt   This seven-story hotel on West End Avenue fills the price and service gap between the Loews Vanderbilt Plaza and the less-expensive motels listed below. Guest rooms are none too large, but units with king-size beds are well suited to business travelers. For the most part, what you get here is a good location, close to Music Row, at prices only slightly higher than those at area motels. A breakfast buffet is available daily, with a choice of cold ($6.95 plus tax) or hot ($9.95 plus tax) foods.

1901 West End Ave., Nashville, TN 37203. www.marriott.com. ⓒ **800/245-1959** or 615/327-9900. Fax 615/327-8127. 223 units. $99–$169 double; $199–$239 suite. AE, DC, DISC, MC, V. Valet parking $16; self-parking $13. **Amenities:** Lounge; exercise room; outdoor pool; whirlpool. *In room:* A/C, TV, hair dryer, Wi-Fi (free).

Hampton Inn & Suites Green Hills   If your Nashville stay will take you to the Green Hills area in the southwestern suburbs of the city, the Hampton Inn is one of the few hotels with close proximity to Nashville's premier shopping destinations

family-friendly HOTELS

Embassy Suites Nashville (p. 116) With an indoor pool and a garden atrium, there is plenty to keep the kids distracted here. The two-room suites also provide kitchenettes and lots of space, including a separate bedroom for parents.

Gaylord Opryland Resort and Convention Center (p. 122) The kids can wander all over this huge hotel's three tropical atria, exploring waterfalls, hidden gardens, fountains, whatever, and then head for one of the pools. There are also enough restaurants under this one roof (the property encompasses nine under glass) to keep everyone in the family happy.

GuestHouse Inn & Suites Music Valley (p. 125) A budget-friendly hotel that is very popular with vacationing families, this clean, comfortable hotel across the street from Opryland is convenient to the interstate and area attractions.

Hyatt Place Opryland (p. 126) Teens and tweens can appreciate a place with huge, in-room plasma TVs with plug-and-play capability. This completely refurbished property also offers spacious rooms with not only beds but also comfy leather ottomans and pullout sofas so the family can spread out.

Marriott Nashville Airport (p. 122) Lower-level rooms are perfect for families whose kids want to spend time in the large indoor/outdoor pool.

(namely Tennessee's first and only Nordstrom, which opened in fall 2011). As with other Hampton properties citywide, the smoke-free hotel features clean, comfortably furnished rooms tailored to business travelers. While the hotel's Green Hills location is great for visiting the nearby mall and the iconic Bluebird Cafe (p. 102), it's not so convenient if you plan to go back and forth to downtown area attractions. Traffic between these areas can be a bear. A cab ride will cost you about $30 one way.

2324 Crestmoor Rd., Nashville, TN 37215. www.hampton-inn.com. © **800/311-5174** or 615/777-0001. Fax 615/986-5200. 77 units. $139–$189 double. Rates include continental breakfast. AE, DC, DISC, MC, V. Free parking. **Amenities:** Exercise room; outdoor pool. *In room:* A/C, TV, hair dryer, kitchenettes, Wi-Fi (free).

Hampton Inn Vanderbilt Exceptionally friendly service sets this reliable chain hotel apart from others of its ilk. Even before its recent, top-to-bottom renovation, this property reportedly had ranked as one of the Hampton chain's busiest in the country. Guest rooms are modern and comfortable. You'll find the king rooms particularly spacious. Situated in a congested area 1 block from Vanderbilt University and 6 blocks from the recording-industry offices of Music Row, the hotel is a good choice for those looking for a variety of excellent restaurants within walking distance.

1919 West End Ave., Nashville, TN 37203. www.hampton-inn.com. © **800/HAMPTON** (426-7866) or 615/329-1144. Fax 615/320-7112. 171 units. $119–$229 double. Rates include cooked breakfast. AE, DC, DISC, MC, V. Free parking. **Amenities:** Exercise room; outdoor pool; valet service. *In room:* A/C, TV, hair dryer, Wi-Fi (free).

Hilton Garden Inn Nashville Vanderbilt ★ Ergonomic Herman Miller chairs, premium bedding, and work-efficient guest rooms are highlights of this hotel, which opened in 2009. Just a few doors down from the larger Embassy Suites, the Hilton Garden Inn is a bit less expensive and a bit more intimate than others in the area. A cheerful, ground-floor cafe looks out into the tree-lined street. Fresh, comfortably appointed rooms come equipped with 36-inch high-definition TVs. An added bonus for guests is the complimentary shuttle service within a 5-mile radius of the hotel.

1715 Broadway, Nashville, TN 37203. www.hiltongardeninn.com. © **866/538-6194** or 615/369-5900. Fax 615/369-5901. 194 units. $129–$159 double; $159–$164 suite. AE, DC, DISC, MC, V. Valet parking $20; self-parking $20. **Amenities:** Restaurant; health club; indoor pool, whirlpool. *In-room:* Fridge, hair dryer, microwave, Wi-Fi (free).

Holiday Inn Select Vanderbilt   With the Vanderbilt University football stadium right outside this 12-story hotel's back door, it isn't surprising that this is a favorite with Vandy alumni and football fans. Guests are also right across the street from Centennial Park, making it a good option for families with children who want a spacious, safe place to run and play. Couples and business travelers will do well to ask for a king room. If you ask for a room on the park side of the hotel, you may be able to see the park's replica of the famous Parthenon. An unexpected perk? All units here have small private balconies.

2613 West End Ave., Nashville, TN 37203. www.holiday-inn.com. © **800/HOLIDAY** (465-4329) or 615/327-4707. Fax 615/327-8034. 300 units. $119–$199 double. AE, DC, DISC, MC, V. Free parking. **Amenities:** Restaurant; lounge; concierge; outdoor pool. *In room:* A/C, TV w/pay movies, hair dryer, Wi-Fi (free).

Inexpensive

Best Western Music Row   This casual, no-frills motel stays booked most of the time with cost-conscious tourists who appreciate affordability and easy access to both downtown and Music Row. Bargain-priced rooms are standard, although the suites offer significantly more space for a few extra dollars; and all rooms offer free local calls. Live music is performed nightly (except Sun) in the lounge.

1407 Division St., Nashville, TN 37203. www.bestwestern.com. © **800/228-5151** or 615/242-1631. Fax 615/244-9519. 103 units. $70–$130 double. Rates include continental breakfast. AE, DC, DISC, MC, V. Free parking. Pets accepted up to 25 lb. ($10 per day). **Amenities:** Lounge; outdoor pool. *In room:* A/C, TV, fridge, hair dryer, microwave, Wi-Fi (free).

> ### Nashville Power Couples
>
> Music stars such as married sweethearts Amy Grant and Vince Gill aren't the only celebrities who hang their hats in Nashville. Oscar-winning actress Nicole Kidman and her country music, heart-throb husband Keith Urban have become another of the city's favorite power couples.

Comfort Inn Downtown–Music Row ★   If you want to stay right in the heart of Music Row and near downtown, try this popular motel. In the lobby, you'll find walls covered with dozens of autographed photos of country music stars who have stayed here in years past. The rooms are fairly standard, though all are clean and comfortable. The seven suites all have whirlpool tubs. Local calls are free here, too.

1501 Demonbreun St., Nashville, TN 37203. www.comfortinnnashville.com. © **800/552-4667** or 615/255-9977. Fax 615/242-6127. 144 units. $79–$89 double; $119–$149 suite. Rates include continental breakfast. AE, DC, DISC, MC, V. Free parking (mobile-home and bus spaces available). Pets accepted, up to 80 lb. ($10 per day). **Amenities:** Nearby golf course; outdoor pool; nearby lighted tennis courts. *In room:* A/C, TV, fridge, hair dryer (on request), microwave, whirlpool (in suites), Wi-Fi (free).

MUSIC VALLEY & THE AIRPORT AREA

If you plan to spend any amount of time at either the Gaylord Opryland Resort or the Opry Mills mall, staying in the Music Valley area will be your best bet. It will also be much more convenient if you plan to attend the *Grand Ole Opry*, where the second of two nightly shows can sometimes extend past midnight. After a night of all that barn-raising music, who wants to drive across town to their hotel?

Very Expensive

Gaylord Opryland Resort and Convention Center ★★★ This palatial property, with its 9 acres of lush indoor botanical gardens, serene waterways, and cascading waterfalls, attracts thousands of visitors daily—and that's on top of those who are actually staying at this massive hotel. The most impressive of the hotel's themed areas is the Delta Atrium, which is set under 4½ acres of glass and surrounded by a ¼-mile-long indoor river. Waterfalls splash across rocky outcroppings, and fountains dance with vibrant colored lights harmonized by lively music. Bridges and meandering pathways add a certain quaint charm. Elsewhere at Opryland, the Magnolia lobby resembles an elegant antebellum mansion, with its classically proportioned double staircase worthy of Tara itself. The resort's indulgent European-inspired spa, Relâche, is the largest spa in Tennessee with 27,000 square feet. Gaylord Springs Golf Links, the resort's Scottish links–style, par-72 course offers 18 challenging holes bordered by limestone bluffs and enhanced by federally protected wetlands.

Opryland's standard guest rooms, while not overly spacious, are comfortable and convenient. All the guest rooms have been updated with new furnishings, including beds with pillowtop mattresses and fine linens. Rooms with atrium views ($75 extra) are charming. Numerous boutiques, cafes, and specialty shops are scattered throughout Opryland. From upscale steak and seafood restaurants to Italian, Mexican, and Southern dining experiences—there's something here for all tastes and budgets. Note that Opryland charges overnight hotel guests an additional $15-per-day resort fee, which includes Wi-Fi, bottled water and coffee daily in room, access to the fitness center and pools, and local calls up to 20 minutes (10¢ per min. thereafter).

> ### Boots Made for Walking
>
> If you're staying at the Gaylord Opryland Resort, comfortable walking shoes are a must. Even if you opt for the valet parking, the distances between drop-off points and your room can be daunting. Each member of the bell staff at Opryland walks an average of 12 miles a day.

2800 Opryland Dr., Nashville, TN 37214. www.gaylordhotels.com. **888/999-OPRY** (6779) or 615/889-1000. Fax 615/871-5728. 2,881 units. $199–$274 double; $319–$3,500 suite. $75 extra for rooms with atrium views. AE, DC, DISC, MC, V. Valet parking $25 plus tax; self-parking $18 plus tax. **Amenities:** 18 restaurants and lounges; concierge; golf course; fitness center; 2 outdoor pools and 1 indoor pool; room service; spa. *In room:* A/C, TV w/pay movies, minifridge, hair dryer, kitchen or kitchenette (in suites), Wi-Fi (included in resort fee).

Expensive

Marriott Nashville Airport ★★ This is one of the airport area's most resort-like hotels, and includes a spacious indoor/outdoor pool with a lovely, landscaped

Nashville Hotels: Music Valley & the Airport Area

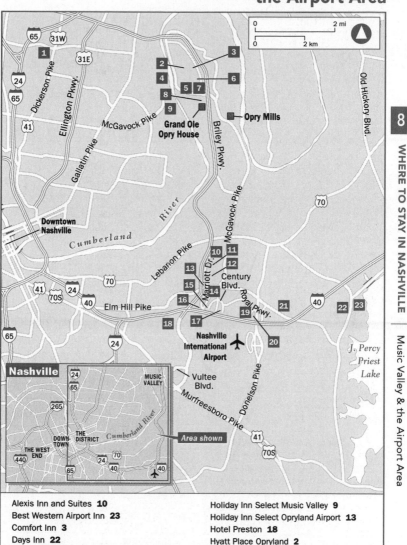

Alexis Inn and Suites **10**
Best Western Airport Inn **23**
Comfort Inn **3**
Days Inn **22**
Doubletree Guest Suites Nashville Airport **11**
Drury Inn and Suites Nashville Airport **20**
Embassy Suites Nashville **15**
Fairfield Inn Opryland **4**
Gaylord Opryland Resort & Convention Center **8**
GuestHouse Inn & Suites Music Valley **6**
Holiday Inn Express Nashville-Opryland **5**

Holiday Inn Select Music Valley **9**
Holiday Inn Select Opryland Airport **13**
Hotel Preston **18**
Hyatt Place Opryland **2**
La Quinta Inn Nashville-Briley Parkway **12**
Nashville Airport Marriott **16**
Radisson Hotel at Opryland **7**
Red Roof Inn-Nashville East **19**
Residence Inn Airport **14**
Sheraton Music City **17**
Sleep Inn Nashville **1**
Springhill Suites by Marriott **21**

patio. Situated on 17 tree-shaded acres, the hotel is ideally suited to business travelers as well as families. Fitness buffs have 24-hour access to a large exercise room with cardio machines and free weights. Guest rooms are larger than average, with corner rooms boasting up to 30% more room than the others. To avoid noise from airplanes taking off and landing, ask for a room on the opposite side from the airport. Outstanding service has always been one of the hallmarks of this immaculate, efficiently run hotel. Its casual restaurant, with a pretty view of the woods outside, is another draw for its delicious breakfast waffles and wide range of pasta and poultry dishes, and generous salads at lunch and dinner.

600 Marriott Dr., Nashville, TN 37214-5010. www.marriott.com. © **800/228-9290** or 615/889-9300. Fax 615/889-9315. 398 units. $105–$189 double; $450–$650 suite. AE, DC, DISC, MC, V. Free parking. **Amenities:** Restaurant; lounge; free airport shuttle; babysitting; concierge; health club; indoor/outdoor pool; room service; sauna; valet service; whirlpool. *In room:* A/C, TV w/pay movies, hair dryer, Wi-Fi ($15 per 24 hr.).

Sheraton Music City   Set on 23 acres in a modern business park near the airport, this large convention hotel (second in size only to Gaylord Opryland) has a commanding vista of the surrounding area. Somewhat dated classic Georgian styling sets the tone and evokes antebellum decor. In the elegant lobby, you can get free Wi-Fi. Comfortable guest rooms are fairly large and feature sleigh beds, work desks, and three telephones. The hotel reserves 20 rooms on the ground-floor level specifically for pet owners.

777 McGavock Pike, Nashville, TN 37214-3175. www.sheratonmusiccity.com. © **800/325-3535** or 615/885-2200. Fax 615/231-1134. 410 units. $109–$189 double; $300–$600 suite. AE, DC, DISC, MC, V. Free parking. Pets accepted (no fee, but must sign nuisance waiver). **Amenities:** Restaurant; lounge; free airport shuttle; concierge; health club w/whirlpool; indoor pool, outdoor pool in quiet central courtyard; valet service. *In room:* A/C, TV, hair dryer, Internet ($9.95 per 24 hr.).

Moderate

Doubletree Guest Suites Nashville Airport   If your flight plans have you taking a red-eye into or out of Nashville, consider staying here—the only hotel in the area offering free 24-hour shuttle service. The spacious suites include separate sleeping and living room areas that include pullout sleeper sofas. Rooms have everything you might need, from a work desk and two telephones to a refrigerator and microwave. And, of course, there's always the Doubletree's trademark lure of fresh-baked cookies to greet each guest upon arrival.

2424 Atrium Way, Nashville, TN 37214. www.doubletree.com. © **615/889-8889.** Fax 615/883-7779. 138 units (all suites). $89–$189 suite. AE, DC, DISC, MC, V. Free parking. **Amenities:** Restaurant; free airport shuttle; exercise room; indoor/outdoor pool. *In-room:* A/C, TV, fridge, hair dryer, microwave, Wi-Fi (free).

Drury Inn and Suites Nashville Airport   One of the few Drury properties in a city overflowing with Marriotts and Hiltons, this reliable, reasonably priced chain is a good choice for travelers who favor friendly informality and convenience. Located on Elm Hill Pike, with easy access to drugstores and fast-food restaurants, the area is less congested than properties closer to the airport. And with value-added perks like free breakfast and airport shuttles and no added fee for having pets in your room, the modest Drury has built a loyal clientele.

555 Donelson Pike, Nashville, TN 37214. www.druryhotels.com. © **866/599-6674** or 615/902-0400. Fax 800/724-9668. 155 units. $119–$137 double. Rates include continental breakfast. AE, DC, DISC, MC, V. Free parking. Pets allowed (no fee). **Amenities:** Free airport shuttle; fitness center; indoor/outdoor pool. *In room:* A/C, TV, fridge, hair dryer, microwave, Wi-Fi (free).

Embassy Suites Nashville ★ ☺ This all-suite hotel makes a great choice and a good value for families, as well as for business travelers. These two-room suites are spacious, modern, and tastefully decorated in warm colors. The centerpiece of the hotel is its large atrium, which is full of tropical plants, including potted palms. A rocky stream runs through the Wi-Fi–accessible atrium, and caged tropical songbirds add their cheery notes to the pleasant atmosphere. *Tip:* The fifth floor of this nine-story hotel is designated for smokers, so you might want to steer clear of the sixth floor as well, if you're sensitive to these odors seeping through walls and ceilings.

10 Century Blvd., Nashville, TN 37214. www.embassysuites.com. ✆ **800/EMBASSY** (362-2779) or 615/871-0033. Fax 615/883-9987. 296 units (all suites). $99–$179 suite. Rates include cooked-to-order breakfast delivered to your room, and an evening manager's reception. AE, DC, DISC, MC, V. Free parking. **Amenities:** Restaurant; bar; free airport shuttle; fitness center; hot tub; indoor pool; room service. *In room:* A/C, TV w/pay movies, fridge, hair dryer, microwave, wet bar, Wi-Fi ($9.95 for 24 hr.).

Fairfield Inn Opryland ★★ One of my favorite affordable hotels when I'm traveling alone on business is this consistently clean, top-notch hotel with a spacious indoor pool and a small, sunlight-filled exercise room. Rooms are set up for productivity and relaxation—with big work desks and large-screen TVs. Bathrooms are modest in size but serviceable, with granite vanities. Staff members are especially welcoming and helpful. Like the other, comparable hotels clustered on this service road next to the freeway and near Opryland, the Fairfield offers the kind of simplicity, convenience, and accessibility that big resorts cannot.

211 Music City Circle, Nashville, TN 37214. www.fairfieldinn.com. ✆ **888/236-2427** or 615/872-8939. Fax 615/872-7230. 109 units. $129–$159 double; suites from $124. Rates include continental breakfast. AE, DISC, MC, V. Free parking. **Amenities:** Exercise room; indoor pool. *In room:* A/C, TV, hair dryer, Wi-Fi (free).

GuestHouse Inn & Suites Music Valley ★ ☺ Especially popular with vacationing families, this four-story red-brick hotel is within walking distance of the Gaylord Opryland Resort and Convention Center, but a free shuttle will take you there, so you don't have to dodge the traffic on foot. Suites feature pullout sofas in addition to king-size beds. Four larger family suites have two queen-size beds and two full-size sleeper sofas, in addition to two vanity areas and kitchenettes.

2420 Music Valley Dr., Nashville, TN 37214. www.guesthouseintl.com. ✆ **800/214-8378** or 615/885-4030. Fax 615/329-4890. 184 units. $99–$129 double. Rates include continental breakfast. AE, DC, DISC, MC, V. Pets accepted ($25). Free self-parking, including in covered garage. **Amenities:** Lounge; free airport and Opryland shuttle; exercise room; hot tub; indoor pool. *In room:* A/C, TV, hair dryer, Wi-Fi (free).

Holiday Inn Express Opryland ★★ A large indoor swimming pool with lovely wooded views is one of the standouts of this newer hotel, which opened in late 2009. Farther away from the interstate, and a bit more secluded than the other budget-friendly chain hotels that have started mushrooming in this suburban area around Music Valley, it offers everything you'd expect: a great lobby and dining area, free parking, and personable service. Crisply appointed guest rooms feature comfortable beds and small kitchenettes with dining room tables under decorative, hanging light fixtures. You'll feel at home here.

2461 McGavock Pike, Nashville, TN 37214. www.holiday-inn.com. ✆ **800/HOLIDAY** (465-4329) or 615/829-7777. Fax 615/829-7799. 113 units. $99–$159 double. Rates include cooked breakfast. AE, DISC, MC, V. Free parking. **Amenities:** 24-hr. exercise room; indoor pool. *In room:* A/C, TV, hair dryer, microwave, Wi-Fi (free).

Holiday Inn Select Opryland Airport   If you're looking for someplace convenient to the airport, this Holiday Inn, just off the Briley Parkway, is a good bet. The lobby features two back-to-back atria, one of which houses the reception desk, a car-rental desk, and a couple of seating areas, while the other contains a swimming pool, lobby/lounge area, and terraced restaurant. Guest rooms are fairly standard, with big TVs and plenty of counter space in the bathrooms. Smoking rooms are available on the fifth floor. The king rooms have a bit more space and are designed with business travelers in mind. On the 14th-floor executive level, you'll receive a complimentary breakfast and other upgraded amenities.

2200 Elm Hill Pike, Nashville, TN 37214. www.holiday-inn.com. ✆ **800/HOLIDAY** (465-4329) or 615/883-9770. Fax 615/391-4521. 382 units. $109–$140 double. AE, DC, DISC, MC, V. Free parking. **Amenities:** Restaurant; lounge; free airport shuttle; exercise room; hot tub; indoor pool; room service; sauna. *In room:* A/C, TV w/pay movies, fridge and microwave (available by request), hair dryer, Wi-Fi (free).

Hotel Preston   Quirky perks such as in-room lava lamps, pet fish, rubber duckies, and art kits are the main selling points of this 11-story boutique hotel. Although fresh and innovative when it first opened a few years ago, the property has become musty and is showing signs of age. Some floors are designated smoke free but the ventilation system doesn't quite do the trick; those sensitive to secondhand smoke may want to book elsewhere. On the plus side, guest rooms are furnished with pillowtop mattresses on the beds (and a menu of pillows from which to choose), comfy chairs, and well-lighted work desks. Aveda bath products and in-room Starbucks coffee and Tazo teas are other nice touches.

733 Briley Pkwy., Nashville, TN 37217. www.hotelpreston.com. ✆ **877/361-5500** or 615/361-5900. Fax 615/367-4468. 196 units. $109–$169 double; $189 suite. AE, DC, DISC, MC, V. Free parking. Pets allowed ($50 nonrefundable fee). **Amenities:** Restaurant and lounge; free airport and Opryland-area shuttle; outdoor pool; valet service. *In room:* A/C, TV w/pay movies, CD player, hair dryer, Wi-Fi (free).

Hyatt Place Opryland ★★ ☺   This mid-rise hotel is located just off Music Valley Drive and is your most comfortable choice in the area if you aren't willing to splurge on the Gaylord Opryland Resort. With the look and feel of a contemporary boutique hotel, this inviting property offers standard rooms that are larger and less expensive than those at nearby Opryland. Cushy pullout sofas and wet bars mean you can stretch out and make yourself at home in front of 42-inch-screen plasma TVs with plug-and-play capability. Beyond the lobby, a sunny breakfast kitchen area features morning cereals, pastries, and breads, served on white china with real silverware. Continental breakfast with freshly brewed Starbucks coffee is complimentary each morning, with hot-cooked entrees and picnic items, such as sandwiches, available for purchase.

220 Rudy's Circle, Nashville, TN 37214. www.hyatt.com. ✆ **888-HYATTHP** (492-8847) or 615/872-0422. Fax 615/872-9283. 123 units. $99–$189 double. Rates include continental breakfast. AE, DISC, MC, V. Free parking. **Amenities:** Exercise room; small outdoor pool. *In room:* A/C, TV, hair dryer, kitchenette, Wi-Fi (free).

Radisson Hotel at Opryland ★   A $9-million renovation in 2011 improved the look and guest amenities (including new flatscreen TVs and Sleep Number beds) of this otherwise standard property, which is owned and operated by Gaylord Hotels. A much smaller and far less extravagant alternative to the Gaylord Opryland Resort and Convention Center, this sister property offers conveniences such as free parking and easier access than the massive resort. Complimentary shuttle service is offered to the resort and is also available to downtown tourist attractions. Another new feature of the refurbished Radisson is its 200-seat restaurant, Opry Backstage Grill, which serves Southern breakfast, lunch, and dinner—by singing waitstaff.

2401 Music Valley Dr. Nashville, TN 37214. www.radisson.com/nashvilletn. © **800/333-3333** or 615/889-0800. Fax 615/883-1230. 303 units. $100–$149 double. Some rates include continental breakfast. AE, DISC, MC, V. Free self-parking. **Amenities:** Restaurant; free shuttle to Opryland and other attractions; indoor pool, sauna. *In room:* A/C, TV, hair dryer, Internet (in exterior rooms only) and Wi-Fi elsewhere (free).

Residence Inn Airport ★   This sprawling, extended-stay Marriott property feels more like a suburban apartment complex than a chain hotel. Studios are a real bargain, considering they include a queen-size bed, pullout sofa, and full kitchens, which, in 2010, were upgraded with new stainless-steel appliances (refrigerators and stoves). For a few dollars more, you can book a two-story loft with two bedrooms. The property is also in the process of upgrading its televisions to high-definition sets. As with all Marriott properties, all units and public spaces are smoke free.

2300 Elm Hill Pike, Nashville, TN 37214. www.marriott.com. © **800/331-3131** or 615/889-8600. Fax 615/871-4970. 168 units. $109–$159 double. Rates include cooked breakfast. AE, DC, DISC, MC, V. Free parking. Pets accepted ($50 nonrefundable fee). **Amenities:** Exercise room; outdoor pool; valet service. *In room:* A/C, TV w/pay movies, hair dryer, Internet (free).

Inexpensive to Moderate

A number of national and regional chain motels, generic but dependable, can be found in the area, including **Alexis Inn and Suites,** 600 Ermac Dr. (© **615/889-4466**), charging $89 to $119 for a double; **Best Western Airport Inn,** 701 Stewart's Ferry Pike (© **615/889-9199**), charging $60 to $70 for a double; **Comfort Inn,** 2516 Music Valley Dr. (© **615/889-0086**), charging $75 to $90 for a double; and **Days Inn,** 2460 Music Valley Dr. (© **615/889-0090**), charging $70 to $90 double (with an outdoor pool and an adjacent miniature-golf course).

In addition, $99 deals can sometimes be found at slightly more expensive properties, including the **Courtyard by Marriott Nashville Airport,** 2508 Elm Hill Pike (© **888/236-2427** or 615/883-9500), where rack rates average $99 to $189; and **Hyatt Place Nashville Airport,** 721 Royal Pkwy. (© **615/493-5200**), where rates average $128 to $210.

Other affordable options include **La Quinta Inn Nashville-Briley Parkway,** 2345 Atrium Way (© **615/885-3000**), charging $65 to $80 for a double; **Red Roof Inn–Nashville East,** 510 Claridge Dr. (© **615/872-0735**), charging $65 for a double; **Sleep Inn Nashville,** 3200 Dickerson Pike (© **866/538-0187**), with rates starting at $65 per night; and **Springhill Suites by Marriott,** 1100 Airport Center Dr. (© **615/884-6111**), charging $89 to $109 for a double.

PRACTICAL INFORMATION

The Big Picture

Deciding where to stay in Nashville needn't be complicated. Grab a map, pinpoint your main areas of interest, and **choose a location** that's convenient to what you want to see and do while you're here. Narrowing it down won't be difficult, because aside from the airport area, you really have only three main choices: downtown, the West End, or Music Valley (also known as the "Opryland" area).

In theory, it's always a good idea to **make a reservation,** although early booking doesn't always ensure the best bargain. Last-minute inquiries, whether online or by telephone, are just as likely to yield the occasional deal as calls made a year ahead of time. However, book in advance if you plan to visit Nashville or Memphis any time April throughout the month of October, when music festivals and special events abound. Demand for rooms soars during two particular weekends: You'll pay a premium for choice reservations in Nashville during the Country Music Association (CMA) Festival in early June. Likewise, a decent room in Memphis during Elvis Week the third week in August will be more expensive than any other time of year. Large conventions, frequent in both Nashville and Memphis, can also skew hotel rates at any given time.

While Nashville hotels offer a variety of room sizes and amenities, services and room features can fluctuate, even within the same hotel chain. In-room fridges and free Wi-Fi might be standard at one hotel, while other properties within the same chain may charge a daily fee for Internet access and offer fridges only by request. The rule of thumb is this: Don't assume anything when making your reservation. If you want to stay at a hotel that has specific amenities, be sure to ask when you're making your reservation. And be sure to clarify fees beforehand, if staying within budget is a priority.

The majority of hotels are now smoke-free properties, although you can still find those with rooms, or entire floors, for smokers. When making a reservation, be sure to request the type of room you need. While multiline phones are often the norm, charges for telephone calls vary widely. Some offer free local calls, while others charge by the minute. (With the universality of cellphones, however, this may be a moot distinction.) Another welcome trend is the inclusion of standard, in-room amenities such as flatscreen TVs and Wi-Fi. Internet fees range from free access to about $12 per day. Increasingly, midpriced and budget hotels have public computers in their lobbies—a nice perk if you don't travel with a laptop or smartphone and you want to check your e-mail.

Major chains operating in and around Nashville and Memphis include leisure-oriented Best Western, Holiday Inn, Hyatt Place, Radisson, and Ramada, as well as business-traveler favorites Hampton Inn & Suites, Hilton, Marriott (in all its incarnations), and Sheraton. Downtown Memphis has a Westin, while Nashville has a Loews. There are few boutique hotels and virtually no luxury operators along the lines of Four Seasons, Mandarin Oriental, or Ritz-Carlton.

Rates in this chapter are for a **double room** (except where noted). The rates quoted here do not include the Tennessee sales tax (9.25%) and state and city room taxes, which altogether will add 16.25% onto your room bill. Keep this in mind when you're searching for rates, because most quotes will not include these taxes. Service fees may also apply when booking through websites. Finally, if you will be driving a car into either downtown Nashville or downtown Memphis, don't overlook the cost of parking your car, which can add up to $26 a night to your hotel bill.

GETTING THE BEST DEAL

The **rack rate** is the maximum rate that a hotel charges for a room. Hardly anybody pays it, however, except sometimes in high season. To cut costs:

○ **Ask for a rate, then ask about special rates or other discounts.** You may qualify for corporate, student, military, senior/AARP, AAA, or other discounts. Nail down the standard rate before you ask for your discount.

- **Book online.** Many hotels offer Internet-only discounts or supply discounted rooms to Priceline, Hotwire, or Expedia at rates much lower than the ones you can get through the hotel or chain. Some chains guarantee that the price on their websites is the lowest available; check anyway.
- **Dial direct.** When booking a room in a chain hotel, you'll often get a better deal from the hotel's reservation desk than from the chain's main number.
- **Remember the law of supply and demand.** Business-oriented hotels are busiest during the week, so you can expect weekend discounts. Leisure hotels are most crowded and expensive on weekends, so discounts may be available midweek.
- **Visit in the winter.** Bargain hunters who don't mind cold and snow (sometimes *lots* of snow) aim for January through March, when hotels offer great deals, especially on weekends.
- **Avoid excess charges and hidden costs.** When you book a room, ask whether the hotel charges for parking—almost every hotel in downtown Nashville and Memphis does—and whether there's a charge for staying in the garage past room checkout time on the last day of your stay. Use your cellphone, prepaid phone cards, or pay phones instead of making expensive calls from hotel phones. If you know you'll be online a lot, seek out a hotel that includes Internet access in the room rate (many older properties and hotels that do a lot of expense-account business don't). And don't be tempted by the minibar: Most hotels charge through the nose for water, soda, and snacks. Finally, ask about local taxes, service charges, and energy surcharges, which can increase the cost of a room by 15% or more.
- **Book an efficiency.** A room with a kitchenette allows you to shop for groceries and even cook. This is a big money saver, especially for families on long stays.
- **Enroll in "frequent guest" programs,** which court repeat customers. Guests can accumulate points or credits to earn free hotel nights, airline miles, in-room amenities, merchandise, concert and event tickets, and more. Some frequent guest members enjoy free Wi-Fi access, saving as much as $15 a day. Many chains partner with other hotel chains, car-rental firms, airlines, and credit card companies to encourage repeat business.

For tips on surfing for hotel deals online, visit **www.frommers.com**.

SIDE TRIPS FROM NASHVILLE

After you've had your fill of Nashville's country music scene, it may be time for a change of scenery—and a taste of the real country. Heading out in any direction from Nashville, you'll hit the Tennessee hills. These are the hills famous for their walking horses and sour mash whiskey. They also hold historic towns and Civil War battlefields that are well worth visiting.

FRANKLIN, COLUMBIA & SCENIC U.S. 31

Franklin is 20 miles south of Nashville; Columbia is 46 miles south of Nashville.

South of Nashville, U.S. 31 leads through the rolling Tennessee hills to the historic towns of Franklin and Columbia. This area was the heart of the middle Tennessee plantation country, and there are still many antebellum mansions along this route. Between Nashville and Franklin, you'll pass by more than a dozen old plantation homes, with still more to the south of Franklin.

Essentials

GETTING THERE The start of the scenic section of U.S. 31 is in Brentwood, at exit 74 off I-65. Alternatively, you can take I-65 straight to Franklin (exit 65) and then take U.S. 31 back north to Nashville. From Columbia, you can head back north on U.S. 31, take U.S. 412/Tenn. 99 east to I-65, or head west on Tenn. 50 to the **Natchez Trace Parkway.** This latter road is a scenic highway administered by the National Park Service.

VISITOR INFORMATION In Franklin, stop in at the tiny **Williamson County Visitor Information Center,** 209 E. Main St. (© **615/591-8514**), open Monday to Friday 9am to 4pm, Saturday 9am to 5pm, and Sunday 1 to 4pm; closed holidays.

Exploring Historic Franklin

At the visitor center—housed in a former doctor's office built in 1839—you can pick up information about various historic sites around the area, including a map to the historic homes along U.S. 31 and a self-guided

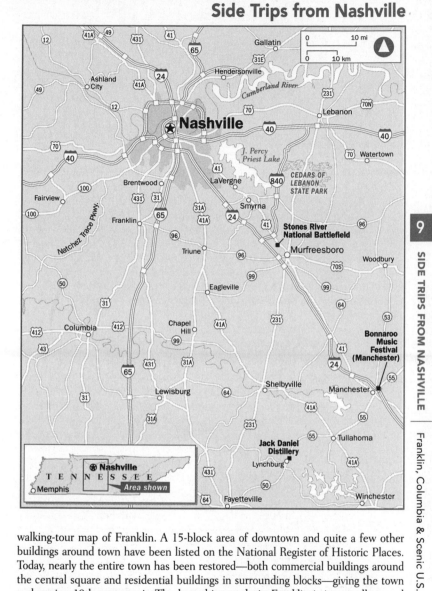

walking-tour map of Franklin. A 15-block area of downtown and quite a few other buildings around town have been listed on the National Register of Historic Places. Today, nearly the entire town has been restored—both commercial buildings around the central square and residential buildings in surrounding blocks—giving the town a charming 19th-century air. The best thing to do in Franklin is just stroll around admiring the restored buildings, browsing through the many antiques stores, shops, and cafes.

After you've worked up an appetite, stop in at **Dotson's,** 99 E. Main St. (© **615/794-2805**), the town's best diner. A local landmark, Dotson's doles out heaping portions of home-style eats like fried chicken and mashed potatoes, biscuits and gravy, and mile-high meringue pies. Meat-and-three plates cost about $8 or $9, but bring your cash because they don't take plastic. The hardworking waitresses might call you darlin', but don't take offense. They're the real deal, and Dotson's is as authentic today as it was half a century ago.

Franklin is best known in Tennessee as the site of the bloody Battle of Franklin during the Civil War. During this battle, which took place on November 30, 1864, more than 6,000 Confederate and 2,000 Union soldiers were killed. Each year on November 30, there are special activities here to commemorate the battle. Among the events are costumed actors marching through town and, after dark, a bonfire. Contact the Visitor Information Center for details.

To learn more about the town's Civil War history, visit the following historic homes.

Carnton Plantation & Battlefield ★   Recently, this somber tourist attraction gained greater visibility as the backdrop for Robert Hicks's best-selling historic novel, *The Widow of the South* (2006). Built in 1826 by Randal McGavock, a former mayor of Nashville, Carnton Plantation is a beautiful neoclassical antebellum mansion with a Greek Revival portico. During the Battle of Franklin, one of the bloodiest battles of the Civil War, this plantation home served as a Confederate hospital, and today you can still see the bloodstains on floors throughout the house. The interior of the stately old home is almost completely restored and houses many McGavock family pieces and other period furnishings. Two years after the battle, the McGavock family donated 2 acres of land to be used as a cemetery for Confederate soldiers who had died during the Battle of Franklin. There are almost 1,500 graves in the McGavock Confederate Cemetery, which makes this the largest private Confederate cemetery in the country.

1345 Carnton Lane. © **615/794-0903.** www.carnton.org. Admission $10 adults, $9 seniors, $5 children 6–12. Mon–Sat 9am–5pm; Sun 1–5pm. Closed major holidays.

The Carter House   Built in 1830, the Carter House served as the Union army command post during the Battle of Franklin. Throughout the bloody fight, which raged all around the house, the Carter family and friends hid in the cellar. Today, you can still see many bullet holes in the main house and various outbuildings on the property. In addition to getting a tour of the restored home, you can spend time in the museum, which contains many Civil War artifacts. A video presentation about the battle that took place here will provide you with a perspective for touring the town of Franklin.

1140 Columbia Ave. © **615/791-1861.** www.carterhouse1864.com. Admission $12 adults, $10 seniors, $6 children 6–13. Apr–Oct Mon–Sat 9am–5pm, Sun 1–5pm; Nov–Mar Mon–Fri 9am–4pm, Sun 1–4pm. Closed major holidays.

Exploring Williamson County

Arrington Vineyards   Napa Valley it ain't, but maybe that's not a bad thing. Country superstar Kix Brooks founded this winery, located about an hour's drive southeast of Nashville in the lovely rural countryside. Neatly trimmed grapes grow in the arbors at the base of a huge hill. At the crest of the hill, a log lodge offers free wine tastings and a gift shop selling merchandise and gourmet picnic foods. Outdoor seating surrounds the lodge, offering breathtaking views of distant farmlands, wooded hillsides, and memorable sunsets. The "Music in the Vines" series invites patrons to bring blankets and picnic baskets as they enjoy live music by the likes of 9-Volt Romeo and the 16th Avenue Jazz Group. Relaxed and friendly, a visit to Arrington offers a low-key but first-rate vineyard experience.

6211 Patton Rd., Arrington, TN. 𝒞 **615/395-0102.** www.arringtonvineyards.com. "Music in the Vines" concerts are held Apr–Nov. Apr events are every Sat 5–9pm; May–Nov concerts are held Fri and Sat evenings and Sun afternoons 2–6pm. Call ahead to confirm scheduled events. Directions: Take I-65 South to Exit 65, go left on Hwy. 96 E. for 7.4 miles. Turn right at Cox Rd. and go 2 miles. Turn left at Patton Rd., and Arrington Vineyards is less than a mile on the right.

Leiper's Fork Another scenic, 20-minute country drive south of downtown Franklin leads to the Village of Leiper's (pronounced "leapers") Fork, a charming, old-timey arts community that's listed as a National Historic District. Squeezed up against a winding, two-lane country road is a cluster of several dozen quaint cottages and old storefronts that stand as fine examples of 19th-century architecture, but it's what lies within that keeps the tourists coming back. Folksy general stores, cafes, and art galleries are ideal for the festival crowds that browse here to enjoy the slow pace, country atmosphere, and sense of community that prevails here. Popular draws include an annual chili cook-off in mid-October, a fall turkey shoot, and the open-air "Lawn Chair Theatre" of live entertainment offerings.

Old Hillsboro Rd. www.leipersfork.com. For more info, contact the Williamson County Visitor's Center, 209 E. Main, Franklin. 𝒞 **615/591-8514.** Directions from Franklin: Take I-65 S. 17 miles to Tenn. 96/Mufreesboro Rd./Franklin TN exit, then follow Tenn. 96 through Franklin 4.9 miles to Tenn. 46/Old Hillsboro Rd. Take a left on Old Hillsboro Rd. and go 4.7 miles to reach Leiper's Fork.

Columbia

Heading south from Franklin on U.S. 31 for about 26 miles will bring you to the small town of Columbia, in Maury County. Maury County is known as the "Antebellum Homes Capital of Tennessee," with more than a dozen Civil War–era homes and three districts listed on the National Register of Historic Places. The best known of these is the **James K. Polk Home** (see below), but to get more details on the county's historic offerings, contact the **Maury County Convention and Visitors Bureau,** 8 Public Sq., Columbia, TN 38401 (𝒞 **888/852-1860** or 931/381-7176; www.antebellum.com).

James K. Polk Home This modest home was where James K. Polk, the 11th president of the United States, grew up and where he lived when he began his legal and political career. Though Polk may not be as familiar a name as those of some other early presidents, he did achieve two very important goals while in office: Polk negotiated the purchase of California and settled the long-standing dispute between the United States and England over where to draw the border of the Oregon Territory. The house is filled with antiques that belonged to Polk's parents when they lived here and to Polk and his family during their time in the White House. There's even a lock of former U.S. President Andrew Jackson's hair.

301 W. Seventh St., Columbia. 𝒞 **931/388-2354.** www.jameskpolk.com. Admission $7 adults, $6 seniors, $4 students 6–18 (maximum of $20 per family for parents with children 17 and under). Apr–Oct Mon–Sat 9am–5pm, Sun 1–5pm; Nov–Mar Mon–Sat 9am–4pm, Sun 1–5pm. Closed major holidays.

DISTILLERIES, HORSES & A BATTLEFIELD

Though Tennessee was last to secede from the Union, the Civil War came early to the state, and 3 years of being on the front lines left Tennessee with a legacy written in blood. More Civil War battles were fought here than in any other state except

Distilleries, Horses & a Battlefield

Virginia, and the bloodiest of these was the Battle of Stones River, which took place 30 miles south of Nashville, near the city of Murfreesboro. Today this battle is commemorated at the **Stones River National Battlefield.**

In the 2 decades that followed the war, Tennessee quickly recovered and developed two of the state's most famous commodities—Tennessee sippin' whiskey and Tennessee walking horses. Another 45 miles or so south of Murfreesboro, you can learn about both of these time-honored Tennessee traditions.

For those who are not connoisseurs of sour mash whiskeys, Tennessee whiskey is *not* bourbon. This latter whiskey, named for Bourbon County, Kentucky, where it was first distilled, is made much the same way, but it is not charcoal-mellowed the way fine Tennessee sour mash whiskey is.

If you have the time, I encourage you to get off the interstate and hit the back roads, which offer lovely countryside vistas and interesting small towns. For more information with links to maps and self-guided driving tours of Civil War sites, distilleries, and Tennessee's portion of the famed Natchez Trace Parkway (southwest of Nashville), visit this Tennessee tourist office website: **www.tntrailsandbyways. com**.

Jack Daniel's Distillery ★   Old Jack Daniel (or Mr. Jack, as he was known hereabouts) didn't waste any time setting up his whiskey distillery after the Civil War came to an end. Founded in 1866, this is the oldest registered distillery in the United States and is on the National Register of Historic Places. It's still an active distillery; you can tour the facility and see how Jack Daniel's whiskey is made and learn how it gets such a distinctive earthy flavor. There are two secrets to the manufacture of Mr. Jack's famous sour mash whiskey. The first of these is the water that comes gushing—pure, cold, and iron free—from Cave Spring. The other is the sugar maple that's used to make the charcoal. In fact, it is this charcoal, through which the whiskey slowly drips, that gives Jack Daniel's its renowned smoothness.

After touring the distillery, you can glance in at the office used by Mr. Jack and see the safe that did him in. Old Mr. Jack kicked that safe one day in a fit of anger and wound up getting gangrene for his troubles. One can only hope that regular doses of Tennessee sippin' whiskey helped ease the pain of his last days. If you want to take home some Jack Daniel's, bottles can be purchased here at the distillery, but nowhere else in this county, which is another of Tennessee's dry counties. (No tastings at the end of the tour, I'm afraid.)

Note: It's easy to get here after visiting the Stones River National Battlefield (above). Continue on I-24 to exit 105, then drive southwest for 10 miles to Tullahoma and follow signs to the distillery in nearby Lynchburg.

182 Lynchburg Hwy., Lynchburg. ✆ **931/759-6319.** www.jackdaniels.com. Free admission. Daily 9am–4:30pm. Tours at regular intervals throughout the day. Reservations not accepted. Closed Thanksgiving, Dec 24–25, Dec 31, and Jan 1. Take Tenn. 55 off I-24 and drive 26 miles southwest to Lynchburg.

Stones River National Battlefield   On New Year's Eve 1862, what would become the bloodiest Civil War battle west of the Appalachian Mountains began just north of Murfreesboro, along the Stones River. Though by the end of the first day of fighting the Confederates thought they were assured a victory, Union reinforcements turned the tide against the rebels. By January 3, the Confederates were in retreat and 23,000 soldiers lay dead or injured on the battlefield. Today, 351 acres of the battlefield are preserved. The site includes a national cemetery and the Hazen Brigade

Monument, which was erected in 1863 and is the oldest Civil War memorial in the United States. In the visitor center you'll find a museum full of artifacts and details of the battle.

3501 Old Nashville Hwy., Murfreesboro. © **615/893-9501.** www.nps.gov/stri. Free admission. Daily 8am–5pm. Closed Dec 25. Take I-24 south from Nashville for about 30 miles to exit 78B.

An Unforgettable Lunch Stop in Lynchburg

Miss Mary Bobo's Boarding House Restaurant ★ SOUTHERN You'll feel as if you should be wearing a hoop skirt or top hat when you see this grand white mansion, with its columns, long front porch, and balcony over the front door (but casual, contemporary clothes are just fine). Miss Mary Bobo's, housed in an antebellum-style mansion built slightly post-bellum (in 1866), opened for business as a boardinghouse back in 1908, and though it no longer accepts boarders, it does serve the best lunch for miles around. Be prepared for filling portions of good Southern home cooking, and remember, lunch here is actually midday dinner. Miss Mary's is very popular, and you generally need to book a weekday lunch 2 to 3 weeks in advance; for a Saturday lunch, you'll need to make reservations at least 2 to 3 *months* in advance.

Main St., Lynchburg. © **931/759-7394.** www.jackdaniels.co.uk/lynchburg/boarding.asp. Reservations required well in advance. Set menu $11 adults, $5 children 9 and under. No credit cards. Lunch seatings Mon–Fri 1pm; Sat 11am and 1pm.

EXPLORING LYNCHBURG

Take some time to explore tiny Lynchburg, population 361, while you're here. There are several historic inns and bed-and-breakfast options, if you'd like to extend your stay. For more information, visit **www.lynchburgtenn.com.**

If you take your whisky seriously, it's also worth driving the few extra miles through the hills of Tullahoma, Tennessee, to visit the **George Dickel Whisky Distillery,** 1950 Cascade Hollow Rd., Tullahoma (© **931/857-4110;** www.dickel.com), while you're in this neck of the woods. George Dickel Whisky is distilled in the Old Scotch tradition (which is why they spell "whiskey" without an "e").

Founded in 1870, the distiller is noted among whisky connoisseurs for using clear, pure Cascade Springs water and for being the only Tennessee whisky maker to chill each batch before it goes through a charcoal filter. Dickel claims this process ensures a smoother taste than competitors' brands.

Free distillery tours are offered from 9am until 3:30pm Tuesdays through Saturdays. To get there from Nashville, take I-24 South to Exit 105. Turn right on Hwy. 41 South, go 1½ miles, and turn right onto Blanton Chapel Road. Go 4 miles and turn left at the stop sign, onto Lyndell Bell Road. Follow the signs to Normandy Dam (3½ miles) and take a right onto Frank Hines Road. Pass by the dam and continue on Frank Hines Road into Normandy. With the railroad crossing on your right, go straight onto Cascade Hollow Road and follow the signs for 1½ miles to the George Dickel Distillery and Visitor's Center.

Tennessee Walking Horse Museum The Tennessee walking horse, named for its unusual high-stepping walking gait, is considered the world's premier breed of show horse, and it is here in the rolling hills of middle Tennessee that most of these horses are bred. Using interactive videos, hands-on exhibits, and other displays, this museum presents the history of the Tennessee walking horse. Though the exhibits here will appeal primarily to equine enthusiasts, there is also much for the

TENNESSEE jammin'

If you're a rock-and-roots music fan planning a Tennessee road trip, don't miss the **Bonnaroo Music and Arts Festival** in Manchester, about 60 miles southeast of Nashville. This epic, 4-day outdoor concert event—held every June since 2001—is one of the hottest live-music events in the country. The setting is a fairly remote 700-acre farm midway between Nashville and Chattanooga, and not too far from Jack Daniel and George Dickel whiskey territory. Bring your camping gear, iPhone or Android (there's an app), credit cards, and a sense of free-spirited abandon—as well as a tolerance for crowds, wilting temperatures, and portable toilets—to Bonnaroo.

If you can get in the right frame of mind, it's worth every minute of the crazy chaos you must endure to truly experience this larger-than-life event. In addition to the eye-popping people-watching opportunities, Bonnaroo offers an eclectic lineup of musical acts. For 4 days straight you can wander the dusty site to catch performances by artists as diverse as Arcade Fire, Jay Z, and Loretta Lynn. 2012 headliners included Radiohead, the Roots, Skrillex, the Avett Brothers, and Trampled by Turtles.

At **Centeroo,** Bonnaroo's eccentric village scene, you'll find vendors and food trucks, a giant water fountain, and even a Ferris wheel. Movies like *8 Mile, Naked Gun,* and *Garden State* play in the 24-hour **Cinema Tent,** while live, stand-up comedy acts with headliners like Lewis Black and John Waters take place in the **Comedy Tent.**

The Broo'ers Festival is a *biergarten* area of haystacks, whiskey barrels, and picnic tables where concertgoers can drink beer from more than 20 different breweries. Another Bonnaroo favorite is the wireless dance party known as **Silent Disco,** where, in the wee hours of the morning, DJs spin music that can be heard only through stereophones, inaudible to sleeping festivalgoers in the sprawling campsites nearby.

Ticket prices to Bonnaroo vary. Those willing to pay more can upgrade to a VIP experience, which includes bleacher seating (all others stand) at the various outdoor concert stages and access to a hospitality tent with luxuries like electricity, cooling fans, and Wi-Fi access. For more information, visit **www.bonnaroo.com**.

Tip: Bonnaroo offers free drinking water, portable toilets, and shower facilities, but with 80,000 fans in attendance, the camping conditions can become trying. If overnight community pods of pup tents is not your style, relax. Manchester has more than 1,300 moderately priced to inexpensive hotel and motel rooms. For more information, contact the **Manchester Area Chamber of Commerce,** 110 E. Main St., Manchester, TN 37355 (📞 **931/728-7635;** www.macoc.org)

casual visitor to learn and enjoy. The annual Tennessee Walking Horse National Celebration, held each August here in Shelbyville, is one of middle Tennessee's most important annual events. Tennessee walkers can also be seen going through their paces at various other annual shows in the Nashville area.

183 Main St., Lynchburg. 📞 **931/759-5747.** www.twhnc.com. Free admission. Tues–Sat 10am–noon and 1–4pm. Closed major holidays.

THE COAL MINER'S DAUGHTER'S MANSION

An hour west of Nashville, several miles north off of Interstate 40, lies Loretta Lynn's version of Graceland (p. 164).

The **Loretta Lynn Ranch,** 44 Hurricane Hills Rd., Hurricane Mills, TN (© **931/296-7700;** www.lorettalynn.com), has clearly been a labor of love for the 76-year-old country music legend.

Nestled on acres of wooded hills, the site has slowly expanded over the years with more attractions and facilities to attract families and country music fans looking for an affordable getaway. Fans can tour the **Loretta Lynn Plantation Home,** a grand Southern-style mansion where she and her husband raised their family. In stark contrast, there's the **Butcher Holler Place,** a re-creation of her backwoods Kentucky birthplace, the log cabin she immortalized in her 1969 hit, *Coal Miner's Daughter.*

With the scope and appearance of a lazy country village, the ranch makes for an enjoyable side trip from Nashville. There's also a **Coal Miner's Daughter Museum,** where self-guided tours are $10 for adults and $5 for children. Other areas of interest include the **Frontier Homestead,** picturesque **Grist Mill Museum, American Artifact Museum,** and **Loretta Lynn's Fan and Doll Museum,** all of which offer free admission.

In addition to occasional concerts, the ranch offers outdoor recreation opportunities including fishing, canoeing, camping, swimming, and trail rides. Accommodations include furnished A-frame log-cabin rentals (rates start at $65 per night) and an RV park with full hookups and a primitive campground. No pets are allowed (in the cabins or leashed outside).

THE BEST OF MEMPHIS

Ask the average American what makes Memphis special, and he or she might cite Graceland, the mansion and final resting place of Elvis Presley. The city's musical influence is much deeper, of course, encompassing the discoveries of blues, rock 'n' roll, rockabilly, and soul. That unmistakable musical mojo may be the magnet that pulls visitors to Memphis, but there's much more to see and do. African-American history sites, fine-art museums, children's attractions, pork-barbecue joints, and the mighty Mississippi River leave lasting impressions of a laid-back Southern city that's unlike any other.

Things to Do   Soak up Memphis music. Tour tiny **Sun Studio,** and stand behind the microphone where Elvis, Johnny Cash, Carl Perkins, and Jerry Lee Lewis sang. Make a pilgrimage to the graffitied gates of **Graceland** and leave your own personal message for The King. Then dance your way through the **Stax Museum of American Soul Music** to funky grooves by Memphis legends Aretha Franklin, Sam & Dave, Isaac Hayes, Earth, Wind & Fire, and the Staples Singers.

Outdoor Pursuits   Play a few rounds at local hero Justin Timberlake's eco-friendly **Mirimichi** golf course, and then head downtown to relax on the grassy banks of the **Mississippi River.** Watch the barges push slowly southward, toward New Orleans and the Gulf of Mexico. Linger long enough, and you can ponder the golden sun setting on the flat Arkansas landscape on the other side of the wide, muddy water.

Eating & Drinking   Indulge in the city's favorite pastime: enjoying pork barbecue. It's as pervasive in Memphis as tacky Elvis souvenirs. So start at **The Rendezvous** and eat your way around town, sampling the sauce-slathered (wet) and spice-rubbed (dry) ribs and pulled-meat sandwiches at mom-and-pop places like **Payne's, A&R,** and **Cozy Corner.**

Nightlife & Entertainment   Do a little "Walking in Memphis," along the 3-block stretch of blues clubs and bars on legendary **Beale Street.** Then ditch the tourists for **Wild Bill's,** a real-deal juke joint off the beaten path. Bring your own booze, grab a seat, and surrender to the house band's hypnotic mix of soulful blues.

THE most unforgettable
MEMPHIS EXPERIENCES

○ **Remembering the Reverend Martin Luther King, Jr.:** Pause for a moment on the balcony of the Lorraine Motel to reflect on the life and legacy of the Reverend Martin Luther King, Jr., who was assassinated on this spot on April 4, 1968. Then consider the slain martyr's lasting impact on humanity as you explore the National Civil Rights Museum that was built around this tragic landmark. See p. 173.

○ **Reveling in Glorious Spring:** Stroll, bike, or drive through town with the car windows down to drink in the beauty of springtime in the South. Centuries-old oaks, flowering pink and white dogwoods, and giant magnolia trees loaded with fragrant blossoms are among spring's pleasures. The iris are in bloom, azalea bushes burst with color, and the weather is ideal—sunny and warm but not yet too humid. Enjoy it while it lasts.

○ **Getting Your First Glimpse of the Jungle Room:** Brace yourself for one of Graceland's cheesiest delights as you begin your tour of the elegant mansion. Politely marvel at the grandeur of the formal living rooms and the kitschy 1960s decor of the TV and billiards rooms, and then—wait for it—shield your eyes from the glaring gaudiness of it all as you're ushered into Elvis' hallowed, faux-Hawaiian Man Cave. See p. 164.

○ **Surrendering to the Blues:** After a long day of sightseeing or business, slip into B.B. King's Blues Club on Beale Street and grab a table for yourself and your friends. Place your order with the bartender and sit back as the city's best musicians and international headliners take the intimate stage for blistering, live blues sets that stretch deep into the night. See p. 103.

○ **Getting Sanctified at Rev. Al Green's Church:** From the pews of Full Gospel Tabernacle, as the gospel choir's impassioned cries shake the rafters and the robed Rev. Green, in trancelike concentration, implores God for mercy on your soul, go ahead: Give it up to your Higher Power, and hum along as Al softly sings "Amazing Grace." See p. 176.

THE most unforgettable
FOOD & DRINK EXPERIENCES

○ **Getting Used to Pork Barbecue Smoke:** Either you love it or you don't, but there's no escaping the hickory-tinged plumes of aromatic smoke that billow from the city's hundreds of barbecue joints. It's in the air. Everywhere.

○ **Giving In to Greasy Goodness:** Maybe you wouldn't want to eat fried chicken every day, but while you're in Memphis, tasting it is a must. Go to **Gus's** (p. 195) for the juicy, crisp-skinned fried chicken platters, and try **Uncle Lou's** (p. 205) for its spicy or honey-sweet versions of this timeless Southern favorite.

○ **Enjoying Soul Food:** Bring the family to the **Four Way Restaurant** and share good, home-style food and conversation over plates of pork chops, turnip greens, mashed potatoes, and macaroni and cheese. Have fun trying to decide whether to choose the banana pudding or the sweet potato pie for dessert. See p. 204.

- **Chowing Down on Burgers & Beer:** Begin with a round or two of cold beer, followed by a hearty, cooked-to-order hamburger and salty, hot french fries. Memphis pub grub at its best is as close as the nearest neighborhood **Huey's.** See p. 195.
- **Feeling Sophisticated:** "Gee, we're not in Memphis anymore" seems to be a common reaction for out-of-towners who realize there's more to Memphis than comfort food and pig meat. As you're savoring a sublime, multicourse meal with wine pairings at posh restaurants such as **Erling Jensen** (p. 199), **Iris** (p. 195), and **Chez Philippe** (p. 196), you'll discover what locals knew all along: The city's got culinary class.

THE best ACTIVITIES FOR FAMILIES

- **Riding the Trolley:** The clickety-clack of wheels on rails and the clang-clang of the antique trolley car bells delight young and old alike on slow-moving **Main Street Trolley** rides through downtown. Enjoy views of the Mississippi River and historic buildings and parks along the way. See p. 258.
- **Taking a Scavenger Hunt:** Get kids and preteens into the spirit of learning by giving them a checklist of objects to find at the **Pink Palace Mansion.** Watch them have fun finding Civil War–era medical instruments, the lock of President Andrew Jackson's hair, an antique dagger, and the shrunken head of an Ecuadoran Indian. See p. 174.
- **Visiting Panda Bears:** Enter the grand, Egyptian-themed gates of the **Memphis Zoo,** and then make a beeline for the China pavilion to see the wildly popular panda bears. As they munch bamboo stalks or frolic lazily in their habitats, you'll be unable to resist the adorableness of Ya Ya and Le Le. See p. 175.
- **Exploring Nature:** Dig in the dirt, go wading in shallow Critter Creek, or climb a treehouse at **Memphis Botanic Garden.** Kids can grab a friend or sibling and try out the two-seater wooden rope swing, and be on constant lookout for garden gnomes hiding in perennial beds and pine groves. See p. 177.
- **Playing Pretend:** Go grocery shopping with the kids in a lifelike market at the **Children's Museum of Memphis,** where youngsters can pluck products from shelves to place in their carts, and then scan them on a real cash register. Then cut the little ones loose to scale the colorful, kid-friendly Skyscraper or to pretend they're on a rescue mission as they climb inside the shiny red fire engine. See p. 179.

THE best FREE & DIRT CHEAP MEMPHIS

- **Watching the Peabody Duck March:** It's become a tourist cliché, but if you've never experienced it, there's nothing quite like the cheap thrill of watching as a posse of well-groomed ducks waddles out of the gilded elevator and marches up to the marble fountain in the lobby of the posh Peabody Hotel. See p. 232.
- **Roaming with the Buffalo:** Whether paddle boating on the lake, biking through wooded trails, or playing Frisbee golf with your dog, a visit to **Shelby Farms** may incite double takes when you realize there are real, live buffalo roaming the grassy fields. See p. 177.

- **Laughing at Tacky Souvenirs:** While scouring the old tabletop bins at **A. Schwab Dry Goods Store,** in business since 1876, you'll be tempted to buy all kinds of crazy stuff, from voodoo potions and velvet Elvis art to plus-size denim overalls, walking canes, and ugly hats. See p. 212.
- **Pondering the Afterlife:** Wandering through historic **Elmwood Cemetery,** you may feel sadness upon seeing mass graves for yellow fever victims of the 1870s, and bemusement at the ornate marble sculptures marking the resting places of prominent wealthy citizens. Beneath it all, find inspiration in the majestic grace of more than 1,500 trees, including oaks, maples, and magnolias. See p. 177.

THE best LOCAL EXPERIENCES

- **Attending a Redbirds Game:** See why Redbirds Stadium is regarded as one of the nation's best minor-league baseball parks while you're sitting in the stands on a warm summer night, and you can actually see all the on-field action without the benefit of a Jumbotron. See p. 185.
- **Hitting the Roof:** Join the young-adult, after-work crowd in downtown Memphis for warm-weather cocktail parties held on the rooftops of premier downtown hotels, including the **Madison Hotel** (p. 232) and **The Peabody** (p. 232). Drink up and dance to live bands as the sun sets on stunning views of Old Man River.
- **Getting Cultured:** Book your **Orpheum Theatre** tickets in advance for the best seats to performances by the critically acclaimed local ballet and opera companies and Broadway touring productions. Or check out a cinema classic during the popular summer series at this former movie palace. See p. 227.
- **Rooting for the Grizzlies:** Memphians take great pride in the dazzling FedEx Forum and in the city's first NBA team, the **Memphis Grizzlies.** Share their enthusiasm, and go with the frenzied post-game flow that ensues when the basketball team's on a winning streak. See p. 185.
- **Embracing the Greenline:** The antidote to all that decadent Southern food is the city's newest outdoor treasure, the extended hiking and bike trail known as The Greenline. Set out on foot, or rent your gear at **Shelby Farms,** and enjoy a healthy workout. Feel your temperature rising? See p. 177.

MEMPHIS IN DEPTH

M
emphis is just a few hours' drive from Nashville, but in many ways it seems worlds away. Though conservative and traditional, the city has spawned several of the most important musical forms of the 20th century—blues, rock 'n' roll, and soul. And although it has been unable to cash in on this musical heritage (at least to the profitable extent that Nashville has with country music), Memphis still seems like a scrappy underdog in its fight to proclaim musical superiority. Less progressive—or, some might say, polished—than Nashville, Memphis still proudly proclaims its significance as the *true* mecca of American music.

MEMPHIS TODAY

Memphis is primarily known for being the city where Graceland is located. Thirty-five years after the entertainer's death, Elvis is still King— Graceland remains the number one tourist attraction in the city. Equally worth visiting are such attractions as Sun Studio, where Elvis made his first recording; the Rock 'n' Soul Museum; and the Memphis Music Hall of Fame, which has displays on Elvis and many other local musicians who made major contributions to rock, soul, and blues music.

But how long can the Elvis craze sustain itself? A city needs diversity and an identity of its own. To that end, in the past few decades Memphis has made considerable progress. One of the greatest hurdles to overcome has been the legacy of racial tension that came to a head with the 1968 assassination here of Martin Luther King, Jr., and the rioting that ensued. Racial tensions are still frequently named as the city's foremost civic problem, even though the casual observer or visitor may not see any signs of these difficulties. Racial tensions have combined with post–World War II white flight to the suburbs, first to East Memphis, and even farther east in more recent years, to more affluent areas including Germantown, Cordova, and Collierville.

That's not to say that downtown and Midtown (Central Memphis) remain utterly abandoned. In fact, downtown has made great strides in the past decade, with a flurry of new developments breathing fresh life into the area and progressive-minded residents reclaiming beautiful old mansions and bungalows. Others have opted for an urban lifestyle in new downtown apartments and condos that have slowly sprung up. Unfortunately, the Great Recession has taken a visible toll, and today grand ideas like the mixed-use Peabody Place retail and entertainment complex sit largely vacant. But downtown Memphis is still the heart and soul of the city, and it has a lot to offer tourists who can keep its ongoing ups and downs in perspective.

Beale Street, billed as the Birthplace of the Blues, is as vibrant and popular as ever. You won't find a lot of locals here unless they're entertaining out-of-town guests, but Beale Street is chock-full of nightclubs offering live music, bars, restaurants, and souvenir shops playing to party-minded people in search of a good time.

LOOKING BACK AT MEMPHIS

GROWTH OF A RIVER PORT The town of Memphis was officially incorporated in 1826, and for the next 2 decades it grew slowly. In 1845, the establishment of a naval yard in Memphis gave the town a new importance. Twelve years later, the Memphis and Charleston Railroad linked Memphis to Charleston, South Carolina, on the Atlantic coast. With the Mississippi Delta region beginning just south of Memphis, the city played an important role as the main shipping port for cotton grown in the delta. This role as river port, during the heyday of river transportation in the mid–19th century, gave Memphis a link and kinship with other river cities to the north. With its importance to the cotton trade of the Deep South and its river connections to the Mississippi port cities of the Midwest, Memphis developed some of the characteristics of both regions, creating a city not wholly of the South or the Midwest, but rather, a city in between.

In the years before the Civil War began, the people of Memphis were very much in favor of secession, but it was only a few short months after the outbreak of the war that Memphis fell to Union troops. Both the Union and the Confederacy had seen the importance of Memphis as a supply base, and yet the Confederates had been unable to defend their city—on June 6, 1862, steel-nosed ram boats easily overcame the Confederate fleet guarding Memphis. The city quickly became a major smuggling center as merchants sold to both the North and the South.

Within 2 years of the war's end, tragedy struck Memphis. Cholera and yellow fever epidemics swept through the city, killing hundreds of residents. This was only the first, and the mildest, of such epidemics to plague Memphis over the next 11 years. In 1872 and 1878, yellow fever epidemics killed thousands of people and caused nearly half the city's population to flee. In the wake of these devastating outbreaks of the mosquito-borne disease, the city was left bankrupt and nearly abandoned.

However, some people remained in Memphis and had faith that the city would one day regain its former importance. One of those individuals was Robert Church, a one-time slave, who bought real estate from people who were fleeing the yellow fever plague. He later became the South's first African-American millionaire. In 1899, on a piece of land near the corner of Beale and Fourth streets, Church established a park and auditorium where African Americans could gather in public.

CIVIL RIGHTS MOVEMENT In the years following the Civil War, freed slaves from around the South flocked to Memphis in search of jobs. Other African-American professionals, educated in the North, also came to Memphis to establish new businesses. The center for this growing community was Beale Street. With all manner of businesses, from lawyers' and doctors' offices to bars and houses of prostitution, Beale Street was a lively community. The music that played in the juke joints and honky-tonks had its roots in traditional musical styles of Africa. During the 19th century, these musical traditions (brought to America by slaves) went through an interpretation and translation in the cotton fields and churches—the only places where African Americans could gather at that time. By the first decade of the 20th century, this music had acquired a name: the blues.

Blues music, the first truly American musical style, was the expression of more than a century of struggle and suffering by African Americans. By the middle of the 20th century, that long suffering had been given another voice—the civil rights movement. One by one, school segregation and other discriminatory laws and practices of the South were challenged. Equal treatment and equal rights with whites was the goal of the civil rights movement, and the movement's greatest champion and spokesman was Dr. Martin Luther King, Jr., whose assassination in Memphis threw the city into the national limelight in April 1968.

In the early months of 1968, the sanitation workers of Memphis, most of whom were African Americans, went on strike. In early April, Dr. King came to Memphis to lead a march by the striking workers; he stayed at the Lorraine Motel, just south of downtown. On April 4, the day the march was to be held, Dr. King stepped out onto the balcony of the motel and was gunned down by an assassin's bullet. Dr. King's murder did not, as perhaps had been hoped, end the civil rights movement. Today, the Lorraine Motel has become the National Civil Rights Museum. The museum preserves the room where Dr. King was staying the day he was assassinated and includes many evocative exhibits on the history of the civil rights movement.

By the time of Dr. King's murder, downtown Memphis was a classic example of urban decay. The city's more affluent citizens had moved to the suburbs in the post–World War II years, and the inner city had quickly become an area of abandoned buildings and empty storefronts. However, beginning in the 1970s, a growing desire to restore life to downtown Memphis saw renovation projects undertaken. By the 1980s, the renewal process was well underway, and the 1990s saw a continuation of this slow but steady revitalization of downtown. The economic downturn of the past 5 years eroded some of these gains, however, prompting the closure of several high-profile restaurants and retail developments. But new shops and eateries continue to open as business owners try to rebound.

The blues, rock 'n' roll, and soul are sounds that defined Memphis music, and together these styles have made a name for Memphis all over the world. Never mind that the blues is no longer as popular as it once was, that Memphis long ago had its title of rock-'n'-roll capital usurped (by Cleveland, home of the Rock and Roll Hall of Fame), and that soul music evolved into other styles. Memphis continues to be important to music lovers as the city from which these sounds first emanated.

BEALE STREET It was here, on Beale Street, that black musicians began to fuse together the various aspects of the traditional music of the Mississippi Delta. In 1909, one of these musicians, a young bandleader named William Christopher Handy, was commissioned to write a campaign song for E. H. "Boss" Crump, who was running for mayor of Memphis. Crump won the election, and "Boss Crump's Blues" became a local hit. W. C. Handy later published his tune under the title "Memphis Blues." With the publication of this song, Handy started a musical revolution that continues to this day. The blues, which developed at about the same time that jazz was first being played down in New Orleans, would later give rise to both rock 'n' roll and soul music.

Beale Street became a center for musicians, who flocked to the area to learn the blues and showcase their own musical styles. Over the next 4 decades, Beale Street produced many of the country's most famous blues musicians. Among these was a young man named Riley King, who first won praise during an amateur music contest.

In the 1940s, King became known as the Beale Street "Blues Boy," the initials of which he incorporated into his stage name when he began calling himself B.B. King. Today, B.B. King's Blues Club is Beale Street's most popular nightclub. A couple of times a year, King performs at the club, and the rest of the year blues bands keep up the Beale Street tradition. Other musicians who developed their style and their first followings on Beale Street include Furry Lewis, Muddy Waters, Albert King, Bobby "Blue" Bland, Alberta Hunter, and Memphis Minnie McCoy.

By the time B.B. King got his start on Beale Street, the area was beginning to lose its importance. The Great Depression shut down a lot of businesses on the street, and many never reopened. By the 1960s, there was talk of bulldozing the entire area to make way for an urban-renewal project. However, in the 1970s, an interest in restoring old Beale Street developed. Beginning in 1980, the city of Memphis, together with business investors, began renovating the old buildings between Second and Fourth streets. New clubs and restaurants opened, and Beale Street once again became Memphis's main entertainment district. Today pure blues music is harder to hear than it once was, as cover bands playing well-known Sun and Stax hits for tourists tend to dominate the street.

HERE COMES THE KING   From the earliest days of Beale Street's musical popularity, whites visited the street's primarily black clubs. However, it wasn't until the late 1940s and early 1950s that a few adventurous white musicians began incorporating into their own music the earthy sounds and lyrics they heard on Beale Street. One of these musicians was a young man named Elvis Presley.

In the early 1950s, Sun Studio owner Sam Phillips began to record such Beale Street blues legends as B.B. King, Howlin' Wolf, Muddy Waters, and Little Milton, but his consumer market was limited to the African-American population. Phillips was searching for a way to take the blues to a mainstream (read: white) audience, and a new sound was what he needed. That new sound showed up at his door in 1954 in the form of a young delivery-truck driver named Elvis Presley, who, according to legend, had dropped in at Sun Studio to record a song as a birthday present for his mother.

Phillips knew that he had found what he was looking for. Within a few months of Elvis's visit to Sun Studio, three other musicians—Carl Perkins, Jerry Lee Lewis, and Johnny Cash—showed up independently of one another. Each brought his own interpretation of the crossover sound between the blues and country (or "hillbilly") music. The sounds these four musicians crafted soon became known as rockabilly music, the foundation of rock 'n' roll. Roy Orbison would also get his start here at Sun Studio.

ROCK 'N' ROLL 'N' SOUL, TOO   In the early 1960s, Memphis once again entered the popular-music limelight when Stax/Volt Records gave the country its first soul music. Otis Redding, Isaac Hayes, Booker T. and the MGs, and Carla Thomas were among the musicians who got their start at this Memphis recording studio.

Some 10 years after Sun Studio made musical history, British bands such as the Beatles and the Rolling Stones latched onto the blues and rockabilly music and began exporting their take on this American music back across the Atlantic. With the music usurped by the British invasion, the importance of Memphis was quickly forgotten. Today, Memphis is no longer the musical innovator it once was, but it still holds cache with pop and rap music fans, who can point to superstar Justin Timberlake and Three 6 Mafia as hometown heroes.

Fame isn't everything, however. And the bottom line is that Memphis clubs are crawling with talented, relatively unknown musicians just as deserving of appreciative audiences as the aforementioned icons. Thankfully, musicians both young and old are keeping alive the music that put the city on the map.

THE LAY OF THE LAND

Located at the far western end of Tennessee, Memphis sits on a bluff overlooking the Mississippi River. Directly across the river lies Arkansas, and only a few miles to the south is the state of Mississippi. The area, which was long known as the "fourth Chickasaw bluff," was chosen as a strategic site by Native Americans as well as French, Spanish, and finally American explorers and soldiers. The most important reason for choosing this site for the city was that the top of the bluff was above the high-water mark of the Mississippi River and thus was safe from floods. Although Memphis started out as an important Mississippi River port, urban sprawl has carried the city's business centers ever farther east—so much so that the Big Muddy has become less a reason for being than simply a way of distinguishing Tennessee from Arkansas.

MEMPHIS IN POP CULTURE

Authors most often associated with Memphis and the Mississippi Delta are an interesting assortment of people. There's Civil War historian Shelby Foote, of course, and literary heavyweight William Faulkner, whose stories of the people and characters of a segregated South are indelibly etched in American pop culture. The great playwright Tennessee Williams also spent formative years in Memphis, and he wrote and produced early works here. But let's face it: No other writer put Memphis on the pop-culture map in a bigger way than John Grisham did in the 1990s.

The former Memphis-area attorney wrote a string of bestselling legal thrillers, including *The Firm*. When Tom Cruise (and then-wife Nicole Kidman, who now calls Nashville home with country-singer hubby Keith Urban) came to Memphis to star in the book's film version, directed by Sydney Pollack, the city was completely star struck. Screaming fans waited on street corners for a glimpse of the famous actor.

DATELINE

1541 Hernando de Soto views Mississippi River from fourth Chickasaw bluff, site of today's Memphis.

1682 La Salle claims Mississippi Valley for France.

1739 French governor of Louisiana orders a fort built on fourth Chickasaw bluff.

1795 Manuel Gayoso, in order to expand Spanish lands in North America, erects Fort San Fernando on Mississippi River.

1797 Americans build Fort Adams on ruins of Fort San Fernando, and the Spanish flee to the far side of the river.

1818 Chickasaw Nation cedes western Tennessee to the United States.

1819 Town of Memphis founded.

1826 Memphis is incorporated.

1840s Cheap land makes for boom times in Memphis.

1857 Memphis and Charleston Railroad completed, linking the Atlantic and the Mississippi.

Locales featured in some of the movie's scenes became tourist hot spots, and a cottage industry sprang up to promote the city's association with the Memphis-area film shoots that followed.

Among the many Grisham films, some are more memorable than others. Susan Sarandon was terrific in *The Client.* Joel Schumacher directed that film, which co-starred Mary Louise Parker and Tommy Lee Jones. Matt Damon and Danny DeVito did star turns in *The Rainmaker,* and Matthew McConaughey became an overnight sensation after his first big starring role in *A Time to Kill.* Less commercially and critically successful was *The Chamber,* with Gene Hackman playing a death row inmate.

There have been several significant non-Grisham movies filmed here as well. European filmmaker Milos Forman chose to film *The People Vs. Larry Flynt* in Memphis. Needless to say, co-stars Woody Harrelson and Courtney Love provided loads of gossipy fodder during their days on location shooting this biopic about the porn pioneer's court cases. Sean Penn and Naomi Watts came to town for the gritty drama *21 Grams.* And director Craig Brewer's *Hustle and Flow,* about an aspiring rapper played by Terrence Howard, drew rave reviews—and even nabbed an Academy Award for local rappers Three 6 Mafia, who were featured in the film's soundtrack. Brewer's follow-up, *Black Snake Moan,* didn't rise to the same level of acclaim as *Hustle and Flow,* but the sultry drama is still one for the collective Memphis scrapbook. It features Samuel L. Jackson, Christina Ricci, and Justin Timberlake, who grew up in Millington, just north of the Memphis city limits.

EATING & DRINKING IN MEMPHIS

Memphis's barbecue smoke is inescapable. It billows from chimneys all across the city, and though it is present all year long, it makes its biggest impact in those months when people have their car windows open. Drivers experience an inexplicable, almost Pavlovian response. They begin to salivate, their eyes glaze over, and they follow the smoke to its source—a down-home barbecue joint.

1862 Memphis falls to Union troops but becomes an important smuggling center.

1870s Several yellow fever epidemics leave the city almost abandoned.

1879 Memphis declares bankruptcy, and its charter is revoked.

1880s Memphis rebounds.

1890s Memphis becomes largest hardwood market in the world, attracting African Americans seeking to share in city's boom times.

1892 First bridge across Mississippi south of St. Louis opens in Memphis.

1893 Memphis regains its city charter.

1899 Church Park and Auditorium, the city's first park and entertainment center for African Americans, are built.

1909 W. C. Handy, a Beale Street bandleader, becomes the father of the blues when he writes first blues song for mayoral candidate E. H. "Boss" Crump.

continues

In a region obsessed with pork barbecue, Memphis lays claim to the title of being the pork-barbecue capital of the world. Non-Southerners may need a primer: Memphis barbecue is pork that has been barbecued over a wood fire, then pulled off the bone and chopped, to be piled onto plates or buns with (or without) your favorite hot sauces.

Barbecued ribs are a particular Memphis specialty; these come either dry-cooked or wet-cooked. If you order your ribs dry-cooked, they come coated with a powdered spice mix and it's up to you to apply the sauce; but if you order wet-cooked, the ribs will have been basted in a sauce. Barbecue is traditionally served with a side of creamy coleslaw and perhaps baked beans or potato salad. In a pulled-pork-shoulder sandwich, the coleslaw tops the sandwich as a lettuce replacement. **Corky's Ribs & BBQ** (p. 201) is the undisputed king of Memphis barbecue, while the **Rendezvous** (p. 193) is famed for its dry-cooked ribs.

The city's other traditional fare is good old-fashioned American food—here, as in Nashville, known as "meat-and-three," which refers to the three side vegetables that you get with whatever type of meat you happen to order. While this is very simple food, in the best meat-and-three restaurants your vegetables are likely to be fresh-cooked (often with pork) and plentiful. Perhaps because of the Southern affinity for traditions, Memphians, both young and old, flock to meat-and-three restaurants for meals just like Mom used to fix.

What if you don't like barbecue or you don't eat meat? Relax. Memphis has a diverse dining scene that includes top-tier gourmet restaurants, moderately priced cafes, and hundreds of ethnic eateries serving everything from sushi and samosas to tagines and tortillas. Burgers, steaks, seafood, pizza, and vegetarian options are abundant in every area of the city.

Yet be forewarned: There's no escaping that pervasive aroma of sizzling pig meat.

WHEN TO GO

Summer is the peak tourist season in Memphis. Unless you're specifically visiting Graceland for Elvis Week in August, you might want to avoid traveling during this time, when hotels sell out and prices go through the roof.

1916 Nation's first self-service grocery store opens in Memphis.

1925 Peabody hotel built. Tom Lee rescues 23 people from sinking steamboat.

1928 Orpheum Theatre opens.

1940 B.B. King plays for first time on Beale Street, at an amateur music contest.

1952 Jackie Brenston's "Rocket 88," considered the first rock-'n'-roll recording, is released by Memphis's Sun Studio.

1955 Elvis Presley records his first hit record at Sun Studio.

1958 Stax Records, a leader in the soul music industry of the 1960s, founded.

1968 Dr. Martin Luther King, Jr., assassinated at Lorraine Motel.

1977 Elvis Presley dies at Graceland, his home on the south side of Memphis.

1983 Renovated Beale Street reopens as tourist attraction and nightlife district.

1991 National Civil Rights Museum opens in former Lorraine Motel.

1992 Memphis elects its first African-American mayor.

Summer is also when both Nashville and Memphis experience their worst weather. During July and August, and often in September, temperatures can hover around 100°F, with humidity at close to 100%. (Can you say "muggy"?) Spring and fall, however, last for several months and both are quite pleasant. Days are often warm and nights cool, though during these two seasons the weather changes, so bring a variety of clothes. Heavy rains can hit any time of year, and if you spend more than 3 or 4 days in town, you can almost bet on seeing some rain. Winters can be cold, with daytime temperatures staying below freezing, and snow is not unknown.

Average Temperature & Rainfall in Memphis

	JAN	FEB	MAR	APR	MAY	JUNE	JULY	AUG	SEPT	OCT	NOV	DEC
Temp. (°F)	40	45	53	63	71	79	83	81	74	63	52	44
Temp. (°C)	4	7	11	17	21	26	28	27	23	17	11	6
Rainfall (in.)	4.7	4.5	5.2	5.6	4.9	3.9	3.9	3.4	3.2	2.9	4.8	5.3

Memphis Calendar of Events

JANUARY

Elvis Presley's Birthday Tribute, Graceland. International gathering of Presley fans celebrate the birthday of The King (© **800/238-2000;** www.elvis.com). Around January 8.

Martin Luther King, Jr.'s, Birthday, citywide. Events to memorialize Dr. King take place on the nationally observed holiday (© **901/521-9699;** www.civilrightsmuseum. org). Mid-January.

FEBRUARY

Beale Street Zydeco Music Festival, along Beale Street. More than 20 acts perform during this 2-day event (© **901/529-0999;** www. bealestreetmerchants.com). Mid-February.

Regions Morgan Keegan Tennis Championship, Racquet Club of Memphis. World-class players compete in this famous tour event (© **901/765-4400;** www.memphis tennis.com). Mid- to late February.

APRIL

Dr. Martin Luther King, Jr., Memorial March, downtown. This somber event remembers the assassination of the civil rights leader (© **901/525-2458**). April 4.

Memphis International Film Festival, Midtown. Filmmakers and cinema lovers converge in Memphis (© **901/273-0014;** www. onlocationmemphis.org). Second week in April.

1993 Two movies based on John Grisham novels, *The Firm* and *The Client,* are filmed in Memphis.

1998 Memphis booms with $1.4 billion in expansion and renovation projects.

2000 Memphis Redbirds baseball team plays its first season in new, $68.5-million AutoZone Park downtown.

2001 Grizzlies move to Memphis, becoming city's first NBA team.

2002 Groundbreaking begins on FedExForum downtown.

2003 Sun Studio founder Sam Phillips dies.

2003 Soulsville USA: Stax Museum of American Soul Music opens in South Memphis.

2004 FedExForum basketball arena and concert venue opens at foot of Beale Street.

2005 Films including *Hustle & Flow, Forty Shades of Blue,* and *Walk the Line* are shot in Memphis.

2006 Craig Brewer's *Black Snake Moan* is shot in Memphis.

continues

Africa in April Cultural Awareness Festival, downtown. The multiday festival showcases African music, dance, theater, exhibits, arts, and crafts (☎ **901/947-2133;** www.africainapril.org). Third week in April.

MAY

Memphis in May International Festival, citywide. More than one million visitors attend this month-long event that celebrates a different country each year with musical, cultural, and artistic festivities. Highlights are the Memphis in May **Beale Street Music Festival** (first weekend in May), the **World Championship Barbecue Cooking Contest** (mid-May), and the **Sunset Symphony** (last weekend of May). Call ☎ **901/525-4611** or visit www.memphisinmay.org. Entire month of May.

Blues Music Awards and International Blues Competition, Memphis Cook Convention Center. The nation's premier blues music awards program is held in the city where W. C. Handy made the genre famous (☎ **901/527-2583,** ext. 12; www.blues.org). Early May.

FedEx Cup St. Jude Classic, Tournament Players Club at Southwind. A benefit for St. Jude Children's Research Hospital, this is a PGA event (☎ **901/748-0534;** www.stjudeclassic.com). Late May to early June.

JUNE

Germantown Charity Horse Show, Germantown Horse Show Arena. This is a 4-day competition in which equestrians compete for prizes (☎ **901/754-0009;** www.gchs.org). Second week in June.

JULY

Blues on the Bluff, downtown. Volunteer- and member-supported radio station WEVL-FM presents two concerts on the grounds of the National Ornamental Metal Museum, overlooking the Mississippi River (☎ **901/528-0560;** www.wevl.org). Late July and early August.

AUGUST

Elvis Week, Graceland and citywide. Festival commemorating the influences of Elvis (☎ **800/238-2000;** www.elvis.com). Second week in August.

SEPTEMBER

Beale Street Labor Day Music Festival, Beale Street. Memphis musicians are featured Labor Day (and night) in restaurants and clubs throughout the Beale Street district (☎ **901/526-0110**). Labor Day weekend.

Memphis Music & Heritage Festival, Center for Southern Folklore. Regional food, music, and art are included in this celebration of the diversity of the South (☎ **901/525-3655;** www.southernfolklore.com). Early September.

2008 Isaac Hayes, Memphis soul singer, dies at age 65.	2010 The 7-mile Shelby Farms Greenline opens to bike riders, joggers, and walkers.
2009 *Memphis,* a musical about the birth of rock 'n' roll, opens on Broadway.	2011 The Great American Steamboat Company announces it will launch overnight cruises along the Mississippi River, with Memphis as its headquarters.
2009 Hometown hero Justin Timberlake opens a golf course, Mirimichi, in the Memphis area.	
2010 Memphis College of Art purchases and renovates a building in the South Main Historic Arts District, bringing more than 100 graduate students and faculty downtown.	

Cooper-Young Festival, Midtown. The popular neighborhood festival features food, arts, crafts, and family activities (📞 **901/276-7222;** www.cooperyoungfestival.com). Mid-September.

Southern Heritage Classic, Midtown. Classic college football rivalry at the Liberty Bowl Memorial Stadium (📞 **901/398-6655;** www.southernheritageclassic.com). Mid-Sept.

OCTOBER

River Arts Festival, South Main Historic District. Painters, jewelers, sculptors, woodworkers, and other artists and musicians converge on the South Main Historic District in downtown Memphis for this high-quality, juried festival (📞 **901/826-3629;** www.river artsfestmemphis.org). Late October.

NOVEMBER

Freedom Awards, downtown. Human rights activists are honored by the National Civil Rights Museum (📞 **901/521-9699;** www. civilrightsmuseum.org) with public lectures and other ceremonies. Past recipients include Oprah Winfrey, Bono, Colin Powell, and Bill Clinton. Late October or early November.

DECEMBER

AutoZone Liberty Bowl Football Classic, Liberty Bowl Memorial Stadium. Intercollegiate game that's nationally televised (📞 **901/274-4600;** www.libertybowl.org). Late December.

Bury Your Blues Blowout on Beale, Beale Street. New Year's Eve celebration both inside the clubs and outside on Beale Street (📞 **901/526-0110**). December 31.

MEMPHIS NEIGHBORHOODS & SUGGESTED ITINERARIES

Many of Memphis's must-see sites are located downtown and in nearby South Memphis. Therefore, it's feasible to tackle a good chunk of the city's best in a single, action-packed day. As with any destination, the seasons and your personal interests will dictate how you proceed. Besides musical attractions, Memphis has much to offer in terms of culture and history. In the spring, summer, and fall, take advantage of the longer days and get outdoors to enjoy some of the city's many parks and natural attractions. Of course, rainy or wintry days make museums, galleries, and antiques shops more practical diversions. Fortunately, most of the city's popular attractions may be enjoyed during any time of year.

When you hit town, you may be surprised, and even a bit baffled, by Memphis. The city is spread out, so getting around can be confusing and frustrating at first. Read this chapter, and your first hours in town should be less bewildering.

ORIENTATION
Visitor Information

The city's main visitor information center, located downtown at the base of Jefferson Street, is the **Tennessee State Welcome Center,** 119 N. Riverside Dr. (© **901/543-6757**). It's open daily 24 hours but staffed only between 8am and 7pm (until 8pm in the summer months). Browse the thousands of brochures and flyers here, and take your camera or smartphone: Inside this large information center, you'll find soaring, photo-worthy statues of both Elvis and B.B. King.

At the airport, you'll find information boards with telephone numbers for contacting hotels, as well as numbers for other helpful services. Other visitor centers are at Elvis Presley Boulevard just north of Graceland, and off of Interstate 40 just east of the Memphis city limits.

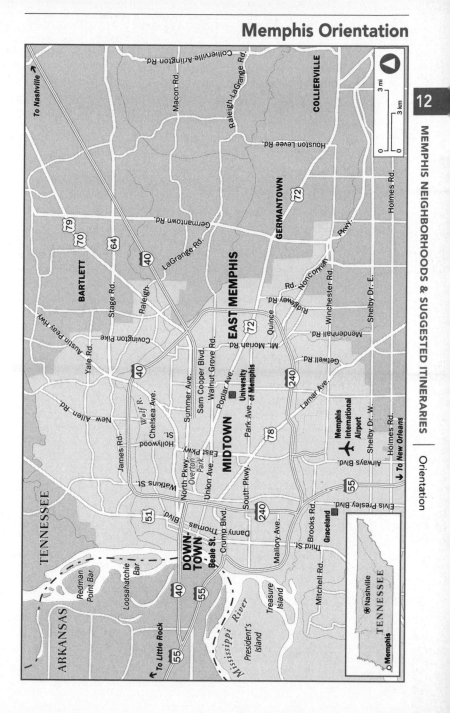

Go, Cat, Go!

Elvis Presley finally has his own Tennessee license plate. Graceland unveiled the automotive honor in February 2008, placing the very first plate, hot off the assembly line, onto the King's purple 1956 Eldorado Cadillac. The white plates feature Elvis's signature, along with a color caricature of the '50s-era Elvis playing a guitar. Profits from the plates benefit the Elvis Presley Memorial Trauma Center at the Regional Medical Center. "The Med," as it's known, is a major Memphis hospital with the only Level-1 trauma center in a five-state region.

City Layout

Memphis, built on the east bank of the **Mississippi River,** lies just above the Mississippi state line. Consequently, growth has proceeded primarily to the east and, to a lesser extent, to the north. The inexorable sprawl of the suburbs has pushed the limits of the metropolitan area far to the east, and today the area known as **East Memphis** is the city's business and cultural center. Despite the fact that the city has a fairly small and compact downtown area, the sprawl of recent years has made getting around difficult for residents and visitors alike. Traffic congestion on main east-west avenues is bad throughout the day, so you're usually better off taking the interstate around the outskirts of the city if you're trying to cross town.

In general, the city is laid out on a grid with a north-south axis. However, there are many exceptions, including downtown, which was laid out with "streets" parallel to the river and "avenues" running perpendicular to the river. Throughout the city you'll find that, for the most part, avenues run east-west and streets run north-south.

MAIN ARTERIES & STREETS   Memphis is circled by **I-40,** which loops around the north side of the city, and **I-240,** which rings the south side. **Poplar Avenue** and **Sam Cooper Boulevard/North Parkway** are the city's main east-west arteries. Poplar, heavily lined with businesses, is narrow, congested, and accident-prone. If you don't want to take the interstate, **Sam Cooper Boulevard** is an alternative route into downtown, as is **Central Avenue** between Goodlett Road in the east and Lamar Avenue in the west. **Union Avenue** is the dividing line between the north and south sides of the city. Other important **east-west roads** include Summer Avenue and Park Avenue. Major **north-south arteries** include (from downtown heading eastward) Third Street/U.S. 61, I-240, Elvis Presley Boulevard/U.S. 51, Airways Boulevard/East Parkway, and Mendenhall Road. Lamar Avenue is another important road.

Out in **East Memphis,** the main east-west arteries are Poplar Avenue and Winchester Road. The main north-south arteries are Perkins Road/Perkins Road Extended, Mendenhall Road, Hickory Hill Road, and Germantown Road.

FINDING AN ADDRESS   Besides going online to find maps to your destination (or, better yet, using a GPS to indicate your route), your second-best bet for finding an address in Memphis is to call the place first and ask for directions or the name of the nearest main cross street. Though address numbers increase the farther you get from downtown, they do not increase along each block in an orderly fashion. It is nearly impossible to determine how many blocks out an address will be. However,

Movie Mogul

Tom Hanks played a dedicated over-night delivery pilot in the film *Castaway*, which included scenes filmed at the world headquarters for FedEx in Memphis. Fred Smith, the company's founder, has a film production company that has done movies including *My Dog Skip; The Sisterhood of the Traveling Pants; Racing Stripes; Insomnia*; and *Dude, Where's My Car?* His daughter, Molly Smith, was also a co-producer on Hillary Swank's 2007 romantic comedy *P.S. I Love You*. That film's supporting cast included Kathy Bates, a former Memphis resident and Academy Award–winning actress.

there are some general guidelines to get you in the vicinity of where you're going. If an address is in the hundreds or lower, you should be downtown. If the address is an avenue or another east-west road in the 2000-to-4000 range, you'll likely find it in Midtown; if the number is in the 5000-to-7000 range, you should be out in East Memphis. If the address is on a street, it will likely have a north or south prefix included. Union Avenue is the dividing line between north and south.

STREET MAPS Because the streets of Memphis can seem a bit baffling at times, you'll definitely need a good map. The **Tennessee State Welcome Center,** 119 N. Riverside Dr. (© **901/543-6757**), offers a simple, free map; you can also buy a more detailed one at any bookstore, pharmacy, or gas station. If you arrive at the airport and rent a car, the rental company will give you a basic map that will at least get you to your hotel or to the information center. Most hotels will also give you a free map at check-in, to help you navigate your way around the city.

If you happen to be a member of **AAA,** you can get free maps of Memphis and the rest of Tennessee either from your local AAA office or from the Memphis office at 5138 Park Ave., Memphis, TN 38117 (© **901/761-5371**); it's open Monday to Friday 9am to 6pm.

The Neighborhoods in Brief

More important than neighborhoods in Memphis are the city's general divisions. These major divisions are how the city defines itself.

Downtown The oldest part of the city, downtown is constructed on the banks of the Mississippi River. After years of efforts toward revitalization, the area saw a boom in development about 15 years ago. However, the recent recession has been a setback, causing many of these new businesses to close. Still, there are scattered openings of new restaurants and shops, too. **Beale Street** remains the city's main entertainment district. Elsewhere downtown, interspersed with the vacant storefronts, are scores of great restaurants, nightspots, and cultural attractions. Unchanged, however, are the breathtaking views of the Mississippi River.

Midtown/Central Memphis This is primarily a residential area, though it's also known for its hospitals, which are themselves collectively known as the Medical Center district. Though a far cry from bustling Beale Street, the **Overton Square** area—once the city's top entertainment district—isn't what it once was. Still, it's where the professional theater companies are located, and there are a few excellent restaurants here, including Restaurant Iris. South of Overton Square, you'll find the proudly Bohemian **Cooper-Young neighborhood**—basically a single intersection with trendy cafes and the city's best and oldest independent bookstore,

Burke's. Midtown is also where you will find lush, heavily wooded **Overton Park,** which envelops the Memphis Zoo, the Memphis Brooks Museum of Art, and the prestigious Memphis College of Art.

East Memphis Heading still farther east from downtown brings you to East Memphis, which lies roughly on either side of I-240 on the east side of the city. From downtown, take Poplar Avenue to get there. It's a maddeningly busy, narrow, and traffic-choked multilane corridor, but it's still the shortest distance between the two points. In East Memphis you'll find malls and strip shopping centers, restaurants, office complexes, and the best hotel options for families and business travelers.

THE BEST OF MEMPHIS IN 1 DAY

Today you will get a taste of the musical legends that put Memphis on the map at the city's best music museums before getting a chance to reflect on the sociopolitical context of the 1950s. Start your day where rock 'n' roll was born: at Sun Studio.

1 Sun Studio ★★

Start your day where it all began: In the early 1950s, a shy teenage truck driver named Elvis Presley sauntered into Sam Phillips's tiny recording studio, asked to cut a birthday song for his mama, and ultimately launched the birth of rock 'n' roll. See p. 170.

2 Soulsville USA: The Stax Museum of American Soul Music ★★★

Albert King, Al Green, Earth, Wind & Fire, Isaac Hayes, and the Staples Singers are just a handful of the musical greats whose inspiring stories unfold in this rousing, interactive museum. The funky music reverberating throughout will make you want to sing, dance, stomp, and shout. See p. 169.

3 Four Way Restaurant 🍴 ★★★

After getting funkdafied by the vibes at Stax, head down the block and hang with the locals at this family-oriented soul food restaurant. Crispy, piping-hot fried chicken, turnip greens, candied yams, and corn bread with butter are the perfect preludes to silky lemon meringue pie. But there's a lot of other comfort food too. 998 Mississippi Blvd. 📞 **901/507-1519.** See p. 204.

4 National Civil Rights Museum ★★★

After spending the morning rocking to the sounds of Memphis music, put some social and political context behind what you've seen and heard. The absorbing and deeply moving National Civil Rights Museum traces the cruel history of slavery and racial discrimination in the American South. See p. 173.

5 South Main Street Arts District

Walk north back toward Beale Street, window-shopping at boutiques and stepping inside cozy art galleries that are beginning to emerge in this revitalized historic district.

6 Beale Street ★

This legendary strip, revered the world over as the birthplace of the blues, can be a rowdy, neon boozefest after dark. But during the day, it's a sea of curious tourists taking pictures, listening to live music at the outdoor W. C. Handy Park, and shopping for souvenirs. Join them. A. Schwab's, a 135-year-old dry goods store, has the best bargains around. (Sadly, after being in the Schwab family for over 100 years, this beloved landmark was recently purchased by a group of private investors.) See p. 164.

7 Blues City Cafe 🍵

Grab a bite at this juke joint and diner, which is my pick as the best of the Beale Street eats. Spicy tamales, lip-smackin' slabs of pork barbecue ribs, cold beer, burgers, and rich gumbo are on the menu. With its weather-beaten booths and rural-Mississippi shack-inspired decor, the mojo here is laid-back. 138 Beale St. © 901/526-3637. See p. 192.

8 Main Street Trolley

Take a ride on one of Memphis's antique restored trolley cars. They're old, they're creaky, their hard wooden seats are uncomfortable, and they're slow. But for a dollar or two you can sit back, relax, and ride the clanging, cumbersome streetcars from one end of downtown to the other, getting glimpses of the Pyramid, the Mississippi River, and other local landmarks. See p. 258.

9 Center for Southern Folklore

Step inside the one-of-a-kind Center for Southern Folklore. Part coffeehouse, part outsider and folk-art gallery, and part intimate performance space, the center is a beloved, locally owned nonprofit that celebrates the region's rich diversity. See p. 217.

THE BEST OF MEMPHIS IN 2 DAYS

Okay, you're goin' to Graceland. If you're an Elvis Presley zealot, you probably couldn't wait until Day 2 to head to the home of the King, so you've already tried to squeeze it into Day 1. Fair enough. True fans should not miss seeing his homey (in a *Beverly Hillbillies* sort of way) mansion and taking the complete tour of all that's offered here. Tourists with no more than a mild interest in Elvis, though, might want to skip the full shebang and do a simple drive-by of the place instead. From here, you'll head back to Midtown and East Memphis for some fine art interspersed with flora and fauna. Cap off your day of critters and culture with a little rest and relaxation in the hip Cooper-Young neighborhood.

1 Graceland ★★

The blue-and-white living room where he and Priscilla entertained guests. The mirrored, yellow TV room where Elvis liked to unwind. His paisley pool room. The Jungle Room! You'll see it all and more on a tour of the mansion where Elvis lived—and where he died. Across the street from the house, you can tour his Austin Powers–ish airplanes, watch Elvis movies, and even admire his car collection. See p. 164.

Suggested Memphis Itineraries

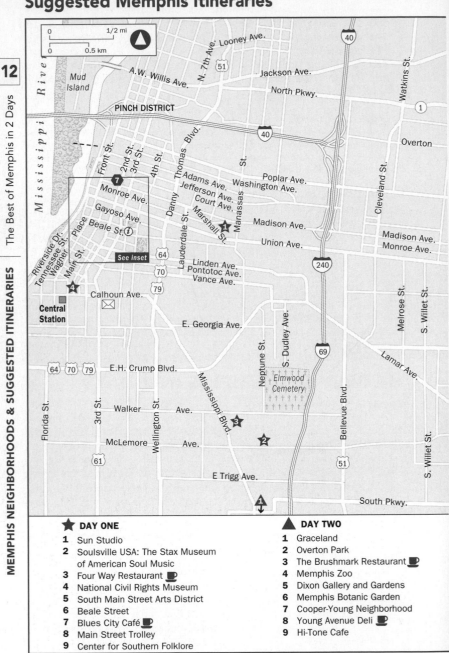

★ **DAY ONE**

1 Sun Studio
2 Soulsville USA: The Stax Museum of American Soul Music
3 Four Way Restaurant ☕
4 National Civil Rights Museum
5 South Main Street Arts District
6 Beale Street
7 Blues City Café ☕
8 Main Street Trolley
9 Center for Southern Folklore

▲ **DAY TWO**

1 Graceland
2 Overton Park
3 The Brushmark Restaurant ☕
4 Memphis Zoo
5 Dixon Gallery and Gardens
6 Memphis Botanic Garden
7 Cooper-Young Neighborhood
8 Young Avenue Deli ☕
9 Hi-Tone Cafe

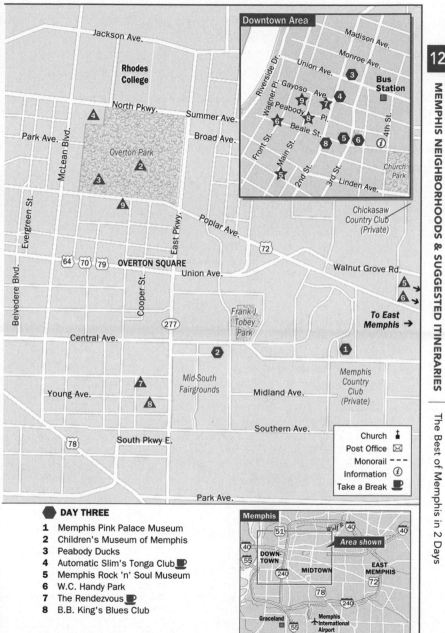

2 Overton Park

Back in Midtown, Overton Park is a sylvan setting that's home to the Memphis Zoo, the Memphis College of Art, and the Brooks Museum of Art. Visit the museum to get an overview of art through the ages. From Medieval and Impressionist to contemporary, a range of styles and media are represented. See p. 176.

3 Brushmark Restaurant ☕

Before or after browsing the masterpieces in the Brooks Museum of Art, take some refreshment in the Brushmark Restaurant. Sit outside on the terrace, order a light lunch, and enjoy the lush views of the wooded park surroundings. 1934 Poplar Ave. ✆ 901/544-6225. See p. 207.

4 Memphis Zoo ★★

The two soulful, cuddly panda bears from China are the reigning stars of this world-class zoo. But there are plenty of other animals and exhibits to see. From snakes and lions to elephants and monkeys, this is where the wild things are. See p. 175.

5 Dixon Gallery and Gardens ★

In East Memphis, you'll find the next two stops on your itinerary: The Dixon Gallery and Gardens and the Memphis Botanic Garden are right across the street from each other. Impressionist works are a highlight of the Dixon, a posh residence-turned-museum. Shaded by towering trees, the meticulously landscaped grounds are perfect for strolling. The gardens are especially gorgeous in the spring, when the dogwoods and azaleas are in bloom. See p. 172.

6 Memphis Botanic Garden ★

Nature enthusiasts will find much to love in this oasis of fragrant roses, iris beds, herb gardens, and acres of other flowering plants, majestic trees, and paved walking trails. The Japanese Garden of Tranquility, with its goldfish ponds, lanterns, and angular evergreens, is a favorite of romantics. See p. 177.

7 Cooper-Young Neighborhood

Drive back toward Midtown and explore the offbeat area known as Cooper-Young. If you like felines, peek inside the **House of Mews,** 933 S. Cooper St. (✆ **901/272-3777**), a storefront converted into a homelike sanctuary for stray cats awaiting adoption. Browse new and used books at **Burke's,** 936 S. Cooper St. (✆ **901/278-7484**), or indulge at one of the casual restaurants clustered around this intersection.

8 Young Avenue Deli ☕

Flop a spell at this sidewalk cafe (2119 Young Ave.; ✆ 901/278-0034; p. 223) and enjoy the eccentric-people-watching the area offers. Or walk half a block to cull the bins at Goner Records for vinyl rarities or other cheesy finds.

9 Hi-Tone Cafe

In the evening, head back over to the Overton Park area to see who's playing or what's happening at this artsy, laid-back venue. See p. 222.

THE BEST OF MEMPHIS IN 3 DAYS

Today begins with a bit of kids' stuff that will appeal to the child in all of us. You'll start at the Pink Palace Museum before heading over to the Children's Museum of Memphis. Then it's downtown to catch the ceremonious march of the Peabody ducks. The remainder of today you're downtown, taking in the Memphis Rock 'n' Soul Museum, W. C. Handy Park on Beale Street, and barbecued ribs at the Rendezvous. Tonight, say farewell to the city in style by taking in some smoldering live music at B.B. King's Blues Club.

1 Memphis Pink Palace Museum ★★★

Grocery-store owner and entrepreneur Clarence Saunders, who pioneered the self-service grocery store with the Piggly Wiggly chain at the beginning of the 20th century, lived in this sprawling mansion built of the palest pink marble. Today it's a museum packed with educational exhibits, along with a planetarium and an IMAX Theatre. See p. 174.

2 Children's Museum of Memphis ★

Kids can climb on a fire engine, daydream in a castle, cash play checks at a bank in a kid-sized city, and fill shopping carts at a grocery store at this Midtown museum, located next to the AutoZone Liberty Bowl Stadium. See p. 179.

3 Peabody Ducks

Sure, it's touristy, but you owe it to yourself to see what all the fuss is about. If you can make it by 11am, you'll get to see the ducks waddle out of the elevator and into the lobby fountain. But if not, they'll be here all afternoon. They make their return trip to their penthouse (yes, really) at 5pm. See p. 232.

4 Automatic Slim's Tonga Club 🍵 ★★

Head downtown for lunch at this funky restaurant. Great food and drinks, along with a vibrant clientele, always keep this hangout buzzing. 83 S. Second St. ✆ 901/525-7948. See p. 192.

5 Memphis Rock 'n' Soul Museum ★

On the plaza outside the FedExForum, you'll find the entrance to this museum that traces the importance of Memphis in the history of rock music, soul, and rhythm and blues. Browse the exhibits, jam to the classics, and learn something new about your favorite musical heroes. See p. 168.

6 W. C. Handy Park

Listen for the sounds of a bluesy rock band, or look for the statue of the early-20th-century trumpeter W. C. Handy that dominates this open-air park and amphitheater. Take a load off at one of the benches, watch the crowds go by, and start tapping your feet to the beat. See p. 170.

7 The Rendezvous ☕ ★★

Make a beeline back down toward Union Avenue, find the alley across from The Peabody, and let your nose lead the way to the source of the sizzling pork barbecue aromas that pervade the area. Feast on the Rendezvous's famous spice-dusted ribs, or try a chopped-pork sandwich. 52 S. Second St. ✆ **901/523-2746.** See p. 193.

8 B.B. King's Blues Club ★★

Kick back and surrender to the blues tonight, taking in whatever act happens to be playing at B.B. King's namesake nightclub on Beale Street. This is the essence of Memphis. See p. 217.`

EXPLORING MEMPHIS

J ust as in Nashville, music is the heart of Memphis, and many of the city's main attractions are related to its musical heritage. The blues first gained widespread recognition here on Beale Street, and rock 'n' roll was born at Sun Studio. W. C. Handy, the father of the blues, lived here for many years, and Elvis Presley made his Memphis home—Graceland—a household word. The history of the Memphis sound comes alive in multiple museums around the city, and each one offers its own unique spin.

Downtown Memphis has weathered its share of hardships over the years. About 10 years ago, the city started to see a long-awaited renaissance, with a flurry of new construction projects taking place. However, the recent U.S. economic recession has hit hard, leaving such visible scars as vacant commercial developments, unleased condos, and closed restaurants.

That's about to change dramatically, however, as two major steamboat companies offering multinight cruises along the Mississippi River prepare ports in Memphis. In 2011, American Cruise Lines, Inc., announced plans to move its headquarters and its *American Queen* steamboat to Memphis, and a competitor, The Great American Steamboat Co., began construction of *The Queen of Mississippi,* which also will dock in Memphis. The influx of tourists who will book overnight stays in Memphis before boarding the boats is expected to spur new restaurants, more shopping, and additional hotels.

Regardless of the prosperity levels at any given point in time, downtown Memphis has always been the heart and soul of the city. To get a sense of what it's all about, you need to stand on the bluff overlooking the Mississippi River, stroll Beale Street to hear live blues being played in B.B. King's nightclub, and "duck" into the city's most beloved historic hotel, The Peabody, to witness its most time-honored tradition (p. 232).

A few blocks south of downtown is the Stax Museum of American Soul Music. This must-see site is one of my favorite attractions, and I never tire of visiting it year in, year out. Stax is located in a grittier neighborhood than downtown, but seeing it may help give you a sense of what Memphis was like a generation or two ago. Besides, it's where Aretha Franklin and scads of other legends grew up. Farther south, you'll want to head on down the highway to Graceland. There are several old-school barbecue joints along the way. Savor all of these things, because they're collectively part of the definitive Memphis tourist experience.

GRACELAND, BEALE STREET & MORE

If you're going to Memphis, you're most likely going to **Graceland,** but there are also several other museums and sites here tied to the history of rock and blues music. Although the blues was born down in the Mississippi Delta, south of Memphis, it was on Beale Street that this soulful music first reached an urban audience. Today, after a period of abandonment, **Beale Street** is once again Memphis's busiest entertainment district. Visitors can hear blues, rock, jazz, country, and even Irish music on Beale Street. To learn more about the various musical styles that originated along the Mississippi River, visit the **Mississippi River Museum,** on Mud Island (p. 173), where there are several rooms full of exhibits on New Orleans jazz, Memphis blues, rockabilly, and Elvis. All of these places are more fully described below.

> ### Impressions
>
> *The seven wonders of the world I have seen, and many are the places I have been. Take my advice, folks, and see Beale Street first.*
> —W. C. Handy

In addition to being the birthplace of the blues and the city that launched Elvis and rock 'n' roll, Memphis played an important role in soul music during the 1960s. Isaac Hayes and Booker T and the MGs recorded here at **Stax Studio.** Other musicians who launched their careers from Memphis include Muddy Waters, Albert King, Al Green, Otis Redding, Sam & Dave, Sam the Sham and the Pharaohs, and the Box Tops.

Below are the sites that music fans won't want to miss while in Memphis.

Beale Street ★ ◉ To blues fans, Beale Street is the most important street in America. The musical form known as the blues—with roots that stretch back to the African musical heritage of slaves brought to the United States—was born here. W. C. Handy was performing on Beale Street when he penned "Memphis Blues," the first published blues song. Shortly after the Civil War, Beale Street became one of the most important streets in the South for African Americans. Many of the most famous musicians in the blues world got their starts here; besides Handy, other greats include B.B. King, Furry Lewis, Alberta Hunter, Rufus Thomas, and Isaac Hayes.

And the blues continues to thrive here. Today, though parts of downtown Memphis look utterly abandoned, Beale Street continues to draw fans of blues and popular music to its nightclubs lining Beale's blocks between Second and Fourth streets. The Orpheum Theatre, once a vaudeville palace, is now the performance hall for Broadway road shows, and the New Daisy Theatre features performances by up-and-coming bands and once-famous performers. Historic markers up and down the street relate the area's colorful past, and two statues commemorate the city's two most important musicians: W. C. Handy and Elvis Presley. In addition to the many clubs featuring nightly live music (including B.B. King's Blues Club and the Hard Rock Cafe), there's also a small often-overlooked museum, the W. C. Handy House—and the museum-like A. Schwab Dry Goods Store. For an update of events, check out www.bealestreet.com. Allow a full afternoon to browse the shops and restaurants, or make a night of it if you're into barhopping and live music.

Graceland ★★ It seems hard to believe, but Graceland, the former home of rock-'n'-roll-legend Elvis Presley and annually the destination of tens of thousands of

Elvis-in-Chief

You probably already knew that former president Bill Clinton's U.S. Secret Service code name was "Elvis." The King and the Commander-in-Chief are further linked in history. Clinton's presidential library, in Little Rock, Arkansas, features his personal collection of Elvis memorabilia. Most of the items are gifts given to the president during his two terms in the White House.

love-struck pilgrims searching for the ghost of Elvis, is the second-most-visited home in America. Only the White House receives more visitors each year. A look around at the crowds waiting in various lines at this sprawling complex makes it clear that Elvis, through his many recordings, numerous movie roles, and countless concerts, appealed to a wide spectrum of people. Today, more than 35 years after Elvis's death in 1977, Graceland draws visitors of all ages from all over the world.

Purchased in the late 1950s for $100,000, Graceland today is Memphis's biggest attraction and resembles a small theme park or shopping mall in scope and design. There are his two personal jets, the Elvis Presley Automobile Museum, the "Sincerely Elvis" collection of Elvis's personal belongings, the *Walk a Mile in My Shoes* video, and, of course, guided tours of the Graceland mansion. If your time here is limited to only one thing, by all means go for the mansion tour. It's the essence of the Big E. All the rest is just icing on Elvis's buttercream-frosted cake.

The Elvis Presley Automobile Museum includes not only his famous 1955 pink Cadillac, a 1956 purple Cadillac convertible, and two Stutz Blackhawks from the early 1970s, but also motorcycles and other vehicles. Accompanying this collection are videos of Elvis's home movies and a fast-paced compilation of car-scene clips from dozens of Elvis movies, which are shown in a sort of drive-in–theater setting.

A re-creation of an airport terminal serves as the entrance to the *Lisa Marie* and *Hound Dog II* private jets. The former was once a regular Delta Air Lines passenger jet that was customized (at a cost of $800,000) after Elvis purchased it in 1975 for $250,000. The *Hound Dog II* is much smaller and was purchased after the *Lisa Marie* was acquired.

"Sincerely Elvis" is Graceland's most revealing exhibit. This is a collection of many of Elvis's personal belongings. Here you'll see everything from some of Elvis's personal record collection (including albums by Tom Jones and Ray Charles) to a pair of his sneakers. One exhibit displays gifts sent to Elvis by fans. Included are quilts, needlepoint, and even a plaque made from woven chewing gum wrappers.

The Graceland exhibits strive to reveal Elvis the man and Elvis the star. Some of the surprising facts passed on to visitors include these: Elvis was an avid reader and always traveled with lots of books; Elvis didn't like the taste of alcohol; and among his favorite movies were *Blazing Saddles* and the films of Monty Python.

In recent years, Graceland's marketing efforts have increased exponentially, resulting in a dizzying array of cross-promotions, new music downloads, touring exhibitions, festivals, cruises, contests, and other programs designed to sustain interest in Elvis and attract younger generations of fans who weren't born until decades after his death in 1977. This makes good business sense, but at the expense of the genuine Graceland tourist experience, which feels more complicated, overwrought, and overpriced than it should. For example, if you buy the most expensive Elvis tour package, you should allow at least 2 to 3 hours or more for the tour. But that doesn't include wait times, including ticket lines and the often long rope lines to board buses that take you from the ticket complex across the highway and inside the gated driveway leading up

Memphis Attractions: Downtown & Midtown

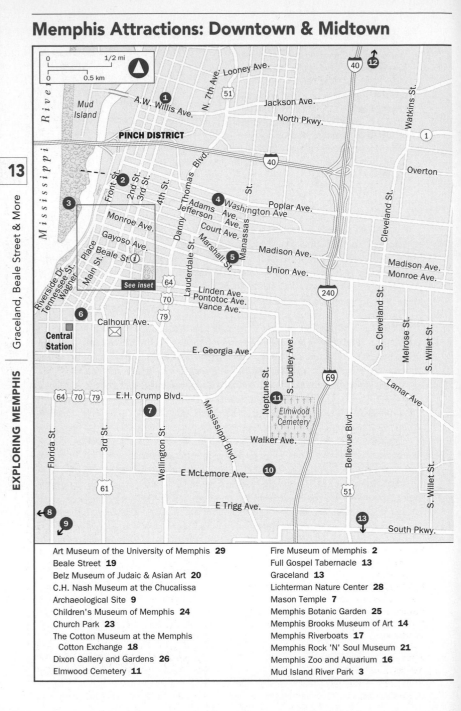

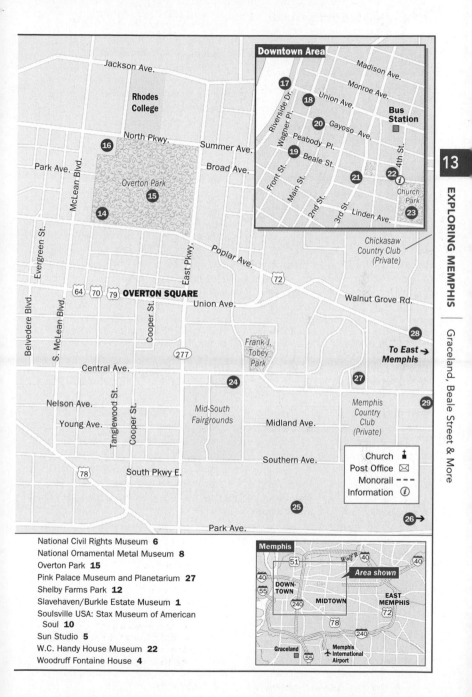

Downtown Area

Jackson Ave.

Rhodes
College

North Pkwy.

16

Overton Park

15

14

Park Ave.

McLean Blvd.

Evergreen St.

Belvedere Blvd.

S. McLean Blvd.

64 70 79 **OVERTON SQUARE**

Central Ave.

Nelson Ave.

Young Ave.

Tanglewood St.

Cooper St.

Cooper St.

78

South Pkwy E.

277

Frank J.
Tobey
Park

24

Mid-South
Fairgrounds

Midland Ave.

Southern Ave.

25

Park Ave.

East Pkwy.

Poplar Ave.

72

Union Ave.

Summer Ave.

Broad Ave.

Madison Ave.

Monroe Ave.

17

Union Ave.

18

20 Gayoso Ave.

Riverside Dr.

Wagner Pl.

Peabody Pl.

19 Beale St.

Front St.

Main St.

2nd St.

3rd St.

21

Linden Ave.

Bus
Station

4th St.

22

Church
Park

23

Chickasaw
Country Club
(Private)

Walnut Grove Rd.

28

**To East →
Memphis**

27

Memphis
Country
Club
(Private)

29

Church
Post Office ✉
Monorail - - -
Information ⓘ

26 →

National Civil Rights Museum **6**
National Ornamental Metal Museum **8**
Overton Park **15**
Pink Palace Museum and Planetarium **27**
Shelby Farms Park **12**
Slavehaven/Burkle Estate Museum **1**
Soulsville USA: Stax Museum of American
   Soul **10**
Sun Studio **5**
W.C. Handy House Museum **22**
Woodruff Fontaine House **4**

Memphis

51

Wolf

40

40

40

55

**DOWN-
TOWN**

240

MIDTOWN

**EAST
MEMPHIS**

72

Area shown

78

240

Graceland

55

**Memphis
✈ International
Airport**

The Men Who Would Be King

Don't call them Elvis impersonators, a derisive term that conjures images of bloated men with bad sideburns squeezed into white jumpsuits and singing "Burnin' Love" with their belly fat jiggling. Ever since Graceland sanctioned its first Elvis competition in 2007, these dubious performers have become known as "Elvis Tribute Artists" (ETAs). Stakes are high as these "Elvi" try to out-snarl each other: In 2011, first prize was a cool $20,000, plus other perks. See www.elvis.com.

to the mansion. If you're up for the experience, these logistical roadblocks may only heighten the thrill of anticipation you'd experience at any major tourist destination. If you just came to see to get a glimpse of the Jungle Room, you may deem the hurdles not worth the hassle.

To steer clear of the crush of the crowds, avoid special events, especially the annual, mid-August Elvis Week (irreverently referred to by locals as "Dead Elvis Week"). Consider a visit during the off season, from Thanksgiving to early New Year's, when Graceland is at its simple best, decorated with Elvis's original Christmas lights and endearingly dated lawn decorations.

Early risers should be aware that most mornings it is possible to visit Elvis's grave before Graceland officially opens. This special free walk-up period is daily from 7:30 to 8:30am.

3734 Elvis Presley Blvd. ✆ **800/238-2000** or 901/332-3322. www.elvis.com. Graceland Mansion Tour $31 adults, $28 seniors and students, $14 children 7–12. The Platinum Tour (includes admission to all Graceland attractions, including Elvis's Automobile Museum, tours of Elvis's custom jets, and other exhibitions) $35 adults, $32 seniors, $17 children 7–12. Graceland Elvis Entourage VIP Tour (includes the "Elvis After Dark" exhibit) $70 for all ages. Tour reservations can be made 24 hr. in advance and are recommended if you have a tight schedule. Mar–Oct Mon–Sat 9am–5pm, Sun 10am–4pm; Nov–Feb 10am–4pm daily. (Dec–Feb mansion tour does not operate Tues.) Closed Thanksgiving, Dec 25, and Jan 1. Take Bellevue S. (which turns into Elvis Presley Blvd.) a few miles south of downtown, past Winchester Ave. Graceland is on the left.

Memphis Rock 'n' Soul Museum ★   With rare recordings and videos, archival photographs and interactive multimedia displays, the past century of American popular music is presented in "Social Crossroads," the first exhibition ever presented by the Smithsonian Institution outside of Washington, D.C. From field hollers and gospel hymns to the turn-of-the-century blues of W. C. Handy, it's all here. Narrated tours on portable audio players allow visitors to customize their tours and musical selections. Allow an hour. *Note:* Call ahead if you're planning a visit, as the museum often closes early to host private parties.

191 Beale St. ✆ **901/205-2533.** www.memphisrocknsoul.org. Admission $11 adults, $8 children 5–17. Daily 10am–7pm (last tour starts at 6:15pm). Downtown at the new FedExForum arena, a half-block south of Beale and Third sts.

The Memphis Music Experience

Want to save $20 on admission to the city's Top 5 music attractions—Graceland, Sun Studio, Stax Museum, Rock 'n' Soul Museum, and the Gibson Guitar Factory? Then purchase your tickets at one of two Memphis visitor centers:

Arlington Road, off Interstate 40, at exit 25, east of the Memphis city limits; and near Graceland in the south Memphis suburb of Whitehaven, at 3205 Elvis Presley Blvd. For more information, call ✆ **888/633-9099.**

elvis TRIVIA

- Elvis's first hit single was "Mystery Train." Recorded at Sun Studio, it made it to number one on the country charts in 1955.

- In 1956, Elvis became the second white person to have a number one single on *Billboard*'s rhythm and blues chart. The song was "Don't Be Cruel." The B-side was "Hound Dog."

- Elvis's first million-selling single and gold record came in 1956, when he recorded "Heartbreak Hotel" as his first release for RCA.

- During his career, Elvis won three Grammy Awards, all of which were for gospel recordings. Two of these awards were for the same song—a studio version and a live version of "How Great Thou Art."

- Elvis made 31 films and sang in all but one of these. *Charro!*, a Western released in 1969, was the only movie in which he didn't break into song at some point.

- The soundtrack to Elvis's movie *G.I. Blues* was on the album chart for a total of 111 weeks, 10 of which were at number one. This was his first movie after returning from service in the army.

- Highway 51 South, which runs past the gates of Graceland, was renamed Elvis Presley Boulevard in 1971, while Elvis was still alive.

- Elvis's first network-television appearance came in January 1956 when he appeared on *Stage Show*, which was hosted by Tommy and Jimmy Dorsey.

- On a night in 1975, Bruce Springsteen, hoping to meet Elvis, jumped the fence at Graceland and ran up to the house. Unfortunately, Elvis wasn't at home, and the guards escorted Springsteen off the property.

- The King holds the record for sold-out shows in Vegas: 837 performances at the Las Vegas Hilton over a 10-year period.

- In 2003, an Elvis CD featuring his 30 number one hits was released and became an international success. To date, sales have reached triple platinum.

- Elvis has sold more than a billion records worldwide, according to some industry estimates. That's more than any other act in recorded history.

Soulsville USA: Stax Museum of American Soul Music ★★★ ⊙ Groove on down to Soulsville USA, one of the city's best attractions, which celebrates Memphis soul music. Opened in spring 2003, the museum sits near the site of the original (sadly, long-ago demolished) Stax recording studio, which during the 1960s and 1970s cranked out world-famous hits by Otis Redding; Booker T and the MGs; The Bar-Kays; Al Green; Aretha Franklin; Earth, Wind & Fire; and others. Don't miss Isaac Hayes's (of *Shaft* and *South Park* fame) gold-plated, shag-carpeted *Superfly* Cadillac, which is on display. First-rate multimedia exhibitions, beginning with a thrilling video introduction in a darkened theater, take visitors back to a place and time when racism deeply divided the South. Stax, however, was an anomaly, a virtually colorblind collaborative where black and white musicians, staff, and studio executives worked together in a shared musical passion. At interactive kiosks, you'll

Chef's Salad Days

One of Memphis's best-loved soul legends died in 2008. Long before he garnered fame at Stax recording studio in Memphis, before the "Theme from Shaft" won him an Academy Award, and way before his gig as the voice of *South Park*'s beloved character Chef made him a household name for a whole new generation of fans, Isaac Hayes worked as a shoeshine boy on Beale Street.

get a chance to hear hundreds of songs and watch archival video. Stax ties to Elvis, the Beatles, and Elton John are mentioned. Elsewhere, Bono, Elvis Costello, and scores of other rock stars offer heartfelt tributes to the lasting legacy of Stax (and Memphis's Sun) recording studios. Allow at least 90 minutes—or an entire afternoon, if you're a true soul sister—to tour the museum. And if the spirit moves, you can also cut loose on its psychedelic dance floor.

926 E. McLemore Ave. ✆ **901/946-2535.** www.staxmuseum.com. Admission $12 adults, $11 seniors, $9 children 9–12, free for children 8 and under with paid adult or senior admission. Apr–Oct Mon–Sat 9am–5pm, Sun 1–5pm; Nov–Mar Tues–Sat 10am–5pm, Sun 1–5pm. Closed major holidays. Take Danny Thomas Blvd. south to Mississippi Blvd. Turn left onto Mississippi Blvd., then left on E. McLemore Ave.

Sun Studio ★★   If Elvis Aaron Presley hadn't come to Sun Studio in the early 1950s to record a song as a birthday present for his mother (so the story goes), musical history today might be very different. Owner and recording engineer Sam Phillips first recorded, in the early 1950s, such local artists as Elvis Presley, Jerry Lee Lewis, Roy Orbison, and Carl Perkins, who together created a sound that would shortly become known as rock 'n' roll. Over the years Phillips also helped start the recording careers of the blues greats B.B. King and Howlin' Wolf, and country giant Johnny Cash. By night, Sun Studio is still an active recording studio and has been used by such artists as U2, Spin Doctors, the Tractors, and Bonnie Raitt. The place has great vibes, and for those who know their music history, touching Elvis's microphone will be a thrill beyond measure. However, if you aren't well versed in this particular area of pop culture, a visit to the singularly themed Sun Studio may leave you wondering what all the fuss is about. Allow an hour.

706 Union Ave. (at Marshall Ave.). ✆ **800/441-6249** or 901/521-0664. www.sunstudio.com. Admission $12 adults, free for children 11 and under accompanied by parent. Children 4 and under not permitted on tours. Daily 10am–6pm (studio tours conducted at the bottom of the hour, 10:30am–5:30pm). Closed some holidays.

W. C. Handy House Museum 🎁   A far cry from the opulence of Graceland, this tiny clapboard shotgun shack was once the Memphis home of the bluesman W. C. Handy—"the father of the blues"—and was where he was living in 1909 when he penned "Memphis Blues." Although the house has only a small collection of Handy memorabilia and artifacts, there are numerous evocative old photos displayed, and the commentary provided by the museum guide is always highly informative. The tour lasts about 20 minutes.

Impressions

Before Elvis, there was nothing.
—John Lennon

352 Beale St. (at Fourth Ave.). ✆ **901/527-3427.** Admission $3 adults, $2 children 4–17, free for children 3 and under. Summer Tues–Sat 10am–5pm; winter Tues–Sat 11am–4pm.

elvis BEYOND THE GATES OF GRACELAND

You've come to Memphis on a pilgrimage and spent the entire day at Graceland. You've cried, you've laughed, you've bought a whole suitcase full of Elvis souvenirs, but still you want more of Elvis. No problem. Elvis is everywhere in Memphis.

If you're a hard-core Elvis fan and plan to visit his grave during the early-morning free visitation period at Graceland, you'll want to find a hotel as close to the mansion as possible. Directly across the street from Graceland are two properties that cater specifically to Elvis fans. Both the **Heartbreak Hotel–Graceland** (p. 242) and the **Days Inn at Graceland** (p. 243) offer round-the-clock, free, in-room Elvis videos. The former hotel actually has a pathway into the Graceland parking lot, and the latter has a guitar-shaped swimming pool.

Also, if you want a hyper-Elvis experience, plan your visit for dates around Elvis's January 8 birthday festivities or during **Elvis Week,** which commemorates his death on August 16. During these festivities, you might catch an all-Elvis concert by the Memphis Symphony Orchestra, the *Taking Care of Business*

Elvis-tribute ballet by Ballet Memphis, or the Elvis laser-light show at the Sharpe Planetarium in the **Pink Palace Museum.**

Any time of year, you can visit **Sun Studio** (p. 170), the recording studio that discovered Elvis and where he made his first recordings. Though the studio isn't very large, its musical history is enough to give people goose bumps and bring tears to their eyes. A highlight of a visit here is a chance to actually touch the microphone that Elvis used to make his first recordings. The late Sam Phillips (who died in 2003) once brought his new musicians here to sign contracts, and Elvis most certainly whiled away many hours here. For a tongue-in-cheek tribute to Elvis, check out the coin-operated shrine to the King at the **Center for Southern Folklore** (p. 217) in Pembroke Square downtown.

To visit the spots around town where Elvis once walked, book a tour with **American Dream Safari** (© **901/527-8870**), which tools guests around town in a 1955 Cadillac to see such Elvis haunts as Humes High School, Sun Studio, and the housing project where he lived as a teenager.

NONMUSICAL MEMPHIS ATTRACTIONS

Museums

Art Museum of the University of Memphis   Memphis takes its name from the ancient capital of Egypt, and here in the Art Museum of the University of Memphis, you can view artifacts from ancient Memphis. An outstanding collection of Egyptian art and artifacts makes this one of the most interesting museums in the city. Among the items on display is a loaf of bread dating from between 2134 B.C. and 1786 B.C. A hieroglyph-covered sarcophagus contains the mummy of Iret-iruw, who died around 2,200 years ago. Numerous works of art and funerary objects show the high level of skill achieved by ancient Egyptian artists. In addition to the Egyptian exhibit, there is a small collection of West African masks and woodcarvings, and there are changing exhibitions in the main gallery. Allow 30 minutes to an hour. *Tip:* Free,

20-minute, guided tours of the African and Egyptian collections are offered week-days. Advance reservations are required.

3750 Norriswood St., CFA Building, Room 142. © **800/669-2678** or 901/678-2224. www.memphis.edu/amum Free admission. Mon–Sat 9am–5pm. Closed university holidays and for changing exhibitions. Turn south off Central Ave. onto Deloach St. (btw. Patterson and Zach Curlin sts.) to Norriswood St.

Belz Museum of Asian & Judaic Art   Founded in 1998 by world travelers and art lovers Jack and Marilyn Belz (he's the owner of The Peabody hotel empire), this unexpected downtown museum features pieces culled from the couple's extensive collection. Chinese art from the Qing and Tang dynasties include stunning silver boxes, imperial tomb figurines, ink-on-paper portraits, and intricate jade and ivory carvings. Alongside these treasures are European art objects, Russian lacquer boxes, and contemporary modern Jewish art. Give yourself about an hour here.

119 S. Main St. © **901/523-ARTS** (2787). www.belzmuseum.org. $6 adults, $5 seniors, $4 students. Tues–Fri 10am–5:30pm; Sat–Sun noon–5pm.

The Cotton Museum at the Memphis Cotton Exchange   "Glorious and notorious." Both adjectives apply to the history of cotton, one of the most significant agricultural crops in the history of the Deep South. African slaves did the backbreaking labor of picking the cotton, while in downtown Memphis, wealthy merchants and brokers bought and sold the lucrative commodity that was loaded onto Mississippi River barges for shipment to the entire world. This interesting museum, on the site of the 1939 Memphis Cotton Exchange building, features exhibits that explore cotton's legacy and its importance to Memphis's growth. Allot half an hour to visit the museum.

65 Union Ave. © **901/531-7826.** www.memphiscottonmuseum.org. Admission $10 adults, $9.50 seniors, $9 students, $8 children 6–12. Mon–Sat 10am–5pm; Sun noon–5pm. Closed Thanksgiving and Christmas.

Dixon Gallery and Gardens ★   The South's finest collection of French and American Impressionist and post-Impressionist artworks resides in this exquisite museum. The museum, art collection, and surrounding 17 acres of formal and informal gardens once belonged to Margaret and Hugo Dixon, who were avid art collectors. After their deaths, the Dixon estate opened to the public and has since become one of Memphis's most important museums. The permanent collection includes works by Henri Matisse, Pierre Auguste Renoir, Edgar Degas, Paul Gauguin, Mary Cassatt, J. M. W. Turner, and John Constable. The museum has strong local support and frequently hosts temporary exhibits of international caliber. Twice a year, the Memphis Symphony Orchestra performs outdoor concerts in the Dixon's formal gardens. Allow an hour for the museum, and more time for the gardens. *Tip:* Admission is free from 10am to noon on Saturdays and offers pay-what-you-can admission on Tuesdays.

4339 Park Ave. © **901/761-5250.** www.dixon.org. Admission $7 adults, $5 seniors and students, $3 children 7–17. Tues–Fri 10am–4pm; Sat 10am–5pm; Sun 1–5pm. Located adjacent to Audubon Park, off Park Ave. at Cherry Rd. (btw. Getwell Rd. and Perkins Rd.).

Memphis Brooks Museum of Art   First opened in 1916 as the Brooks Memorial Art Gallery, this is the oldest art museum in Tennessee; it contains one of the largest art collections of any museum in the mid-South. With more than 7,000 pieces in the permanent collection, the Brooks frequently rotates works on display. The museum's emphasis is on European and American art of the 18th through the 20th centuries, with a very respectable collection of Italian Renaissance and baroque paintings and sculptures as well. Some of the museum's more important works include pieces by Auguste Rodin, Pierre Auguste Renoir, Thomas Hart Benton, and Frank Lloyd Wright. Take a break from strolling through the museum with a stop in the Brushmark Restaurant. Allow an hour to 90 minutes. *Tip:* On Wednesdays, admission is pay-what-you-can from 10am to 4pm.

Overton Park, 1934 Poplar Ave. (btw. N. McLean Blvd. and E. Parkway N.). © **901/544-6200.** www. brooksmuseum.org. Admission $7 adults, $6 seniors, $3 students, free for children 5 and under. Wed and Fri 10am–4pm; Thurs 10am–8pm; Sat 10am–5pm; Sun 11am–5pm.

Mud Island River Park ☺ Mud Island is more than just a museum. The 52-acre park on Mud Island is home to several attractions, including the **River Walk** and the **Mississippi River Museum.** If you have seen any pre-1900 photos of the Memphis waterfront, you may have noticed that Mud Island is missing from the photos. This island first appeared in 1900 and became permanent in 1913. In 1916, the island joined with the mainland just north of the mouth of the Wolf River, but a diversion canal was dug through the island to maintain a free channel in the Wolf River.

To learn all about the river, you can follow a 5-block-long scale model of 900 miles of the Mississippi River. Called the **River Walk,** the model is complete with flowing water, street plans of cities and towns along the river, and informative panels that include information on the river and its history.

On Mud Island you can rent bicycles, kayaks, and paddle boats (the latter two are not for use on the Mississippi River itself, of course) by the hour or half-day, allowing plenty of time for a leisurely exploration of the area. Evenings during the summer, the **Mud Island Amphitheater** hosts such touring acts as Jimmy Buffett, Norah Jones, and Rob Thomas. Allow an hour, or make a day of it.

125 N. Front St. (at Adams Ave.). © **800/507-6507** or 901/576-7241. www.mudisland.com. Mississippi River Museum $8 adults, $6 seniors, $5 children 5–12; grounds only free. Summer Tues–Sun 10am–8pm; spring and fall Tues–Sun 10am–5pm. Closed Nov–Mar. To reach Mud Island, take the monorail from Front St. at Adams Ave.

National Civil Rights Museum ★★★ 📷 Dr. Martin Luther King, Jr., came to Memphis in early April of 1968 in support of the city's striking garbage collectors. He checked into the Lorraine Motel, as he always did when visiting Memphis. On April 4, he stepped out onto the balcony outside his room and was shot dead by James Earl Ray. The assassination of King struck a horrible blow to the American civil rights movement and incited riots in cities across the country. However, despite the murder of the movement's most important leader, African Americans continued the struggle for the equal rights that were guaranteed to them under the U.S. Constitution.

Saved from demolition, the Lorraine Motel was remodeled and today serves as the nation's memorial to the civil rights movement. In evocative displays, the museum chronicles the struggle of African Americans from the time of slavery to the present. Multimedia presentations and life-size, walk-through tableaux include historic exhibits: a Montgomery, Alabama, public bus like the one on which Rosa Parks was riding when she refused to move to the back of the bus; a Greensboro, North Carolina, lunch counter; and the burned shell of a Freedom-Ride Greyhound bus. Allow 2 to 3 hours.

450 Mulberry St. (at Huling Ave.). © **901/521-9699.** www.civilrightsmuseum.org. Admission $13 adults, $11 seniors and students, $9.50 children 4–17, free for children 3 and under. Free admission

Mon after 3pm for Tennessee residents. Wed–Sat and Mon 9am–5pm, Sun 1–5pm; June–Aug open until 6pm. Closed major holidays.

National Ornamental Metal Museum ★ 🎒   Set on parklike grounds on a bluff overlooking the Mississippi, this small museum is dedicated to ornamental metalworking in all its forms. There are sculptures displayed around the museum's gardens, a working blacksmith shop, and examples of ornamental wrought-iron grill-work such as that seen on balconies in New Orleans. Sculptural metal pieces and jewelry are also prominently featured both in the museum's permanent collection and in temporary exhibits. Be sure to take a look at the ornate museum gates; they were created by 160 metalsmiths from 17 countries and feature a fascinating array of imaginative rosettes. Just across the street is a community park that includes an ancient Native American mound. Allow 1 hour or more.

374 Metal Museum Dr. ✆ **877/881-2326** or 901/774-6380. www.metalmuseum.org. Admission $6 adults, $5 seniors, $4 students and children 5–18, free for children 4 and under. Tues–Sat 10am–5pm; Sun noon–5pm. Closed major holidays, for exhibition changes, and when Memphis City Schools are closed due to weather. Take Crump Blvd. or I-55 toward the Memphis-Arkansas Bridge and get off at exit 12-C (Metal Museum Dr.), which is the last exit in Tennessee; the museum is 2 blocks south.

Pink Palace Museum ★★ ☺   "The Pink Palace" was the name locals gave to the ostentatious pink-marble mansion that grocery store magnate Clarence Saunders built shortly after World War I. It was Saunders who revolutionized grocery shopping with the opening of the first Piggly Wiggly self-service market in 1916. Unfortunately, Saunders went bankrupt before he ever finished his "Pink Palace," and the building was acquired by the city of Memphis for use as a museum of cultural and natural history.

Among the exhibits here is a full-scale reproduction of the maze of aisles that constituted an original Piggly Wiggly. Other walk-through exhibits include a pre–Piggly Wiggly general store and an old-fashioned pharmacy with a soda fountain. Memphis is a major medical center; accordingly, this museum has an extensive medical-history exhibit. On the lighter side, kids enjoy such exhibits as a life-size mechanical triceratops, a real mastodon skeleton, and a hand-carved miniature circus that goes into animated action. In the planetarium, there are frequently changing astronomy programs as well as rock-'n'-roll laser shows (the annual Aug. Elvis laser show is the most popular). There is also an IMAX movie theater here. Allow 1 to 2 hours.

3050 Central Ave. (btw. Hollywood and Highland). ✆ **901/320-6320** or 901/763-IMAX (4629) for IMAX schedule. www.memphismuseums.org. Museum $9.75 adults, $9.25 seniors, $6.75 children 3–12, free for children 2 and under. Exhibitions and IMAX $15 adults, $14 seniors, $9.50 children 3–12. Other combination tickets available. Call for IMAX showtimes. Museum Mon–Sat 9am–5pm; Sun noon–5pm. Closed Thanksgiving, Christmas, and New Year's.

Historic Buildings

Mason Temple   It's rarely listed in travel guidebooks, and it's not a tourist attraction, but anyone with even a passing interest in civil rights history should at least drive by this stately house of worship. The Reverend Martin Luther King, Jr., delivered his prophetic "Mountaintop" speech in this church on April 3, 1968, the eve of his assassination.

930 Mason Ave. (btw. Chelsea and Bicknell aves.). ✆ **901/947-9300.**

Slavehaven Underground Railroad Museum/Burkle Estate 🎒 Secret
tunnels and trapdoors evoke a period before the Civil War, when this house was a
stop on the underground railroad used by runaway slaves in their quest for freedom.
The house is filled with 19th-century furnishings and has displays of artifacts from
slavery days. It takes about an hour to get through the house.

826 N. Second Ave. (btw. Chelsea and Bicknell aves.). ℂ **901/527-3427.** Admission $6 adults, $4
students. Summer Mon–Sat 10am–4pm; winter Wed–Sat 10am–4pm.

Woodruff-Fontaine House   Within the leafy downtown neighborhood known
as Victorian Village, the Woodruff-Fontaine House displays an elaborate charm. Built
in 1870 in a French architectural style, the fully restored 16-room home contains
period furnishings. Mannequins throughout the house display the fashions of the late
19th century. *Tip:* There is no elevator in the three-story mansion, making the upper
floors inaccessible to visitors in wheelchairs. Only the ground floor of the three-story
home is wheelchair accessible. Allow 30 minutes.

Victorian Village, 680 Adams Ave. ℂ **901/526-1469.** Admission $10 adults, $8 seniors, $6 stu-
dents. Wed–Sat noon–4pm. Guided tours every 30 min. Btw. Neely and New Orleans sts., next to
Mallory-Neely House.

Other Memphis Attractions

C.H. Nash Museum at the Chucalissa Archaeological Site ☺   The main
drawback of this site is its rather isolated, hard-to-find location, several miles south
of nearly everything else in Memphis. (That is, unless you do this on your way to or
from Tunica, MS.) The Chucalissa Archaeological Museum is built on the site of a
Mississippian-period (A.D. 900–1600) Native American village. Dioramas and displays of artifacts discovered in the area provide a cultural history of Mississippi River
Valley Native Americans. The reconstructed village includes several family dwellings,
a shaman's hut, and a chief's temple atop a mound in the center of the village compound. The chance to walk through a real archaeologist's trench and to explore a
Native American village thrills most children. Allow 1 to 2 hours.

1987 Indian Village Dr. ℂ **901/785-3160.** www.memphis.edu/chucalissa. Admission $5 adults, $3
seniors and children 4–11, free for children 3 and under. Tues–Sat 9am–5pm; Sun 1–5pm. South of
Memphis off U.S. 61 and adjacent to the T. O. Fuller State Park. Closed major holidays.

Memphis Zoo ★★ ☺   Locals take great pride in this clean, efficiently managed
world-class zoo, which consistently gets raves from tourists as well. The accolades are
well deserved, especially given new exhibits like Teton Trek. Opened in 2009, it
showcases wildlife of the Greater Yellowstone ecosystem—with grizzly bears, elk, grey
wolves, sandhill cranes, and trumpeter swans. Polar bears, seals, and sea lions inhabit
the Northwest Passage area. Elsewhere, a pair of adorable panda bears from China
are top draws at this great zoo. Built to resemble an ancient Egyptian temple, the zoo's
entry is covered with traditional and contemporary hieroglyphics. The attraction also
includes a 5-acre primate habitat, an exhibit of nocturnal animals, and an extensive
big-cat area with habitats that are among the best zoo exhibits in the country. Next
up for the zoo? The Zambezi River Hippo Camp, slated to open in 2012. Allow 3
hours or up to a full day.

Overton Park, 2000 Prentiss Place. ℂ **901/276-WILD** (9453). www.memphiszoo.org. Admission $13
adults, $12 seniors, $8 children 2–11. Admission free to TN residents Tues after 2pm. Parking $3
during summer season. Mar to late Oct daily 9am–5pm; late Oct to Feb daily 9am–4pm. Located
inside Overton Park off Poplar Ave. (2000 block), btw. N. McLean Blvd. and E. Parkway N.

Would it be sacrilegious to include soul legend Al Green's **Full Gospel Tabernacle,** 787 Hale Rd. ((℗ **901/396-9192**), as a tourist "attraction" in this chapter? Perhaps. But it would be a sin of omission *not* to recommend the church's Sunday morning worship services, which rank among the most authentic and memorable Memphis experiences you'll ever have. The Grammy Award–winning singer shot to fame in the 1970s with hits like "Let's Stay Together," "Love and Happiness," and "Tired of Being Alone," but in later years, he followed a spiritual calling to save souls rather than to merely sing soul music. You'll find Green most Sundays in the pulpit of the modest Full Gospel Tabernacle, a few blocks south of Graceland. Members of his congregation, as well as tourists from all over the world, fill the wooden pews for the 11:30am worship service. Expect to be blown away by the spine-tingling power of the small but mighty gospel choir, but keep in mind this is a church service and not a performance. Rev. Al preaches the gospel of God's love with passion and conviction, and he lapses into song from time to time, as the spirit moves him. The congregation is welcoming and tolerant of tourists who are respectful of their surroundings. So participate in the service. Put a little money in the collection plate. And when Rev. Al asks somebody for an "amen," offer it with all your heart. More info: www.algreenmusic.com/fullgospeltabernacle.html.

Parks & Gardens

In downtown Memphis, between Main Street and Second Avenue and between Madison and Jefferson avenues, you'll find **Court Square,** the oldest park in Memphis. With its classically designed central fountain, restored gazebo, and stately old shade trees, this park was long a favored gathering spot of Memphians. Numerous historic plaques around the park relate the many important events that have taken place in Court Square. (*Tip:* Don't sit here and expect to enjoy a snack or picnic lunch—you'll be accosted by dive-bombing pigeons and aggressive, overweight squirrels.)

A block to the west, you'll find **Jefferson Davis Park,** which overlooks Mud Island and Riverside Drive. Several Civil War cannons face out toward the river from this small park. Below Jefferson Davis Park, along Riverside Drive, you'll find **Tom Lee Park,** which stretches for 1½ miles south along the bank of the Mississippi and is named after a local African-American hero who died saving 32 people when a steamer sank in the Mississippi in 1925—even though Lee himself could not swim. This park is a favorite of joggers and is the site of various festivals, including the big Memphis in May celebration. A parallel park called **Riverbluff Walkway** is the newest development atop the bluff on the east side of Riverside Drive. And just north of the Pyramid in Harbor Town, an exclusive, 950-home planned community neighborhood, lies **Greenbelt Park.** Its tree-shaded trails and pristine picnic area offers the city's most picturesque, unspoiled views of the Mississippi River.

Located in Midtown and bounded by Poplar Avenue, East Parkway North, North Parkway, and North McLean Boulevard, **Overton Park** is one of Memphis's largest parks and includes not only the Memphis Zoo but also the Memphis Brooks Museum of Art, the Memphis College of Art, and the Overton Park Municipal Golf Course, as well as tennis courts, hiking and biking trails, and an open-air theater. The park's large, old shade trees make this a cool place to spend an afternoon in the summer, and the surrounding residential neighborhoods are some of the wealthiest in the city.

Elmwood Cemetery Victims of war, disease, and natural causes are buried in this historic garden cemetery on the outskirts of downtown Memphis. Dating back to 1852, the majestic, 80-acre sanctuary is brimming with elaborate marble sculptures, simple headstones, and towering shade trees. Take a guided tour or stroll the grounds alone to get a sense of the city's rich history. Descendants such as 1920s bandleader Jimmie Lunceford, Civil War historian and author Shelby Foote, and African-American civil rights photographer Ernest Withers are laid to rest here. Most haunting, however, is "No Man's Land," public lots marking the gravesites of 1,500 victims of the 1878 yellow fever epidemic. Maps are available in the Victorian Garden Cottage that serves as the Visitors Center. Allot 1 to 2 hours for a visit here.

824 S. Dudley St. © **901/774-3212.** www.elmwoodcemetery.org. Free admission (donations accepted). Grounds daily 8am–4:30pm; office closed Sat at noon and Sun.

Lichterman Nature Center Often overlooked by tourists, this well-maintained, wooded nature preserve in the heart of East Memphis is one of the city's most family-friendly attractions. Open year-round, the center offers hiking trails, scientific demonstrations, and other hands-on activities on 65 acres and within its museumlike Backyard Wildlife Center. With a grassy meadow and lake as well as woods, there are plenty of educational opportunities for learning about various wildlife habitats. Lichterman is part of the Memphis Museum System, which also includes the Pink Palace and other sites. *Tip:* Admission is free on Tuesdays after 1pm. Give yourself 2 to 3 hours here.

5992 Quince Rd. © **901/767-7322.** www.memphismuseums.org. $6 adults, $5.50 seniors, $4.50 children 3–12. Tues–Thurs 9am–4pm; Fri–Sat 9am–5pm.

Memphis Botanic Garden ★ With 20 formal gardens covering 96 acres, this rather large botanical garden requires a bit of time to visit properly. You'll find something in bloom at almost any time of year, and even in winter the Japanese garden offers a tranquil setting for a quiet stroll. In April and May the Ketchum Memorial Iris Garden, one of the largest in the country, is in bloom, and during May, June, and September the Municipal Rose Garden is alive with color. A special Sensory Garden is designed for people with disabilities and has plantings that stimulate all five senses. In 2009, a new 2½-acre Children's Garden opened, offering a "tree top adventure" that ascends into the tree line, and a tunneling excursion that offers kids a worm's-eye point of view. Allow at least 2 hours.

Audubon Park, 750 Cherry Rd. © **901/576-4100.** www.memphisbotanicgarden.com. Admission $5 adults, $4 seniors and students, $3 children 3–12. Mar–Oct Mon–Sat 9am–6pm, Sun 11am–6pm. Located across from Audubon Park Golf Course on Cherry Rd., btw. Southern and Park aves. Closed Thanksgiving, Christmas, and New Year's.

Shelby Farms Park ★★ An estimated one million people each year visit Shelby Farms, a 4,500-acre sanctuary for outdoor enthusiasts located in eastern Shelby County a short drive from downtown Memphis. Wooded hiking and biking trails, horseback riding, fishing, and an off-leash dog park are just a few of the active pursuits you'll find here. The 65-acre Patriot Lake provides calm waters for canoes, kayaks, and Stand Up Paddle (SUP) boarding, while kids find hours of entertainment in the new $1-million Woodland Discovery Playground, with its forts and tunnels.

Picnic sites and shelters are available, as is a disc golf course and fields designated for kite flying and model-airplane flying. But by far the most surprising feature of Shelby Farms is its herd of live buffalo. Doing what these legendary American animals do best, the buffaloes actually roam, in pastures maintained by the Shelby Farms Park Conservancy.

Shelby Park Farms Visitor Center, 500 N. Pine Lake Dr. ©**901/767-PARK** (7275). www.shelby farmspark.org. Free admission. Fees vary for boat and bike rentals, horseback riding, and so on. Park operates daily sunrise–sunset. Visitors Center Mon–Fri 8am–5pm.

AFRICAN-AMERICAN HERITAGE IN MEMPHIS

For many people, the city of Memphis is synonymous with one of the most significant, and saddest, events in recent American history: the assassination of Dr. Martin Luther King, Jr. The Lorraine Motel, where King was staying when he was shot, has in the years since the assassination become the **National Civil Rights Museum** (p. 173).

Long before the civil rights movement brought King to Memphis, the city had already become one of the most important cities in the South for blacks. After the Civil War and the abolition of slavery, Memphis became a magnet for African Americans, who came here seeking economic opportunities. **Beale Street** (p. 164) was where they headed to start their search. Beale Street's most famous citizen was W. C. Handy, the father of the blues, who first put down on paper the blues born in the cotton fields of the Mississippi Delta. **W. C. Handy Park,** with its statue of the famous blues musician, is about halfway down Beale Street, and Handy's small house, now the **W. C. Handy House Museum** (p. 170), is also now on Beale Street. At the **Memphis Rock 'n' Soul Museum** (p. 168), just a block off Beale Street, you can learn more about Handy and other famous African-American blues musicians who found a place for their music. Best of all is the **Soulsville USA: Stax Museum of American Soul Music** (p. 169), which has been drawing rave reviews since it opened a few years ago in a resurgent South Memphis neighborhood. Another museum with exhibits on famous black musicians is the **Pink Palace Museum** (p. 174).

Church Park, on the corner of Beale and Fourth streets (and once the site of a large auditorium), was established by Robert R. Church, a former slave and Memphis businessman who became the city's first black millionaire. The park was a gathering place for African Americans in the early 1900s, when restrictive Jim Crow laws segregated city parks.

Gospel music was part of the inspiration for the blues that W. C. Handy wrote, and that music came from the churches of the black community. The tradition of rousing musical accompaniment in church continues at many of the city's churches, but none is more famous than the **Full Gospel Tabernacle,** 787 Hale Rd. (© **901/396-9192**), which is where one-time soul music star Al Green now takes to the pulpit as a minister. Sunday service is at 11:30am (p. 176). **Mason Temple Church of God in Christ,** 930 Mason St. (© **901/947-9300**), is the international headquarters of the Church of God in Christ and was where Dr. Martin Luther King, Jr., gave his "I've been to the mountaintop" speech shortly before his death. Tourists are welcome to visit and step inside. Donations are accepted. Sunday services are no longer held here, however.

If you'd like a guide to lead you through the most important sites in Memphis's African-American heritage, contact **Heritage Tours** (© **901/527-3427**), which offers both a 1-hour Beale Street Walking Tour ($5) and a 3- to 4-hour Memphis Black Heritage Tour ($25 adults, $15–$20 children). Heritage Tours also operates both the W. C. Handy House Museum and the Slavehaven/Burkle Estate Museum.

Heritage Tours also visits another worthwhile out-of-town attraction, the **Alex Haley House Museum** (© **731/ 738-2240**). If you prefer to go on your own, it's a pleasant day trip by car to reach the small town of Henning, about 45 miles north of downtown Memphis on U.S. 51. The home is now a museum containing memorabilia and old portraits of the Haley family. Nearby is the family burial site, where Haley (author of *Roots: The Saga of an American Family*) and many of his ancestors, including Chicken George, are buried. The museum is open Tuesday to Saturday 10am to 5pm and Sunday by appointment only. Admission is $6 for adults and $4 for students.

13

> ### Sexy Swing
>
> Grammy-winning pop star and avid golfer **Justin Timberlake** bought and renovated an old country club near the northern suburb of Millington, where he's from. The new **Mirimichi Golf Club,** an 18-hole championship, par-72 course, features more than 7,400 yards, 80 bunkers, four waterfalls, six lakes, and two creeks that run between holes. It is also the first eco-friendly course certified by the Audubon Classic Sanctuary Program. To reserve a tee time, or get directions to the course, contact Mirimichi Golf Club, 6195 Woodstock Cuba Rd., Millington, TN (© **901/259-3800;** www.mirimichi.com).

ESPECIALLY FOR KIDS

Many of Memphis's main attractions will appeal to children as well as to adults, but there are also places that are specifically geared toward kids. In addition to the attractions listed below, see also the Pink Palace Museum (p. 174), the Memphis Zoo (p. 175), the Chucalissa Archaeological Museum (p. 175), the Mud Island/Mississippi River Museum (p. 173), and the Peabody Ducks (p. 232).

Attractions for Kids

Children's Museum of Memphis ★ Located adjacent to the Liberty Bowl Memorial Stadium, the children's museum offers fun, hands-on activities that can be enjoyed by children and adults alike. A real fire engine invites climbing, while the museum's kid-sized city lets little ones act like grown-ups: They can go shopping for groceries, stop by the bank to cash a check, try their hand at broadcasting the news, or climb up through a 22-foot-tall skyscraper. Special traveling exhibitions are often booked at the museum, so call ahead to find out what special programs are being offered during your stay. Allow 2 to 3 hours.

2525 Central Ave. © **901/458-2678.** www.cmom.com. Admission $10, free for babies under 1. Daily 9am–5pm; June–July open until 7pm. Closed Easter, Thanksgiving, and Christmas. Btw. Airways and Hollywood.

Fire Museum of Memphis Billed as the only fire museum in the country that combines history with an interactive fire-safety educational program, this often-overlooked kids' attraction has lots to offer, and safety lessons to teach. Highlights include Ol' Billy the talking horse and a simulation that allows visitors to feel as if they are standing inside a burning house. Though it's far from being a "thrill-ride" experience, parents should keep in mind that the scene, which includes a sofa bursting into flames and a rise in temperature as the fire engulfs the house, may be too intense for easily frightened youngsters. *Tips:* Two-for-one admission is offered on Tuesdays. Allow an hour and a half for a visit.

118 Adams St. ✆ **901/320-5650.** www.firemuseum.com. $6 adults, $5 children 3–12. Mon–Sat 9am–5pm.

Golf & Games Family Park   Located on the east side of town just off I-40 at exit 12A, this miniature golf and games complex claims to be the largest of its kind in the world; whether or not that claim is true, your kids will find plenty to do. There are more than 50 holes of miniature golf, a driving range, baseball batting cages, a go-kart track, a swimming pool, a video game room, and picnic tables. A laser-tag arena and ropes course are other active options. Allow 2 to 3 hours.

5484 Summer Ave. (at Pleasant View Rd.). ✆ **901/386-2992.** www.golfandgamesmemphis.com. 1-day passes range from $19 for 3 attractions to $55 for 10 attractions. Sun–Thurs 8am–11pm; Fri–Sat 8am–midnight. (Closes 1 hr. earlier during school year.)

STROLLING AROUND MEMPHIS

If you like to walk, consider doing the tour outlined below, which takes in some of the city's best attractions, including Beale Street and the National Civil Rights Museum.

WALKING TOUR: DOWNTOWN MEMPHIS

START:	**The Peabody hotel, on the corner of Union Avenue and Second Street.**
FINISH:	**Cotton Row and the Cotton Museum at the Memphis Cotton Exchange, corner of Front Street and Union Avenue.**
TIME:	**Approximately 2 hours, not including time spent at museums, shopping, meals, and other stops. It's best to plan on spending the whole day doing this walking tour.**
BEST TIMES:	**Spring and fall, when the weather isn't so muggy, and Friday and Saturday, when the Rendezvous is open for lunch.**
WORST TIMES:	**Summer days, when the weather is just too muggy for doing this much walking. Be mindful of safety, and don't attempt this walking tour after dark.**

Start your tour of Memphis's main historic districts at:

1 The Peabody hotel

This is the home of the famous Peabody ducks, which spend their days contentedly floating on the water of a marble fountain in the hotel's lobby. The ducks make their grand, red-carpet entrance each morning at 11am (and the crowds of onlookers begin assembling before 10:30am).

Walking Tour: Downtown Memphis

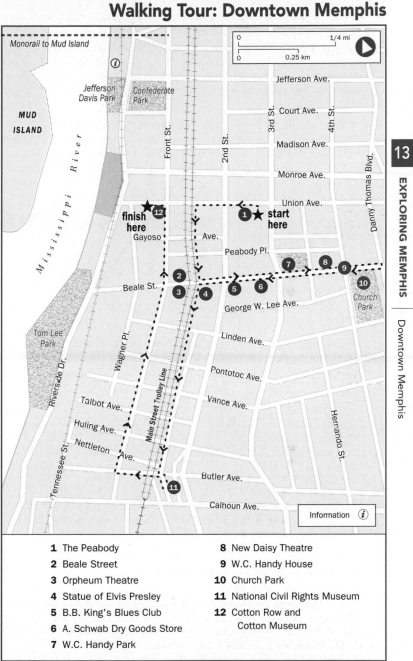

1 The Peabody
2 Beale Street
3 Orpheum Theatre
4 Statue of Elvis Presley
5 B.B. King's Blues Club
6 A. Schwab Dry Goods Store
7 W.C. Handy Park
8 New Daisy Theatre
9 W.C. Handy House
10 Church Park
11 National Civil Rights Museum
12 Cotton Row and
    Cotton Museum

2 The Rendezvous ☕

By the time the crowds thin out and you've had a chance to ogle The Peabody's elegant lobby, you may already be thinking about lunch. If it's a Friday or Saturday, you can fortify yourself at The Rendezvous, one of Memphis's favorite barbecue spots. 52 S. Second St. ⓒ **901/523-2746.** See p. 193.

From The Peabody, walk 1 block west to Main Street, a pedestrian mall down which runs an old-fashioned trolley. Turn left, and in 2 blocks you'll come to:

3 Beale Street

This is where W. C. Handy made the blues the first original American music when he committed "Memphis Blues" to paper. Today, this street of restored buildings is Memphis's main evening-entertainment district.

On the corner of Main and Beale, you can't miss the:

4 Orpheum Theatre

Originally built as a vaudeville theater in 1928, the Orpheum features a classic theater marquee and beautiful interior decor. Today, it's Memphis's main performing arts center.

Across Main Street from the theater stands a:

5 Statue of Elvis Presley

A visit to this statue is a must for Elvis fans. Bring your camera.

Continuing east on Beale Street to the corner of Second Street will bring you to:

6 B.B. King's Blues Club

Named for the Beale Street Blues Boy himself, this is the most popular club on the street, and though B.B. King plays here only twice a year, there is still great live blues here almost every night.

A few doors down the street, you'll come to the:

7 A. Schwab Dry Goods Store

This store has been in business at this location since 1876, and once inside, you may think that nothing has changed since the day the store opened. You'll find an amazing array of the odd and the unusual. *Note:* The Schwab family recently sold the store to a group of private investors. The future of the store is uncertain at this time.

At Beale and Third streets, you can take a breather in:

8 W. C. Handy Park

There always seems to be some live music in this park, also the site of a statue of Handy.

A block south along Beale Street from this park you'll find the:

9 New Daisy Theatre

This is a popular venue for contemporary music, including rock, blues, and folk.

A few doors down from the New Daisy, you'll find the restored:

10 W. C. Handy House

Though it wasn't always on this site, this house was where Handy lived when making a name for himself on Beale Street.

Diagonally across the intersection is:

11 Church Park

Robert Church, a former slave who became the city's first African-American millionaire, gave the African-American citizens of Memphis this park in 1899.

Now head back up Beale Street and take a left on Main. This is the street down which the trolley runs, so if you're feeling tired, you can hop on the trolley and take it south a few blocks. If you walk, turn left on Butler Street, and if you ride, walk east on Calhoun Street. In a very short block, you'll come to the:

12 National Civil Rights Museum

Once the Lorraine Motel, it was here that Dr. Martin Luther King, Jr., was assassinated on April 4, 1968. The motel has been converted into a museum documenting the struggle for civil rights.

After visiting this museum, head west on Butler Street and turn right on Front Street. You will now be walking through:

13 Cotton Row and the Cotton Museum

In the days before and after the Civil War, and continuing into the early part of the 20th century, this area was the heart of the Southern cotton industry. Most of America's cotton was once shipped through the docks 2 blocks away. This area of warehouses and old storefronts is now a designated historic district, and many of the buildings have been renovated.

ORGANIZED TOURS

River Tours

Although the economic heart of Memphis has moved to the eastern suburbs, this is still a Mississippi River town; no visit to Memphis would be complete without spending a bit of time on Ole Man River. **Memphis Riverboats,** 45 S. Riverside Dr. (© **800/221-6197** or 901/527-5694; www.memphisriverboats.net), operates several paddle-wheelers, all of which leave from a dock on "the cobblestones" at the foot of Monroe Avenue in downtown Memphis. From March to November, there are 1½-hour sightseeing cruises, and in the summer, there are sunset dinner cruises and party cruises. The barbecue-buffet dinner cruises include live music. The 1½-hour sightseeing cruise costs $20 for adults; $17 for seniors, military, and students; $10 for children 4 to 17 (free for children 3 and under). The evening dinner cruise costs $45 for adults, $43 for seniors and military, and $30 for children.

City Tours

"There's only two reasons to go to a juke joint full of blues: because you feel good, or because you feel bad." That's the perfectly logical reasoning behind Memphis's most authentic and in-depth tour operator, **American Dream Safari** (© **901/527-8870;** www.americandreamsafari.com). This is your chance to be chauffeured around town in a '55 Cadillac, with stops at Humes High School (where Elvis went to school), Johnny Cash's house, and countless other gems found only in Memphis. Owner-driver Tad Pierson, one of the coolest guys in town, has an encyclopedic knowledge of rock and blues history, he has great taste in music, and he can tailor your experience to fit your mood. Whether you want him to escort you to Rev. Al Green's Full Gospel Tabernacle on Sunday morning, and then to Gus's for fried chicken afterward, or if you'd rather take the "Drive By Shooting" photographer's tour, he will not only get you there but provide as much context and conversation as you want him to. He charges a flat rate, starting at about $200 for 3 hours, money well spent for the serious music tourist. The car seats five passengers.

Backbeat Tours, 140 Beale St. (© **866/392-BEAT** [2328] or 901/272-2328; www.backbeattours.com), does a booming business from its convenient Beale Street ticket office. For these guys, "Rockin' Rides Through Memphis Music History" is more than just a tag line. In this case, these fun-loving tour operators are talented musicians who sing and strum guitars on the bus, performing Sun-era songs while showing off the local sites. Best of all is the actual bus, "Miss Claudy." She's a 1959 cream-and-crimson-colored, city-transit beauty. Fully restored, the comfy bus still has those cheesy Naugahyde seat covers. Tour-package pricing starts at $26 for adults for the 90-minute Mojo Tour ($24 for seniors, $14 children 7–12) to $42 per adult for the Big Mojo Tour, which includes legendary Sun Studio Graceland ($40 for seniors and students, and $31 for children 7–12).

Blues City Tours of Memphis, 325 Union Ave. (© **901/522-9229;** www.bluescitytours.com), offers more than two dozen itineraries for varied interests, from music sites to shopping and nightlife. Before taxes, the 3-hour city tour costs $24 for adults and $16 for children; the Elvis Graceland Tour, $50 for adults and $40 for children. They also offer tours to the Tunica, Mississippi, casinos—a smart bet if you plan to drink alcohol while you're there and want to leave the driving to someone else.

Why be chauffeured around an unfamiliar city when you can do it on your own two feet, getting a good overview of the area and your exercise to boot? The unique **Rockin' Runnin' Tours,** 778 N. McLean (© **901/461-3139;** www.rockinrunning tours.com), is Memphis's newest tour-group operator. Led by running enthusiasts who will customize any tour to suit a customer's needs, the tours are priced at $25 per person for a 3-mile tour ($5 for each additional mile), or $20 per person for groups of three or more. Kids in strollers are free, and children 12 and older are half-price; call ahead to make arrangements for children under age 12). A variety of tours is offered. The Rockin' Downtown Loop (3- or 6-mile options) follows a "greatest hits" route that starts at The Peabody and includes glimpses of the South Main Historic District, the National Civil Rights Museum, Cotton Row, and Beale Street. The 6-mile version adds Sun Studio and views of the Mississippi River. Designed to showcase lesser-known, hidden gems in Central Memphis is the Midtown Hipster Run that features the simple ranch house where Johnny Cash lived, as well as Overton Park, the Cooper-Young district, and lovely residential neighborhoods Central Gardens and the Evergreen Historic District. All tours include a T-shirt, water bottle, and snack, as well as a digital photo of you during the run.

Finally, **Carriage Tours of Memphis** (© **901/527-7542;** www.carriagetour sofmemphis.com) specializes in old-fashioned, horse-drawn carriage rides that can be tailored to be as romantic or family-friendly as you choose. The graceful carriages glide through historic downtown neighborhoods and parks, past Beale Street, and through late-19th-century Court Square. The pretty carriages, which can seat six people, are available for a flat rate of $45 for 30 minutes and $75 for an hour. Tours are available year-round, weather permitting. You can make advance reservations or just walk up to the carriages in front of The Peabody (149 Union Ave.) and along Beale Street at Second and Third streets.

OUTDOOR ACTIVITIES

GOLF Golfers were thrilled when, in September 2010, hometown megastar Justin Timberlake opened **Mirimichi**, 6195 Woodstock Cuba Rd., Millington (☏ **901/259-3800**), an eco-friendly public golf course in north Memphis. Memphis's other public courses include the **Stoneridge Golf Course,** 3049 Davies Plantation Rd. (☏ **901/382-1886**), as well as those operated by the Memphis Parks Commission: **The Links at Audubon Park,** 4160 Park Ave. (☏ **901/683-6941**); **Fox Meadows Park,** 3064 Clark Rd. (☏ **901/362-0232**); **The Links at Galloway,** 3815 Walnut Grove Rd. (☏ **901/685-7805**); and The Links at **Overton Park,** 2080 Poplar Ave. (☏ **901/725-9905**).

TENNIS The Memphis Parks Commission operates seven public tennis courts all over the city. The most convenient to downtown and Midtown is **Leftwich,** 4145 Southern Ave. (☏ **901/685-7907**).

SPECTATOR SPORTS

BASEBALL The **Memphis Redbirds Baseball Club,** 175 Toyota Plaza, Ste. 300 (☏ **901/721-6050;** www.memphisredbirds.com), a Triple-A affiliate of the St. Louis Cardinals, plays at AutoZone Park, located 2 blocks east of The Peabody hotel on Union Avenue.

BASKETBALL The **Memphis Grizzlies** (☏ **901/205-1234;** www.grizzlies.com) are the city's first NBA team, having relocated from Vancouver, British Columbia, in 2001. Since 2004, they have played at their new downtown arena, the FedExForum. Grizzlies fever was at an all-time high during the 2010–11 season, when the team made the playoffs.

The **University of Memphis Tigers** (☏ **888/867-UOFM** [8636] or 901/678-2331; www.gotigersgo.com) regularly pack in crowds of 20,000 or more people when they play the FedExForum. The Tigers often put up a good showing against nationally ranked NCAA teams, which makes for some exciting basketball. Call for ticket and schedule information.

FOOTBALL The **AutoZone Liberty Bowl Classic** (☏ **901/729-4344;** www.libertybowl.org) is the biggest football event of the year in Memphis and pits two of the country's top college teams in a December postseason game. As with other postseason college bowl games, the Liberty Bowl is extremely popular and tickets go fast. This game is held at the **Liberty Bowl Memorial Stadium** (www.libertybowl.org), on the Mid-South Fairgrounds at the corner of East Parkway South and Central Avenue.

GOLF TOURNAMENTS The **St. Jude Classic** (☏ **901/748-0534;** www.stjudeclassic.com), a PGA charity tournament, is held each year in late spring at the Tournament Players Club at Southwind.

GREYHOUND RACING Across the river in Arkansas, greyhounds race at the **Southland Greyhound Park Gaming and Racing,** 1550 N. Ingram Blvd., West

Memphis, Arkansas (© **800/467-6182** or 870/735-3670). Matinee post time is at 12:30pm; evening races start at 7:30pm.

HORSE SHOWS   Horse shows are popular in Memphis, and the biggest of the year is the **Germantown Charity Horse Show** (© **901/754-0009;** www.gchs. org), held each June at the Germantown Horse Show Arena, which is just off Poplar Pike at Melanie Smith Lane in Germantown.

TENNIS   The **Regions Morgan Keegan Championships** and **Cellular South Cup** (© **901/765-4401** or 901/685-ACES [2237]; www.memphistennis.com), part of the ATP Tour, are held each year in February at the Racquet Club of Memphis. Call for ticket and schedule information.

WHERE TO EAT IN MEMPHIS

M ention Memphis food, and one of two things may come to mind: pork barbecue (world-famous), or Elvis's fried peanut-butter-and-banana sandwiches (infamous). Although both these and other Southern staples like fried chicken, vegetables simmered with ham, corn bread, and sweet iced tea are abundant here, Memphis's unexpectedly diverse dining scene also boasts its fair share of gourmet establishments with noteworthy chefs and extensive wine lists, as well as great burger joints and steakhouses. Vegetarians needn't feel marginalized. For such a pork-centric place, Memphis has a laudable array of places focused on offering organic, farm-fresh, and meat-free menu choices. The restaurants recommended here are some of the city's best. The price categories below represent what you could expect to pay for a full meal, for one person (not including alcohol, tax, or tip).

BEST RESTAURANT BETS

- **Best Restaurant for Sharing:** The new **Flight Restaurant and Wine Bar,** 39 S. Main, puts the fun in fine dining with its delectable international cuisine. Salads, appetizers, entrees, even desserts are offered individually or in flights of three small plates, allowing patrons to sample a plethora of flavors in a single sitting. See p. 188.
- **Most Romantic:** Rising culinary star Kelly English presides over unforgettable, multicourse meals at his French-Creole **Restaurant Iris,** 2146 Monroe Ave. Ensconced in a lovely Victorian home, the restaurant also offers the best service in town. Expect to be pampered. See p. 195.
- **Best for Kids:** The cavernous **Spaghetti Warehouse,** 40 W. Huling, has been a tried-and-true kids' favorite for many years. Families can dine inside an old trolley car while deciding whether to order burgers or plates of pasta and meatballs. See p. 195.
- **Best Restaurant for Dinner & Cocktails:** Vibrant, Louisiana-inspired dishes like shrimp and grits, bread pudding, and pan-seared redfish are delicious at **Felicia Suzanne's,** 80 Monroe Ave.—especially after a few Creole Martinis. That's vodka shaken with pickled okra, jalapeño juice, green beans, and tomatoes. See p. 188.
- **Oldest Diner:** Young Elvis ate here, and you can too. Grab a booth and order a plate lunch at the **Arcade Restaurant,** 540 S. Main St., a last-of-its-kind diner that has anchored this downtown corner since 1919. See p. 194.

PRICE CATEGORIES

Expensive	$41 and up
Moderate	$20–$40
Inexpensive	Under $20

o **Best Soul Food:** The beloved **Four Way Restaurant,** 998 Mississippi Blvd., is Memphis's oldest soul food restaurant, serving the most sublime sweet potato pie, fried pork chops, and collard greens you're ever likely to taste. See p. 204.

o **Best Breakfast:** Scrumptious eggs, buttermilk biscuits, blintzes, and sausages pull early risers into **Brother Juniper's,** 3519 Walker Ave. This quaint, family-run eatery also offers Greek specialties, like spanakopita omelets. See p. 202.

o **Best Farm-to-Fork Restaurant:** Chef Mac Edwards's cheerful **Elegant Farmer,** 262 S. Highland, showcases seasonal farmers' market fare in a charming cottage. Here you'll find fresh, comfort food favorites like salmon patties, creamy corn pudding, garden-fresh salads, and killer chocolate cake. See p. 201.

o **Best Splurge:** Danish-born chef Erling Jensen, owner of **Erling Jensen,** 1044 S. Yates Rd., is one of the most revered chefs in town. With fastidious attention to detail, he presides over gourmet preparations of everything from escargots, silky bisques, and wild game dishes to exquisite sorbets and crème brûlée in one of the most strikingly chic dining rooms in the city.

o **Best Bang for Your Buck:** Juicy burgers, crispy fries, and cold beer are an unbeatable, budget-friendly combo at **Huey's,** with locations in all areas of town. See p. 195.

DOWNTOWN
Expensive

Felicia Suzanne's ★★ CREOLE   Perhaps the best-known female chef in Memphis, Felicia Suzanne seems to be hitting her stride after nearly a decade at the helm of her eponymous restaurant in downtown's historic Brinkley building (original site of The Peabody hotel back in the 1920s). Drawing on Louisiana and Carolina Low-Country culinary traditions, she offers vibrant, Southern-inspired dishes, like shrimp and grits with andouille sausage, and the mile-high bacon, tomato, and lettuce sandwich, stacked with crispy fried green tomatoes. Dramatic lighting and contemporary art and furnishings make the spacious bar a great place for cocktails such as the Creole Martini (vodka shaken with pickled okra, jalapeño juice, green beans, and tomatoes). The intimate, wrought-iron fenced courtyard is reminiscent of Old New Orleans. Bread pudding is among the desserts, but I'll forgo it every time for the intensely chocolatey baked fudge, a puddle of pure sin.

80 Monroe Ave. ✆ **901/523-0877.** www.feliciasuzanne.com. Entrees $22–$28; AE, MC, V. Tues-Sat 5–10pm; Fri 11:30am–2pm.

Flight Restaurant and Wine Bar ★★★ TAPAS   Happily, one of Memphis's newest fine-dining restaurants is also one of its consistently best. Go with a group of friends, agree to taste off of each other's plates, and you've got a fun feast that will allow you to sample dozens of delicious dishes. At Flight, patrons may choose trios of any given course—appetizers, salads, entrees, desserts, and wines. A Seafood Flight might include lobster tail, crab cakes, and shrimp scampi, all artfully plated and served side-by-side on rectangular white platters. The Feathered Flight features chicken, quail, and duck dishes. For dessert, consider the Cupcake Flight that includes yellow, strawberry, and s'more cupcakes—the latter with a graham-cracker crust, liquid chocolate center, and toasted marshmallows. Large plates (as well as trios of small plates) of any menu item also are available. Choose your flights with wine, if you like. Extremely attentive service, a posh, two-tier dining room, plus a lovely outdoor patio also help make Flight the perfect place to impress a date or business client.

39 S. Main. Ⓒ **901/521-8005.** www.flightmemphis.com. Lunch $10–$14; dinner $27–$39. AE, DISC, MC, V. Daily lunch and dinner.

The Inn at Hunt Phelan CREOLE/BRUNCH   What's so much fun about dining at the Inn at Hunt Phelan is how cozy and welcome you can feel in such a grand, storied place. The restaurant—made up of a collection of small dining rooms on the first floor of a restored 1828 antebellum mansion—is a welcome retreat just outside the hustle of downtown Memphis. Inside the mansion, now a lovely B&B, the restaurant caters to inn guests and to outside visitors. On a recent visit here, the salad of artichokes, wild boar pancetta, and olive vinaigrette were a delightful beginning. The morel mushrooms with a grit cake, fava beans, and okra were rich and a nice tip of the hat to Southern-food tradition, but the lamb with couscous entree proved that the chef is definitely not living in the past. An impressive dessert and wine list round out the menu—your waiter will be happy to make recommendations, should you not know where to begin.

533 Beale St. Ⓒ **901/525-8225.** www.huntphelan.com. Reservations recommended. Main courses $27–$34 dinner; Sun brunch $11–$24. AE, DC, MC, V. Wed–Sat 5–11pm; Sun brunch 10am–2:30pm.

McEwen's on Monroe ★ SOUTHERN   The exposed brick walls, white tablecloths, and well-spaced tables are your first clue that McEwen's is a classy, comfortable kind of place. A lunchtime favorite with the business crowd, McEwen's "Southern fusion" menu is a mind-twisting mix that includes appetizers like sweet potato empanadas, barbeque duck confit enchiladas, and buttermilk fried oysters. Pan-seared scallops with stone-ground cheddar grits are one of the tastiest entrees. Also delicious is the watercress salad, with mandarin oranges, roasted red and yellow bell peppers, and a cotija cheese blood-orange vinaigrette. For dessert, nothing will make you happier than McEwen's famous banana cream pie. The award-winning confection will make you swoon, Southern-style.

122 Monroe Ave. Ⓒ **901/527-7085.** http://mcewensmemphis.com. Main courses $7–$12 lunch; $20–$29 dinner. AE, DC, MC, V. Mon–Fri 11am–2pm; Mon–Thurs 5:30–10pm; Fri–Sat 5:30–11pm. Bar open later.

Spindini ★ ITALIAN   Opened to much fanfare in 2007 by chef Judd Grisanti in downtown's South Main arts district, Spindini is still holding its own. Grisanti recently departed, but that hasn't dimmed Spindini's star. The long, narrow dining room is flanked by a banquette with tightly spaced tables and a classy bar adorned with decorative glass sculptures. A wood-burning oven emits a warm glow, as the kitchen churns out steaks, seared fish, pizzas, and fresh pasta dishes. The Tuscan Butter may be one of the best appetizers in town—an ice-cream-sized scoop of spreadable mascarpone and goat cheese drenched in a tangy tomato sauce and served with soft, slender slices of warm garlic bread.

Memphis Restaurants: Downtown & Midtown

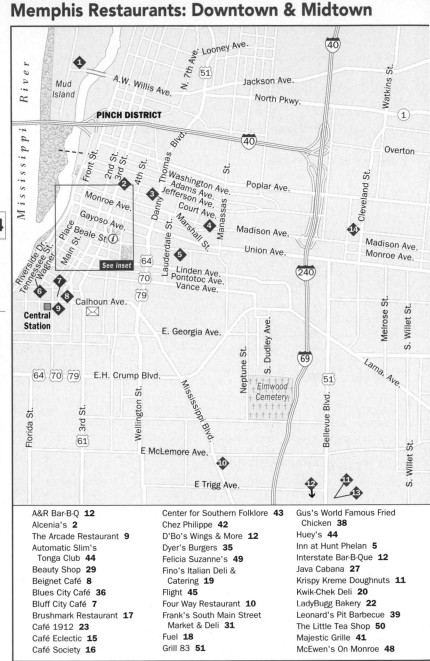

A&R Bar-B-Q **12**
Alcenia's **2**
The Arcade Restaurant **9**
Automatic Slim's
  Tonga Club **44**
Beauty Shop **29**
Beignet Café **8**
Blues City Café **36**
Bluff City Café **7**
Brushmark Restaurant **17**
Café 1912 **23**
Café Eclectic **15**
Café Society **16**

Center for Southern Folklore **43**
Chez Philippe **42**
D'Bo's Wings & More **12**
Dyer's Burgers **35**
Felicia Suzanne's **49**
Fino's Italian Deli &
  Catering **19**
Flight **45**
Four Way Restaurant **10**
Frank's South Main Street
  Market & Deli **31**
Fuel **18**
Grill 83 **51**

Gus's World Famous Fried
  Chicken **38**
Huey's **44**
Inn at Hunt Phelan **5**
Interstate Bar-B-Que **12**
Java Cabana **27**
Krispy Kreme Doughnuts **11**
Kwik-Chek Deli **20**
LadyBugg Bakery **22**
Leonard's Pit Barbecue **39**
The Little Tea Shop **50**
Majestic Grille **41**
McEwen's On Monroe **48**

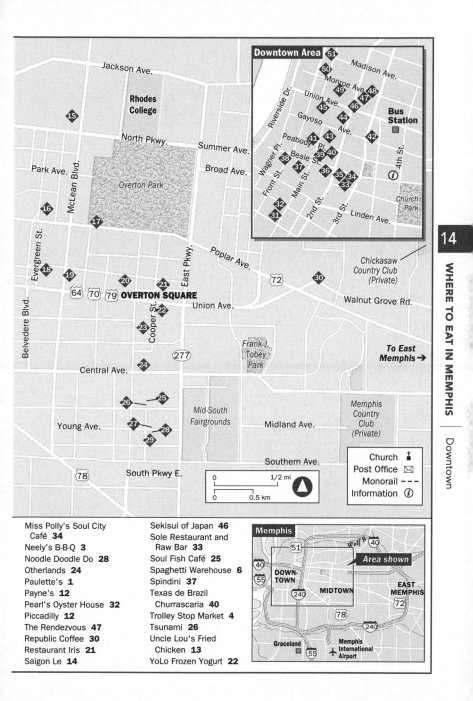

Downtown Area

Jackson Ave.

Rhodes College

North Pkwy.

Summer Ave.

Park Ave.

McLean Blvd.

Overton Park

Broad Ave.

Poplar Ave.

Evergreen St.

Belvedere Blvd.

Cooper St.

East Pkwy.

OVERTON SQUARE

Union Ave.

Frank J. Tobey Park

Central Ave.

Mid-South Fairgrounds

Young Ave.

Midland Ave.

Southern Ave.

South Pkwy E.

Chickasaw Country Club (Private)

Walnut Grove Rd.

To East Memphis →

Memphis Country Club (Private)

Madison Ave.

Monroe Ave.

Union Ave.

Riverside Dr.

Gayoso

Peabody Pl.

Beale St.

Wagner Pl.

Front St.

Main St.

2nd St.

3rd St.

Linden Ave.

Bus Station

4th St.

Church Park

14

WHERE TO EAT IN MEMPHIS | Downtown

Church ✝
Post Office ✉
Monorail - - -
Information ⓘ

0   1/2 mi
0   0.5 km

Miss Polly's Soul City Café **34**
Neely's B-B-Q **3**
Noodle Doodle Do **28**
Otherlands **24**
Paulette's **1**
Payne's **12**
Pearl's Oyster House **32**
Piccadilly **12**
The Rendezvous **47**
Republic Coffee **30**
Restaurant Iris **21**
Saigon Le **14**

Sekisui of Japan **46**
Sole Restaurant and Raw Bar **33**
Soul Fish Café **25**
Spaghetti Warehouse **6**
Spindini **37**
Texas de Brazil Churrascaria **40**
Trolley Stop Market **4**
Tsunami **26**
Uncle Lou's Fried Chicken **13**
YoLo Frozen Yogurt **22**

Memphis

Wolf

Area shown

DOWN-TOWN

MIDTOWN

EAST MEMPHIS

Graceland

Memphis International Airport

383 S. Main St. ✆ **901/578-2767.** www.spindinimemphis.com. Reservations recommended. Pizzas and main courses $13–$32. AE, DC, DISC, MC, V. Sun–Wed 5–10pm; Thurs–Sat 5–11pm.

Texas de Brazil Churrascaria BRAZILIAN/STEAK   A carnivore's dream, this exotic (for Memphis), all-you-can-eat, special-occasion restaurant draws diners intent on overindulging. Sizzling filet mignon, flank steak, sausages, pork, and chicken specialties are slow-roasted over an open pit, and carved from long, swordlike skewers, right at your table by waiters. These "gauchos" will keep bringing meats to your table as long as you keep eating it. Gimmickry aside, the food is first-rate. You'll find authentic Brazilian favorites like hearts of palm on the vast salad bar, which has it all—sushi, imported cheeses, even Italian salami. You'll have to pay extra for desserts ($7.50 to $8.50 each) and alcohol. Pretend you're in Rio and order a *caipirhina*, a sugar-cane rum and lime cocktail, or choose a South American wine from the extensive cellar.

150 Peabody Place. ✆ **901/526-7600.** www.texasdebrazil.com. Lunch $22 adults, dinner $43 adults; both meals half-price for kids 6–12. AE, DC, DISC, MC, V. Dinner nightly and lunch Wed–Fri.

14 Moderate

Automatic Slim's Tonga Club AMERICAN   Ownership changes have affected consistency at this once-hot restaurant, but it's still a fun place to hang for a late-night bite of fried fish, jerk chicken, or tobacco fries. The name "Automatic Slim" comes from an old blues song, and the Tonga Club was a local teen hangout popular in the early 1960s. Artists from New York and Memphis created the decor (they're credited on the menu), including zebra-print upholstered banquettes, slag-glass wall sconces, and colorfully upholstered bar stools. Be sure to try a cocktail with some of the fruit-soaked vodka.

83 S. Second St. ✆ **901/525-7948.** www.automaticslimsmemphis.com. Reservations accepted. Main courses at dinner $17–$26; late-night plates $10–$15. AE, DC, MC, V. Mon–Sat 11am–3am; Sun 10am–4pm.

Blues City Cafe ★★ STEAKS/BARBECUE   Far and away the best and most authentic restaurant on Beale Street, Blues City Cafe has been a favorite with locals for more than two decades. Signature dishes are aged, hand-cut porterhouse and

---

😊 FAMILY-FRIENDLY RESTAURANTS

Corky's Ribs & BBQ (p. 201)   Kids and grandparents alike love Corky's boisterous atmosphere, rollicking rock oldies music, and big pork platters paired with sky-high stacks of onion rings.

Four Way Restaurant (p. 204)   Old-fashioned home cooking means kids might be asked to eat their vegetables along with fried chicken and pork chops. But when the green beans are seasoned with pork and the mashed potatoes are drenched in butter, who but the fussiest little eaters would object?

The Majestic Grille (p. 193)   Vintage Popeye cartoons and silent movies play on a large video screen at one end of this upscale-ish but affordable family restaurant with enough menu choices for all tastes.

Spaghetti Warehouse (p. 195)   Antique trolley cars and hearty Italian comfort food, including thick slabs of lasagna and kid-friendly spaghetti and meatballs, make this inexpensive restaurant a family favorite.

T-bone steaks, tender beef tamales that melt in your mouth, and spicy seafood gumbo. Barbecue fanatics swear by the hickory-smoked pork ribs, slathered in sauce. All platters come with baked beans, coleslaw, and steak fries. Weathered signs and old booths enhance the laid-back, down home vibe here.

140 Beale St. ℭ **901/526-3637.** www.bluescitycafe.com. Entrees $7.95–$18 (steaks about $15 per pound). AE, DC, DISC, MC, V. Daily from 11am.

The Majestic Grille ★ ☺ AMERICAN/STEAK   Silent movies, old Popeye cartoons, and Marx Brothers comedies play on a big screen in this stylish bistro and early 1900s movie palace. Today the interior is polished and sophisticated, a large dining room with tables and booths set on two levels. Something for everyone can be found on the extensive menu: Filet mignon, rib-eyes, and the pork tenderloin are best bets for big eaters. Signature flatbreads (thin-crust pizzas) come with a choice of toppings, and sandwiches and burgers are served with tendrils of crispy Parmesan fries. Shot glasses contain desserts like key lime pie and cheesecake, providing just a few bites to satisfy the sweet tooth.

145 S Main St. ℭ **901/522-8555.** www.majesticgrille.com. Main courses $12–$29. AE, DISC, MC, V. Mon–Thurs 11am–11pm; Fri–Sat 11am–midnight; Sun 11am–9pm.

Pearl's Oyster House ★ CAJUN/SEAFOOD   An old warehouse in downtown's South Main Street district has found renewed energy as a spacious, laid-back Gulf Coast–style seafood joint. Platters of plump oysters can be ordered raw or fried, or try the juicy pan-roasted mussels. Cajun gumbos and étouffée are rich, roux-based soups studded with chunks of andouille sausage and fish. Fried-shrimp po' boys are encased in shredded lettuce inside chewy French baguettes. More substantial fare includes fresh catfish fried in butter, and the seasonal crawfish boil—a spicy-hot favorite with corn-on-the-cob and new potatoes.

299 S. Main St. ℭ **901/522-9070.** www.pearlsoysterhouse.com. Main courses $10–$19. AE, DC, DISC, MC, V. Mon–Sat from 11am; closing times vary.

The Rendezvous ★★ 📷 BARBECUE   The Rendezvous has been a downtown Memphis institution since 1948, and it has a well-deserved reputation for serving the best ribs in town. You can see the food being prepared in an old open kitchen as you walk in, but more importantly, your sense of smell will immediately perk up as the fragrance of hickory-smoked pork wafts past. You'll also likely be intrigued by all manner of strange objects displayed in this huge but cozy cellar. And when the waiter comes to take your order, there's no messin' around; when you come in, you're expected to know what you want—an order of ribs. Also be sure to ask if they still have any of the red beans and rice that are served nightly until the pot is empty. This Memphis landmark is tucked along General Washburn Alley, across from The Peabody. Upstairs, you'll find a large bar.

52 S. Second St. ℭ **901/523-2746.** www.hogsfly.com. Main plates $6.50–$18. AE, DC, DISC, MC, V. Tues–Thurs 4:30–10:30pm; Fri 11am–11pm; Sat 11:30am–11pm.

Sekisui of Japan ★★ JAPANESE/SUSHI   Unlike Japanese restaurants that almost go overboard on tranquillity, Sekisui is a noisy and active place, especially on weekends. The sushi bar prepares platters of assorted fish, from appetizer tidbits to a huge sushi boat that includes octopus, conch, snapper, and flying-fish-roe sushi. Fiery wasabi, a splash of soy, and shredded ginger add zing. Tempura, teriyaki, and *yakizakana* dinners come with rice, a wonderful miso soup, and salad. Some locations offer a separate *robata* grill menu. Among the other Sekisui locations are those at

25 S. Belvedere St. (© **901/725-0005**) in Midtown, and under the name **Sekisui Pacific Rim,** at 4724 Poplar Ave. (© **901/767-7770**), in East Memphis.

Inside the Holiday Inn Select downtown, 160 Union Ave. © **901/523-0001.** www.sekisuiusa.com. Reservations recommended Sat–Sun. Main courses $9–$26. AE, DC, DISC, MC, V. Mon–Fri 11:30am–2pm; Sun–Thurs 5–9pm; Fri–Sat 5–10pm.

Inexpensive

Alcenia's SOUTHERN   This down-to-earth breakfast/lunch hangout looks like the kind of place where Stella got her groove back. The decor is shabby chic, where orange walls and purple beaded curtains blend right in with the potted plants, African artwork, and tulle draped from the ceiling. Best known for its homemade preserves, Alcenia's serves up salmon croquettes, pancakes, and biscuits for breakfast. Sandwiches and Southern-style munchies are available at other hours. Call ahead to see if Alcenia's famous bread pudding is on the menu that day.

317 N. Main St. © **901/523-0200.** Main courses $7–$9. AE, DC, MC, V. Tues–Fri 11am–5pm; Sat 9am–1pm. (Occasionally open evenings for special events; call ahead.)

The Arcade Restaurant ★ AMERICAN   Established in 1919, the Arcade stands as a reminder of the early part of the century when this was a busy neighborhood, bustling with people and commerce. Although this corner is not nearly as lively as it once was, the restaurant attracts loyal Memphians and out-of-towners who stop by for the home-style cooking and pizzas. Because the proprietors have an annoying habit of closing down when business is slow, you might want to call ahead if you're making the Arcade your destination.

540 S. Main St. © **901/526-5757.** www.arcaderestaurant.com. Breakfast $6–$8; lunch $6–$8; pizza $7–$20. DC, DISC, MC, V. Daily 7am–3pm.

Beignet Café ★ 🍴 BRUNCH/CREOLE   With hot, crisp, sugar-dusted beignets every bit as mouthwatering as the famed Café Du Monde's in New Orleans—and some of the best jambalaya in town—this cute cafe is a hidden gem. Run by an enterprising foodie from Louisiana, this eatery is tucked off a side street behind the National Civil Rights Museum. On one of my visits (during the River Arts Fest in the South Main Historic District), succulent ribs were being grilled on an outdoor smoker at the corner. Full of unpretentious charm and friendly people enjoying such comfort food as po' boys, bread pudding, and fried macaroni-and-cheese balls, this place is one of my new favorites.

124 G. E. Patterson Blvd. © **901/527-1551.** Under $10. MC, V. Tues–Thurs 8am–8pm; Fri–Sat 8am–9pm; Sun 9am–3pm.

Dyer's Burgers 🍔 BURGERS   I feel obliged to include this retro diner only because it's garnered so much attention on Food Network, the Travel Channel, and in several national and international magazines. Why? Sure, it's got an appealing, old-timey look, but the greasy spoon's notoriety is their claim that they've been deep-frying their hamburgers and French fries in the same vat of cooking oil—for nearly a century. Let me set you straight: With food that's average at best, this place is just another novelty for easy-to-please bar-hoppers on Beale Street. But if you're dying for a deep-fried Twinkie, it's your funeral.

205 Beale St. © **901/527-3937.** Under $10. AE, DC, MC, V. Sun–Thurs 11am–1am; Fri–Sat 11am–5am.

Gus's World Famous Fried Chicken ★★★ SOUTHERN   In a decidedly dingy juke-joint setting off the beaten path downtown sits this franchise of the legendary Gus's in Mason, Tennessee. Black and white, young and old, hip and square—they and every other demographic all converge here for spicy-battered chicken, beans, slaw, and pies. Service is friendly but slow, so don't go here if you're in a hurry. (If you'd like to take a road trip to the Real McCoy, the original Gus's is at 505 Hwy. 70 W., Mason; ☎ **901/294-2028.** Call ahead for hours.)

310 S. Front St. ☎ **901/527-4877.** Main courses $6–$9. AE, MC, V. Daily 11am–9pm (Sat–Sun until 10pm).

Huey's ★★ 🔥 BURGERS   Ask Memphians where to get the best burger in town, and you'll invariably be directed to Huey's. With a fine sheen of grease and a layer of melting cheese, the thick, perfectly cooked hamburgers are substantial enough to require two hands to eat. Fries are addicting: crisp around the edges and full of creamy potato flavor within. This affordably priced, good-times tavern also has one of the most extensive beer selections in town. The original Huey's, at 1927 Madison Ave. (☎ **901/726-4372**), in the Overton Square area, is still in business. In recent years, suburban locations have also sprouted up in East Memphis and beyond.

77 S. Second St. ☎ **901/527-2700.** www.hueyburger.com. Reservations not accepted. Main courses $5–$10. AE, DISC, MC, V. Daily 11am–3am.

Spaghetti Warehouse ★ ☺ AMERICAN/ITALIAN   Families and tourists on budgets seek out this sprawling, noisy old warehouse brimming with antiques and amusing collectibles. Food is middle-of-the-road. Simple American burgers are served alongside Italian staples such as lasagna and spaghetti. Though this longtime Memphis eatery may lack the buzz of newer restaurants, it certainly has staying power.

40 W. Huling. ☎ **901/521-0907.** www.meatballs.com. Main plates $6–$16. AE, MC, V. Sun–Thurs 11am–10pm; Fri–Sat 11am–11pm.

MIDTOWN/CENTRAL MEMPHIS

For locations of restaurants in this section, see the "Memphis Restaurants: Downtown & Midtown" map on p. 190.

Expensive

Beauty Shop ★★ AMERICAN   The first and most important thing you need to know is *not* that this hip eatery sits inside an old 1960s-style beauty shop, but that it's the brainchild of Karen Blockman Carrier, the creative force behind Memphis's coolest restaurant (Automatic Slim's). Yes, the atmosphere is kitschy and fun. You can indeed dine in refurbished hair-dryer chairs. But what keeps the place packed with all the beautiful people is the fantastic food: globally inspired salads (I loved the Thai Cobb), entrees such as the whole striped bass, or the best BLTA (bacon, lettuce, tomato, and avocado sandwich) you've ever tasted.

966 S. Cooper St. ☎ **901/272-7111.** Reservations highly recommended. Main courses $19–$26. AE, MC, V. Mon–Sat 11am–2pm; brunch Sun 10am–3pm; dinner Mon–Sat Thurs 5–10pm.

Restaurant Iris ★★★ CAJUN/CREOLE/FRENCH   Chef/owner Kelly English, named one of *Food & Wine*'s Best Chefs of 2009, has been garnering rave reviews—and fully booked tables—at his Midtown fine-dining restaurant. Opened in 2008, it occupies a charming Victorian home that once housed the city's esteemed La

hotel RESTAURANTS

Nearly every large hotel has a restaurant, but which ones are worthy destinations if you're not booking a stay? These are the cream-of-the-crop: In 2011, **Paulette's,** 2110 Madison Ave. (© **901/726-5128**), which had been a Midtown fixture for decades, replaced Currents as the flagship restaurant at the swank Inn at Harbor Town. Gone is the French country décor of old, but not the restaurant's iconic filet mignon, strawberry-buttered popovers, and Hungarian specialties such as *gulyas.* Tucked into a corner of the Embassy Suites Hotel, **Frank Grisanti's** (© **901/761-9462**) serves some of the most authentic Italian food in Memphis. The atmosphere evokes the Old South far more than it does the trattorias of Rome, and the clublike setting attracts a well-heeled clientele. Meaty lasagna, rich pasta dishes, and creamed spinach are excellent choices here. Breakfast, lunch and dinner—as well as afternoon tea—are served in **Grill 83** (© **901/333-1224**), the chic restaurant and lounge adjacent to the Madison Hotel. Vintage black-and-white photographs adorn the walls of the narrow dining room, where succulent sea bass and 16-ounce Kansas City steaks are specialties. Of course, the opulent **Chez Philippe** (© **901/529-4188**) at The Peabody continues to impress patrons with its very expensive, prix-fixe menus of classic French cuisine. The ritzy landmark has also begun offering a reasonably priced tapas menu some evenings in the hotel lobby. Afternoon tea is served here, as well. Oysters on the half shell, and fresh-market-catch specials on such selections as Hawaiian sunfish, Maine lobster, and blue prawns are best bets at **Sole Restaurant & Raw Bar** (© **901/334-5950**), a business-casual seafood restaurant in one corner of the Westin Beale Street. With its soft lighting and warm, wood-paneled booths and tables set with ocean-blue napkins, you'll have a front-row seat to the activity across the street at the FedEx Forum arena.

Tourelle restaurant (where another noteworthy local chef, Erling Jensen, got his start). Raised in Louisiana and trained at the famed Culinary Institute of America, English excels in combining French and Creole influences in creative and inspired dishes that are never over the top. Already a menu staple is the lobster-knuckle sandwich, along with other generously portioned appetizers including bacon-braised Brussels sprouts salad. Friendly servers are extremely knowledgeable about food and wine, and their professionalism greatly enhances the dining experience here.

2146 Monroe Ave. © **901/590-2828.** www.restaurantiris.com. Reservations recommended. Main courses $25–$36. AE, MC, V. Mon–Sat 5–10pm; Sun brunch one Sunday a month.

Tsunami ★★★ PACIFIC RIM/SEAFOOD   Consistently ranked by locals as one of their favorite restaurants in Memphis, Tsunami serves creative Pacific Rim cuisine. Tropical colors over cement floors and walls enliven the otherwise uninspired setting. But the food's the thing. Appetizers run the gamut from pot sticker dumplings with chili-soy dipping sauce to shrimp satay with Thai peanut sauce. Among chef/owner Ben Smith's other specialties are roasted sea bass with black Thai rice and soy beurre blanc, wasabi-crusted tuna, and duck breast with miso-shiitake risotto. Crème brûlée fans should not miss Smith's sublime Tahitian-vanilla version of this classic. A judicious list of Australian and French wines includes champagne and a handful of ports.

928 S. Cooper St. © **901/274-2556.** www.tsunamimemphis.com. Reservations recommended. Main courses $20–$30; small plates $12–$15. AE, MC, V. Mon–Fri 11am–2pm; Mon–Sat 5:30–10pm.

Moderate

Cafe 1912 AMERICAN   At the edge of the Cooper-Young district in Midtown, this casual bistro and bar is especially popular with neighborhood residents. Rickety wooden tables and straw-seat chairs line the painted cement floor in the main dining room, behind which is a separate bar area. (Ask for a table away from the front door, where it can become cold and drafty in chilly weather.) Daily specials include fresh fish and soups, or try the perennially popular beef tenderloin encrusted with smoked olive tapenade, served with potato puree and red-wine sauce. The best dessert here is the ample fruit-and-cheese plate, featuring generous wedges of soft, semisoft, and hard cheeses.

243 S. Cooper ✆ **901/722-2700.** Main courses $16–$25. www.cafe1912.com. AE, DC, DISC, MC, V. Mon–Thurs 5:30–9:30pm; Fri–Sat 5:30–10:30pm; Sun 5:30–9pm.

Café Society AMERICAN   Named after a Parisian cafe, this lively bistro has a vague country-inn feel about it and is a popular ladies' lunch spot and pre-theater restaurant. As in a French cafe, you'll find convivial conversations at the small bar and outdoor seating on the street where you can sit and people-watch. Start out with some French onion soup or honey-baked brie, followed up with the likes of salmon with a sesame-seed and poppy-seed crust or braised lamb shank with a pear brandy and walnut glaze. Lunches are reasonably priced and offer a chance to sample some of the same fine food that is served at dinner. There are also monthly four-course wine and food tastings, for which reservations are required.

212 N. Evergreen St. ✆ **901/722-2177.** Reservations recommended. Main courses $13–$27. AE, DC, MC, V. Mon–Fri 11:30am–2pm; Mon–Sun 5–10:30pm.

Fuel Café ★ AMERICAN/BRUNCH   Even if it wasn't built into a 1920s-era filling station and garage, Fuel would still be one of the coolest new eateries in Memphis. Another farm-to-fork restaurant, the emphasis here is on organic and sustainably raised foods. Grass-fed bison burgers, beef medallions and wild-caught seafood are hallmarks, but here's the surprise: Co-owner Carrie Mitchum (actor Robert's grand-daughter) is a Le Cordon Bleu-trained chef who also happens to be vegan. Thus, Fuel has become a go-to eatery for diners who want delicious meat- and dairy-free choices that run the gamut from quiche to crème brûlée. Fuel is renowned for its fries, which are twice-fried, medium-cut potatoes sprinkled with sea salt and served with a trio of sauces: Thai chili, white truffle, and garlicky mayo.

1761 Madison. ✆ **901/725-9025.** www.fuelcafememphis.com. Entrees $15–$20. DC, DISC, MC, V. Tues-Fri 11am–2:30pm and 5–9:30pm; Sat 11am–3pm and 5–10pm; Sun brunch 11am–3pm.

Inexpensive

Café Eclectic SANDWICHES   Near Rhodes College and the Memphis Zoo, in the pretty residential neighborhood known as Vollintine-Evergreen, this new cafe and coffee shop is a gathering place for students and families. Although it doesn't sell alcohol (you can bring your own wine, for a corkage fee), there's a comfy bar counter-top and stools, quirky artwork on the walls, and a sofa strewn with pillows. Try the bacon, avocado, and tomato with a side of roasted sweet potatoes. Baguettes and other loaves of fresh-baked bread are sold from a glass case near the cash register.

603 N. McLean Blvd. ✆ **901/725-1718.** www.cafeeclectic.net. Main dishes under $10. DC, DISC, MC, V Mon–Wed 6:30am–10pm; Thurs–Sat 6:30am–10pm (coffees, pastries, and ice cream until 1am); Sun 9am–3pm (coffees, pastries, and desserts until 10pm).

High Point Pizza ★ 🎒 PIZZA   Red-and-white-checked tablecloths adorn the few small tables within this quintessential neighborhood pizza place. Freshly prepared sandwiches, salads, subs and all the standard pizza favorites are here, along with beer and wine. Bring the kids, or your dog on a leash, and linger over supper outside on the sidewalk seating area along this tree-shaded residential street. Friendly and welcoming, the eatery does a brisk takeout business and also boasts an old-school classic Ms. Pac-Man game machine.

477 High Point Terrace. ⓒ **901/452-3339.** www.facebook.com/HighPointPizza. Slices $2.50–$3.50; pizzas $8–$18. AE, DISC, MC, V. Sun–Thurs 11am to 9pm; Fri–Sat 11am–10pm.

Kwik-Chek Deli DELI   A slab of meat roasting on a spit is the most out-of-place thing you'll immediately notice about this nondescript convenience store in Midtown. Order the falafel or the Hey Zeus, a tortilla wrap with turkey, roast beef and a tangy blast of marinated veggies. Gyros and other sandwiches, made (while you wait) from freshly sliced meats and cheeses have kept loyal folks coming back here for years.

2013 Madison Ave. ⓒ **901/274-9293.** Under $10. MC, V. Mon–Sat 10am–9pm; Sun 10am–7pm.

Noodle Doodle Do JAPANESE   Spare furnishings in this brick storefront overlooking the intersection of Cooper and Young streets in Midtown keep the focus on people-watching and tasting. Celebrated local restaurateur and caterer Karen Blockman Carrier is the force behind this sushi restaurant, called Do (pronounced "dough"), where the menu includes everything from sashimi rolls and seaweed salad to noodle dishes and soups. Clean, vibrant flavors and friendly, knowledgeable service are hallmarks here.

964 Cooper St. ⓒ **901/272-0830.** Main courses under $10. AE, DC, DISC, MC, V. Tues–Sat 11:30am–4pm; Mon–Sat 5–11pm.

Saigon Le ★ VIETNAMESE   A popular lunch spot, Saigon Le is in an urban neighborhood close to the medical-center district and is popular with hospital workers. Friendly service and generous portions of Chinese and Vietnamese dishes are the standards here. The Kung Pao beef is spicy, and the vegetable egg foo yong is plump with vegetables. Saigon Le's Vietnamese specialties include flavorful noodle, meat, fish, and vegetable dishes such as charbroiled pork, spring rolls with vermicelli, and clear noodle soup with barbecued pork, shrimp, and crabmeat. At just under $6, the lunch special may be the best bargain in town.

51 N. Cleveland St. ⓒ **901/276-5326.** www.saigon-le.com. Main courses $6–$15. DC, DISC, MC, V. Mon–Sat 11am–9pm.

Soul Fish Cafe ★★ 🍴 SOUTHERN/SEAFOOD   The crispiest, most mouthwatering fried catfish in town is served at this wildly popular new haunt at the edge of the Cooper-Young area. A narrow old house has been filled with tables and a short bar against the far end of the room. Sit here at one of the bar stools to admire the fishing lures embedded in the countertop, while sipping a cold beer or iced tea. Baskets of fried catfish come with lettuce, tomatoes, and creamy rémoulade sauce. Abundant sides include home-style macaroni and cheese, green beans, and Cajun cooked cabbage (it's great, packing a tomato-ey, sweet-and-sour zip). The hush puppies alone are worth the trip. Eat in or order for takeout. And try to avoid going on Friday nights, when there's a line outside the door.

862 S. Cooper St. ⓒ **901/725-0722.** www.marksmenus.com. Main courses under $12. AE, MC, V. Mon–Sat 11am–10pm; Sun 11am–9pm.

EAST MEMPHIS
Expensive

Andrew Michael Italian Kitchen ITALIAN   Fresh produce, meats, and cheeses from local farms and food purveyors are hallmarks of this new rustic Italian eatery located in a converted East Memphis house. Known for their handmade potato gnocchi, ravioli, and other pastas, the young chefs—Andrew Ticer and Michael Hudman—are childhood friends who recently fulfilled their dream to open a restaurant. Besides pasta, menu standouts are seafood dishes like calamari, halibut, and swordfish boosted by leeks, fennel, tarragon, and other piquant flavors. At dinner, black-olive tapenade comes with warm, crusty loaves of bread. In season, the Caprese salad of heirloom tomatoes, freshly shredded buffalo mozzarella, and pesto is divine. The lovely restaurant, with dark hardwood floors and elegant furnishings, has a nice patio out back. There's also a full bar.

712 W. Brookhaven Circle. (C) **901/347-3569.** www.andrewmichaelitaliankitchen.com. Reservations recommended. Main courses $18–$32. AE, MC, V. Mon–Sat 5–10pm.

Circa ★★ SOUTHERN/BRUNCH   French-trained chef John Bragg made a splash with the 2007 opening of his downtown, fine-dining restaurant. He relocated to East Memphis a few years later. Polished service, including expert wine recommendations made from an extensive list, makes meals here feel special. Start with the seared foie gras, and then try the seared five-spice-encrusted tuna with wasabi mashed potatoes or the sorghum-cured rack of lamb. Get your shrimp and grits at Sunday brunch, or think outside the box and order the Nutella crepes.

6150 Poplar Ave. (C) **901/746-9130.** www.circamemphis.com. Reservations recommended for dinner. Main courses $26–$37. AE, DC, DISC, MC, V. Sun–Thurs 5–9:30pm; Fri–Sat 5–10pm. Sun brunch 10:30am–2:30pm.

Erling Jensen ★★★ CONTINENTAL   Chef Erling Jensen made a name for himself at the popular La Tourelle a decade ago before venturing out on his own at this eponymous restaurant located in a converted home just off Poplar Avenue at I-240. Understated elegance and contemporary art set the tone for Jensen's innovative cuisine. The Danish-born chef offers a "deconstructed" lobster Bolognese ravioli and other appetizers, including crispy oysters over mixed greens with roasted corn relish and Pernod-scented buttermilk dressing. A diverse entree assortment makes decisions difficult. Options might range from seared ahi tuna with ratatouille and truffled basil coulis, to more than a dozen meat and game dishes, including lamb, bison, beef, and veal. Sorbets and soufflés anchor a constantly updated dessert menu. Staff is well trained to provide exemplary service.

1044 S. Yates St. (C) **901/763-3700.** www.ejensen.com. Reservations highly recommended. Main courses $31–$46. AE, DC, MC, V. Daily 5–10pm.

Folk's Folly Prime Steak House ★★ STEAK   There are better-known chain steakhouses in Memphis, but none is more beloved than this local institution. You'll find Folk's Folly just off Poplar Avenue—it's the corner building with the royal-blue awning. Just off the parking lot is a tiny butcher shop that's part of the restaurant; in the meat cases inside, you'll see the sort of top-quality meats they serve here (the likes of which you'll probably never see at your neighborhood market). Steaks are the specialty of the house, and steaks are what they do best. However, you can start your meal with anything from blackened catfish to seafood gumbo or even fried pickles.

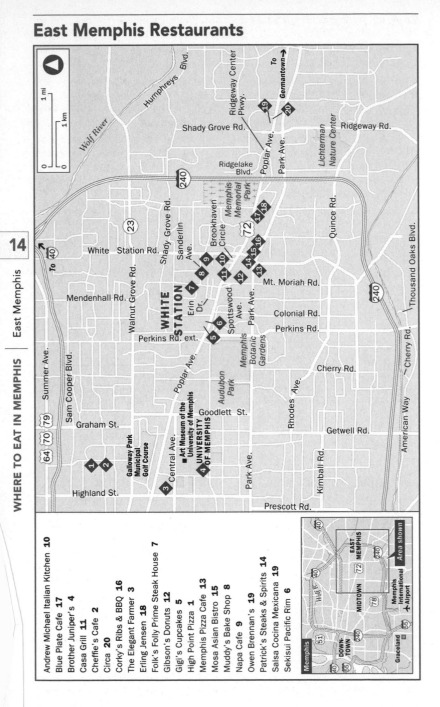

Andrew Michael Italian Kitchen **10**
Blue Plate Cafe **17**
Brother Juniper's **4**
Casa Grill **11**
Cheffie's Cafe **2**
Circa **20**
Corky's Ribs & BBQ **16**
The Elegant Farmer **3**
Erling Jensen **18**
Folk's Folly Prime Steak House **7**
Gibson's Donuts **12**
Gigi's Cupcakes **5**
High Point Pizza **1**
Memphis Pizza Cafe **13**
Mosa Asian Bistro **15**
Muddy's Bake Shop **8**
Napa Cafe **9**
Owen Brennan's **19**
Patrick's Steaks & Spirits **14**
Salsa Cocina Mexicana **19**
Sekisui Pacific Rim **6**

Among the prime cuts of beef are aged sirloins, filet mignons, and T-bones. Seafood offerings include Alaskan king crab legs, salmon filets, and jumbo Maine lobsters.

551 S. Mendenhall Rd. ✆ **901/762-8200.** www.folksfolly.com. Reservations recommended. Main courses $20–$45. AE, DC, MC, V. Mon–Thurs 5:30–10pm; Fri–Sat 5:30–11pm; Sun 5:30–9pm.

Napa Café CALIFORNIAN   In an upscale East Memphis shopping center near the Doubletree Hotel, this classy restaurant has been serving inspired California cuisine for more than a decade. The comfy, low-key dining room is conducive to conversation, which makes Napa Café a good choice for either a romantic evening or lunch with friends. Aesthetically pleasing presentations of dishes such as the potato-encrusted halibut and the rack of lamb make even relatively informal meals feel special. As its name implies, Napa Café has an award-winning wine list. What's more, private dinners for parties of two or more are available in the restaurant's cozy wine cellar if you book them in advance.

5101 Sanderlin Dr., Ste. 122. ✆ **901/683-0441.** www.napacafe.com. Reservations recommended. Main courses $16–$29. AE, DC, DISC, MC, V. Mon–Fri 11am–2pm; Mon–Thurs 5–9pm; Fri–Sat 5–10pm.

Moderate

Casa Grill ★★ MEDITERRANEAN   Craving a "Big Mac of the Middle East"? You can get the so-called falafel pita sandwich at this comfortably exotic eatery that recently relocated from the Cooper-Young neighborhood to East Memphis. The chef/ owner imports all his spices and ingredients, such as olive oil, from his native Middle East. A hardworking, congenial host, he mingles with customers and offers helpful suggestions for appetizers such as baba ghanouj, puréed lentil soup, and silky hummus served with a basket of soft, warm pita bread. You can also indulge in generously stuffed gyros or Greek salads, including tabbouleh or crisp lettuce with olives and feta cheese. Entrees include grilled rack of lamb with mango sauce, and Holy Land shish kebab. Exotic Moroccan tagine dishes—seafood or lamb baked in clay pots—serve two people.

5030 Poplar Ave. ✆ **901/725-8557.** www.casablancamemphis.com. Main courses $10–$18; sandwiches $6–$12. AE, DC, DISC, MC, V. Daily 11am–10pm.

Corky's Ribs & BBQ ★★ ☺ BARBECUE   Corky's is good-natured and boisterous, with rock-'n'-roll tunes piped both indoors and out. Aromatic barbecue permeates the air. An argument over which is the best barbecue restaurant in Memphis persists, but this one pretty much leads the pack when it comes to pulled-pork-shoulder barbecue topped with tangy coleslaw. Photographs and letters from satisfied customers line the rough-paneled lobby, where you always have to wait for a table. Corky's even has a toll-free number you can call (✆ **800/9-CORKYS** [926-7597]) to get their delicious ribs shipped "anywhere." There's also a drive-up window for immediate barbecue gratification. A downtown location, at 175 Peabody Place (✆ **901/529-9191**), is right around the corner from Beale Street. The suburbs have a Corky's at Dexter Road in Cordova (✆ **901/737-1988**).

5259 Poplar Ave. ✆ **901/685-9744.** www.corkysbbq.com. Reservations not accepted. Main courses $4–$20. AE, DC, DISC, MC, V. Sun–Thurs 10:45am–9:30pm; Fri–Sat 10:45am–10pm.

The Elegant Farmer ★★★ AMERICAN   Flowers and shrubs adorn the exterior of this storybook cottage on a side street near the busy intersection of Poplar and Highland. Cozy as an old farmhouse, and adjoining an upscale antiques shop, this is noted local chef Mac Edwards's new farm-to-table restaurant. Using locally sourced ingredients, the kitchen staff finesses wholesome comfort foods such as pot roast, collard greens, and salmon patties served with Creole mustard sauce. Flaky biscuits, creamy corn pudding, and killer macaroni (rigatoni) and cheese are among the sublime sides. Portions are huge, leading light eaters to consider salads and such, perhaps with a glass of wine. In season, red and yellow tomato slices are wedged between house-made ricotta and basil pesto and drizzled with balsamic vinaigrette. Luscious chocolate layer cake, or sliced pound cake piled with strawberries and house-made whipped cream, make ordering dessert irresistible.

262 S. Highland. © **901/324-2221.** www.theelegantfarmerrestaurant.com. Entrees $10–$19. AE, DC, DISC, MC, V. Tues–Sat 11am–2:30pm and from 5:30pm. Reservations accepted for parties of 5 or more.

Owen Brennan's ★ BRUNCH/CAJUN/CREOLE Located in one of East Memphis's most upscale shopping plazas and used as a set in the movie *The Firm,* Owen Brennan's has long been an East Memphis tradition, particularly for power lunches. The interior manages to conjure up the Big Easy with its Mardi Gras jesters and float decorations. Cuisine is flamboyant Cajun and Creole, from fluffy crab beignets to silky turtle soup. House specialties include the requisite blackened dishes, as well as hearty gumbos bursting with seafood. Desserts are so heavy they might make you woozy: The dense bread pudding is moistened with rum, and the caramelized bananas Foster is drenched in it as well.

Regalia Shopping Center, 6150 Poplar Ave. © **901/761-0990.** www.brennansmemphis.com. Reservations recommended. Main courses $11–$23. AE, DC, DISC, MC, V. Mon–Thurs 11am–9pm; Fri 11am–10pm; Sat 9:30am–10:30pm; Sun 10am–2pm.

Inexpensive

Blue Plate Cafe SOUTHERN Hearty breakfasts brimming with fried sausage, bacon, ham, and eggs at this cottage help Memphis retain its ranking as one of the most overweight populations in the United States. Southern-style grits and buttermilk biscuits with gravy also do their part. Lunch and dinner are also served, featuring home-style meat-and-three choices in plentiful portions. The food is better than the service, which can be blunt.

5469 Poplar Ave. © **901/761-9696.** Main courses $5–$9. AE, MC, V. Mon–Sat 6am–8pm; Sun 7am–2pm.

Brother Juniper's ★★ BREAKFAST/BRUNCH In the University of Memphis area, one of the best breakfast spots in town occupies a plain little house behind a white picket fence. Inside, it's cheerful but nothing fancy, and there's limited seating. As a result, a steady stream of diners are perpetually at the door, beginning at the crack of dawn, waiting for a table at which to sample scrumptious eggs, buttermilk biscuits, blintzes, sausages, and gyros. The family-run eatery is vegetarian-friendly, too, with such offerings as the feta-rich spanakopita omelet and a breakfast tofu stir-fry.

3519 Walker Ave. © **901/324-0144.** www.brotherjunipers.com. Breakfasts under $10. AE, DC, DISC, MC, V. Tues–Fri 6:30am–1pm; Sat 7am–12:30pm; Sun 8am–1pm.

Gibson's Donuts ★★ DONUTS Donut lovers will think they've died and gone to donut heaven when they step inside this old-fashioned, family-owned bakery that does one thing and does it better than anyone else. The glass display cases seem to groan under the weight of the plump crullers, cream horns, and apple fritters within.

All types of round donuts—glazed, yeast, blueberry, cake, jelly-filled, and chocolate-iced with colorful sprinkles—are up for grabs. A few booths and tables allow for eager patrons to get instant gratification from their donuts and coffee, but Gibson's does a steady takeout business as well.

760 Mt. Moriah. ⓒ **901/682-8200.** Donuts 60¢–75¢ each, or $6.50–$7.50 per dozen. AE, DISC, MC, V. Open 24 hr. Closed Christmas.

Memphis Pizza Cafe PIZZA   Consistently rated by customers as having the best pizza in Memphis, this locally owned restaurant is wildly popular. Known for its thin crust, fresh toppings, and sheer variety of pizzas, Memphis Pizza Cafe also serves salads, calzones, and subs. Cheeses, meat, veggies, and more are among the variety of fresh toppings available. For something different, try the barbecued chicken pizza. The local chain has several other Memphis-area locations, including 2087 Madison Ave. (ⓒ 901/726-5343).

5061 Park Ave. ⓒ **901/684-1306.** www.memphispizzacafe.com. Slices $2.45–$2.90; pizzas $9.15–$15. MC, V. Sun–Thurs 11am–10pm; Fri–Sat 11am–11pm.

Mosa Asian Bistro ★ THAI   Rice plates, red and green curries, and noodle dishes fill the extensive menu at this busy Asian bistro, which recently opened in the White Station area of East Memphis. Eat inside the pleasant dining room, or call ahead for takeout orders, which are meticulously packaged, sacked, and securely taped shut—and include chopsticks. Crab-cheese wontons and pot stickers are more traditional appetizers, but my favorites are the basil rolls—glass noodles, cucumbers, carrots, bean sprouts, and a fresh basil leaf wrapped in rice paper. An ice cooler by the cash register is stocked with bottles of beer and other cold drinks.

850 S. White Station Rd. ⓒ **901/683-8889.** www.mosaasianbistro.com. Main courses under $10. AE, DC, DISC, MC, V. Mon–Thurs 11am–9pm; Fri–Sat 11am–10pm; Sun 11am–8:30pm.

Patrick's Steaks & Spirits SOUTHERN   The daily plate lunches are what keep the loyal clientele coming back to this popular diner. Homemade yeast rolls and fat corn bread muffins are served warm from the oven. Whether you order the calf's liver smothered in onions, the Tuesdays-only fried chicken, or the hefty homemade meat-loaf, you can be sure the portions will be large. Entrees come with your choice of two vegetables from a long list that includes fried okra, turnip greens, purple-hull peas, and cheesy baked-macaroni shells.

Park Ave., at Mt. Moriah. ⓒ **901/682-2852.** www.patricksmemphis.net. Main courses $8–$18. AE, DISC, MC, V. Daily 11am–10pm.

Salsa Cocina Mexicana ★★ MEXICAN   For more than 15 years now, my favorite Mexican restaurant has remained a stalwart. Salsa is a locally owned gem tucked into an upscale shopping center behind Ruth's Chris Steakhouse. Mexican standards are scrumptious, as are the flavorful chicken in citrus-chipotle sauce, and a sirloin steak topped with grilled poblano peppers. You can even relish the side dishes, including creamy refried beans and a robust salsa picante. Wash it all down with an icy margarita. Service is attentive—they really care that you enjoy your meal. Mexican music plays softly in the background. When vast platters of enchiladas, guacamole, and rice show up at your table, you'll know that you've come to the right place.

Regalia Shopping Center, 6150 Poplar Ave. ⓒ **901/683-6325.** Reservations accepted only for parties of 6 or more. Main courses $5–$14. AE, DC, DISC, MC, V. Mon–Sat 11am–10pm.

SOUTH MEMPHIS & GRACELAND AREA

Inexpensive

D'Bo's Wings n' More ★ AMERICAN   Order a beer and a basket of wings and watch the game on TV, or call ahead and take home a couple hundred of these succulent chicken drummies and tips that are deep-fried and then slathered in mild, hot, or "suicidal" red sauces. Entrepreneur David Boyd and his wife started D'Bo's more than a decade ago, selling wings out of a food trailer at area festivals. Their lip-smacking wings caught on like wildfire. Now there are D'Bo's locations throughout the city and beyond. If wings aren't your thing, the restaurant also serves great hamburgers and fries. D'Bo's has a nice location (there are others throughout the area), near the Reverend Al Green's church, Full Gospel Tabernacle, but unfortunately, this particular location isn't open on Sundays.

4407 Elvis Presley Blvd. ✆ 901/345-9464. www.dboswings.com. Main courses $5–$9. AE, DC, DISC, MC, V. Mon–Thurs 11am–10pm; Fri–Sat 11am–midnight.

Four Way Restaurant ★★★ 🍴 ☺ SOUTHERN   If you're looking for the legendary Four Way Grill, this is it. The cherished South Memphis family restaurant serves the tastiest soul food in town. Eat dessert first. Try the velvety sweet-potato pie or strawberry cake. Then dig into some juicy fried green tomatoes, pork chops, catfish, or chicken, and round it out with black-eyed peas and crumbly corn bread. If he's not too busy, ask the proprietor to reminisce about the old days of this historic black neighborhood, which locals hope is poised for a comeback. The restaurant doesn't serve soft drinks or alcohol, so plan on ordering lemonade or iced tea with your meal.

998 Mississippi Blvd. ✆ 901/507-1519. Reservations recommended for large groups. Main courses $6–$9. MC, V. Tues–Sat 11am–7pm; Sun 11am–5pm.

Interstate Bar-B-Que ★ BARBECUE   Corky's Ribs & BBQ may be a bit flashier, but Interstate Bar-B-Que has the kind of grit and street cred that no suburban East Memphis eatery could muster. Located off I-55 on South Third Street (a great stop-off if you're driving south from downtown to Graceland), Interstate is a former grocery-store-turned-barbecue-joint. Insurance agent Jim Neely launched the biz in the 1970s in a then-dicey part of town. Though urban renewal efforts seem to have eluded the still-blighted neighborhood, Interstate Bar-B-Que is a bright, welcoming spot. Long before *USA Today* proclaimed it the best place in America for a pork barbecue sandwich, locals and tourists already knew it. Along with pork and beef ribs and shredded barbecue, Interstate smokes a mean, spice-rubbed turkey breast. Chicken halves are slow-roasted in hickory-wood pits, to achieve a tender, moist flavor. Sides include sugary baked beans, coleslaw, potato salad, and barbecued spaghetti. For worldwide delivery, call ✆ 888/227-2793.

2265 S. Third St. ✆ 901/775-2304. www.interstatebarbecue.com. Sandwiches $4.85–$5.30; dinner platters $6.25–$8.75. MC, V. Mon–Thurs 11am–10pm; Fri–Sat 11am–11pm; Sun 11am–5pm.

Krispy Kreme Doughnuts BREAKFAST   Perhaps you've experienced one of these heavenly grease bombs—deep-fried pillows of dough that have been drenched in a tooth-achingly sugary glaze. You may catch a drift of that unmistakable, yeasty aroma before you spot the big red-and-green sign along Elvis Presley Boulevard. If

South Memphis & Graceland Area

WHERE TO EAT IN MEMPHIS

you're lucky, you'll get to place your order when the doughnuts are still warm, and at their most mouthwateringly decadent.

4244 Elvis Presley Blvd. ✆ **901/332-0620.** www.krispykreme.com. Dozen donuts $6.54. AE, MC, V. Drive-through 24 hr.; inside daily 5am–10pm.

Piccadilly ★AMERICAN/SOUTHERN   Elvis would've left the building (nearby Graceland, that is) for a meal at this down-home cafeteria, had it been around when he was still living in the neighborhood. One of the better restaurant suggestions in this otherwise fast-food-rampant part of town, Piccadilly is a refreshing change of pace. A clean, well-run chain restaurant, it packs people in for old-fashioned fried chicken, roast beef, baked fish, and hefty portions of sides and desserts. This is one of Piccadilly's several Memphis locations. So if you're in town to see the King's quarters, skip the mediocre, overpriced food courts within the Graceland compound, and come here instead.

3968 Elvis Presley Blvd. ✆**901/398-5186.** www.piccadilly.com. Most entrees under $10. AE, DC, V. Daily 11am–8:30pm.

Uncle Lou's Fried Chicken ★ 📷SOUTHERN   If you're craving a fried baloney sandwich and you're brave enough to venture into this dicey neighborhood, you won't be disappointed with Uncle Lou's. This is the real deal, a locally owned eatery that serves up its mouthwatering fried chicken in several variations. The honey hot-sauced version is tasty, but the crisp-skinned, lightly salted original nears perfection. Moist and flavorful, the chicken is every bit as good as Gus's (p. 195) but doesn't get as much glory. Creamy, rich potato salad and fried okra are excellent, while the deep-fried corn nuggets may be more of an acquired taste. Uncle Lou's is a tidy, efficiently run restaurant where you place your order at the counter and eat at booths or small tables. A map of the USA along one wall is studded with colorful pushpins and ringed by photos of satisfied customers from all over the country. Add yours before you head out—but wash the grease off your fingers first.

3633 Millbranch Rd. ✆ **901/332-2367.** www.unclelousfriedchicken.com. Chicken under $10. Mon–Thurs 11am–8pm; Fri–Sat 11am–10pm; Sun noon–6pm.

BARBECUE

Memphis claims to be the barbecue capital of the world, and with more than 100 barbecue restaurants and the annual Memphis in May World Championship Barbecue Cooking Contest, it's hard to argue the point. The standard barbecue here comes in two basic types—hand-pulled pork shoulder (pulled off the bone rather than cut off) and pork ribs. The latter can be served wet or dry (that is, with or without sauce). The best pulled pork shoulder in town is at **Corky's Ribs & BBQ** (p. 201), and the best ribs are served at **The Rendezvous** (p. 222).

If you're unsure about all the fuss, or if you're new to 'que, graze the chafing dishes at **Leonard's Pit Barbecue,** downtown at 103 N. Main St. (✆ **901/528-0882**). At their daily buffet, you can have an absolute pork pigout while sampling soul foods including pulled pork shoulder, fried catfish, barbecued beans, hush puppies, and coleslaw. They have an East Memphis location too, at 5465 Fox Plaza Dr. (✆ **901/360-1963**).

Looks can be deceiving, as in this case of the foreboding hole in the wall known as **Cozy Corner,** 745 N. Parkway (✆ **901/527-9158**). Step inside, and make yourself at home. The friendly little barbecue spot is a Midtown landmark. Even before the

Food Network brought fame and fortune to its "down-home," lovey-dovey husband-and-wife owners, **Neely's B-B-Q,** 670 Jefferson Ave. in downtown (✆ **901/521-9798**), and at 5700 Mt. Moriah Rd. in East Memphis (✆ **901/795-4177**), was a local favorite. They do it all, including barbecued spaghetti and barbecued bologna. Down near Graceland, there is an abundance of timeworn, no-frills barbecue joints and bona fide dives. Try **Payne's,** 1393 Elvis Presley Blvd. (✆ **901/942-7433**), **Interstate Bar-B-Que** (p. 204), and **A&R Bar-B-Q,** 1802 Elvis Presley Blvd. (✆ **901/774-7444**), all of which draw universal raves for barbecue authenticity.

COFFEE SHOPS

Sure, there's a Starbucks at practically every other intersection, but wouldn't you really rather patronize a coffee shop where you can soak up some local atmosphere? If so, your first stop should be downtown, to the **Center for Southern Folklore,** Pembroke Square (✆ **901/525-3655**). It's a one-of-a-kind cafe of culture where you can belt back a cappuccino while admiring local crafts and outsider art, and hear great music almost any time of day. Another cozy nook is **Bluff City Coffee,** 505 S. Main St. (✆ **901/405-4399**), where you can park yourself in an overstuffed chair and leaf through an actual newspaper (remember those?) while refueling with caffeine.

At the edge of the gay-friendly Cooper-Young neighborhood, you can quaff a cup o' joe and listen to live music or poetry at **Otherlands,** 641 S. Cooper St. (✆ **901/278-4994**). Farther down the street and around the corner, you'll find **Java Cabana,** 2170 Young Ave. (✆ **901/272-7210**), a bohemian shop with a cement floor and flea-market furnishings. Good coffee, muffins, and brownies are just right over a game of chess or during one of the frequent open-mic nights.

Farther east, cavernous **Republic Coffee,** 2924 Walnut Grove (✆ **901/590-1578**), is hipster central, where young adults meet up over chai tea or fruit-juice smoothies. Solo patrons bury themselves in corner booths, laser-focused on their smartphones or laptops, while sipping coffee. Fresh-baked cookies, muffins, and even macaroni and cheese are among the munchies on the menu.

CAFES & DELIS

In downtown Memphis, **The Little Tea Shop,** 69 Monroe Ave. (✆ **901/525-6000**), has been doling out excellent Southern home cooking for decades. Although the menu changes daily, you can expect fried chicken, catfish, mashed potatoes, and (vegetarians, rejoice) meatless turnip greens—a real rarity in the pork-simmered South. Iced sweet tea is a must. In the South Main Historic District, **Frank's South Main Street Market and Deli,** 327 S. Main (✆ **901/523-0101**), is a friendly little storefront that's built its reputation on smoked turkey sandwiches and specialty subs made from slow-roasted meats. And if you're down on Beale Street, there are tons of bars, restaurants, and places to grab a quick bite or a cup of coffee. One of the homiest is **Miss Polly's Soul City Cafe,** 154 Beale St. (✆ **901/527-9060**), where you can get a cheap morning-after breakfast of waffles, eggs, and fried potatoes.

For hefty, New York–style subs layered with meats and cheeses, **Fino's Italian Deli and Catering,** 1853 Madison Ave. (✆ **901/272-3466**), has been a local favorite for generations. The Midtown shop also stocks kitchen pantry products like imported pasta and sauces. Generous portions of farm-fresh American cooking anchor the extensive menu at **Trolley Stop Market,** 704 Madison (© **901/526-1361**). This is truly a something-for-everyone kind of place, where huge sandwiches, burgers, and salads are available along with the hearty plate lunches. On Monday nights, the Market offers an all-vegan menu.

In a lovely, Central Memphis residential neighborhood known as High Point Terrace is a newcomer that's earning rave reviews. **Cheffie's Café,** 483 High Point Terrace (© **901/343-0488**), is a build-your-own salad and sandwich shop set within a spacious, contemporary store that also sells recumbent bicycles (appropriate, considering its location just steps away from Memphis's new Greenline hiking and biking trail). Like an upscale Subway, Cheffie's allows diners to choose the ingredients they want, as staff assembles the dishes for you from behind a cafeteria-style counter. Kids and adults alike love the Cheffie's gelato, too.

The most bucolic cafe view in town can be found inside the Memphis Brooks Museum of Art, where noted local chef Wally Joe oversees the elegant **Brushmark Restaurant,** 1934 Poplar Ave. (© **901/544-6225**). Whether you sit inside or out on the terrace, this is the kind of place that encourages you to linger over glasses of wine while you drink in the lush greenery of Overton Park, with its centuries-old trees. Classics like quiche Lorraine and the niçoise salad, as well as sandwiches and soups (try the African peanut soup) are first-rate. You don't have to pay museum admission to dine at The Brushmark, but the Brooks' collections are well worth a visit while you're here.

BAKERIES & ICE CREAM

Old-fashioned, chocolate ice-cream sodas and thick, hand-dipped milkshakes are served up, as they have been for generations, from behind the soda fountain of Memphis's oldest independent drugstore, **Wiles-Smith Drugs,** 1635 Union Ave. (© **901/278-6416**). Spoon it up or use your straw; either way, you'll feel like it's 1961, the year this local gem opened.

Light-years away from that experience is **YoLo Frozen Yogurt,** 6 S. Cooper (© **901/343-0438**), a bright, modern corner shop specializing in soft-serve frozen yogurt, ice cream, and tons o' toppings. The store shares space with **LadyBugg Bakery,** where you can get sinful desserts like two-fisted, cream-filled peanut butter whoopee pies, as well as daily vegan specials like the scrumptious strawberry muffins.

In East Memphis, there are a couple of popular bakeries riding the nationwide cupcake craze. **Muddy's Bake Shop,** 5101 Sanderlin Ave. (© **901/683-8844**), touts its use of organic ingredients. Small, simply decorated cupcakes come in a slew of flavors. The selection of sweets varies each day, so before you get your heart set on Snickerdoodles, call ahead to see what kinds of pies, cakes, and cookies have been baked that day. And **Gigi's Cupcakes,** 4709 Poplar (© **901/888-2253**), is beloved for its nearly obscene buttercream-to-cupcake ratio, available in such descriptive flavors as Scarlett's Red Velvet and Hunka Chunka Banana Love.

SHOPPING IN MEMPHIS

Tacky Elvis souvenirs and made-in-China trinkets can be found all over town, especially on Beale Street and in the shops surrounding Graceland. For more discriminating tastes, The Peabody hotel downtown has some high-priced boutiques offering designer clothes, fine art, jewelry, and collectibles. Otherwise, your best shopping bets are going to be in East Memphis and the suburbs. Although downtown and Midtown have attracted a good array of new retail tenants over the past few years, the recession has left many vacant storefronts in their wake. Hopes are high that the scene will eventually rebound, however. Meanwhile, there are plenty of upscale boutiques, offbeat specialty shops, and other retail therapy options throughout the metro area.

15

As in Nashville and other cities of the New South, the shopping scene in Memphis is spread out. If you want to go shopping in this city, you'll need to arm yourself with a good map, get in the car, and start driving. Most people head to the shopping malls and plazas (there are dozens) in East Memphis to find quality merchandise. However, in recent years, a few funky shops and worthwhile boutiques have started to pop up in the South Main Historic District of downtown.

Shopping malls and department stores are generally open Monday to Saturday 10am to 9pm and Sunday noon to 6pm. Many smaller mom-and-pop stores located outside malls and shopping centers are closed on Sundays. Call ahead to check store hours.

SHOPPING A TO Z

Antiques

Flashback With 1950s furniture becoming more collectible with each passing year, it should come as no surprise that Memphis, the birthplace of rock 'n' roll in the early 1950s, has a great vintage furniture store. In addition to 1950s furnishings and vintage clothing, this store sells stuff from the '20s, '30s, and '40s, including a large selection of European Art Deco furniture. 2304 Central Ave. ✆ **901/272-2304.** www.flashbackmemphis.com.

Toad Hall Antiques Furniture, primitives, lamps, and mirrors make up the eclectic merchandise selection at this Cooper-Young landmark. Look for the frog in checked tights, painted on the outside of the brick building. Inside, browse for French and English as well as American decorative objects, jewelry, and other affordably priced gifts. 2129 Central Ave. ✆ **901/726-0755.** www.toadhallmemphis.com.

Art

David Lusk Gallery   In the most sophisticated, upscale art gallery in town, owner David Lusk showcases the South's finest contemporary artists. A wide variety of media are represented, including glass and photography. Lively receptions, educational events, and charitable efforts make this one of the most active galleries in the city. Laurelwood Center, 4540 Poplar Ave. ℂ **901/767-3800.** www.davidluskgallery.com.

The Folklore Store ★★   Folk-art finds, including colorful mixed-media pieces and homespun, one-of-a-kind crafts, are sold in this authentically local souvenir shop operated by the nonprofit Center for Southern Folklore. Take home a boll of fresh-picked cotton and a Moon Pie, a copy of Peter Guralnick's bestselling Elvis biography *Careless Love,* and a handful of Memphis CDs by the likes of the Daddy Mack Blues Band and Mose Vinson. All proceeds help sustain this beloved Memphis gem, which strives to preserve the region's culture, art, history, stories, food, and live music. 123 S. Main. ℂ **901/525-3655.** www.southernfolklore.com.

Joysmith Gallery ★ 🎁   Brenda Joysmith, a longtime San Francisco–area artist who trained at the Art Institute of Chicago, had earned an international reputation before she returned to her native Memphis a few years ago. Best known for her pastel portraits of African-American women and children, Joysmith's works are featured in many national museums, in corporate collections, in books, and on the sets of popular television shows. Maya Angelou and Oprah Winfrey are among her celebrity fans. There's a retail shop in her studio selling affordable prints and other merchandise. *Tip:* Hours are by appointment only; but the artist is usually working in her second-floor studio, so if you'd like to visit, call ahead. 46 Huling Ave. ℂ **901/543-0505.**

Bikes

Midtown Bike Co.   Full-service bicycle sales, repair, and rentals are offered at this great little shop in the historic South Main historic downtown. Check out the choice selection of two-wheelers, helmets, and other essentials. Then chat up the knowledgeable store clerks to get the lowdown on the best bike trails, including the Mississippi River Trail that passes through Memphis on its way from northern Minnesota to New Orleans. 509 S. Main St. ℂ **901/522-9757.** www.midtownbikeco.com.

Books

Burke's Book Store ★ 🎁   After decades in the same location, the region's best and most beloved independent bookstore relocated to new digs in the flourishing Cooper-Young neighborhood. Burke's specializes in used, old, and collectible books. However, they have a good selection of new books as well. When favorite Memphis son John Grisham pens a new bestseller, this is usually where he holds his first book signing before embarking on national tours. 936 S. Cooper. ℂ **901/278-7484.** www.burkesbooks.com.

Department Stores

Dillard's   Dillard's is a Little Rock, Arkansas–based department store that has expanded across the country. Good prices and plenty of choices make this store a favorite of Memphis shoppers. You'll find Dillard's department stores in the **Oak Court Mall** (ℂ **901/685-0382**), **Wolfchase Galleria** (ℂ **901/383-1029**), and **The Avenue Carriage Crossings** (ℂ **901/850-2229**).

Macy's   Macy's department stores are the most upscale in Memphis. The **Oak Court Mall** location, at 4545 Poplar Ave. (ℂ **901/766-4199**), is probably the most convenient for visitors to the city. Other stores can be in the **Wolfchase Galleria,** 2760 N. Germantown Pkwy. (© **901/937-2600**), and **The Avenue Carriage Crossings** (© **901/850-2229**).

Discount Shopping

Casino Factory Shoppes If you're willing to make the drive south to Mississippi—or if you're planning a day trip there anyway, to take in some Tunica casino action—you'll want to hunt for some bargains at the Mid-South's best outlet mall. Casino Factory Shoppes is a 40-store center boasting such brand names as Bass, Izod, Lane Bryant, GNC, Hibbett Sports, Nautica, Old Navy, rue21, and Zales. 13118 U.S. Hwy. 61 N., Robinsonville, MS. © **662/363-1940.** www.casinofactoryshoppes.com.

Williams-Sonoma Clearance Outlet Williams-Sonoma, one of the country's largest mail-order companies, has a big distribution center here in the Memphis area, and this store is where they sell their discontinued lines and overstocks. If you're lucky, you just might find something that you wanted but couldn't afford when you saw it in the catalog. 4708 Spottswood Ave. © **901/763-1500.** www.williams-sonoma.com.

Fashion

MEN'S

Baer's Den Owner Jeremy Baer's upscale men's clothing store offers a shopping experience unmatched in Memphis. The impeccably furnished store, with its leather couches and dark colors, feels masculine and denlike. It's the backdrop for all styles of men's outerwear, tees, jeans, and shoes, with top-tier brands including Hugo Boss, Citizens of Humanity, and Diesel. 4615 Poplar Ave. © **901/684-6001.** www.thebaersden.com.

James Davis You'll find Giorgio Armani here for both men and women. In addition to tailored and casual clothing, sportswear, outerwear, and shoe brands such as Bruno Magli and Cole Haan, they carry women's apparel, as well as glamorous evening gowns. In addition to costume jewelry, the store offers merchandise through Mednikow Jewelers. Laurelwood Center, 400 Grove Park Rd. © **901/767-4640.** www.jamesdavisstore.com.

Lansky's ★ For the most stylish selection of jeans and clothing for young men, look to Lansky's—best known as "Clothier to The King." The Lansky Brothers have a long history dating back to the 1950s, when they dressed a young Elvis Presley in flashy threads. This shop, as well as three other Lansky-brand clothing and gifts stores, is located in the lobby of the Peabody hotel in downtown Memphis. 149 Union Ave. © **901/529-9070.** www.lanskybros.com.

WOMEN'S

Crazy Beautiful Dramatic fashions for young women are the forte of this edgy shop in the University of Memphis area. Well-known brands such as Trashy Diva and Iron Fist are for sale. Accessories and jewelry are also part of the mix. 3536 Walker Ave. © **901/452-6905.** www.facebook.com/crazybeautifulclothing.

Delphinium ★ 👜 Hand-cut, scented soaps and a wide array of cosmetics, including Bare Escentuals, Mario Badescu, and Smashbox, are among the trendy brands offered in this vibrant new boutique. Reasonably priced jewelry and gifts are arranged in creative displays. Hot buys include hand-woven neck scarves and embroidered coin purses, as well as supple black satchels made of recycled bicycle tires. 107 G. E. Patterson Ave. © **901/522-8600.** www.delphiniumboutique.com.

Hoot + Louise One of the newest boutiques in downtown Memphis, Hoot + Louise has a fresh, youthful vibe reflective of its owner, who stocks the store with well-chosen vintage as well as new women's clothing. Handmade housewares and other interesting items make browsing here fun. 109 G. E. Patterson Ave. ✆ **901/746-8683**. www.facebook.com/hootandlouise.

Isabella   This chic women's boutique carries designers not usually found in other Memphis stores, including Anlo, Rachel Pally, Trina Turk, and Ella Moss. If you're craving a stylish new pair of jeans, this is the place to scour. You might even find a belt or other invaluable accessory. Laurelwood Collection, 4615 Poplar Ave. ✆ **901/683-3538**.

Muse   In the South Main Historic District, boutique owner Lisa Doss has created one of the most popular women's apparel shops in downtown Memphis in a converted warehouse space with red-brick walls and velvet dressing room drapes. Designer-name dresses, tops, jeans, and accessories attract finicky customers who enjoy the personalized service in an urban setting. 546 S. Main St. ✆ **901/526-8738**. www.museinspiredfashion.com.

The Pink Door   If you're looking for classic, preppy clothing and accessories, check out this Lilly Pulitzer signature store in East Memphis. In addition to Lilly Pulitzer, the boutique carries such brands as Vineyard Vines, Elegant Baby, Molly B, and Lacoste. 4615 Poplar Ave. ✆ **901/682-2107**. www.thepinkdoormemphis.com.

CHILDREN'S

Cotton Tails   Customers with deep pockets can indulge the babies and children in their lives at this locally owned retailer. It's not all smock dresses and pinafores. The adorably decorated store has a wide selection of casual and dressy boys', girls', and infant and toddler clothing, accessories like leggings and backpacks, and nursery furnishings. Laurelwood Shopping Center, 389 Perkins Exit. ✆ **901/685-8417**. www.cotton-tails.com.

Pinocchio's Children's Book Store   With the closure of two of the city's biggest bookstore chains in recent years, shoppers have found a renewed appreciation for this unassuming little shop, located in a colorfully painted house in East Memphis. Hardback and paperback books for very young children through junior-high age are the focus. A weekly story time is held on Friday mornings. 688 W. Brookhaven Circle. ✆ **901/767-6586**.

The Village Toymaker   Thomas the Tank Engine merchandise, Melissa & Doug wooden puzzles, arts and crafts kits, and other nonelectronic toys fill this storefront in an East Memphis shopping center. The knowledgeable, friendly sales staff will help guide customers in finding just the right gift for the child on their shopping list. 4615 Poplar Ave. ✆ **901/240-5380**. www.thevillagetoymaker.com.

Food

Dinstuhl's Fine Candies   Southern favorites, such as buttered-nut brittles, divinity, and chocolate-covered marshmallow "hash," are specialties at this local proprietor. The Dinstuhl family has been making fudge, chocolates, and other candies in Memphis for five generations. You'll find these sweets sold in venues around town, including many hotel gift shops. Laurelwood Shopping Center, 436 Grove Park. ✆ **901/682-3373**. www.dinstuhls.com.

Lucchesi's   Fettuccine, tortellini, and other fresh-made pastas, along with homemade sauces, hearty breads, and take-and-bake pizzas, are prepared daily at this East Memphis market. Green garden salads as well as creamy prepared salads (potato, pasta, chicken, and the like) are available by the pound, along with Gorgonzola, balsamic, and other dressings. Sandwiches, panini, and ready-to-heat entrees such as eggplant lasagna and ravioli with meat sauce also tempt hungry shoppers. 540 S. Mendenhall (at Sanderlin). ✆ **901/766-9922**. www.lucchesis.com.

Miss Cordelia's ★★   Picnic goodies such as deli sandwiches, bakery-style cookies and cakes, and fresh fruits are available at this small local grocery store and market in Harbor Town, just north of the Pyramid. Bottled juices, teas, and even prepackaged sushi kits (chopsticks and wasabi included) from local restaurant Sekisui make it easy to grab a meal to enjoy at nearby Greenbelt Park on the Mississippi River. 737 Harbor Bend Rd. ✆ **901/526-4772.** www.misscordelias.com.

The Peanut Shoppe ☺   In business since 1951, this tiny but mightily aromatic shop is easily spotted: Look for the larger-than-life Mr. Peanut character tapping with his cane on the front window of the shop. Inside, you'll inhale the warm, toasty scent of all kinds of nuts—freshly roasted on the premises and still displayed on nostalgic glass counters and then weighed on old-fashioned scales. For fans of the monocled big guy, there's also lots of Mr. Peanut memorabilia on display. 24 S. Main St. ✆ **901/525-1115.** www.memphispeanutshoppe.com.

Whole Foods Market ★   Hands down the city's best grocery store, Whole Foods acquired this former Wild Oats Market in 2008. Along with the national chain's usual mix of organic produce, bins of bulk beans, rice and grains, and health-conscious frozen and packaged foods, there are deli-style counters offering fresh salads, meats, cheeses, sandwiches, pastries, breads, and other baked goods. 5022 Poplar Ave. ✆ **901/685-2293.** www.wholefoods.com.

Gifts & Souvenirs

A. Schwab Dry Goods Store ★★★ ☺ 📷   Owned by the same family for generations, this Memphis institution was recently sold to a group of private investors, so its future is in question. Enjoy it while you can. With its battered wood floors and tables covered with everything from plumbing supplies to religious paraphernalia, A. Schwab is a step back in time to the days of general stores. The offerings here are fascinating, even if you aren't in the market for a pair of size-74 men's overalls. You can still check out the 44 kinds of suspenders, the wall of voodoo love potions and powders, and the kiosk full of Elvis souvenirs. What else will you find at Schwab's? Bongo drums and crystal balls; shoeshine kits and corncob pipes; long thermal underwear and cotton petticoats; voodoo potions and praying hands; and plastic back-scratchers. Don't miss this place! 163 Beale St. ✆ **901/523-9782.**

Champion's Pharmacy and Herb Store 💼   Offbeat doesn't begin to describe this one-of-a-kind medicine-wagon museum and old-school drugstore. Champion's sells an eye-popping array of herbal remedies and nostalgic patent medicines with such names as Packer's Pine Tar Soap, Lydia E. Pinkham Tonic, Red Clover Salve, and Old Red Barn Ointment. 2369 Elvis Presley Blvd. (2¼ miles north of Graceland). ✆ **901/948-6622.** www.theherbalman.com.

Viking Culinary Arts ★   This spacious retail store and demonstration area for Greenwood, Mississippi–based Viking ranges and appliances offers top-of-the-line cookware and gadgets galore, making it a great place to shop for the cooking enthusiast on your gift list. 1215 Ridgeway Blvd. ✆ **901/763-3747.** www.vikinghomechef.com.

Jewelry

Mednikow   Open since 1891, this is one of the largest and most highly respected jewelry stores in Memphis, offering exquisite diamond jewelry, Rolex and Cartier timepieces, Mikimoto pearls, David Yurman designs, and other beautiful baubles. 474 Perkins Rd. Extended. ✆ **901/767-2100.** http://mednikow.com.

Timna Adjacent to the East Memphis Doubletree, Timna features hand-woven fashions and hand-painted silks by nationally acclaimed artists. A broad selection of contemporary jewelry includes fanciful pieces made of metals and stones, as well as harder-edged industrial designs, with prices ranging from $40 to several hundred dollars. 5101 Sanderlin Centre. ✆ **901/683-9369.**

Malls/Shopping Centers

The Avenue Carriage Crossing The metropolitan area's newest mall is an open-air shopping plaza in the far southeastern reaches of Shelby County, near the FedEx World Headquarters in Collierville, Tennessee, and close to the Mississippi state line. Dillard's and Macy's department stores anchor the center, which also includes scores of men's and women's apparel stores such as Aeropostale, Hollister, Talbots, and Jos. A. Bank. Specialty stores include Yankee Candle, Build-A-Bear Workshop, Bed Bath & Beyond, and Barnes & Noble. Among the dozens of eateries are upscale chains Carrabba's Italian Grill and Bonefish Grill, along with a Starbucks and Ben & Jerry's. From downtown Memphis, take I-40 west to I-240 south, to the Bill Morris Parkway (Hwy. 385), and exit at Houston Levee Road. ✆ **901/854-8240.** www.shoptheavenue.com.

Chickasaw Oaks Village ★ La Baguette bakery and Just for Lunch, a cafe popular with well-to-do ladies who lunch, are top dining draws at this indoor shopping center in Midtown. Interior designers, salons, and galleries such as Perry Nicole Fine Art, and upscale ladies' clothing boutiques Ella and the Kittie Kyle Kollection, have beautifully appointed shops here, where you can spend a delightful afternoon of retail therapy. 3092 Poplar Ave. ✆ **901/794-6022.** www.chickasawoaksvillage.com.

Laurelwood ★★ Conveniently located in East Memphis, about halfway between downtown and the suburbs of Germantown and Cordova, this upscale shopping plaza has an enviable variety of thriving retail options, including popular restaurants such as Grove Grill and the wonderful Davis-Kidd Booksellers. The immaculate stores here specialize in top-quality antiques, home furnishings, stationery, and apparel, featuring well-known chains such as Chico's. Poplar Ave. and Perkins Rd. Extended. ✆ **901/682-8436.** www.laurelwoodmemphis.com.

Oak Court Mall ★ With both a Macy's and a Dillard's and dozens of specialty shops, this mall has parklike landscaping with mature shade trees in the heart of the city. It's also the shopping mall that's most conveniently located to downtown and East Memphis. 4465 Poplar Ave., at Perkins Rd. ✆ **901/682-8928.** www.oakcourtmall.com.

The Regalia Several vacant storefronts also haunt this once-swank shopping plaza next door to the Embassy Suites Hotel and just off I-240; yet, it's worth a look. Oak Hall does steady business selling upscale men's and women's apparel. In addition to a Ruth's Chris Steakhouse, the center has four of Memphis's best locally owned restaurants—Salsa, Circa, Owen Brennan's, and (inside Embassy Suites) Grisanti's. Poplar Ave. and Ridgeway Rd. ✆ **901/767-0100.**

The Shops of Saddle Creek Technically located in the city of Germantown, Saddle Creek is considered part of the greater Memphis area. The affluent bedroom community's premier shopping area includes familiar national chain stores such as Coldwater Creek, Banana Republic, Crabtree & Evelyn, Ann Taylor, and GapKids, as well as restaurants and small shops. If you're tech needs find you looking for an Apple store while you're in the Memphis area, it's here. 5855 River Bend Rd. ✆ **901/761-2571.** www.shopsofsaddlecreek.com.

Wolfchase Galleria   The Cordova suburb's biggest mall is this mammoth (more than 1-million-sq.-ft.) retail center out near the interstate. It includes Dillard's and Macy's department stores, plus scores of restaurants and specialty shops. From Pottery Barn finds and Godiva chocolates to Looney Tunes toys at the Warner Brothers store, this always-crowded mall also has a children's carousel and a multiplex cinema with stadium-style seating. 2760 N. Germantown Pkwy. © **901/381-2769.** www.wolfchase galleria.com.

Markets

Memphis Farmers' Market ☺   Each Saturday morning at the train station downtown, farmers from throughout the region bring their produce to sell at this open-air market. Look for red-ripe Tennessee tomatoes; turnip, mustard, and collard greens; and other Southern crops. Children's activities and great community camaraderie pervade this market, which operates seasonally from May to the end of October. 545 S. Main St.© **901/575-0580.** www.memphisfarmersmarket.com.

Memphis Flea Market   A bargain browser's paradise or a junk collector's dream, this flea market, known locally as "The Big One," is held on the third weekend of every month. Hundreds of vendors hawk all manner of goods, from discount jeans and perfumes to antiques and other collectibles. 955 Early Maxwell Blvd., Mid-South Fairgrounds.© **901/276-3532.** www.memphisfleamarket.com.

Music

Goner Records ★   Take a stroll in the Cooper-Young neighborhood, and you'll stumble across this homegrown late-'70s-style record shop. Punk, funk, rock, rhythm and blues, and everything in between, coexist here. Flip through bins of vinyl LPs, old 45s, and CDs for affordably priced finds like late Delta-blues great Junior Kimbrough's releases on the Fat Possum label. Sun, Stax, Volt, Loverly, and Goner are among the other better-known Memphis-label rarities here. Goner also sells turntables and doubles as a fledgling indie record company. While you're here, ask for details about Gonerfest, one of the region's most buzzed-about, up-and-coming annual music events. 2152 Young Ave.© **901/722-0095.** www.goner-records.com.

Memphis Music   Recordings by legendary blues men such as Leadbelly and Memphis Minnie are a specialty of this otherwise touristy music shop that also sells Memphis souvenirs and T-shirts with images of iconic blues, rock, and jazz musicians. Watch your wallet (pickpockets are not unknown here), and you may want to consider doing your shopping *before* imbibing in the Beale Street bars. 149 Beale St.© **901/526-5047.**

River Records   The weathered little storefront on the scabby outskirts of the University of Memphis campus may look abandoned, but it's not. Once the city's premier record shop for serious collectors, River Records is still in business after 4 decades, selling comic books, posters, and vinyl records. 822 S. Highland St.© **901/324-1757.**

Shangri-La Records ★★ 📖   With Memphis's best selection of new and used rockabilly, as well as soul, R & B, reggae, and rock, Shangri-La is a bona fide gold mine for bargain browsers with offbeat musical appetites. It's all stuffed inside this nondescript old house in Midtown. Hang here to get the latest on what's happening in the local music scene. 1916 Madison Ave.© **901/274-1916.** www.shangri.com.

Musical Instruments

Amro Music Stores   A family-owned and -operated store that's been in business since 1921, Amro is a name that has become synonymous with music. The small business sells a large array of musical instruments, as well as sheet music and accessories. There are several locations around town, but this large showroom in Midtown is the flashiest. 2918 Poplar Ave. ✆ **901/323-8888.** www.amromusic.com.

Consignment Music   New and vintage guitars, drums, amplifiers, and other accessories. Specializing in restringing, repairs. Open daily. There's also a 24-hour vending machine stocked with strings, reeds, drum keys, picks, and the like. 4040 Park Ave. ✆ **901/458-2094.** www.memphisvintageguitar.com.

Gibson Beale Street Showcase   Not only can you watch Gibson guitars being manufactured, and hear them played, but you may also purchase a variety of Gibson and Epiphone stringed instruments and other merchandise. Public tour times vary, so call ahead and make a reservation before you head out. 145 Lt. George W. Lee Ave. ✆ **800/444-2766** or 901/544-7998. www.gibson.com.

Memphis Drum Shop ★   At the edge of the Cooper-Young district is this Midtown retailer that's been selling drums for 3 decades. The knowledgeable staff will help you find new, used, vintage, and custom drums, cymbals, parts, and accessories. Percussion instruments are also repaired, and can even be rented, at this fun shop. 878 S. Cooper St. ✆ **901/276-2328.** www.memphisdrumshop.com.

St. Blues Guitar Workshop   After relocating this guitar shop from Nashville back to their hometown of Memphis in 2011, the co-owners of this specialty instrument shop have a singular focus: building handmade acoustic and electrical guitars in a variety of styles. 645 Marshall Ave. ✆ **901/578-3588.** www.saintblues.com.

Shoes & Boots

In addition to the following shoe and boot stores, you'll find an excellent selection of shoes at the **Dillard's** department store in the Mall of Memphis shopping mall.

DSW Shoe Warehouse   An excellent selection of major-label shoes, with savings of 20% to 50% off standard retail prices. Open 7 days a week. Germantown Village Sq., Germantown Pkwy., at Poplar Ave. ✆ **901/755-2204.** www.dswshoe.com.

Oak Hall   Men with exquisite taste and plenty of disposable income have turned to this exclusive clothier for nearly 150 years. The store sells men's and women's clothing as well as top-of-the-line shoes by Mark Mason, Gravati, Ermenegildo Zegna, and Canali. 6150 Poplar Ave. ✆ **901/761-3580.** www.oakhall.com.

Peria   If Carrie Bradshaw shopped for shoes in Memphis, it would be at this eponymous shop run by 30-something trendsetter Peria Gober. Shoes, handbags, clutches, and accessories are in stock, with brands ranging from Sam Edelman and Poetic Licence to Apepazza. Whether you're looking for pointy-toed ballet flats, opentoe heels, or over-the-knee boots, you're likely to find them here. 1680 Union Ave. at Belvedere. ✆ **901/274-8488.** www.periashoes.com.

Rack Room Shoes   In East Memphis, 1 block west of Poplar Avenue, this large store offers good discounts on Timberland, Rockport, Nike, Reebok, and Bass shoes, among other lines. Eastgate Shopping Center, 5110 Park Ave. ✆ **901/682-1584.** www.rackroomshoes.com.

MEMPHIS ENTERTAINMENT & NIGHTLIFE

For a century, Memphis has nurtured one of the liveliest club scenes in the South, and the heart and soul of that nightlife has always been Beale Street. Whether your interest is blues, rock, opera, ballet, or Broadway musicals, you'll probably find entertainment to your liking on this lively street. However, there is more to Memphis nightlife than just Beale Street. In downtown Memphis, historic South Main Street has emerged as a fledgling arts community, with galleries, boutiques, and a growing number of buzz-worthy restaurants. You'll also find several theater companies performing in Midtown near Overton Square, which has several popular bars, restaurants, and a few clubs. Nightlife is livelier in the gay-friendly Cooper-Young neighborhood, at the intersection of Cooper Street and Young Avenue. Delis, boutiques, and a handful of excellent restaurants keep the young crowds coming.

Other places to check for live music are downtown alleys and the respective rooftops of the Peabody hotel and the Madison Hotel. Each summer, the hotels sponsor sunset cocktail parties that offer breathtaking views of the Mississippi River. Sometimes, after-work parties are held in alleyways closed off from traffic.

To find out about what's happening in the entertainment scene while you're in town, check with the *Memphis Flyer* (www.memphisflyer. com), Memphis's free arts-and-entertainment weekly, which comes out on Thursday. You'll find it in convenience, grocery, and music stores; some restaurants; and nightclubs. You could also check the website of the *Commercial Appeal,* Memphis's morning daily newspaper. The Friday edition has thorough events listings.

For tickets to sporting events and performances at the FedExForum and other venues, your best bet is to contact **Ticketmaster** (© **800/745-3000;** www.ticketmaster.com).

BEALE STREET & DOWNTOWN

Beale Street is the epicenter of Memphis's nightclub scene. This street, where the blues gained widespread recognition, is now the site of bars, restaurants, and souvenir shops. Relatively tame and family-friendly by day, the neon district gets quite rowdy after dark, when barricades allow for pedestrian traffic only. While blues purists looking for authenticity may be disappointed at the predominance of local rock and soul cover bands that reign here, others, including curious conventioneers and hard-drinking partiers, seem eager enough to accept the commercialism that has homogenized much of Beale Street. For links to various clubs and other businesses along Beale, click on **www.bealestreet.com**.

> **Impressions**
>
> *Beale Street is the life to me. We that play the blues, we're proud of it. It's somethin' religious.*
>
> —B.B. King

Alfred's ★ This spacious club on the corner of Third and Beale has rock 'n' roll most weekends, with a variety of bands currently packing the house. With its corner location and upstairs, outdoor patio, Alfred's also makes a great vantage point for people-watching and late-night drinking and eating. The kitchen's open until 3am. 197 Beale St. ✆ **901/525-3711.** www.alfredsonbeale.com. Cover $5–$10.

B.B. King's Blues Club ★★ 📷 Yes, the club's 80-something namesake "King of the Blues" does play here occasionally, though not on a regular basis. However, any night of the week you can catch blazing blues played by one of the best house bands in town. Because of the name, this club attracts famous musicians who have been known to get up and jam with whoever is onstage that night. Upstairs, a new third-floor restaurant, called Itta Bena, is named for B.B.'s Mississippi hometown. 147 Beale St. ✆ **800/443-0972** or 901/524-5464. www.bbkingsclub.com. Cover $7–$10 (usually $50–$170 for B.B.'s increasingly infrequent, but always sold-out, concerts).

Blues City Cafe ★★ This lively spot across the street from B.B. King's Blues Club takes up two old storefronts, with live blues wailing in one room (called the Band Box) and an excellent, casual restaurant serving steaks, tamales, and barbecue in the other. If you're looking to tank up on good food before a night of crawling the clubs along Beale Street, this is the best place to do it. 138–140 Beale St. ✆ **901/526-3637.** www.bluescitycafe.com. Cover $4–$5.

Center for Southern Folklore ★ 🎁 After bouncing between various locations on or around Beale Street, this offbeat treasure that's part coffeehouse/part folk-art flea market has landed in Pembroke Square. Warm and welcoming, it's a laid-back space where you can get a meal or some munchies and sip a latte or a beer. The Delta's most authentic roots-music artists often choose to play this venue. Kate Campbell is a perennial favorite. 119 S. Main St. ✆ **901/525-3655.** www.southernfolklore.com. No cover.

Earnestine & Hazel's ★ 📷 Although it's actually 4 blocks south of Beale Street, this downtown dive, which was once a sundry store that fronted for an upstairs brothel, has become one of Memphis's hottest nightspots. In 2011, Justin Timberlake and Free Sol featured it in the single "Hoodies On, Hats Low," and in 2004 Jack White and Loretta Lynn filmed a video here. On Friday and Saturday nights, there's a piano bar early; and then later in the night, the best jukebox in Memphis keeps things on a slow simmer. Things don't really get cookin' here until after midnight. 531 S. Main St. ✆ **901/523-9754.** No cover.

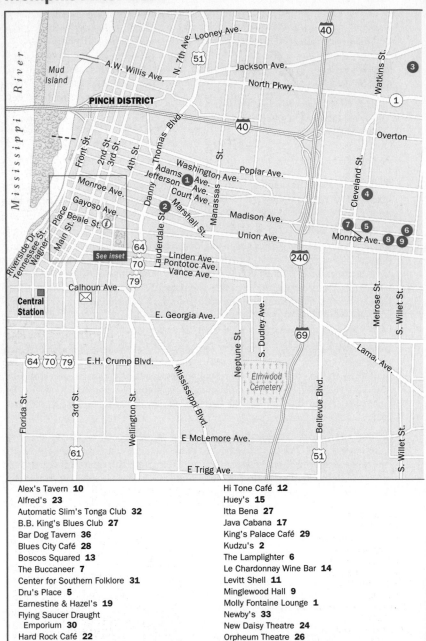

Alex's Tavern **10**
Alfred's **23**
Automatic Slim's Tonga Club **32**
B.B. King's Blues Club **27**
Bar Dog Tavern **36**
Blues City Café **28**
Boscos Squared **13**
The Buccaneer **7**
Center for Southern Folklore **31**
Dru's Place **5**
Earnestine & Hazel's **19**
Flying Saucer Draught
  Emporium **30**
Hard Rock Café **22**

Hi Tone Café **12**
Huey's **15**
Itta Bena **27**
Java Cabana **17**
King's Palace Café **29**
Kudzu's **2**
The Lamplighter **6**
Le Chardonnay Wine Bar **14**
Levitt Shell **11**
Minglewood Hall **9**
Molly Fontaine Lounge **1**
Newby's **33**
New Daisy Theatre **24**
Orpheum Theatre **26**

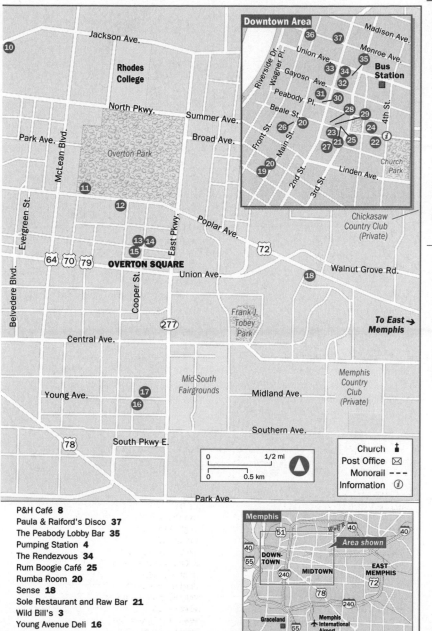

P&H Café **8**
Paula & Raiford's Disco **37**
The Peabody Lobby Bar **35**
Pumping Station **4**
The Rendezvous **34**
Rum Boogie Café **25**
Rumba Room **20**
Sense **18**
Sole Restaurant and Raw Bar **21**
Wild Bill's **3**
Young Avenue Deli **16**

Hard Rock Cafe   If you want the obligatory T-shirt, you'll want to check out this Hard Rock location that's, as expected, packed with rock and blues memorabilia. Look for gold musical notes on the brick sidewalk out front that celebrate famous Memphis musicians through the years. Live music is offered only occasionally, and it's usually staged in conjunction with local charity benefits. Impress your friends with this bit of trivia: The global Hard Rock Cafe chain was founded by Isaac Tigrett, a philanthropist-entrepreneur and former Memphis resident. 315 Beale St. ✆ **901/529-0007.** www.hardrock.com. Cover usually around $5 after 9pm.

> **Impressions**
>
> *I'd rather be here than any place I know.*
> —W. C. Handy, referring to Beale Street

King's Palace Café ★   With its battered wood floor, this bar has the most authentic, old-time feel of any club on Beale Street. Though primarily a restaurant serving decent Cajun food, including a knockout gumbo, there's frequent live jazz and blues on tap here. Popular with tour groups and locals alike, King's Palace has been a consistently good Beale Street venue for many years now. 162 Beale St. ✆ **901/521-1851.** www.kingspalacecafe.com. No cover.

New Daisy Theatre   The stage at the New Daisy has long been the place to see regional and national rock bands, but these days the theater books a surprisingly wide variety of entertainment, from boxing matches to touring alternative-rock bands. Bob Dylan filmed a video here from his Grammy-winning *Time Out of Mind* CD (fitting, because Memphis musicians were featured on that work). More recent acts to have played the venue include hometown heroes Justin Timberlake and the North Mississippi Allstars. 330 Beale St. ✆ **901/525-8981.** www.newdaisy.com. Ticket prices vary according to event.

Rum Boogie Cafe   Dozens of autographed guitars, including ones signed by Carl Perkins, Stevie Ray Vaughan, Joe Walsh, George Thorogood, and other rock and blues guitar wizards, hang from the ceiling at the Rum Boogie. There's live music nightly, with guest artists alternating with the house band, which plays everything from blues to country. 182 Beale St. ✆ **901/528-0150.** www.rumboogie.com. Cover $3–$5 after 9pm.

THE REST OF THE CLUB & MUSIC SCENE

Acoustic, Rock & Soul

Levitt Shell   In lovely Overton Park, this Hollywood Bowl–like amphitheater has a fascinating history. Built during the Depression by the WPA, it initially hosted musical theater and orchestral concerts. But on July 30, 1954, a relatively unknown Elvis Presley opened for Slim Whitman, in what some musicologists call the first-ever rock-'n'-roll show. Over the years, musicians ranging from Johnny Cash to the Grateful Dead took to the stage, before it fell into disrepair. Preservationists rallied to revitalize the hall, which is now the site of free outdoor live-music events of all styles. In 2011, acts as diverse as New Orleans's Rebirth Brass Band, Memphis soul supergroup The Bo-Keys, and kiddie-popsters Jack and the Zinghoppers all staged shows here. 1930 Poplar Ave. ✆ **901/272-5159.** www.levittshell.org. Ticket prices vary.

Minglewood Hall ★ The most popular live-music venue in town, Minglewood emerged a few years ago from a Midtown warehouse bread factory turned music store. The midsize hall has an elevated stage and can hold up to 1,500 dance-happy concertgoers. Neko Case, Old Crow Medicine Show, and Wanda Jackson are among the entertainers who've played here so far. Plan to arrive early and stay late at Minglewood, which has lounges for grabbing coffee and sandwiches, a cool cereal bar (wall-mounted dispensers filled with more than a dozen of your favorite not-just-for-breakfast treats) and an oxygen bar where you can chill by deep breathing filtered or "flavored" air. 1555 Madison Ave. ✆ **901/312-6058.** www.minglewoodhall.com. Ticket prices vary.

Newby's Located close to the University of Memphis, this cavernous club is a popular college hangout with two stages—one large, one small. There's live rock, mostly by local and regional acts, most nights of the week. Funk and alternative rock have been pretty popular here of late. While you're there, try their new infamous specialty cocktail known as the Rock Star, which is a Long Island Iced Tea "jacked up" with energy drink. 539 S. Highland St. ✆ **901/452-8408.** www.newbysmemphis.com. Cover $5–$10.

Wild Bill's ★★★ Beer sells by the quart, but you'll have to bring your own hard liquor to this gritty urban juke joint that's also as many light-years away from the glitz of Beale Street as you can get. Locals and rhythm-and-blues-loving tourists pack the nondescript room and sit in hard-back chairs at long tables before the band starts cranking out soul and blues classics. The music is hypnotizing, and sweaty patrons—young and old, black and white—drink and dance with abandon. If you want an authentic Memphis music experience, check it out. But call first, as the place is open only on weekends. 1580 Vollintine Ave. ✆ **901/726-5473.** Cover $5–$10.

> ### Impressions
>
> *People ask me what I miss about Memphis. And I said, "Everything."*
> —Elvis Presley

Folk

Java Cabana Located just down from the corner of Cooper and Young streets, this 1950s retro coffeehouse has occasional poetry readings and live acoustic music, singer-songwriters, and open-mic nights. Although you can't get alcohol here, you can indulge in all manner of coffees—and enjoy a smoke-free environment. 2170 Young St. ✆ **901/272-7210.** No cover.

BARS, PUBS & LOUNGES

Bars

DOWNTOWN

Automatic Slim's Tonga Club With funky decor, a cool menu, and live music on weekends, Automatic Slim's Tonga Club attracts the arty and upscale 20-, 30-, and 40-something crowd. Yummy Popsicle-flavored cocktails are a bar specialty, and the mimosas are popular for Sunday brunch. 83 S. Second St. ✆ **901/525-7948.** www.automaticslimsmemphis.com.

Bar Dog Tavern ★ A slightly classier cousin to your average corner bar and grill, this dark, noisy tavern with red-brick walls and soft couches draws young adults who like to socialize over cocktails or beer. Smoking is allowed in the main bar area, but a downstairs dining room is smoke free. Italian subs, club sandwiches, and the bar's signature sliders are a notch above the usual pub grub, making this a popular hangout for late-night eats. They also offer free delivery in the downtown area. 73 Monroe Ave. ✆ 901/275-8752. www.bardog.com.

Itta Bena ★★   Named for the tiny Mississippi town where B. B. King was born, this restaurant on the third floor of the blues legend's namesake nightclub seems more like a sophisticated speakeasy or a cabaret lounge than just another eatery. It's got dark lighting from blue chandeliers and windows that look down onto Beale Street, and a cozy bar that's perfect for enjoying a meal and drinks. Having a glass of wine or a cocktail here, above the rowdy blues club below, feels like a secret indulgence. Be aware that you must climb two flights of stairs to reach this bar, which is inaccessible to people in wheelchairs or those with limited mobility. 143 Beale St. ✆ **901/578-3031.** www.ittabenamemphis.com.

Mollie Fontaine Lounge ★   Tucked away on a leafy residential street near the Medical Center in Midtown, Mollie's is a beautifully restored Victorian house that dates back to 1886. A classy yet comfortable place to enjoy mellow piano music while sipping a martini in fashionable surroundings, Mollie's is best known for delicious tapas and other small-plate items. Beloved local restaurateur Karen Blockman Carrier is the owner. Music starts at 9pm, and there's no cover. 679 Adams Ave. ✆ **901/524-1886.**

The Peabody Lobby Bar ★   There's no more elegant place in Memphis for a drink, but be sure you drop in well after the crowds—who gather to watch the Peabody ducks do their daily march—have dispersed, usually shortly after 5pm. Piano music is featured in the evenings. If you're a middle-aged or older traveler with refined tastes and an appreciation of historic, Old South charm, you'll feel right at home relaxing here with a glass of bourbon or merlot. You can also order affordably priced small plates from Chez Philippe, the hotel's ritzy fine-dining restaurant. The Peabody, 149 Union Ave. ✆ **901/529-4000.** www.peabodymemphis.com.

The Rendezvous   Although best known for its barbecued ribs and waiters with attitude, the Rendezvous also has a big beer hall upstairs from the restaurant. It's a convivial spot, and a convenient place to start a night on the town or kill some time while you wait for a table in the restaurant. 52 S. Second St. ✆ **901/523-2746.** www.hogsfly.com.

MIDTOWN

Alex's Tavern   Bikers, working professionals, barflies, and nearby Rhodes College students all feel at home at this laid-back bar. You won't find many tourists here, but if you want to hang with the locals, play a little shuffleboard, and groove to the jukebox, stop in for a cheeseburger, chicken wings, or pork ribs and an ice-cold beer. 1445 Jackson Ave. ✆ **901/278-9086.**

The Buccaneer   Servers can be surly at times, but that shouldn't deter you from scouting out this local landmark, which is one of Midtown's bona fide dives. The Buc is beloved by laid-back barflies and after-hours partiers, who end up here late at night to hang with like-minded beer lovers. Occasional live music gigs are another reason to visit. Singer-songwriter Amy LeVere was a regular here every Wednesday night before she hit it big with a national tour in 2011. 1368 Monroe. ✆ **901/278-0909.**

Hi-Tone Cafe ★★   Acts as diverse as Michelle Shocked, Trampled By Turtles, Southern Culture on the Skids, and the Meat Puppets have all played late-night gigs at this ultrahip hangout near the Memphis College of Art in Overton Park. Elvis Costello liked it so much he and the Imposters filmed their DVD release *Club Date: Live in Memphis* here. 1913 Poplar Ave.℗ **901/278-8663.** www.hitonememphis.com.

Huey's Midtown   Other locations in the locally owned Huey's chain may be cleaner and more modern, but they can't hold a candle to the greasy, graffiti-littered original, a Midtown Memphis institution known for its mouthwatering burgers. Huey's is a definitive place to sip a beer and listen to live blues on Sunday evenings. Spitting cocktail toothpicks at the ceiling is another favorite pastime of patrons. 1927 Madison Ave.℗ **901/726-4372.** www.hueyburger.com.

Kudzu's   Named for the creeping wild vines that smother Southern landscapes in Chia Pet–like green shag carpeting, Kudzu's is a longtime local bar favorite with an unmistakable, deep-green paint job. Wildly popular for its trivia quiz nights, the place has a friendly Irish-pub sort of vibe. Pints of Guinness, along with other beers, are available, as is wine. The grub is pretty good, too; Kudzu's has excellent burgers, along with patty melts, Reubens, and other pub favorites. 603 Monroe Ave.℗ **901/525-4924.** No website.

The Lamplighter   If you're a fan of singer-songwriter Cat Power, who hails from Memphis, you're probably already hip to this Midtown dive bar that served as the backdrop to her 2006 "Lived in Bars" video. And if not, well, duck inside this dilapidated little hole in the wall for a late-night patty melt and a cold PBR. 1702 Madison.℗ **901/726-1101.**

Le Chardonnay Wine Bar   Near the ragged-looking former entertainment district known as Overton Square sits Memphis's original wine bar. With a dark, wine-cellar feel, Le Chardonnay tends to attract casual executive types, as well as theatergoers from nearby Playhouse on the Square. Consistently lauded for having one of the best wine lists in town, Le Chardonnay has been a time-honored institution for generations of Memphis residents. Have a drink here if you want to feel like one of the locals. 2094 Madison.℗ **901/725-1375.**

P & H Cafe   A dilapidated-looking hole in the wall as well as a beloved neighborhood landmark, the P & H ("Poor and Hungry") is a smoke-choked bar that has been a favored hangout for drinking, smoking, and shooting pool since 1961. Beer flows freely, washing down such cheap eats as spaghetti and meat sauce, stuffed burgers, and chicken-fried steak (about $7 each). It would have been unthinkable a generation ago, but the P & H now hosts karaoke on some nights. 1532 Madison Ave.℗ **901/726-0906.** www.pandhcafe.com.

Sole Restaurant & Raw Bar   Inside the Westin Beale Street is this contemporary nightspot where patrons can sip wine, suck down some oysters, or watch the game on TV over some beers. Located in a corner nook of the hotel just steps from the FedExForum and the Gibson Guitar factory, this is a perfect place to kick back with friends and just chill. Westin Hotel, 221 S. Third.℗ **901/334-5950.**

Young Avenue Deli ★   Buzzing with activity at all times of the afternoon and evening, this hangout is not so much a delicatessen as a trendy gathering place for young adults who like to shoot pool and drink coffee and/or alcohol. Way laid-back, the deli and sidewalk patio out front are at the epicenter of coolness in the Cooper-Young neighborhood. There's an impressive list of beers by the bottle and draft, and munchies such as Greek salads, quesadillas, and the best chili-cheese fries in town. 2119 Young Ave. ℗ **901/278-0034.** www.youngavenuedeli.com. Cover $5–$20, depending on bands playing.

EAST MEMPHIS

Belmont Grill   A quintessential neighborhood bar, Belmont is a go-to watering hole for Memphians looking for a place to unwind after a day at the office. As plain as a run-down roadhouse, it's unpretentious and casual. The eatery, which some might call a "greasy spoon," also happens to serve terrific cheeseburgers and fried catfish po' boys. 4970 Poplar Ave. (©*901/767-0305.*

Fox and Hound   Perhaps the most gregarious sports bar in town, this clubby pub is within walking distance of the East Memphis Doubletree Hotel. It's a favorite choice for fans who want to catch a game on a big screen while kicking back with buddies over beer and billiards. Corporate types, road warriors, and all manner of business travelers will also feel at home here. 5101 Sanderlin Ave. (©*901/763-2013.* www. fhrg.com.

Brewpubs

Boscos Squared ★★   Live jazz sizzles on Sundays at this popular, locally owned, Overton Square brewpub, known for its Famous Flaming Stone Beer. Boscos also boasts a top-notch restaurant menu featuring delicious pizzas baked in a wood-fired oven. An outdoor patio attracts large parties. If you're a cheap date (or you just like saving money), you'll appreciate that parking is free and much less hassle than at the downtown and Beale Street brewpubs. Plus, the food is better. 2120 Madison Ave. (©*901/432-2222.* www.boscosbeer.com.

Flying Saucer Draught Emporium   Open-air seating makes for great people-watching at this beer lovers' paradise right around the corner from Beale Street. College kids seem to love this place, with its frequent music and a lively pub atmosphere. Diversions such as trivia contests keep the blues at bay and patrons satisfied—and coming back for more. 130 Peabody Place. (©*901/523-8536.* www.beerknurd.com.

Dance Clubs

Paula & Raiford's Disco   Legendary Memphis DJ Robert "Hollywood" Raiford retired in 2007, after 32 years at the helm of his dance club on Vance Avenue downtown. In 2009 his daughter Paula brought the gold-toothed, Jheri-curled, cape-draped legend back for an encore. Fog machines, mirrored neon walls, disco balls, and throbbing disco hits keep the two-story club packed on Fridays and Saturdays, the only two nights Raiford's is open. 14 S. Second St. (©*901/521-2494.* www.paularaiford.com. Cover $10–$13.

Rumba Room ★   Learn to salsa on Friday and Saturday nights, listen to live and DJ-led reggae music on Wednesdays, and relax with poetry night on Mondays. Now in its third year, the Rumba Room draws a friendly, diverse crowd that embraces the eclectic nature of this one-of-a-kind Memphis dance club's offerings. 303 S. Main. (©*901/523-0020.* www.memphisrumbaroom.com. Cover $10. Women 21 and over get in free until 10pm.

Senses   A nondescript warehouse in a dreary part of Midtown by day, this steamy dance club comes alive late at night. A strict dress code (no jeans) helps maintain the upscale vibe, as gorgeous male and female 20-somethings weave between Senses' six different clubs, sipping fancy cocktails and grinding into the wee hours. 2866 Poplar Ave. (©*901/454-4081.* www.sensesmemphis.com. Cover $5–$10.

Gay Bars

Dru's Place A neighborhood bar and grill that draws mostly women, Dru's Place is the newest incarnation of the old Jungle Club in Midtown. The current owners have worked hard to make this a place that embraces community activism as well as fun. Fundraisers for worthy causes, as well as Karaoke, trivia contests, live music from singer-songwriters, beer busts, and drag shows are offered with equal measure. 1474 Madison Ave. (✆ **901/275-8082.** www.drusplace.com.

The Pumping Station Darts, billiards, and explicit videos are after-hours pursuits at this discrete Midtown haunt. There's also a crudely constructed treehouse on the patio out back. A strictly gay-male bar, it's known for catering to a slightly more mature crowd. *Tip:* You can park in the Kroger lot next door. 1382 Poplar Ave. ✆ **901/272-7600.** www.pumpingstationmemphis.com.

THE PERFORMING ARTS

With Beale Street forming the heart of the city's nightclub scene, it seems appropriate that Memphis's main performance hall, the Orpheum Theatre, is located here as well. A night out at the theater can also include a visit to a blues club after the show.

Classical Music, Opera & Ballet

Although blues and rock 'n' roll dominate the Memphis music scene, the city also manages to support a symphony, an opera, and a ballet. The symphony performs, and big-name performers and lecturers often appear, at the 2,100-seat **Cannon Center for the Performing Arts,** 255 N. Main St. (✆ **800/726-0915;** www.thecannoncenter.com), adjacent to the downtown center. Another of the city's premier performing arts venues is the **Orpheum Theatre,** 203 S. Main St. (✆ **901/525-3000;** www.orpheum-memphis.com), which was built in 1928 as a vaudeville hall. The ornate, gilded plasterwork on the walls and ceiling gives this theater the elegance of a classic opera house and makes this the most spectacular performance hall in the city.

In addition to performing at the Cannon Center, the orchestra also occasionally performs at other venues, including the suburban Germantown Performing Arts Center and outdoor concerts at the lovely Dixon Gallery and Gardens. The extremely popular **Sunset Symphony,** an outdoor extravaganza held on the banks of Tom Lee Park overlooking the Mississippi River each year as part of the Memphis in May International Festival, is always a highlight of the symphony season and one of the city's definitive Memphis experiences. The **Memphis Symphony Orchestra** (✆ **901/324-3627;** www.memphissymphony.org) box office is at 3100 Walnut Grove Rd. (tickets $12–$76).

Opera Memphis (✆ **901/257-3100;** www.operamemphis.org) also performs at both the Orpheum and Cannon Center, annually staging three or four operas (tickets $20–$70). The company, which for more than 50 years has been staging the best of classical opera and innovative new works for appreciative Memphis audiences, also has built a reputation for its extensive educational outreach program.

Ballet Memphis (✆ **901/737-7322;** www.balletmemphis.org), widely regarded as the city's crown jewel of performing arts groups, performs at both the Orpheum and Cannon Center (tickets $20–$70). For sentimentalists, the highlight of each

gambling ON THE MISSISSIPPI

From one of the poorest counties in the U.S. to the nation's third-largest gambling center, Tunica, Mississippi, has undergone an amazing transformation over the past 2 decades. While not on par with Las Vegas and Atlantic City, Tunica lures between 40,000 and 50,000 tourists a day to this cluster of casinos located about 20 miles south of Memphis, Tennessee.

Back in the heyday of paddle-wheelers on the Mississippi River, showboats and gamblers cruised the river, entertaining the masses and providing games of chance for those who felt lucky. Long gone are the dusty Delta cotton fields that once stretched out over the vast, flat landscape, but the Mississippi River is still here. The "Big Muddy," as it's known, is a fitting backdrop to the nine casino resorts offering everything from 24/7 slots, table games, poker rooms, nightclubs, and concert venues to three championship golf courses, outlet mall shopping, RV parks, and more than 6,000 hotel rooms.

From Memphis, take either Tenn. 61 or I-55 south. If you take the interstate, get off at either the Miss. 304 exit or the Miss. 4 exit, and head west to the river, watching for signs as you drive. www. tunicatravel.com.

- **Bally's,** 1450 Bally's Blvd. (© **800/38-BALLY** [382-2559]).
- **Fitz Casino & Hotel,** 711 Lucky Lane (© **800/766-LUCK** [5825] or 662/363-5825).
- **Goldstrike Casino Resort,** 1010 Casino Center Dr. (© **888/24K-PLAY** [245-7529] or 866/245-7511).
- **Harrah's,** 1100 Casino Strip Blvd. (© **800/HARRAHS** [427-7247] or 662/363-7777).
- **Hollywood Casino,** 1150 Commerce Landing (© **800/871-0711** or 662/357-7700).
- **Horseshoe Casino & Hotel,** 1021 Casino Center Dr. (© **800/303-SHOE** [7463]).
- **Resorts Casino,** 1100 Casino Strip Resort Blvd. (© **866/676-7070**).
- **Sam's Town Hotel & Gambling Hall,** 1477 Casino Strip Blvd. (© **800/456-0711** or 662/363-0711).
- **Tunica Roadhouse Casino & Hotel,** 1107 Casino Center Dr. (© **800/391-3777**)

season is the annual holiday performance of *The Nutcracker,* but exciting world premieres and contemporary dance works also rate high priority on the company's mission.

Theater

Memphis has a relatively well-developed theater scene with numerous opportunities to attend live stage productions around the city. **Theatre Memphis,** 630 Perkins Rd. Extended (© **901/682-8323;** www.theatrememphis.org), is a commendable community theater that's been around for more than 75 years. Located on the edge of Audubon Park, it has garnered regional and national awards for excellence. There are two stages here—a 435-seat main theater that does standards, and a 100-seat, blackbox theater, known as Next Stage, where less mainstream productions are staged.

Staging productions of a higher artistic caliber are two sister theaters in Midtown: **Circuit Playhouse,** 1705 Poplar Ave. (© **901/726-4656**), and **Playhouse on the Square,** 51 S. Cooper St. (© **901/726-4656;** www.playhouseonthesquare.org), are the only professional theaters in Memphis, and between them they stage about 25 productions each year. Off-Broadway plays are the rule at the Circuit Playhouse (with the occasional premiere), while at Playhouse on the Square, Broadway-worthy dramas, comedies, and musicals dominate.

Another good option is the **Hattiloo Theatre,** 656 Marshall (© **901/502-3486;** www.hattilootheatre.org), Memphis's Black repertory theater. Recent productions included *Ain't Misbehavin'* and *For Colored Girls Who Have Considered Suicide When the Rainbow Is Enuf.*

The Orpheum Theatre ★ Best known for hosting touring Broadway productions, as well as performances by local opera and ballet groups, the Opheum is the crown jewel of downtown's live entertainment venues. The restored 1928 movie palace also presents a classic movie series every weekend throughout the summer.

In October 2011, the Orpheum also experienced a first when it launched the national touring production of the Tony-winning Broadway musical *Memphis*. It's the story of a white man who falls in love with a black soul singer. 203 S. Main. © **901/525-7800.** www.orpheum-memphis.com.

Other Venues

Since its opening in 2004, the 18,400-seat **FedExForum,** 191 Beale St. (© **901/205-1234;** www.fedexforum.com), though primarily the venue for the NBA Memphis Grizzlies team, has booked big-name concert acts such as Justin Timberlake, Elton John, Bon Jovi, and the Rolling Stones.

From late spring to early fall, Memphians frequently head outdoors for their concerts, and the **Mud Island River Park Amphitheatre,** 125 N. Front St. (© **800/507-6507** or 901/576-7241; www.mudisland.com), is where they head most often. With the downtown Memphis skyline for a backdrop, the 5,000-seat Mud Island Amphitheatre is the city's main outdoor stage. The concert season includes many national acts with the emphasis on rock and country music concerts; 2011 headliners included Bob Dylan, Death Cab for Cutie, and Garrison Keillor. Though the monorail usually runs only during the summer months, it runs here year-round on concert evenings.

WHERE TO STAY IN MEMPHIS

Where you stay in Memphis will depend on what brings you here. Families and business travelers looking for convenience and affordability will find abundant chain-hotel choices in East Memphis, but Elvis fans on pilgrimage to Graceland have only a few motel options near Presley's gated mansion in the seedy south end of town. Wisely, most tourists interested in Memphis's rich musical and cultural heritage stay downtown. In addition to iconic views of the beautiful Mississippi River, it's here that you'll find the widest choice of unique accommodations, from the sleek Westin to the quirky Talbot Heirs.

BEST HOTEL BETS

- **Most Romantic:** The intimate **Madison Hotel,** 79 Madison Ave., is an upscale boutique property offering sumptuous furnishings, first-class service, and rooftop river views. See p. 232.

- **Best for Families:** Spacious suites with kitchens and comfy sectional-style sofas around 42-inch flatscreen TVs make **Hyatt Place,** 1220 Primacy Pkwy., in East Memphis, my top pick for vacationing families. Close to restaurants and such kid-friendly attractions as the Lichterman Nature Center, it also offers a convenient, central location for exploring the city. See p. 240.

- **Best for Business Travelers:** Travelers with high expectations and pinched pocketbooks get the best of both worlds at the **Hampton Inn & Suites–Shady Grove,** 962 S. Shady Grove Rd., an exceptionally well-run, affordable hotel in a beautiful residential section of East Memphis. See p. 241.

- **Best Downtown Pool:** From its plum, rooftop perch at the **Comfort Inn,** 100 N. Front St., this outdoor pool does double duty, offering killer views of the Mississippi River and relief from Memphis's sweltering summer heat and humidity. See p. 235.

- **Best Splurge & Best Service:** Open for only a few years now, the **River Inn of Harbor Town,** 50 Harbor Town Sq. is still somewhat of a hidden gem—a 28-room, European-style hotel offering exquisite furnishings, gourmet food, impeccable service, and lovely picnic areas along the grassy banks of the Mississippi River. See p. 234.

- **Best for Nightlife:** If your plans revolve around partying on Beale Street, this one's a no-brainer: Book a room at the **Hampton Inn & Suites–Beale Street,** 175 Peabody Place. Billed as the chain's top-selling property in the world, it offers perks like fresh-baked cookies, as well as free earplugs, and has balconies overlooking the clubs and bars along world-famous Beale Street, birthplace of the blues. See p. 233.

- **Best Bang for Your Buck:** One of the newest and most popular downtown hotels is the **Residence Inn by Marriott,** 110 Monroe Ave., a sophisticated stunner that occupies a 12-story Art Deco building dating back to the 1930s. With large suites including kitchens, plus value-added perks like complimentary breakfast and light dinner Monday through Thursday, you get much more for your money than in comparably priced and even more expensive hotels downtown. See p. 234.

- **Best Historic Hotel:** Even if **The Peabody,** 149 Union Ave., weren't the *only* historic hotel in the city, it would likely still be the best. That ambience is mainly experienced in the lobby, with its marble fountain full of pampered live ducks. See p. 232.

- **Best for Elvis Fans: Lauderdale Courts,** 252 N. Lauderdale, the housing project where the shy future entertainer lived while attending high school, is now known as **Uptown Square.** The complex has been renovated as upscale condos—except for the simple Presley apartment, which has been preserved as it was in 1949–53, when Gladys, Vernon, and their son shared it. See p. 243.

- **Best Hotel Near the Airport:** Though not located within the undesirable airport area per se, the well-maintained **Marriott East,** 2625 Thousand Oaks Blvd., provides the nicest hotel option *near* the airport area. Polished service, extensive amenities, and free transportation to and from the terminals and other nearby destinations also add value to this surprisingly affordable high-rise. See p. 242.

- **Best Place to Rock Out:** Guests at the **Westin Memphis Beale Street,** 170 Lt. George W. Lee Ave., can call down to the front desk to have a classic 1956 Les Paul Goldtop VOS or one of several other Gibson guitars delivered to their rooms along with a virtual amp and headphones. See p. 235.

DOWNTOWN

If you want to be where the tourist action is, your first choice ought to be downtown. Besides Beale Street, this area is also where the majority of the city's major sporting events, concerts, and cultural performances take place. If you want to feel as though you've been to Memphis, you need to experience the riverfront heart of it all.

Very Expensive

Memphis Marriott Downtown As one of the city's primary convention hotels, this upscale Marriott in the north end of downtown always seems crowded. Although the 19-story hotel is a bit off the beaten track, surrounded mostly by government buildings, it's accessible to the trolley that will take you up and down Main Street to where there's more action. The lobby is built on a grand scale with soaring ceilings, marble floors, and traditional furnishings. Corner guest rooms have angled walls that provide a bit more character than others. For views of the Mississippi, ask for a room on the 10th floor or higher. As with all Marriott hotels, the property does not permit smoking.

250 N. Main St., Memphis, TN 38103. www.marriott.com. © **800/557-8740** or 901/527-7300. Fax 901/214-3711. 600 units. $209 and up double; $349–$500 suite. AE, DC, DISC, MC, V. Valet parking $20; self-parking $12. **Amenities:** Restaurant; lounge; concierge; exercise room; hot tub; large indoor pool; room service. *In room:* A/C, TV, hair dryer, Internet ($13 per 24 hr.).

Memphis Hotels: Downtown & Midtown

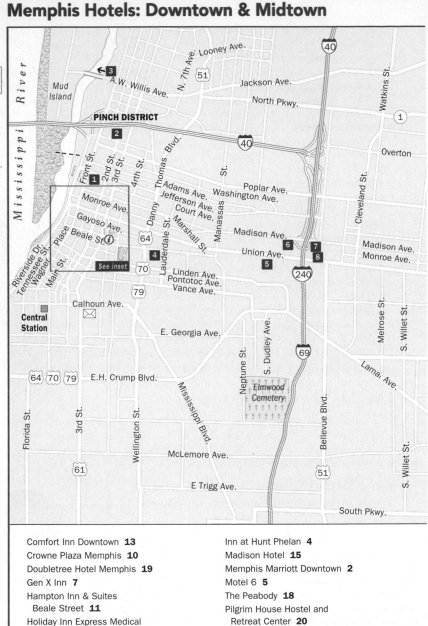

Comfort Inn Downtown **13**
Crowne Plaza Memphis **10**
Doubletree Hotel Memphis **19**
Gen X Inn **7**
Hampton Inn & Suites
  Beale Street **11**
Holiday Inn Express Medical
  Midtown **8**
Holiday Inn Select Downtown **17**

Inn at Hunt Phelan **4**
Madison Hotel **15**
Memphis Marriott Downtown **2**
Motel 6 **5**
The Peabody **18**
Pilgrim House Hostel and
  Retreat Center **20**
Residence Inn by Marriott Memphis
  Downtown **16**

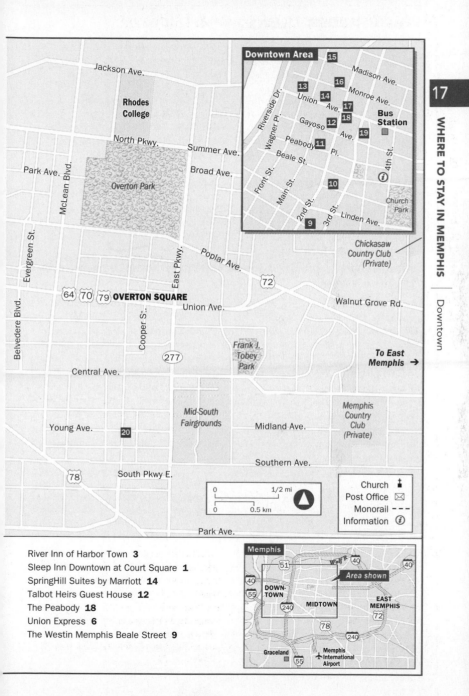

Downtown Area

Madison Ave.

Monroe Ave.

Union Ave.

Gayoso Ave.

Peabody Pl.

Beale St.

Riverside Dr.

Wagner Pl.

Front St.

Main St.

2nd St.

3rd St.

4th St.

Linden Ave.

Bus Station

Church Park

Chickasaw Country Club (Private)

Jackson Ave.

Rhodes College

North Pkwy.

Summer Ave.

Broad Ave.

Park Ave.

McLean Blvd.

Overton Park

Evergreen St.

Poplar Ave.

East Pkwy.

72

64 70 79 **OVERTON SQUARE**

Union Ave.

Belvedere Blvd.

Cooper S..

277

Central Ave.

Frank J. Tobey Park

Walnut Grove Rd.

To East Memphis →

Young Ave.

20

Mid-South Fairgrounds

Midland Ave.

Memphis Country Club (Private)

Southern Ave.

78

South Pkwy E.

Park Ave.

| 0 | | 1/2 mi |
| 0 | 0.5 km | |

Church ✝
Post Office ✉
Monorail - - -
Information ⓘ

River Inn of Harbor Town **3**
Sleep Inn Downtown at Court Square **1**
SpringHill Suites by Marriott **14**
Talbot Heirs Guest House **12**
The Peabody **18**
Union Express **6**
The Westin Memphis Beale Street **9**

Memphis

51

Wolf R.

40

40

40

55

DOWN-TOWN

240

MIDTOWN

Area shown

EAST MEMPHIS

72

78

240

Graceland

Memphis International Airport

55

THE PEABODY ducks

It isn't often that you find live ducks in the lobby of a luxury hotel. However, ducks are a fixture at **The Peabody.** Each morning at 11am, the Peabody ducks, led by a duck-master, take the elevator down from their penthouse home, waddle down a red carpet, and hop into the hotel's Romanesque travertine-marble fountain. And each evening at 5pm they waddle back down the red carpet and take the elevator back up to the penthouse. During their entry and exit, the ducks waddle to John Philip Sousa tunes and attract large crowds of curious onlookers that press in on the fountain and red carpet from every side.

The Peabody ducks first took up residence in the lobby in the 1930s when Frank Schutt, the hotel's general manager, and friend Chip Barwick, after one too many swigs of Tennessee sippin' whiskey, put some of his live duck decoys in the hotel's fountain as a joke (such live decoys were legal at the time but have since been outlawed as unsportsmanlike). Guests at the time thought the ducks were a delightfully offbeat touch for such a staid and traditional establishment, and, since then, ducks have become a beloved fixture at The Peabody.

The Peabody ★ For years, The Peabody has enjoyed a reputation as "the South's grand hotel." In its present location since the 1920s (the original site at Main and Monroe dates back to the late 1880s), The Peabody appeals to well-heeled travelers looking for a slice of Memphis history. However, no longer best known for the genteel, white-glove service that defined The Peabody generations ago, today it is The Peabody's reputation as a tourist attraction that keeps it fully booked much of the time. Although standard rooms aren't overly spacious or extraordinary, the public spaces dazzle. Marble columns, hand-carved and burnished woodwork, and ornate gilded plasterwork on the ceiling give the lobby the air of a palace. Its dominant feature is its Romanesque marble fountain. Here, the famous Peabody ducks, one of Memphis's biggest attractions, splash away each day, drawing throngs of tourists in search of that definitive photo opportunity.

149 Union Ave., Memphis, TN 38103. www.peabodymemphis.com. ✆ **800/PEABODY** (732-2639) or 901/529-4000. Fax 901/529-3677. 464 units. $260–$350 double; $750 and up suite. AE, DC, DISC, MC, V. Valet parking $24; self-parking $18. **Amenities:** 2 restaurants; 2 lounges; concierge; athletic facility; indoor pool; room service; sauna; shoeshine service; steam room; valet service; massage. *In room:* A/C, TV, hair dryer, Wi-Fi ($9.95 per day).

Expensive

Madison Hotel ★★★ 📷 A member of the prestigious Small Luxury Hotels of the World, this intimate hotel occupies the site of a former bank building. The graceful Beaux Arts architecture belies the bold, contemporary furnishings inside. From the chic lobby, with its grand piano and musical instrument motif, to the rich, solid colors in the guest rooms, the Madison is a contrast between classic and modern. Completely smoke free, the hotel offers nightly turndown and twice-daily housekeeping service to keep guests feeling pampered. Take the elevator to the rooftop for breathtaking views of the Mississippi River and surrounding downtown. Every Thursday evening from April to mid-October, the hotel hosts sunset parties here featuring live music.

79 Madison Ave., Memphis, TN 38103. www.madisonhotelmemphis.com. © **866/44-MEMPHIS** (446-3674) or 901/333-1200. Fax 901/333-1212. 110 units. $171–$290 double; $256–$360 suite. AE, DC, DISC, MC, V. Valet parking $23; self-parking $6 (no in-and-out privileges). **Amenities:** Restaurant/lounge; concierge; fitness room; indoor pool; room service. *In room:* A/C, TV, hair dryer, minibar, MP3 docking stations, Wi-Fi (free), make-up mirror.

Hampton Inn & Suites–Beale Street ★★

You can't get closer to spending the night on Beale Street unless you pass out on the pavement after a blues-soaked binge of barhopping. This award-winning property is not your typical chain hotel; in fact, it's touted by Hampton as their top hotel in the world. This stylish, curved building sits on a corner lot, jutting out into the heart of the action along Beale and Peabody Place. (Try to get a corner room with an iron balcony and watch the revelry like it's Mardi Gras.) You'll want to keep your earphones (or earplugs, free at front desk) at the ready if you plan to do any sleeping while you're here. It stays pretty rowdy all night long and into the wee hours. Other pluses of this all-smoke-free hotel include all-day coffee and cookies, and exceptionally eager-to-please service.

175 Peabody Place, Memphis, TN 38103. www.hampton-inn.com. © **901/260-4000.** Fax 901/260-4012. 144 units. $185 double; $265 suite. Rates include continental breakfast. AE, DC, DISC, MC, V. Parking $20. **Amenities:** Exercise room; indoor pool. *In room:* A/C, TV w/pay movies, Wi-Fi (free).

Holiday Inn Select Downtown ★

Across the street from The Peabody, this Holiday Inn is in the heart of the downtown action. The guest rooms, though not large, have comfortable chairs and big windows. But be advised that some of those windows butt up against other concrete buildings. Rooms facing south afford the best views of the bustle along Union Avenue below. Some suites have fridges and microwaves. Foodies may appreciate that the hotel is mere footsteps away from the city's best barbecue rib joint—**The Rendezvous** (p. 193)—not to mention across the corner from **Huey's,** Memphis's beloved burger-and-beer joint. The hotel also houses one of the freshest sushi bars in town (**Sekisui,** p. 193).

160 Union Ave., Memphis, TN 38103. www.ihg.com. © **888/HOLIDAY** (465-4329) or 901/525-5491. Fax 901/529-8950. 192 units. $159–$199 double. AE, DC, DISC, MC, V. Parking $12. **Amenities:**

STARTING THE CHAIN: THE STORY OF THE
holiday inn

Wherever in the world your travels take you, the next time you're looking to book a clean, comfortable hotel room, you might want to thank Kemmons Wilson. The Memphis entrepreneur founded the first Holiday Inn back in 1952, before there was such a concept as chain hotels that aimed for consistency and reliability across many locations. The Holiday Inn franchise went international in 1960; today the brand is owned by the Intercontinental Hotel Group (IHG), which operates properties worldwide.

Wilson, who was known in Memphis as somewhat of a character, died in 2003. His autobiography, *Half Luck and Half Brains,* tells the interesting story of the Holiday Inn. His legacy lives on at the University of Memphis, where the Kemmons Wilson School at the Fogelman College of Business and Economics trains new generations of hoteliers and tourism professionals.

The university's Holiday Inn is at 3700 Central Ave., Memphis, TN 38111 (© **901/678-8200;** www.holidayinn.com).

Restaurant; lounge; off-site health club ($7 per day); modest outdoor pool on 4th-floor terrace; room service. *In room:* A/C, TV, hair dryer, Wi-Fi (free).

The Inn at Hunt-Phelan
If you want to get a taste of being a wealthy plantation owner in the Old South, you'll most likely love this antebellum bed-and-breakfast. But if you find that Confederate mind-set sort of pretentious, you might want to book elsewhere. Built in the 1820s, the mansion is said to have served as General Ulysses S. Grant's temporary headquarters during the Civil War. Furnished with period antiques, the postcard-pretty inn sits in a rather seedy area about a $5 cab ride away from Beale Street's tourist attractions. Inside the security-gated estate, however, you'll find five elegant guest rooms and five condos (all smoke free) that include living rooms and full kitchens. All have private bathrooms. The upscale restaurant specializes in French Creole dishes. Call well in advance if you want to make a weekend reservation here; the entire inn sometimes gets booked for weddings and private parties.

533 Beale St., Memphis, TN 38103. www.huntphelan.com. © **901/525-8225.** Fax 901/523-2509. 10 units. $159 rooms; $295 condo. Rates include continental breakfast. AE, DC, DISC, MC, V. Free parking. Pets accepted in 2 condos ($50 fee). **Amenities:** Restaurant; lounge. *In room:* A/C, TV, Wi-Fi (free).

Residence Inn by Marriott Memphis Downtown ★★ 🔥
One of the newer hotels in downtown Memphis is located in a 12-story Art Deco building that dates back to the 1930s. The fully renovated high-rise features 90 suites, ranging from studio rooms with queen and sofa beds to two-bedroom units with fully stocked kitchens and sitting rooms with pullout sofas and fireplaces. Close to attractions, great restaurants, and the Main Street Trolley line, its location is ideal. Value-added perks include a complimentary social hour each weekday evening, as well as daily breakfast with freshly made waffles. The lobby offers free Wi-Fi, and within a year all rooms will have it as well.

110 Monroe Ave., Memphis, TN 38103. www.marriott.com. © **901/578-3700.** Fax 901/578-3999. 90 units (all suites). $159–$259 suite. Rates include cooked-to-order breakfast and social hour. AE, DISC, MC, V. Valet parking $16; off-site self-parking $8. Pets accepted (nonrefundable $100 cleaning fee). **Amenities:** Exercise room; rooftop Jacuzzi; Wi-Fi (free, in lobby and breakfast area); valet service. *In room:* A/C, TV, hair dryer, Internet (free), fully furnished kitchens.

River Inn of Harbor Town ★★★
As close to perfect as it gets, this posh, 28-room boutique hotel may be Memphis's best-kept secret. Opened in late 2007, the inn is ensconced in the upscale community of Harbor Town, on a small island a few blocks north of the Pyramid. With a west-facing, rooftop terrace offering breathtaking sunsets over the Mississippi River, the inn has a charming European flavor (the general manager is Austrian). The hotel brims with fresh roses and fine furnishings, and rooms are sumptuously furnished with four-poster beds, Frette linens, and Gilchrist & Soames bath products. A wood-burning fireplace in the cozy lobby, as well as free champagne or wine, welcomes guests at check-in. Nightly turndown includes chocolate truffles and port. Popular with couples and female executives, it's also ideal for fitness-minded folks who relish early-morning or sunset workouts. Manicured walking trails and picnic areas on the Mississippi River bank are just steps away. Service is exceedingly gracious and intuitive, with staff ready to anticipate guests' every request.

50 Harbor Town Sq., Memphis, TN 38103. www.riverinnmemphis.com. © **877/222-1531** or 901/260-3333. Fax 901/260-3291. 28 units. $189–$340 double; $375–$595 suite. Rates include gourmet breakfast. AE, DISC, MC, V. Free parking. **Amenities:** 2 restaurants; concierge; exercise room. *In room:* A/C, TV, hair dryer, MP3 docking stations, Wi-Fi (free).

The Westin Memphis Beale Street ★★ Downtown's newest full-service luxury hotel is a few years old now, but it's still a stunner: The city's first (and only) Westin has a plum perch at the foot of famed Beale Street. Exquisitely appointed two-room corner suites overlook the NBA Grizzlies' FedExForum and the Gibson Guitar plant. Hotel guests can call down to the front desk to have a classic 1956 Les Paul Goldtop VOS or one of several other Gibson guitars delivered to their rooms, along with a virtual amp and headphones. The perk is free, and not just for VIPs. Other hotel features include a 24-hour business center with computers and free Internet access. Westin's signature "Heavenly Beds," with plush pillowtop mattresses and 250-thread-count sheets, as well as thick bathrobes and oversized showers with dual massaging shower heads, nurture relaxation.

170 Lt. George W. Lee Ave., Memphis, TN 38103. www.westin.com/bealestreet. ©️ **800/WESTIN1** (937-8461) or 901/334-5900. Fax 901/334-5919. 203 units. $170–$269 double; $649–$1,299 suite. AE, DISC, MC, V. Valet parking $24; self-parking $18. Dogs 40 lb. and under permitted; no fee. **Amenities:** Restaurant; lounge; concierge; health club; room service; shoeshine stand. In room: A/C, TV w/pay movies and video games, hair dryer, Internet ($6.95–$13), minibar, MP3 docking stations, makeup mirror.

Moderate

Comfort Inn Downtown ★★ 🐾 Memphis's only rooftop swimming pool is the best boast of this Front Street property overlooking the Mississippi River. The all-suites hotel is a good value for the money, considering its location and perks, including free local calls and full complimentary breakfast. Quite often, you'll see busloads of school and tour groups staying at the hotel. Yet the cheerful staff and exceptional customer service help maintain a welcoming atmosphere for all guests. Both smoking and smoke-free rooms are available.

100 N. Front St., Memphis, TN 38103. www.choicehotels.com. ©️ **901/526-0583.** Fax 901/525-7512. 71 units. $120–$140 double and suite. AE, DC, DISC, MC, V. Parking $8. **Amenities:** Outdoor pool; Wi-Fi (free, in lobby and pool area). In room: A/C, TV, hair dryer, Wi-Fi (free).

Crowne Plaza Memphis The 11-story Crowne Plaza offers an excellent location if your trip will take you to the nearby convention center or to St. Jude Children's Research Hospital. However, if you're a tourist who wants to be closer to the action of Beale Street and good restaurants, I don't recommend this property in downtown's dull north end. Perhaps because of the transition in ownership, the hotel feels a bit isolated and out of the loop, like a place that is used mainly for overflow from other hotels. When I visited recently, service was indifferent at best. All units have standard amenities, including work desks and 32-inch flatscreen TVs.

300 N. Second St., Memphis, TN 38103. www.ichotelsgroup.com. ©️ **901/525-1800.** Fax 901/524-1859. 230 units. $149 single or double. AE, DC, DISC, MC, V. Valet parking $15; self-parking $10. **Amenities:** Restaurant/lounge; exercise room; outdoor pool. In room: A/C, TV w/pay movies, hair dryer, Wi-Fi (free).

Doubletree by Hilton Memphis Because it's located across the street from AutoZone Park baseball stadium and adjacent to the downtown bus station, this otherwise nondescript high-rise is a practical choice for travelers with modest expectations. Rooms are a bit larger than expected, but furnishings are outdated. If you arrive by car, be aware that the small, congested front entrance can get backed up with vehicles and valet parking attendants trying to navigate the tight driveway off of busy Union Avenue.

185 Union Ave., Memphis, TN 38103. www.doubletree.hilton.com. ✆ **800/222-8733** or 901/528-1800. Fax 901/524-0795. 280 units. $119–$299 double; $219–$309 suite. AE, DC, DISC, MC, V. Valet parking $21; no self-parking. **Amenities:** Restaurant; lounge; small exercise room; outdoor pool. *In room:* A/C, TV w/pay movies, hair dryer, Wi-Fi (free).

SpringHill Suites by Marriott ★   A good value for tourists who want a clean, comfortable suite at a reasonable price in a great location, this property is just a block from the Mississippi River. Step out the back door and hop on the trolley to reach Beale Street and other attractions. A cheerful lobby and adjacent breakfast room provide guests with a welcome greeting. Suites are spacious and tastefully decorated, and include well-lighted work spaces with multiline speakerphones, kitchenettes, and soft couches. Rooms with south-facing windows have nice views of Court Square, a leafy park that dates back to the late 1800s. On the ground floor in front of the hotel, the small outdoor pool is gated and landscaped, though not very private.

21 N. Main St., Memphis, TN 38103. www.marriott.com. ✆ **901/522-2100.** Fax 901/522-2110. 148 units. $139 double. AE, DC, DISC, MC, V. Parking $12. **Amenities:** Outdoor pool; valet service. *In room:* A/C, TV w/pay movies, fridge, hair dryer, Wi-Fi (free).

Talbot Heirs Guesthouse ★ 🎁   Rich colors and simple, contemporary styling are hallmarks of the rooms in this unique downtown bed-and-breakfast. The eight guest rooms vary in size from large to huge. Many have kilim rugs. Call ahead with your grocery list, and they'll have the fridge stocked for your arrival (for an added fee). Lots of interesting contemporary art further adds to the hip feel of this inn. You can't beat the location, across the street from The Peabody and within easy walking distance of Beale Street and dozens of excellent restaurants.

99 S. Second St., Memphis, TN 38103. www.talbothouse.com. ✆ **800/955-3956** or 901/527-9772. Fax 901/527-3700. 8 units. $130–$275 double. Rates include continental breakfast. AE, DC, DISC, MC, V. Parking $10. **Amenities:** Concierge; massage. *In room:* A/C, TV, CD player, hair dryer, MP3 docking station, Wi-Fi (free).

Inexpensive

Sleep Inn–Downtown at Court Square ★   You can't beat the location of this smoke-free motel, which fills up quickly during weekends when there is a lot happening downtown. Wedged between nostalgic Court Square and the banks of the Mississippi River, it's also on the Main Street trolley line. At only six stories, this motel is dwarfed by surrounding buildings. The modern design and economical rates, along with wireless access throughout, ensure its appeal. Most rooms are large and comfortable, and business-class rooms come with fax machines, work desks, and dual phone lines. The motel shares a parking lot with the adjacent SpringHill Suites.

40 N. Front St., Memphis, TN 38103. www.sleepinn.com. ✆ **877/424-6423** or 901/522-9700. Fax 901/522-9710. 118 units. $95–$170 double. Rates include continental breakfast. AE, DC, DISC, MC, V. Parking $12. **Amenities:** Small exercise room. *In room:* A/C, TV, fridge, hair dryer, microwave, Wi-Fi (free).

MIDTOWN

Midtown probably isn't the best area of town to stay as a tourist, but there are some moderate to inexpensive choices here. One of the newest places is a small boutique hotel that took over a rather ugly office building near the Southern College of Optometry in the medical center area. But don't judge a hotel by its building: **Gen X Inn,** 1177 Madison (✆ **901/692-9136**), is a smoke-free Best Western property with a spare, modern look, clean rooms, free Wi-Fi throughout, and plenty of free parking. It appeals primarily to students and other budget-conscious travelers who don't mind its location, a short cab ride from downtown. Rates average around $99 per night weekdays ($115 weekends).

Other reasonably priced options include the **Holiday Inn Select Medical Center/ Midtown,** 1180 Union Ave. (© **901/276-1175**), charging as low as $89 for a double; **Union Express,** 42 S. Camilla St. (© **901/526-1050**), charging $69 for a double; and **Motel 6,** 210 S. Pauline St. (© **901/528-0650**), charging $55 for a double.

Another option to consider is the **Pilgrim House Hostel and Retreat Center,** 1000 S. Cooper (© **901/278-6787**), which offers inexpensive accommodations in the Cooper-Young neighborhood. Bunk beds in shared rooms cost $15; for an extra $15 you can have a private room and shower. Linens, sheets, and towels are provided to guests. No teenagers are allowed unless they're part of a youth group. For more information, visit www.pilgrimhouse.org.

EAST MEMPHIS

If your visit to Memphis brings you to any of the suburban business parks in the perimeter of the city, East Memphis is a smart choice. It's centrally located between downtown hot spots and outlying suburbs, where top employers such as FedEx and International Paper have their corporate headquarters. Budget-conscious travelers and families will find an array of affordably priced rooms—all with free parking, which has become all but obsolete for downtown hotels, where the expense averages about $20 per night.

Expensive

Doubletree Hotel Memphis This East Memphis Hilton-owned hotel is a bit closer to Midtown museums than other hotels in this area. Within walking distance of a couple of recommended restaurants, it's also a very short drive to Corky's Ribs & BBQ, one of the best barbecue joints in town. The eight-floor hotel is built around an atrium, and has glass elevators so you can enjoy views as you rise. Most rooms here are designed with the business traveler in mind and have two phones, radio/television speakers in the bathrooms, and large desks. Angled windows make the rooms seem a bit larger than standard hotel rooms.

5069 Sanderlin Ave., Memphis, TN 38117. www.doubletree.com. © **800/445-8667** or 901/767-6666. Fax 901/683-8563. 276 units. $179–$279 double; $219–$259 suite. AE, DC, DISC, MC, V. Free parking. **Amenities:** Restaurant; lounge; exercise room; indoor/outdoor pool; room service. *In room:* A/C, TV w/pay movies, fridge, hair dryer, Wi-Fi (free).

Hilton Memphis This gleaming, round high-rise dominates the skyline in an upscale East Memphis area that makes it convenient to the suburbs of Germantown, Cordova, and Collierville. Each room has huge, floor-to-ceiling windows looking out over the surrounding freeway intersection and beyond. In 2011 guest rooms were upgraded with 32-inch flatscreen TVs. The property's popularity as the largest East Memphis hotel is evidenced by the brisk party, conference, and wedding reception business it does. As a result, common areas and elevators can become very crowded.

939 Ridge Lake Blvd., Memphis, TN 38120. www.hilton.com. © **800/774-1500** or 901/684-6664. Fax 901/762-7496. 405 units. $179–$219 double; $350 suite. AE, DC, DISC, MC, V. Valet parking $10; free self-parking. Located off Ridgeway Center Pkwy., at I-240 and Poplar Ave., exit 15 east.

East Memphis Hotels

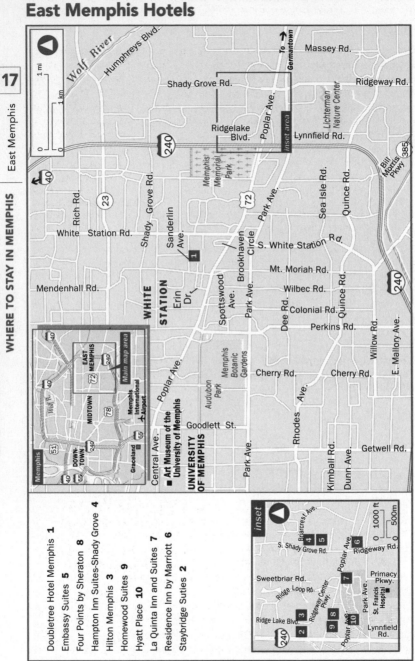

Doubletree Hotel Memphis **1**
Embassy Suites **5**
Four Points by Sheraton **8**
Hampton Inn Suites-Shady Grove **4**
Hilton Memphis **3**
Homewood Suites **9**
Hyatt Place **10**
La Quinta Inn and Suites **7**
Residence Inn by Marriott **6**
Staybridge Suties **2**

Amenities: Restaurant; lounge; free airport shuttle; health club; hot tub; outdoor pool; room service; Wi-Fi ($9.95 per day); valet service. *In room:* A/C, TV w/pay movies, hair dryer.

Moderate

Embassy Suites ★ ☺   The courtyard-style lobby is rather dark and a bit outdated, despite pretty landscaping with tropical plants. Yet the spacious surroundings and open-air ambience are clean and welcoming. All the guest rooms here are fairly large two-room suites that have kitchenettes, dining tables, two televisions, two phones, and sofa beds. Accommodations here are a safe bet for families and business travelers alike. The complete, cooked-to-order breakfast is served in the atrium, where, in the evening, there's also a complimentary manager's reception with free drinks. The moderately priced **Frank Grisanti's Italian Restaurant,** just off the atrium, serves lunch and dinner and is one of the best Italian restaurants in the city.

1022 S. Shady Grove Rd., Memphis, TN 38120. www.embassysuites.com. **℗ 800/EMBASSY** (362-2779) or 901/684-1777. Fax 901/685-8185. 220 units (all suites). $139–$219 suite. Rates include full breakfast and nightly manager's reception. AE, DC, DISC, MC, V. Free parking. **Amenities:** Restaurant; lounge; free airport transfers; exercise room; hot tub; indoor pool; room service; sauna; Wi-Fi (free, in business center); valet service. *In room:* A/C, TV w/pay movies and video games, fridge, hair dryer, Wi-Fi ($9.95 per day; free for Hilton Honors members).

Four Points by Sheraton   The lackluster former Park Place Hotel was purchased and renovated as a Sheraton property in spring of 2011. The transformation is impressive, with its colorful, contemporary design features and comfortable new furnishings. Completely smoke free, the clean, compact property has become increasingly popular with families and budget-conscious frequent travelers. Its odd location, at the intersection of a busy interstate and the Poplar Avenue business corridor, is a mixed blessing. You might expect some traffic noise, but it's convenient to shopping areas and to quickly getting to other parts of the city.

5877 Poplar Ave., Memphis, TN 38120. www.fourpoints.com/memphis. **℗ 866/716-8133** or 901/767-6300. Fax 901/767-0098. 124 units. $109–$139 double. Breakfast $10. AE, DC, DISC, MC, V. Free parking. **Amenities:** Free airport transfers; exercise room; outdoor pool. *In room:* A/C, TV w/pay movies, fridge, hair dryer, Wi-Fi (free).

 FAMILY-FRIENDLY HOTELS

Homewood Suites (p. 240)   With a pool and basketball court and grounds that resemble an upscale apartment complex, this East Memphis hotel is a good bet for families. Plus, the evening social hour includes enough food to serve as dinner (and thus save you quite a bit on your meal budget).

Hyatt Place (p. 240)   Larger-than-expected suites have comfy, sectional-style furniture and ottomans, ideal for spreading out to nap or to watch sports or play video games on the massive flatscreen TV. With spacious kitchenettes and plush beds, this affordably priced hotel offers all the comforts of home in a safe, convenient location.

Staybridge Suites (p. 240)   Large suites include bedrooms and separate sitting areas and kitchenettes. Free breakfast, a pleasant outdoor pool, and barbecue grills allow guests to make themselves at home.

Homewood Suites ☺   The Homewood Suites offers clean, casual accommodations in a less-than-ideal location (on a wedge of property surrounded by interstate traffic). The suites, which are arranged around a landscaped central courtyard with a swimming pool and basketball court, resemble an apartment complex rather than a hotel. The lobby features pine furnishings and artwork. There are two televisions in every suite, with separate rooms for bedroom and living room. Full kitchens include refrigerators, stoves, and microwaves, while the bathrooms offer plenty of counter space. There is also a complimentary social hour on weeknights that includes enough food to pass for dinner.

5811 Poplar Ave. (just off I-240), Memphis, TN 38119. www.homewood-suites.com. © **800/CALL-HOME** (225-5466) or 901/763-0500. Fax 901/763-0132. 140 units (all suites). $134–$209 suite. Rates include cooked breakfast. AE, DC, DISC, MC, V. Free parking. Dogs only accepted ($50 fee). **Amenities:** Free airport transfers; exercise room; hot tub; outdoor pool; basketball court. *In room:* A/C, TV, kitchen, Wi-Fi (free). Pets allowed ($50 fee).

Residence Inn by Marriott ★   This extended-stay property offers spacious studio, one-bedroom, and two-bedroom suites with fully furnished kitchens, including a refrigerator with ice maker, stove, toaster, and toaster oven. The smoke-free hotel also benefits from being within walking distance of several excellent restaurants. Some suites have rooms that open onto the lobby, while others have windows to the outside and tiny triangular balconies. The popular property is in demand, so book in advance. Be sure to ask for a room on the side away from the railroad tracks.

6141 Old Poplar Pike, Memphis, TN 38119. www.marriott.com. © **800/331-3131** or 901/685-9595. Fax 901/685-1636. 105 units (all suites). $134–$209 suite. Rates include continental breakfast and light dinner (Mon–Thurs 5:30–7pm). AE, DC, DISC, MC, V. Free parking. Pets accepted ($100 fee). **Amenities:** Fitness room, outdoor pool; sports court; Wi-Fi (free, in lobby). *In room:* A/C, TV w/ pay movies, hair dryer, Internet (free).

Staybridge Suites ★ ☺   With the number of moderately priced, family-oriented hotels in this clean, secure area of East Memphis increasing, competition is keen. Travelers looking to compare similar properties may be swayed by one or two amenities that are important to them. For instance, this all-suite hotel offers rates and features comparable to the nearby Four Points by Sheraton, but the Staybridge Suites also accepts pets and includes free breakfast in the room rate. Guest suites include bedrooms and sitting areas with sofa beds, work desks, and fridges. Outdoors, there are barbecue grills for guests' use, and the pool is set in a sunny, neatly landscaped area.

1070 Ridge Lake Blvd., Memphis, TN 38120. www.staybridge.com. © **877/859-5095** or 901/682-1722. Fax 901/682-5078. 114 units. $100–$120 double. Rates include buffet breakfast. AE, DC, DISC, MC, V. Pets under 80 lb. accepted ($75 fee for 1–7 days or $150 for more than 7 days). Free parking. **Amenities:** Free airport transfers; fitness room; outdoor pool; hot tub. *In room:* A/C, TV, fridge, hair dryer, Wi-Fi (free).

Hyatt Place ★★ ☺   This place is ideal for families. Larger-than-expected suites have comfy, oversized sofa sleepers and large ottomans, making them ideal for stretching out to nap or to watch sports or movies on the 42-inch, high-definition plasma TVs. With spacious kitchenettes and plush beds, this smoke-free, contemporary hotel is a great choice for travelers looking for above-average accommodations in a safe, convenient location close to restaurants and shopping.

In addition to complimentary breakfast, the home-style guest kitchen off of the main lobby offers freshly prepared appetizers, sandwiches, and pizza, as well as Starbucks coffee, beer, and wine.

1220 Primacy Pkwy., Memphis, TN 38119. www.hyattplace.com. ⓒ **901/680-9700.** Fax 901/681-0102. AE, DC, DISC, MC, V. 126 units. $103–$129 double. Rates include breakfast. Free parking. **Amenities:** Exercise room; outdoor pool. *In room:* A/C, TV, hair dryer, MP3 docking station, Wi-Fi (free).

Hampton Inn & Suites–Shady Grove ★ 🎁 Located next door to the Embassy Suites off Poplar Avenue in East Memphis, this 12-year-old property is an overlooked gem. Tucked into a tree-shaded, affluent neighborhood surrounded by great restaurants, it appeals to travelers with high expectations and stretched budgets. This is a lot of hotel for the money, with a large lobby that has the look and feel of a coffee shop and Internet cafe. There's also a cozy fireplace, oversized leather chairs, and a separate kitchen area with granite countertop island, white cabinets, and stashes of fresh fruits and beverages. Rooms are immaculate, furnished with crisp linens and "lap" desks stocked with snacks and the TV remote, as well as standard work desks and comfortable seating. Fridges and microwaves are available upon request.

962 S. Shady Grove Rd., Memphis, TN 38119. www.hamptoninn.com. ⓒ **800/HAMPTON** (426-7866) or 901/762-0056. Fax 901/962-0033. 130 units. $98–$149 double. AE, DC, DISC, MC, V. Free parking. **Amenities:** Free airport shuttle; fitness room; small outdoor pool; room service from adjacent Frank Grisanti's Restaurant. *In room:* A/C, TV w/pay movies, Wi-Fi (free).

Inexpensive

La Quinta Inn & Suites 🌂 ☺ Adjacent to the Hyatt Place is this familiar chain hotel with the Spanish-style architecture. Also an excellent choice for families, this clean, well-maintained hotel offers rates as low as $69 per night. With an array of amenities throughout the large property, you almost certainly won't find a better deal on a comparable hotel anywhere in town. Some rooms have microwaves and refrigerators, making them ideal for frugal extended stays.

1236 Primacy Pkwy., Memphis, TN 38119. www.lq.com. ⓒ **901/680-9700.** Fax 901/374-0330. 131 units. $69–$99 double. Rates include breakfast. Free parking. **Amenities:** Exercise room; outdoor pool. *In room:* A/C, TV, hair dryer, Wi-Fi (free).

THE AIRPORT & GRACELAND AREAS

Obviously, if you need to be near the airport, any of these properties will suit your needs. But truthfully, the airport area encompasses neighborhoods in which locals and tourists don't feel safe. To get a sense of what Memphis is all about, you really should try to stay in or near downtown. Besides, with the plethora of tour buses and shuttle services available, access to Graceland is as easy from downtown as it is from the airport area. Still, if you want to go it alone, be aware that there is not much besides Elvis's former home to offer tourists in this area. Along Elvis Presley Boulevard there are many cheap motels scattered among the fast-food restaurants, gas stations, cash-advance stores, and other businesses, but book these at your own risk.

Moderate

Courtyard Memphis Airport ★   This clean, well-maintained property, located a few miles from the main airport terminal, has earned a reputation as the airport area's top choice among corporate road warriors. Located in a pleasant, secure office park, the hotel offers rooms (including 10 suites) well equipped for business travelers. There are large work desks, daily newspaper delivery, and dinner delivery service from local restaurants.

1780 Nonconnah Blvd., Memphis, TN 38132. www.marriott.com. ✆ **901/396-3600.** Fax 901/332-0706. 145 units. $144–$169 double; $159 suite. AE, DC, DISC, MC, V. Free parking. **Amenities:** Exercise room; outdoor pool; whirlpool. *In room:* A/C, TV w/pay movies, hair dryer, Wi-Fi (free).

Elvis Presley's Heartbreak Hotel–Graceland ★ ⬛   If you will be visiting Graceland and want to stay overnight in the immediate area, you can't get much closer than this Graceland-operated hotel near Elvis's former home. In the lobby, you'll find two big portraits of The King and garish decor that would fit right in at the mansion. In the back courtyard, there's a smallish, heart-shaped outdoor pool. Indoors, four themed suites include the irresistibly named "*Burning Love* Suite." (Feel your temperature rising?) If you don't want to shell out big bucks for the entire suite, ask to split it and just rent a portion (or one room) of the suite. Many guests do this, I'm told.

3677 Elvis Presley Blvd., Memphis, TN 38116. www.elvis.com/epheartbreakhotel. ✆ **877/777-0606** or 901/332-1000. Fax 901/332-1636. 128 units. $138 double; $153 regular suite; $223–$378 themed suite. Rates include continental breakfast. AE, DC, DISC, MC, V. Free parking. **Amenities:** Heart-shaped outdoor pool. *In room:* A/C, TV w/24-hr. Elvis movies, fridge, hair dryer, microwave.

Marriott Thousand Oaks ★★ ✒   In the years since this once-premier property anchored the area surrounding the Mall of Memphis (now demolished), it has weathered some rough years. The surrounding area hasn't entirely rebounded, but the hotel's location on the outskirts of the airport area—and its proximity to both Midtown and East Memphis—are keeping it viable. Today, the hotel looks polished and well maintained, and customer service is notably poised and professional. With its large, open lobby, marble floors, and well-appointed sitting areas, this Marriott has the look and feel of an expensive hotel. Yet with rates as low as $119 a night, it's an excellent value for price-conscious travelers who want to feel pampered. Rooms are of average size but are fresh and comfortably furnished.

2625 Thousand Oaks Blvd., Memphis, TN 38118. www.marriott.com/MEMTN. ✆ **800/627-3587** or 901/362-6200. Fax 901/362-7221. 315 units, 4 suites. $119–$139 double; $250 suite. AE, DC, DISC, MC, V. Free parking. **Amenities:** Restaurant/lounge; free airport transfers; exercise room; hot tub; indoor and outdoor pools; room service; valet service. *In room:* A/C, TV, hair dryer, Wi-Fi ($13).

Regency Inn & Suites Memphis Airport   If you're in town for an airport-area business meeting or you plan to arrive in Memphis very late at night, this hotel right on the grounds of the airport fits the bill. The rooms themselves are rather dark and not very memorable, but many are set up for business travelers with a desk and comfortable chair. The outdoor pool is set in a pleasant (though sometimes noisy) sunken garden area between two wings of the hotel, which is smoke free throughout.

2411 Winchester Rd., Memphis, TN 38116. www.regencymemphis.com. ✆ **901/332-2370.** Fax 901/398-4085. 211 units. $119 double; suites are being renovated. AE, DC, DISC, MC, V. Free parking. **Amenities:** Restaurant/lounge; free airport shuttle; exercise room; outdoor pool (seasonal); room service; 2 tennis courts. *In room:* A/C, TV, hair dryer, Wi-Fi (free).

Elvis Slept Here

You might not mistake this former housing project for an upscale hotel, but, then again, this is Memphis—where offbeat surprises seem to lurk around every corner.

Elvis Presley lived here at Lauderdale Courts with his parents, Vernon and Gladys, when he was still a wide-eyed teenager (1949–53). Spared from demolition, in recent years the site has been transformed into **Uptown Square,** 252 N. Lauderdale, a trendy apartment complex that has preserved its sole historic unit as **"The Elvis Suite."**

For $250 a night, tourists may rent this first-floor apartment, which includes a 1950s-style kitchen and sleeping room for four people. Before you book, be aware that this is a smoke-free property without wheelchair access, and that there's a 2-night minimum and 6-night maximum stay. Blackout dates apply during Elvis week (Aug) and other tourist-heavy times, when the property is in demand for guided tours but not for overnight lodging. For reservations, call ⓒ **901/523-8662** (www.lauderdale courts.com). If you don't want to spend the night, you can still take a peek. Tours are offered from 9am to 3pm weekdays for a $10 fee

Inexpensive

Days Inn at Graceland With Graceland right across the street, it's no surprise that Elvis is king at this budget motel. Just look for the Elvis mural on the side of the building and the neon guitar sign out front, and you'll have found this unusual Days Inn. In the lobby, and on the room TVs, are round-the-clock Elvis videos. Service here is usually very friendly, too.

3839 Elvis Presley Blvd., Memphis, TN 38116. www.daysinn.com. ⓒ **800/329-7466** or 901/346-5500. Fax 901/345-7452. 61 units. $79–$89 double. Rates include continental breakfast. AE, DC, DISC, MC, V. Free parking. **Amenities:** Guitar-shaped outdoor pool. *In room:* A/C, TV, Wi-Fi (free).

SIDE TRIPS FROM MEMPHIS

18

The Mississippi Delta begins in Memphis, Tennessee, and extends southward along the Mississippi River, all the way to New Orleans, Louisiana. From downtown Memphis, it's just a few miles to the Mississippi state line. A 75-mile road trip down historic Hwy. 61 will take you into the land of the Delta blues. This is the mother lode for blues lovers, who come here from all over the world to trace the steps of local legends like Robert Johnson, Muddy Waters, and B.B. King. Another accessible Mississippi day trip from Memphis is the picturesque college town of Oxford, home of literary legend William Faulkner, and one of the best used bookstores in the country.

CLARKSDALE, MISSISSIPPI

An unmistakable vibe pervades the languid Mississippi Delta town of Clarksdale, about an hour's drive south of Memphis, Tennessee. It's by turns eerie and endearing, a flat landscape where fertile fields, endless railroad tracks, and run-down shacks are giving way to pockets of progress and commercialization—an upscale restaurant, a few strip malls with discount stores and fast-food chains, and a must-see museum celebrating the blues music that took root here in the early 20th century.

Clarksdale also happens to be Tennessee Williams country. The cherished American playwright, author of such masterworks as *A Streetcar Named Desire* and *The Glass Menagerie,* grew up here. Young Tom, who later adopted the name "Tennessee," lived in the parsonage of St. George's Episcopal Church, where his grandfather was pastor.

If you don't plan to return to Memphis the same day and you're up for an extended road trip, Clarksdale is a good place to begin a driving tour of legendary **Hwy. 61 (U.S. 61),** the two-lane road that took blues legends such as Muddy Waters, Robert Johnson, and B.B. King from the impoverished cotton plantations of the South to the cities of Memphis and Chicago in the North. For today's tourists, the long drive south from Memphis takes you through the proverbial dusty Delta towns and cities such as Greenville, Vicksburg, and Natchez, where Mississippi meets Louisiana.

Essentials

GETTING THERE **By Car** The major route into Clarksdale is **Hwy. 61** from Memphis to the north.

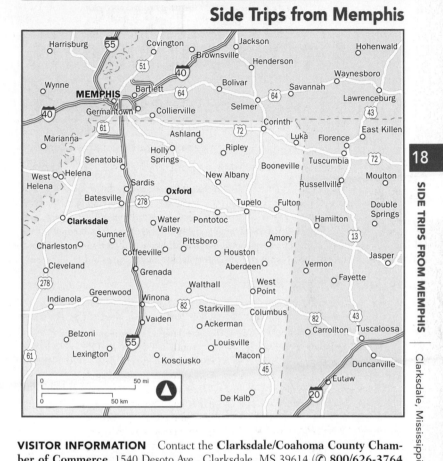

Harrisburg 55 Covington Jackson Hohenwald
Brownsville
51 Henderson
40 Waynesboro
Wynne Bartlett Bolivar Savannah
MEMPHIS 64 64 Lawrenceburg
Germantown Collierville Selmer
40 43
61 Corinth
Marianna Ashland 72 Luka Florence East Killen
Holly Ripley Tuscumbia 72
Senatobia Springs Booneville
West Helena New Albany Russellville Moulton
Helena Sardis
Batesville 278 Oxford Fulton Double
Clarksdale Water Tupelo Hamilton Springs
Sumner Valley Pontotoc 13
Charleston Coffeeville Pittsboro Amory Jasper
Cleveland Houston Vermon
278 Grenada Aberdeen Fayette
Indianola Greenwood Walthall West
Winona Point
Vaiden 82 Starkville Columbus
Belzoni Ackerman 82 43
55 Carrollton Tuscaloosa
61 Lexington Louisville Duncanville
Kosciusko Macon
45 Eutaw
De Kalb 20

0   50 mi
0   50 km

VISITOR INFORMATION   Contact the **Clarksdale/Coahoma County Chamber of Commerce,** 1540 Desoto Ave., Clarksdale, MS 39614 (© **800/626-3764** or 662/627-7337; www.visitclarksdale.com).

What to See & Do

As you ease into town, your first stop should be at the **Crossroads,** at the intersection of Hwy. 49 and Hwy. 61. Though there's little to see here, the site is steeped in superstition and folklore as the place where bluesman Robert Johnson (1911–38) is said to have sold his soul to the devil in exchange for the guitar prowess that has made him one of the most revered musicians of the past century. Marking the spot is a weird, faded guitar statue, one of the most photographed landmarks in this region.

From here, your next stop should be the **Delta Blues Museum,** 1 Blues Alley (© **662/627-6820;** www.deltabluesmuseum.org). Housed in a renovated train depot built in 1918, it includes a treasure-trove of old blues memorabilia, including the actual log cabin where Muddy Waters grew up, on a cotton plantation not far from here. There are displays, musical instruments, and costumes of some of the Mississippi-born greats, such as Albert King, James Cotton, and Son House. Admission is $7 adults, $5 children 6 to 12; it is open Monday through Saturday.

Beyond the museum, it's easy to navigate your way around town for an overview of everything you might want to see. Bessie Smith fans can do a drive-by tour of the **Riverside Hotel,** 615 Sunflower Ave. (© 662/624-9163), the former blacks-only hospital where the great blues singer died after a car crash in 1937. Blues legends Sonny Boy Williamson II, Ike Turner, Robert Nighthawk, and even politician Robert F. Kennedy once stayed here. Today it still operates as a motel, but most visitors see it only through their windshields.

Mississippi *Help*

The Help, the 2011 hit movie about black maids serving white housewives in the 1960s segregated South, was filmed in Jackson, Mississippi, as well as in Clarksdale and Greenwood.

While downtown, don't miss **Cathead Delta Blues & Folk Art,** 252 Delta Ave. (© 662/624-5992; www.cathead.biz). The store sells new blues CDs, DVDs, and books, as well as eye-catching—and affordable—folk and outsider art. The hepcat-cool hot spot also serves as a clearinghouse for what's going on around town. Check Cathead's chalkboard that tells of weekly music events and updates. The store also occasionally has book signings and special events. You'll likely find the owner chatting up European tourists who've made the sojourn here for some serious blues sightseeing.

Where to Stay & Eat

Clarksville's overnight lodging options are limited and offbeat. In addition to the circa-1935 Hopson Plantation (see **Shack Up Inn** (p. 247), there's **The Riverside Inn,** since 1944 a no-frills, blues-travelers' roadhouse with simple rooms and shared baths. Famous guests have included Sonny Boy Williamson, Ike Turner, and JFK Jr., but it's best known as the former hospital where blues singer Bessie Smith died after a car accident in 1937.

Happily, you won't go hungry in Clarksdale. Locals love **Abe's Bar-B-Que,** 616 State St. (© 662/624-9947), for generously portioned pork sandwiches and ribs. Same can be said of **Hick's Tamales & BBQ Shop,** 305 S. State St. (© 662/624-9887), which also draws foodies on pilgrimages for the deliciously grease-glistened, spicy beef tamales slow-cooked in corn husks.

Morgan Freeman, who grew up in the area and is still seen around town from time to time, is a partner in **Ground Zero Blues Club,** 364 Delta Ave., a former cotton warehouse that's been fashioned into an old-timey juke joint with nightly live music. More authentic for blues purists, but somewhat less reliable for tourists on tight schedules, is **Red's,** 395 Sunflower Ave. (no phone), a foreboding-looking hole in the wall where live music gets underway late, often extending until sunrise.

OXFORD, MISSISSIPPI

Home to the University of Mississippi, "Ole Miss," Oxford is a quaint small town where daily life revolves around its 150-year-old Court Square. A popular weekend destination for out-of-towners and visiting alumni, Oxford offers an enticing array of great art galleries, bookstores, restaurants, and historic homes. Although its proximity

In the lodging category of too creepy for anyone but the most die-hard blues fan, there's the one-of-a-kind **Shack Up Inn,** 001 Commissary Circle (© **662/ 624-8329;** www.shackupinn.com), on old Hwy. 49 south of Clarksdale. Billed as Mississippi's oldest B&B (and that stands for Bed and Beer), the property sits amid a weedy rural cotton gin littered with rusting antique farming implements, old road signs, and crumbling sharecropper shacks that have been modernized enough to accommodate easy-to-please travelers in search of a good time and a place to crash. In recent years, the plantation's former gin house has been converted into private rooms, or "gin bins." Rates, which range from $65 to $95 per room, include a Moon Pie on your pillow. If you're thinking about booking a shack or bin when there's a blues music festival or another big event going on in the Clarksdale area, advance reservations are essential. Far from being a place of last resort, this genuinely offbeat joint has become so popular it's often booked solid.

18

SIDE TRIPS FROM MEMPHIS | Oxford, Mississippi

to Memphis makes it a doable day trip, Oxford's offbeat charms might entice you to stay a day or two.

Essentials

GETTING THERE   By Car   The major route into Oxford is **I-55** from both the north (Memphis) and south (Jackson). It's about a 90-minute drive.

VISITOR INFORMATION   Contact the **Oxford Convention & Visitors Bureau,** 107 Courthouse Sq., Ste. 1, Oxford, MS 38655 (© **800/758-9177** or 662/234-4680; www.touroxfordms.com).

Exploring the Area

Oxford's favorite son is Nobel Prize–winning author William Faulkner, whose residence from 1930 until his death in 1963 was his beloved home, **Rowan Oak,** Old Taylor Road (© **662/234-3284**). A tour of the grounds, with its graceful magnolias and old farm buildings, is a trip back in time. Inside, literary enthusiasts can still marvel at the author's old manual typewriter, and read his handwritten outline for *A Fable,* which is scrawled on the wall of his study. It's closed Mondays and major holidays. Admission is free on Wednesdays but costs $5 other days.

The most popular pastime in Oxford is simply strolling **The Square,** where travelers might spot former local residents such as bestselling author John Grisham, returning to town for his latest book-signing event. **Square Books,** 160 Courthouse Sq. (© **662/236-2262;** www.squarebooks.com), in business since 1870, is regarded as one of the best independent bookstores in the country. Down the street is its bargain-priced annex, **Off Square Books,** 129 Courthouse Sq. (© **662/236-2828**). Thousands of discounted and remaindered books cram shelves and bins. It's also the site of Square Books' author signings and readings, as well as *Thacker Mountain Radio,* Oxford's original music and literature radio show. Bestselling authors such as Robert Olen Butler, Elmore Leonard, and Ray Blount, Jr., have read their works on the live show. Musical guests have run the gamut from Elvis Costello and Marty Stuart to the

Del McCoury band and the North Mississippi Allstars. The show is recorded live on Thursdays from 6 to 7pm.

Next door, **Southside Gallery,** 150 Courthouse Sq. (© **662/234-9090**), is an always-interesting place that showcases everything from photography, painting, and sculpture to outsider art by the likes of Howard Finster.

WHERE TO STAY & EAT

Because of its proximity to Memphis, Oxford is a popular day-trip destination for many travelers. Perhaps as a result, there are only a handful of hotels and motels, most of them chains on the outskirts of town that cater to the parents of college kids and other travelers to the university.

Among the cleanest and most reliable choices are the **Holiday Inn Express Hotel & Suites,** 112 Heritage Rd. (© **662/236-2500**; $85), and the adjacent **Hampton Inn & Suites,** 110 Heritage Rd. (© **662/232-2442**; $159).

Call ahead and book early if you want to reserve a room at one of the city's bed-and-breakfast properties, which are often booked during weekends when Ole Miss has home football games or other major events. You won't see it advertised much because the place is always full, but try to book a stay at **Puddin' Place,** 1008 University Ave. (© **662/816-5292**), a spotless, cheerfully decorated 1892 house that has two large suites with private bathrooms. Gourmet breakfasts are included in the room rates, which usually run $145 for a double (during Ole Miss football season it's $350 for the 2-night minimum weekend stay, and it sells out these weekends months in advance).

Another option is the newly renovated **5 Twelve,** 512 Van Buren Ave. (© **662/234-8043**). The white-columned, red-brick structure has a welcoming front porch packed with potted plants and flowers. There are six modern, comfortable guest rooms, all with private bathroom. Rates run $105 to $175 for a double; continental breakfast is available weekdays, and a full breakfast is served on weekends.

Oxford is a fabulous restaurant town, thanks in large part to one well-known chef. John Currence, a contestant on Bravo TV's *Top Chef Masters* 3 in 2011 (he was the tall guy with the bandana around his head for much of the season), was well known even before that gig. For years he has helmed **City Grocery,** 152 Courthouse Sq. (© **662/232-8080**; www.bigbadbreakfast.com), one of the best restaurants in Mississippi. New Orleans–born Currence finesses Southern dishes such as spicy cheese grits topped with plump shrimp, mushrooms, and smoked bacon. City Grocery churns out tempting gourmet salads, soups, and Cajun delicacies. Sandwiches, salads, soups, and entrees range from $11 to $15 at lunch. Dinner entrees run $25 to $29. Reservations are recommended.

Currence has branched out with several other eateries: **Boure,** 309 N. Lamar (© **662/234-1968**), serving casual Creole fare; **Big Bad Breakfast,** 719 N. Lamar (© **662/236-2666**), specializing in biscuits, gravy, cured meats, and steel-cut oatmeal dishes; and **Snackbar,** 721 N. Lamar (© **662/232-2442**), an oysters-and-whiskey kind of place he dubbed a "Bubba Brasserie."

Bottletree Bakery, 923 Van Buren Ave. (© **662/236-5000**), is a must if you crave caffeine and the aroma of warm muffins being pulled from the oven. The cheery nook serves pastries and freshly baked breads, as well as fine coffees, sandwiches, and salads.

Oxford's favorite dive bar is **Proud Larry's,** 211 S. Lamar Blvd. (© **662/236-0050**), where live music and drink specials augment a simple menu of burgers, pasta, salads, and hand-tossed pizzas.

SOUTHERN FOODWAYS ALLIANCE: IT'S gravy

Even if you're not a foodie, you've got to love an organization whose newsletter is called *Gravy*. That's the fun and informative missive of the **Southern Foodways Alliance** (SFA), an institute of the Center for the Study of Southern Culture at the University of Mississippi.

Led by noted food writer and author John T. Edge (*Southern Food: At Home, on the Road, in History; Cornbread Nation: The Best of Southern Food Writing;* and *Southern Belly: The Ultimate Food Lover's Companion to the South*), the nonprofit SFA is based at the Ole Miss campus in Oxford. However, its reach extends across several states, from Louisiana and Alabama to the Carolina Low Country and the Appalachians. With about 800 members, the SFA celebrates and documents Southern cooking traditions through its publications, oral history projects, and events such as the Potlikker Film Festival.

An annual symposium includes an array of lectures, discussions, and social outings focused on such topics as turnip greens, vine-ripened tomatoes, hoe-cakes, corn bread, and fried chicken. Chefs, farmers, barbecue champs, academics, and people who simply love to eat and to learn about food are participants in this eclectic group.

The SFA also bestows lifetime achievement awards to people who uphold high culinary and cultural standards. The awards are named for Craig Claiborne, *New York Times* food editor, who was raised in the small Mississippi Delta town of Sunflower, not far from Oxford.

To get helpful travel advice on where to go and what to eat, go online to download the SFA's "Mississippi Delta Hot Tamale Trail," "Southern BBQ Trail," "Southern Boudin Trail," and "Southern Gumbo Trail." You can also sign up for field trips and special events, by contacting the SFA (© **662/915-5993;** www. southernfoodways.org).

INDIANOLA, MISSISSIPPI

If you can, devote an entire day to this getaway that's essential for blues aficionados. Opened in 2008, the **B.B. King Museum and Delta Interpretive Center,** 400 Second St., Indianola, MS (© **662/887-9539;** www.bbkingmuseum.org), is a world-class tourist attraction tucked along a flat stretch of rural Hwy. 82 between Greenwood and Greenville. Getting to tiny Indianola takes a while. It's about a 2½-hour drive south of Memphis, and just out of the way enough to make it impractical to do in combination with any other serious sightseeing in Clarksdale or Oxford. Trust me, and make a day of it. If you're a music lover and a fan of B.B. King, the interactive, multimedia exhibits will lure you into a blissful state of total immersion.

Riley B. King was born in 1925, on a plantation in nearby Itta Bena. A poor share-cropper and tractor driver, King's rags-to-riches story is given context through photo murals, film clips, and news archives tracing segregation in the Delta in the '30s, through the Civil Rights struggles of the '60s.

Along the way, there are in-depth explorations of musical styles and influences on B.B. King. Stop and listen to full-length songs by all the greats, from Muddy Waters and Albert King to little-known jug bands and country-church gospel choirs. Most of all, take the time to stop and experience B.B.'s music, from career-making hits like "The Thrill Is Gone" to gratifying collaborations with Eric Clapton and countless

THE blind side: A MEMPHIS MOVIE

Despite being filmed in Georgia rather than in Tennessee, the blockbuster 2009 movie *The Blind Side,* starring Sandra Bullock (who won an Academy Award and a Golden Globe for Best Actress) and Nashville country singer Tim McGraw, is based on a heartwarming, real-life story from Memphis. Movie fans, of course, know the plot: Sean and Leigh Anne Tuohy, a well-to-do suburban white couple, adopted Michael Oher, a 300-pound, homeless, black teenager from the projects.

Against all odds, Oher became a football star at Memphis's elite Briarcrest Christian School, before going on to play at Ole Miss (the University of Mississippi).

In 2009, he was a first-round draft pick of the NFL's Baltimore Ravens, signing a contract worth more than $13 million. He started every game of his rookie season on the Ravens' offensive line.

The Blind Side stars Academy Award–winning actress (and former Memphis resident) Kathy Bates as Oher's tutor, Miss Sue. The movie was produced by FedEx founder Fred Smith's Alcon Entertainment company, with daughter Molly Smith as an executive producer. Their company also produced the 2010 Denzel Washington hit, *The Book of Eli.* For more about the Smiths and the films they have worked on, see the "Movie Mogul" box, in chapter 12.

others. In short, the museum offers a staggering array of musical listening experiences, so pace yourself.

Self-guided museum tours begin and end with a well-made, high-definition movie theater experience that gives you a front-row seat to the octogenarian's recent concert performances. The documentary takes viewers behind the scenes with B.B. on his tricked-out tour bus, as he and his band members travel from city to city, always greeted by adoring fans. The museum is open year-round, and is closed on Mondays November through March. Admission is a bargain at $10 for adults, $5 for seniors and students, and free to children 5 and under.

PLANNING YOUR TRIP TO NASHVILLE & MEMPHIS

Nashville and Memphis have many things in common. But boiled down to basics, both are large, modern cities that retain the flavor and hospitality of the American South— and both are bona fide, world-renowned tourist destinations for fans of American music, including the blues, folk, rock, soul, and, of course, country and bluegrass. So it makes sense that if you're traveling a significant distance to get here, you might as well do both destinations in a single trip.

Nashville and Memphis are within a half-day's drive of each other, making it feasible to stay a few nights in one city before heading down the highway to the other. You'll have to drive, or book an escorted tour that covers both locales. A good place to start planning is the **Tennessee Department of Tourism Development,** P.O. Box 23170, Nashville, TN 37202 (© **800/452-5395** or 615/741-2158). For more information and suggested itineraries, visit their website at www.tnvacations.com. However, it's not necessary to do both cities. Both are equally accessible to travelers throughout the U.S. and around the world.

Before heading to Music City, you can get more information by contacting the **Nashville Convention & Visitors Bureau,** 150 Fourth Ave. N. (© **800/657-6910** or 615/259-4700). Ask about booking money-saving travel packages that include hotel accommodations, discounts to popular attractions, and tickets to the hottest events in town.

You can also find information about Nashville at the following websites:

- Nashville Convention & Visitors Bureau: **www.visitmusiccity.com**
- *Nashville Scene,* Nashville's main arts and entertainment weekly: **www. nashvillescene.com**
- *The Tennessean,* Nashville's morning daily newspaper: **www. tennessean.com**

For information on Memphis, contact the **Memphis Convention & Visitors Bureau,** 47 Union Ave., Memphis, TN 38103 (📞 **800/8-MEMPHIS** [863-6744] or 901/543-5300). You can also get information online at **www.memphistravel.com** and the following websites:

○ The *Memphis Flyer* is Memphis's main arts and entertainment weekly: **www.memphisflyer.com**

○ *The Commercial Appeal* is Memphis's morning daily newspaper: **www.commercialappeal.com**

For additional help in planning your trip and for more on-the-ground resources, please turn to "Fast Facts: Nashville & Memphis," on p. 260.

GETTING THERE
Getting to Nashville & Memphis
BY PLANE

Nashville (airport code: BNA) is served by the following major airlines: **Air Canada** (📞 888/247-2262); **American Airlines** (📞 800/433-7300); **Continental Express** (📞 800/525-0280); **Delta** (📞 800/221-1212); **Frontier Airlines** (📞 800/432-1359); **Southwest** (📞 800/435-9792); **United Airlines** (📞 800/241-6522); and **US Airways** (📞 800/428-4322).

Southwest is the city's largest carrier, with some 87 daily flights out of the city. Most Southwest flights will depart and arrive from the airport's Concourse C. Southwest Airlines also offers air/hotel packages. For details, visit **Southwest Airlines Vacations** online at **www.swavacations.com**, or call 📞 **800/423-5683.**

Memphis is served by the following airlines: **American Airlines** (📞 800/433-7300); **Delta** (📞 800/221-1212); **KLM** (📞 800/374-7747); **Northwest** (📞 800/225-2525); **Southwest** (📞 800/435-9792); **United Airlines** (📞 800/241-6522); and **US Airways** (📞 800/428-4322).

Some large airlines offer transatlantic or transpacific passengers special discount tickets under the name **Visit USA,** which allows mostly one-way travel from one U.S. destination to another at very low prices. Unavailable in the U.S., these discount tickets must be purchased abroad in conjunction with your international fare. This system is the easiest, fastest, cheapest way to see the country.

Getting into Nashville from the Airport

Nashville International Airport (📞 615/275-1600) is located about 8 miles east of downtown Nashville and is just south of I-40. It takes about 15 minutes to reach downtown Nashville from the airport. See below for information on car-rental facilities at the airport. Many hotels near the airport offer a complimentary shuttle service, while others slightly farther away have their own fee shuttles; check with your hotel when you make your reservation.

The **Super Shuttle International** (📞 800/258-3826 or 615/361-6034) offers transportation from the airport to Nashville and surrounding areas. Departures leave the airport every 15 minutes, and they leave downtown and West End hotels for the airport every 30 minutes. The **Gray Line Airport Express** (📞 615/275-1180) operates shuttles between the airport and downtown and West End hotels. These shuttles leave from the airport every 15 to 30 minutes daily between 6:15am and 11pm; in addition to the hotels listed below, a few other hotels are on call. The downtown shuttle stops at the following hotels: Hilton, Union Station, Courtyard by

Marriott (Fourth and Church), Holiday Inn Express, Renaissance Nashville Hotel, Nashville Sheraton, The Hermitage, and Doubletree Hotel Nashville. The West End shuttle stops at the following hotels: Loews Vanderbilt Plaza Hotel, Embassy Suites–West End, Holiday Inn Select, Courtyard by Marriott, Marriott-Vanderbilt, Guest House Inn, Hampton Inn–Vanderbilt, Hampton Inn and Suites–Elliston Place, and Days Inn–Vanderbilt. Rates are $16 one-way and $25 round-trip.

Metropolitan Transit Authority **buses** connect the airport and downtown Nashville. Buses run 7 days a week. One-way fares are $2. All-day, unlimited-ride passes are $4.80. Buses from the airport leave at the ground-level curbside. Buses to the airport leave from the new Music City Central downtown transit station, at 400 Charlotte Ave. It's located between Fourth Avenue North and Fifth Avenue North. For current schedule information, call © **615/862-5950** Monday to Friday 6:30am to 6pm and Saturday 8am to 1pm.

Taxi service is another option. There is a $25 flat fare in the triangle between the airport, downtown, and Gaylord Opryland Resort and Convention Center. Between any two points, the fare is $25 for up to four people. Outside this geographical triangle, the meter starts at $7. Taxis are available on the ground level of the airport terminal. For information, call the Transportation Licensing Commission (TLC) at © **615/862-6777.**

Getting into Memphis from the Airport

The **Memphis International Airport** (© **901/922-8000**) is located approximately 11 miles south of downtown Memphis, off I-240. From the airport to East Memphis, it's about 9 miles. The route into either downtown or East Memphis is on I-240 all the way. Generally, allow about 20 minutes for the trip between the airport and downtown, and 15 minutes between the airport and East Memphis—up to an hour more during rush hour. See below for information on car-rental facilities at the airport.

Although there is no direct bus service from the airport to downtown Memphis, it is possible (though impractical), with a change of bus en route, to get downtown on **Memphis Area Transit Authority (MATA)** buses (© **901/274-6282**). These buses, however, do not run very often and are not very convenient for visitors. The buses run every 1 to 2 hours until about 5:30pm Monday through Saturday, and until 5:15pm on Sunday, and the fare is $1.75. From the lower level at the airport, take no. 32, the East Parkway/Hollywood bus, and transfer to no. 10, the Lamar bus (which runs about every hour Mon–Fri, fewer times on Sat), or the no. 56, the Union/Kimball bus (running about every half-hour Mon–Fri), which will take you downtown. If you want to take the bus, the best bet is to call MATA or ask a bus driver for the latest schedule information.

A taxi from the airport to downtown Memphis will cost about $35; to East Memphis it will cost about $30. There are usually plenty of taxis around, but if you can't find one, call **Yellow/Checker Cab** (© **901/577-7777**) or **City Wide Cab Company** (© **901/324-4202**). The first mile is $3.80; after that, it's $1.90 per mile. Each additional passenger is $1 extra.

BY CAR

Nashville is a hub city intersected by three interstate highways. **I-65** runs north to Louisville, Kentucky, and south to Birmingham, Alabama. **I-40** runs west to Memphis and east to Knoxville, Tennessee. **I-24** runs northwest toward St. Louis and southeast toward Atlanta. Downtown Nashville is the center of the hub, encircled by interstates 40, 65, and 265. Briley Parkway on the east, north, and west and I-440 on the south form a larger "wheel" around this hub.

Here are some driving distances from selected cities: Atlanta, 250 miles; Chicago, 442 miles; Cincinnati, 291 miles; Memphis, 210 miles; New Orleans, 549 miles; and St. Louis, 327 miles.

If you're heading into downtown Nashville, follow the signs for I-65/24 and take either exit 84 or exit 85. If you're headed to Music Valley (Opryland Resort), take I-40 east to the Briley Parkway exit and head north. If your destination is the West End/Music Row area, take I-40 around the south side of downtown and get off at the Broadway exit.

To limit frustration, try to avoid hitting the interstates around either city at morning or afternoon rush hour. Traffic tie-ups and lengthy delays are becoming increasingly common, especially in Nashville. Ongoing freeway construction and renovation projects further congest the roadways. To find out about lane closures and other headaches, call the **Tennessee Department of Transportation**'s construction hot line at ✆ **800/858-6349.** Snow and ice storms may also make road conditions hazardous. For updates, call the state's inclement weather/road closure hot line (✆ **800/342-3258;** www.tdot.state.tn.us/tdotsmartway).

Memphis lies at the southwestern tip of Tennessee, bordering Mississippi and Arkansas. Interstate 40 connects Memphis with Nashville to the east and Little Rock, Arkansas, to the west. Interstate 55 connects Memphis with Mississippi to the south, and St. Louis to the north. Both interstates intersect with I-240, which loops around the city's north, east, and southern suburbs. The western edge of downtown Memphis is the Mississippi River.

For Memphis, here are some driving distances from other cities: Atlanta, 390 miles; Chicago, 534 miles; Little Rock, 135 miles; New Orleans, 395 miles; St. Louis, 284 miles.

If you are a member of the **American Automobile Association (AAA)** and your car breaks down, call ✆ **800/222-4357** for 24-hour emergency road service. The **local AAA office** in Nashville is at 2501 21st Ave. S., Ste. 1 (✆ **615/297-7700**), and is open Monday to Friday 8:30am to 5:30pm and Saturday 9am to 1pm.

There is no plane service between Nashville and Memphis. You will have to rent a car and drive the 3-hour distance between the two cities. Interstate 40, also known as "The Music Highway," has several interesting diversions along the way (see "Side Trips from Memphis," p. 244, and "Side Trips from Nashville," p. 130).

The speed limit is 70 mph for much of the stretch between Nashville and Memphis, which also offers access to clean rest stops and dozens of service stations and restaurants. For travel information at any time, dial ✆ **511** on your cellphone.

If you're visiting from abroad and plan to rent a car in the United States, keep in mind that foreign driver's licenses are usually recognized in the U.S., but you should get an international one if your home license is not in English.

Check out **Breezenet.com,** which offers domestic car-rental discounts with some of the most competitive rates around.

International visitors should note that insurance and taxes are almost never included in quoted rental-car rates in the U.S. Be sure to ask your rental agency about additional fees for these. They can add a significant cost to your car rental.

BY BUS

Greyhound (✆ **800/231-2222;** www.greyhound.com) is the sole nationwide bus line. International visitors can obtain information about the **Greyhound North**

American Discovery Pass. The pass, which offers unlimited travel and stopovers in the U.S. and Canada, can be obtained from foreign travel agents or through www. discoverypass.com.

Greyhound offers service to **Nashville** from around the country. These buses operate along interstate corridors or local routes. The Greyhound bus station is on the south side of downtown Nashville at 200 Eighth Ave. S.

The Greyhound bus station in **Memphis** is in downtown Memphis, at 203 Union Ave.

BY TRAIN

Amtrak (© 800/872-7245; www.amtrak.com) serves Memphis (but not Nashville) with a route that goes from Chicago through Memphis (about 11 hr. travel time) en route to New Orleans (about 8 hr.) on the *City of New Orleans.* If you arrive in Memphis on an Amtrak train, you'll find yourself at **Central Station,** 545 S. Main St. (© 901/526-0052), near Calhoun Street. This historic railway station has been completely renovated into a combination transportation center with public bus and Main Street Trolley connections and retail complex. However, the neighborhood around the station remains quite run-down. *Warning:* The area can be unsafe on foot, especially after dark. If arriving by train, you should take a cab or the Main Street Trolley to your hotel.

> ### Tuneful Tidbit
>
> *There is no richer, more illuminating showcase of musical roots in the country than in this 220-mile stretch of highway.*
> —Esteemed rock music critic Robert Hilburn of the *Los Angeles Times,* describing the 3-hour drive between Nashville and Memphis along I-40.

International visitors planning to visit several U.S. cities can buy a **USA Rail Pass,** good for 5, 15, or 30 days of unlimited travel on **Amtrak** (© 800/USA-RAIL [872-7245]; www.amtrak.com). The pass is available online or through many overseas travel agents. See Amtrak's website for the cost of travel within the western, eastern, or northwestern United States. Reservations are generally required and should be made as early as possible. Regional rail passes are also available.

GETTING AROUND

Getting Around Nashville

BY CAR

As mentioned earlier, driving between Nashville and Memphis is the only practical way to see both cities. Interstate 40 connects the two.

Because Nashville and its many attractions are quite spread out, the best way to get around is by car. It's surprisingly easy to find your way around the city and to find parking, even downtown. But bring plenty of cash. Parking can cost a few coins in the meter or upwards of $20 during special events. Some self-service lots also accept credit cards. The only time driving is a problem is during morning and evening rush hours. At these times, streets leading south and west out of downtown can get quite congested.

RENTAL CARS All the major rental-car companies and several independent ones have offices in Nashville. Fortunately, most of the companies have desks conveniently located on the lower level at the Nashville International Airport. Major car-rental companies in Nashville include **Alamo Rent A Car,** at the airport (© 800/327-9633 or 615/340-6546; www.alamo.com); **Avis Rent A Car,** at the airport (© 800/831-2847 or 615/361-1212; www.avis.com); **Budget Rent A Car,** at 1816 Church St., 1525 N. Gallatin Pike, and the airport (© 800/763-2999 or 615/366-0822; www.budget.com); **Dollar Rent A Car,** at the airport (© 800/800-4000 or 615/367-0503; www.dollar.com); **Enterprise Rent-A-Car,** at the airport (© 800/325-8007 or 615/275-0011; www.enterprise.com); **Hertz,** at the airport (© 800/654-3131 or 615/361-3131; www.hertz.com); **National Car Rental,** at the airport (© 800/227-7368 or 615/361-7467; www.nationalcar.com); and **Thrifty Car Rental,** 1201 Briley Pkwy., at Vultee Boulevard, and at the airport (© 800/367-2277 or 615/361-6050; www.thrifty.com).

PARKING   In downtown Nashville, there are a variety of parking lots, ranging from $6 to more than $20 per day. Drop your money into the self-service machine at the end of the parking lot. Downtown parking is also available in other municipal and private lots and parking garages.

When parking on the street, be sure to check the time limit on parking meters. Also be sure to check whether you can park in a parking space during rush hour (4–5:30pm), or your car may be ticketed and towed. On-street parking meters are free after 6pm on weekdays, after noon on Saturday, and all day Sunday. For more downtown-parking information, check out the new website **www.parkitdowntown.com**.

DRIVING RULES   A right turn at a red light is permitted after coming to a full stop, unless posted otherwise, but drivers must first yield to vehicles that have a green light or pedestrians in the walkway. Children under 4 years of age must be in children's car seats or other approved restraints when in the car.

Tennessee has a very strict DUI (driving under the influence of alcohol) law, and has a law that states a person driving under the influence with a child under 12 years of age in the vehicle may be charged with a felony.

BY BUS

Although Nashville is served by the extensive and efficient **Metropolitan Transit Authority (MTA)** bus system, it is generally not practical for tourists to get around this way. Except for the downtown circuits, the citywide bus system is neither promoted to tourists nor heavily used by them. It's possible, of course, to take the bus, but the city is so spread out that a car or cab is the best way to get around. For more information on the MTA, call the Customer Service Center (© **615/862-5950**), which is open Monday to Friday 6:30am until 6pm. The MTA information center and ticket booth, located at 400 Charlotte Ave., is open Monday to Friday 6:30am to 6:30pm and on Saturday 8am to 1pm. MTA bus stops are marked with blue-and-white signs; in the downtown area, signs include names and numbers of all the routes using that stop. All express buses are marked with an X following the route number.

Adult **bus fares** are $1.60 ($2.10 for express buses); children 3 and under ride free. Exact change is required. You can purchase a weekly pass, good for unlimited local rides from Sunday to Saturday, for $22 per adult or $10 for ages 19 and under; a picture ID is required. Seniors and riders with disabilities qualify for an 80¢ fare with an MTA Golden Age, Medicare, TenneSenior, or Special Service card. Call © **615/862-5950** to register for this discount. For more information, visit **www.nashvillemta.org**.

The **Music City Circuit** is another way to navigate downtown. The Blue Circuit/Bicentennial Mall route goes to Bridgestone Arena, the Nashville Farmers Market,

Hatch Show Print, Municipal Auditorium, Ryman Auditorium, Tennessee Performing Arts Center, and the Tennessee State Museum. It runs from 6:30am to 6:30pm weekdays. The Green Circuit/Gulch goes to Cummins Station, the Country Music Hall of Fame and Museum, the Frist Center for the Visual Arts, Gulch bars and restaurants, Second Avenue, the Nashville Convention Center, and the Schermerhorn Symphony Center. It runs from 6:30am to midnight, weekdays. On Saturdays, the Green Circuit runs 11am to midnight, while the Blue Circuit runs 11am to 6pm. For more info, visit www.nashvillemta.org.

BY TAXI

For quick cab service, call **Music City Taxi** (© 615/262-0451), **Checker Cab** (© 615/256-7000), **United Cab** (© 615/228-6969), or **Yellow Cab** (© 615/256-0101). The flag-drop rate is $3; after that it's $2.10 per mile, plus $1 for each additional passenger. There is a flat-fare triangle between the airport, downtown, and Opryland. Between any two points in the triangle, the fare is set at $25 for up to four passengers.

ON FOOT

With the exception of the quaint, strollable Germantown neighborhood just north of downtown, the heart of downtown Nashville is the only area where you're likely to do much walking around. In this area, especially around lower Broadway, you can visit attractions, do some shopping, have a good meal, and even go to a club, all without having to get in your car. The suburban strips can't make that claim.

Getting Around Memphis
BY CAR

Memphis is a big sprawling city, and the best—and worst—way to get around is by car. A car is nearly indispensable for traveling between downtown and East Memphis, yet traffic congestion can make this trip take far longer than you'd expect (45 min. isn't unusual). Avenues running east-west and almost any road in East Memphis at rush hour are the most congested. Parking downtown is not usually a problem, but stay alert for tow-away zones and watch the time on your meter. Out in East Memphis, there is usually no parking problem. When driving between downtown and East Memphis, you'll usually do better to take the interstate.

CAR RENTALS   All the major car-rental companies and several independent companies have offices in Memphis. Some are located near the airport only, and some have offices near the airport and in other areas of Memphis. Be sure to leave yourself plenty of time for returning your car when you head to the airport to catch your return flight. None of the companies has an office in the airport itself, so you'll have to take a shuttle van from the car drop-off point to the airport terminal.

Major car-rental companies in Memphis include **Avis,** 2520 Rental Rd. (© 800/577-1521 or 901/345-6129; www.avis.com); **Budget Rent A Car,** 2650 Rental Rd. (© 800/527-0700; www.budget.com); **Dollar/Thrifty Auto Group,** 2600 Rental Rd. (© 800/800-4000; www.dollar.com); **Enterprise Rent-A-Car,** 2909 Airways Blvd. (© 866/799-7965 or 901/396-3736; www.enterprise.com); **Hertz,** 2560 Rental Rd. (© 800/654-3131 or 901/345-5680; www.hertz.com); and **Thrifty Car Rental,** 2680 Rental Rd. (© 877/283-0898 or 901/345-0170; www.thrifty.com).

PARKING   Parking in downtown Memphis is a lot more expensive than it used to be. There are plenty of parking lots behind the Beale Street clubs; these charge big bucks. Metered parking on downtown streets is becoming increasingly scarce; if you're lucky enough to snag a spot close to your destination, be sure to check the time limit on the meter. Downtown parking is also available in municipal and private lots and parking garages. Again, most require a stiff fee. The good news is, many of the automated parking kiosks now accept credit and debit cards for payment, eliminating the need to carry a lot of change.

In Midtown, where parking is rarely a problem, there is a free lot in Overton Square, between Madison Avenue and Monroe Avenue.

DRIVING RULES   A right turn at a red light is permitted after coming to a full stop, unless posted otherwise, but drivers must first yield to vehicles proceeding through a green light or to pedestrians in the walkway. Children under 4 years of age must be in a child's car seat or other approved child restraint when in the car.

BY BUS

The **Memphis Area Transit Authority** (**MATA**; ✆ **901/274-MATA** [6282]; www. matatransit.com) operates citywide bus service, but I do not recommend it for tourists. Public transportation here is poor and does not offer convenient connections between most hotels and tourist sites. Bus stops are indicated by green-and-white signs. For schedule information, ask a bus driver or call the MATA number above. The standard fare is $1.75, and exact change is required. Transfers from bus to bus cost 10¢, but there's no transfer fee to the trolley (see below). MATA offers a 50% discount for travelers with disabilities and senior citizens with ID cards. (**Note:** To qualify for the discounted fare, however, you need to show a Medicare card or obtain a MATA ID card by bringing two forms of identification to the MATA Customer Service Center at 444 N. Main St., open Mon–Fri 7am–7pm.)

BY TROLLEY

The **Main Street Trolley** (✆ **901/577-2640**) operates renovated 1920s trolley cars (and modern reproductions) on a circular route that includes Main Street from the Pyramid to the National Civil Rights Museum and Central Station, and then follows Riverside Drive, passing the Tennessee State Visitors Center. It's a unique way to get around the downtown area. The fare is $1.25 each way, with a special lunch-hour rate of 50¢ between 11am and 1:30pm. An all-day pass is $3.50; exact change is required, and passengers may board at any of the 20 stations along Main Street. Trolleys are wheelchair accessible.

BY TAXI

For quick cab service, call **Checker/Yellow Cab** (✆ **901/577-7777**) or **City Wide Cab Company** (✆ **901/324-4202**), or have your hotel or motel call one for you. The first mile is $3.80; after that, it's $1.80 per mile. Each additional passenger is $1 extra. There is also a $2 gas surcharge.

ON FOOT

Downtown Memphis is walkable, though the only areas that attract many visitors are the Beale Street area and Main Street from the National Civil Rights Museum north to the Pyramid. The rest of the city is not walkable.

SUSTAINABLE TOURISM

Being environmentally conscious isn't the main concern of most music fans visiting Nashville and Memphis, yet Tennessee has begun taking steps to change that. After all, it is the home state of former U.S. Vice President Al Gore, whose bestseller, *Earth in the Balance,* launched intense scrutiny of global warming.

Increasingly, hotel chains in Nashville and Memphis are trying to be more environmentally friendly, by giving guests the option of requesting fresh linens and towels on a nightly basis. For example, the **Hutton Hotel,** in Nashville, is a pioneer in sustainable luxury. See p. 118.

Perhaps most noticeably, green living begins with what people eat. Restaurants such as Nashville's **tayst** (p. 73)—the city's first green-certified eatery—are drawing kudos for their efforts and encouraging other restaurants to take similar measures.

In Memphis, **Project Green Fork** rewards restaurateurs for composting and recycling materials and for using environmentally friendly, nontoxic cleaning products; for reducing water and energy consumption; and for properly controlling their pollution output.

In both Nashville and Memphis, chefs and restaurant owners are beginning to emphasize organic and/or locally grown and raised produce, cheese, and meat sources for their menu items. Both cities also have vibrant farmers' markets, allowing residents and tourists alike to shop for the fresh foods and ingredients.

In the pork-barbecue-loving cities of Nashville and Memphis, it's not always easy to avoid eating greasy, meat-heavy meals. But the situation is light-years better than it used to be. An abundance of ethnic eateries can be found in both cities, and vegetarian options at mainstream restaurants are much more common than they were, say, a decade ago.

Increasingly, coffeehouses such as Bongo Java in Nashville feature fair-trade coffees in their own, distinctive blends.

SPECIAL-INTEREST TRIPS & ESCORTED GENERAL-INTEREST TOURS

Special-Interest Trips

Most large tour operators, including **Sweet Magnolia** (see below, under "Escorted General-Interest Tours"), tailor some of their trip offerings to music guests. Others have options for Civil War buffs, including tours of historic battlegrounds and plantations. African-American history tours include sites related to the American Civil Rights movement.

Food Trips

If you're more interested in barbecue and turnip greens cooked in "pot likker" than you are in Tennessee's music attractions, you probably already know about the **Southern Foodways Alliance,** P.O. Box 1848, University, MS 38677 (© **662/915-5993;** www.southernfoodways.com). Based at the University of Mississippi in Oxford, about an hour's drive south of Memphis, the fun-loving and highly regarded nonprofit organization specializes in culinary tourism. Special events, field trips, and symposia often sell out, so check their website for special activities that may be scheduled when you plan to visit the area.

Escorted General-Interest Tours

The convention and visitors bureaus' websites in Nashville and Memphis allow tourists to book vacation packages that include hotel and attractions options. Packages vary by theme and activity and can be customized online, allowing you to book additional nights and add attractions to your itinerary.

Sweet Magnolia Tours (www.sweetmagnoliatours.com) is one of the few tour operators in Tennessee with offices in both Nashville and Memphis. In 2008, the company began offering specific vacation packages that combine the best of both cities. The land-only packages include hotel and attractions. For more information, call ✆ **800/235-5295** or 615/646-0030 in Nashville, and ✆ **901/369-9838** in Memphis.

For European travelers interested in touring Tennessee as well as Atlanta and New Orleans, check out the website www.deep-south-usa.de.

For more information on escorted general-interest tours, including questions to ask before booking your trip, see www.frommers.com/planning.

FAST FACTS: NASHVILLE & MEMPHIS

African-American Travelers   Because Tennessee is so rich in African-American heritage, the convention and visitors bureaus in both cities offer free, specialized resources for travelers in black history and multicultural heritage.

For general information, contact the Nashville Black Chamber of Commerce (✆ **615/876-9634**), or the Nashville Area Hispanic Chamber of Commerce (✆ **615/216-5737**).

For further suggestions and direction, contact **Authentic Tours of Historic Black Nashville and Beyond** (✆ 615/299-5626; www.tnvacations.com). Trained historians offer sightseeing tours and act as step-on guides.

Memphis visitors interested in obtaining a directory of African-American businesses can contact the **Black Business Association** (✆ **901/526-9300;** http://bbamemphis.blogspot.com).

Area Codes   The telephone area code in Nashville is **615.** The area code in Memphis is **901.**

Automobile Organizations   Motor clubs will supply maps, suggested routes, guidebooks, accident and bail-bond insurance, and emergency road service. The **American Automobile Association (AAA)** is the major auto club in the United States. If you belong to a motor club in your home country, inquire about AAA reciprocity before you leave. You may be able to join AAA even if you're not a member of a reciprocal club; to inquire, call AAA at ✆ **800/222-4357** (www.aaa.com), which is also their nationwide emergency road service number.

Business Hours   In **Nashville,** banks are generally open Monday to Thursday 9am to 4pm, Friday 9am to 5 or 6pm, and Saturday morning. Office hours are usually Monday to Friday 8:30am to 5pm. In general, stores in downtown Nashville are open Monday to Saturday 10am to 6pm. Shops in suburban Nashville malls are generally open Monday to Saturday 10am to 9pm and Sunday 1 to 6pm. Bars in Nashville are frequently open all day and are allowed to stay open daily until 3am, but might close between 1 and 3am.

In **Memphis,** banks are generally open Monday to Thursday 8:30am to 4pm, with later hours on Friday. Office hours are usually Monday to Friday 8:30am to 5pm. In general, stores located in downtown Memphis are open Monday to Saturday 10am to 5:30pm.

Shops in suburban Memphis malls are generally open Monday to Saturday 10am to 9pm and on Sunday 1 to 5 or 6pm. Bars are allowed to stay open until 3am, but may close between 1 and 3am.

Customs **What You Can Bring into the U.S.** Every visitor more than 21 years of age may bring in, free of duty, the following: (1) 34 ounces of wine or hard liquor; (2) 200 cigarettes, 100 cigars (but not from Cuba), or 3 pounds of smoking tobacco; and (3) $100 worth of gifts. These exemptions are offered to travelers who spend at least 72 hours in the United States and who have not claimed them within the preceding 6 months. It is forbidden to bring into the country almost any meat products (including canned, fresh, and dried meat products such as bullion, soup mixes, and such). Generally, condiments including vinegars, oils, spices, coffee, tea, and some cheeses and baked goods are permitted. Avoid rice products, as rice can often harbor insects. Bringing fruits and vegetables is not advised, though not prohibited. Customs will allow produce depending on where you got it and where you're going after you arrive in the U.S. International visitors may carry in or out up to $10,000 in U.S. or foreign currency with no formalities; larger sums must be declared to U.S. Customs on entering or leaving, which includes filing form CM 4790. For details regarding U.S. Customs and Border Protection, consult your nearest U.S. embassy or consulate, or **U.S. Customs** (www.cbp.gov).

What You Can Take Home from the U.S. For information on what you're allowed to bring home, contact one of the following agencies:

Canadian Citizens: Canada Border Services Agency (© **800/461-9999** in Canada, or 204/983-3500; www.cbsa-asfc.gc.ca).

U.K. Citizens: HM Revenue & Customs (© **0845/010-9000,** or 020/8929-0152 from outside the U.K.; www.hmce.gov.uk).

Australian Citizens: Australian Customs and Border Protection Service (© **1300/363-263;** www.customs.gov.au).

New Zealand Citizens: New Zealand Customs Service, The Customhouse, 17–21 Whitmore St., Box 2218, Wellington (© **04/473-6099** or 0800/428-786; www.customs. govt.nz).

Disabled Travelers Most disabilities shouldn't stop anyone from traveling in the U.S. There are more options and resources out there than ever before.

Almost all hotels and motels in Nashville offer wheelchair-accessible accommodations, but when making reservations be sure to ask. Additionally, the MTA public bus system in Nashville either has wheelchair-accessible regular vehicles or offers special transportation services for travelers with disabilities. To find out more about special services, call **Access Ride** (© **615/880-3970**).

The **Disability Information Office,** Howard Office Building (© **615/862-6492**), provides a referral and information service for visitors with disabilities. The *Nashville City Vacation Guide,* available through either this office or the Nashville Convention & Visitors Bureau, includes information on accessibility of restaurants, hotels, attractions, shops, and nightlife around Nashville. Similarly, the **Memphis Center for Independent Living,** 1633 Madison Ave. (© **901/726-6404;** www.mcil.org), is a consumer-oriented organization that helps people with disabilities.

Wheelchair Getaways of Memphis, Tennessee (© **800/642-2042;** www.wheelchair-getaways.com), rents specialized vans with wheelchair lifts and other features for those with disabilities.

Doctors If you need a doctor in **Nashville,** call 3rd and Church Healthcare at © **255-7902** or Tri-Star Medline at © **800/265-8624** or 615/342-1919; or contact the Vanderbilt Medical Group Physician Referral Service at © **615/322-3000.**

In **Memphis,** call **Methodist Healthcare,** at 1211 Union Ave. ((C) **800/288-5000**), or the **Regional Medical Center/Elvis Presley Trauma Center,** at 877 Jefferson Ave. ((C) **901/545-7100**).

If you have dental problems in either city, a nationwide referral service, known as 1-800-DENTIST ((C) **336-8478**), will provide the name of a nearby dentist.

You may want to ask the concierge at your hotel to recommend a local doctor—even his or her own. This will probably yield a better recommendation than any toll-free number would.

You can also try the emergency room at a local hospital. Many hospitals also have walk-in clinics for emergency cases that are not life threatening; you may not get immediate attention, but you won't pay the high price of an ER visit.

If you suffer from a chronic illness, consult your doctor before your departure. Pack prescription medications in your carry-on luggage, and carry them in their original containers, with pharmacy labels—otherwise they won't make it through airport security. Visitors from outside the U.S. should carry generic names of prescription drugs. For U.S. travelers, most reliable healthcare plans provide coverage if you get sick away from home. Foreign visitors may have to pay all medical costs upfront and be reimbursed later.

Drinking Laws   The legal age for purchase and consumption of alcoholic beverages is 21; proof of age is required and often requested at bars, nightclubs, and restaurants, so it's always a good idea to bring ID when you go out.

Bars are allowed to stay open until 3am every day. Beer can be purchased at convenience, grocery, or package stores, but wine and liquor are sold through package stores only.

Do not carry open containers of alcohol in your car or any public area that isn't zoned for alcohol consumption. The police can fine you on the spot. Don't even think about driving while intoxicated.

Driving Rules   See "Getting Around," p. 255.

Electricity   Like Canada, the United States uses 110 to 120 volts AC (60 cycles), compared to 220 to 240 volts AC (50 cycles) in most of Europe, Australia, and New Zealand. Downward converters that change 220 to 240 volts to 110 to 120 volts are difficult to find in the United States, so bring one with you.

Embassies & Consulates   All embassies are located in the nation's capital, Washington, D.C. Some consulates are located in major U.S. cities, and most nations have a mission to the United Nations in New York City. If your country isn't listed below, call for directory information in Washington, D.C. ((C) **202/555-1212**) or check **www.embassy. org/embassies**.

The embassy of **Australia** is at 1601 Massachusetts Ave. NW, Washington, DC 20036 ((C) **202/797-3000;** www.usa.embassy.gov.au).

The embassy of **Canada** is at 501 Pennsylvania Ave. NW, Washington, DC 20001 ((C) **202/682-1740;** www.canadianembassy.org). Other Canadian consulates are in Buffalo (New York), Detroit, Los Angeles, New York, and Seattle.

The embassy of **Ireland** is at 2234 Massachusetts Ave. NW, Washington, DC 20008 ((C) **202/462-3939;** www.embassyofireland.org). Irish consulates are in Boston, Chicago, New York, San Francisco, and other cities. See website for complete listing.

The embassy of **New Zealand** is at 37 Observatory Circle NW, Washington, DC 20008 ((C) **202/328-4800;** www.nzembassy.com). New Zealand consulates are in Los Angeles, Salt Lake City, San Francisco, and Seattle.

The embassy of the **United Kingdom** is at 3100 Massachusetts Ave. NW, Washington, DC 20008 ((C) **202/588-7800;** ukinusa.fco.gov.uk). Other British consulates are in Atlanta, Boston, Chicago, Cleveland, Houston, Los Angeles, New York, San Francisco, and Seattle.

Emergencies   Dial 🕻 **911** for fire, police, emergency, or ambulance. If you get into desperate straits, call **Travelers' Aid** of the Nashville Union Mission, 639 Lafayette St. (🕻 **615/255-2475** or 615/780-9471). It's primarily a mission that helps destitute people, but if you need help in making phone calls or getting home, they might be able to help.

Gasoline (Petrol)   At press time, the average price for a gallon of gasoline in Tennessee was about $3.75. Taxes are already included in the printed price. One U.S. gallon equals 3.8 liters or .85 imperial gallons.

Holidays   Banks, government offices, post offices, and many stores, restaurants, and museums are closed on the following legal national holidays: January 1 (New Year's Day), the third Monday in January (Martin Luther King, Jr., Day), the third Monday in February (Presidents' Day), the last Monday in May (Memorial Day), July 4 (Independence Day), the first Monday in September (Labor Day), the second Monday in October (Columbus Day), November 11 (Veterans Day/Armistice Day), the fourth Thursday in November (Thanksgiving Day), and December 25 (Christmas). The Tuesday after the first Monday in November is Election Day, a federal government holiday in presidential-election years (held every 4 years, and next in 2012).

For more information on holidays see "Calendar of Events," p. 17 and p. 149.

Hospitals   **Nashville:** The following hospitals offer emergency medical treatment: **St. Thomas Hospital,** 4220 Harding Rd. (🕻 **615/222-2111**), and **Vanderbilt University Medical Center,** 1211 Medical Center Dr., in the Vanderbilt area (🕻 **615/322-5000**).

Memphis: Major hospitals in the downtown/Midtown areas are **Methodist Healthcare,** at 1211 Union Ave. (🕻 **901/516-7000**), and the **Regional Medical Center/Elvis Presley Trauma Center,** at 877 Jefferson Ave. (🕻 **901/545-7100**).

Insurance   For information on traveler's insurance, trip-cancellation insurance, and medical insurance while traveling, please visit www.frommers.com/planning.

Internet Access   Most coffee shops and hotels, along with many restaurants in Nashville and Memphis, have free Wi-Fi access. Internet access is also available (along with computers) at public-library branches and FedEx Office locations.

Nashville was at the forefront of the connectivity trend a few years ago, when its Centennial Park, in the city's affluent West End, became one of the first in the nation to offer free Wi-Fi.

Legal Aid   If you are "pulled over" for a minor infraction (such as speeding), never attempt to pay the fine directly to a police officer; this could be construed as attempted bribery, a much more serious crime. Pay fines by mail, or directly into the hands of the clerk of the court. If accused of a more serious offense, say and do nothing before consulting a lawyer. Here the burden is on the state to prove a person's guilt beyond a reasonable doubt, and everyone has the right to remain silent, whether he or she is suspected of a crime or actually arrested. Once arrested, a person can make one telephone call to a party of his or her choice. International visitors should call their embassy or consulate.

LGBT Travelers   While lacking the vibrancy of many larger U.S. cities, both Nashville and Memphis have much to offer gay travelers. Church Street near downtown is the most well-known gay district in Nashville. Nashville has several gay and lesbian newspapers, including the entertainment weekly *Xenogeny* (🕻 **615/831-1806**).

In Memphis, volunteers staff the **Memphis Gay and Lesbian Community Center,** 892 S. Cooper (🕻 **901/278-6422;** www.mglcc.org), nightly. The Cooper-Young neighborhood is widely regarded as the most gay-friendly area of town. For more information, look for the Memphis *Triangle Journal*, a free weekly newspaper that's available at local bookstores, libraries, and other locations.

Mail   At press time, domestic postage rates were 28¢ for a postcard and 44¢ for a letter. For international mail, a first-class letter of up to 1 ounce costs 98¢ (75¢ to Canada and

79¢ to Mexico); a first-class postcard costs the same as a letter. For more information go to **www.usps.com**.

If you aren't sure what your address will be in the United States, mail can be sent to you, in your name, c/o General Delivery at the main post office of the city or region where you expect to be. (Call ✆ **800/275-8777** for information on the nearest post office.) The addressee must pick up mail in person and must produce proof of identity (driver's license, passport, and the like). Most post offices will hold your mail for up to 1 month, and are open Monday to Friday from 8am to 6pm, and Saturday from 9am to 3pm.

Always include zip codes when mailing items in the U.S. If you don't know your zip code, visit www.usps.com/zip4.

Medical Requirements   Unless you're arriving from an area known to be suffering from an epidemic (particularly cholera or yellow fever), inoculations or vaccinations are not required for entry into the United States.

Money & Costs   It's always advisable to bring money in a variety of forms on a vacation: a mix of cash and credit cards. You should also exchange enough petty cash to cover airport incidentals, tipping, and transportation to your hotel before you leave home, or withdraw money upon arrival at an airport ATM.

Nashville and Memphis are moderately priced compared with larger U.S. cities such as New York and Atlanta. While rapid growth and developments caused costs for downtown parking, hotels, and restaurants to spike in both cities in recent years, the recent U.S. economic recession has led many of these destinations to offer discounted rates or added perks to entice travelers.

ATMs are prevalent in Nashville and Memphis. Debit cards are widely accepted.

THE VALUE OF THE U.S. DOLLAR VS. OTHER POPULAR CURRENCIES

US$	C$	£	€	A$	NZ$
1.00	1.00	0.64	0.76	0.94	1.20

Frommer's lists exact prices in the local currency. The currency conversions quoted above were correct at press time. However, rates fluctuate, so before departing consult a currency exchange website such as **www.oanda.com/convert/classic** to check up-to-the-minute rates.

WHAT THINGS COST IN NASHVILLE & MEMPHIS	US$
Cup of coffee	1.50
Taxi from airport to downtown	25.00–35.00
Moderate 3-course dinner for one, without alcohol	30.00
A night in a moderately priced hotel room	150.00
Self-guided tour of the Ryman Auditorium	12.95
Admission to Country Music Hall of Fame and Museum, and Historic RCA Studio B	33.00
Ticket to the *Grand Ole Opry*	28.00–53.00
Graceland Mansion Tour	31.00
Tootsie's Orchid Lounge and Nashville's honky-tonks	Never a cover

Newspapers & Magazines   The *Tennessean* is Nashville's morning daily and Sunday newspaper. The alternative weekly is the *Nashville Scene.*

The *Commercial Appeal* is Memphis's daily newspaper. The arts-and-entertainment weekly is the *Memphis Flyer.*

Passports   Virtually every air traveler entering the U.S. is required to show a passport. All persons, including U.S. citizens, traveling by air between the United States and Canada, Mexico, Central and South America, the Caribbean, and Bermuda are required to present a valid passport. *Note:* U.S. and Canadian citizens entering the U.S. at land and sea ports of entry from within the Western Hemisphere must now also present a passport or other documents compliant with the Western Hemisphere Travel Initiative (WHTI; see www.getyouhome.gov for details). Children 15 and under may continue entering with only a U.S. birth certificate, or other proof of U.S. citizenship.

Police   For police emergencies, phone ⓒ **911.**

Safety   **Nashville** is a friendly city where travelers can feel safe both downtown and in outlying neighborhoods. Cautious tourists may want to be aware that the nightlife along Broadway downtown can become rowdy after dark.

Although it's full of friendly people, **Memphis** also has a serious crime problem, with rampant gang activity and one of the highest violent crime rates in the U.S. Although tourists aren't necessarily targeted, neither are they immune. Avoid walking or driving in unpopulated or inner-city areas alone, especially after dark. Be mindful of your surroundings, and take prudent precautions to avoid becoming a victim, such as keeping valuables hidden and your car locked.

Smoking   Smoking is banned from most workplaces and restaurants (outdoor patios are an exception), but smoking is allowed in over-21 venues including bars, and in certain hotel and motel rooms.

Taxes   The United States has no value-added tax (VAT) or other indirect tax at the national level. Every state, county, and city may levy its own local tax on all purchases, including hotel and restaurant checks and airline tickets. These taxes will not appear on price tags.

Nashville: In Davidson County, the combined state and local sales tax is 9.25%. This tax applies to goods as well as all recreation, entertainment, and amusements. However, in the case of services, the tax is often already included in the admission price or cost of a ticket. The Nashville hotel and motel room tax is 5%, which when added to the 9.25% makes for a total hotel room tax of 15.25% plus $2 city tax, per night. Car-rental taxes total 13.25%.

Memphis: The state sales tax is 9.25%. An additional room tax of 6.7% on top of the state sales tax brings the total hotel-room tax to a whopping 15.95%.

Telephones   Many convenience groceries and packaging services sell **prepaid calling cards** in denominations up to $50; for international visitors these can be the least expensive way to call home. Many public pay phones at airports now accept American Express, MasterCard, and Visa credit cards. **Local calls** made from pay phones in most locales cost either 25¢ or 35¢. Most long-distance and international calls can be dialed directly from any phone. **For calls within the United States and to Canada,** dial 1 followed by the area code and the seven-digit number. **For other international calls,** dial 011 followed by the country code, the city code, and the number you are calling.

Calls to area codes **800, 888, 877,** and **866** are toll-free. However, calls to area codes **700** and **900** (chat lines, bulletin boards, "dating" services, and so on) can be very expensive—usually a charge of 95¢ to $3 or more per minute, and they sometimes have minimum charges that can run as high as $15 or more.

For **reversed-charge or collect calls,** and for person-to-person calls, dial the number 0, then the area code and number; an operator will come on the line, and you should specify whether you are calling collect, person-to-person, or both. If your operator-assisted call is international, ask for the overseas operator.

For **local directory assistance** ("information"), dial 411; for long-distance information, dial 1, then the appropriate area code and 555-1212.

Time   Nashville and Memphis are in the Central Time Zone—and observe Central Standard Time (CST) or Central Daylight Time (CDT), depending on the time of year—making it 2 hours ahead of the West Coast and 1 hour behind the East Coast.

Daylight saving time is in effect from 2am on the second Sunday in March to 2am on the first Sunday in November. Daylight saving time moves the clock 1 hour ahead of standard time.

Tipping   In hotels, tip **bellhops** at least $1 per bag ($2–$3 if you have a lot of luggage) and tip the **chamber staff** $1 to $2 per day (more if you've left a disaster area for him or her to clean up). Tip the **doorman** or **concierge** only if he or she has provided you with some specific service (for example, calling a cab for you or obtaining difficult-to-get theater tickets). Tip the **valet-parking attendant** $1 every time you get your car.

In restaurants, bars, and nightclubs, tip **service staff** and **bartenders** 15% to 20% of the check, tip **checkroom attendants** $1 per garment, and tip **valet-parking attendants** $1 per vehicle.

As for other service personnel, tip **cab drivers** 15% of the fare; tip **skycaps** at airports at least $1 per bag ($2–$3 if you have a lot of luggage); and tip **hairdressers** and **barbers** 15% to 20%.

Toilets   You won't find public toilets or "restrooms" on the streets in most U.S. cities, but they can be found in hotel lobbies, bars, restaurants, museums, department stores, railway and bus stations, and service stations. Large hotels and fast-food restaurants are often the best bet for clean facilities. Restaurants and bars in resorts or heavily visited areas may reserve their restrooms for patrons.

Visas   The U.S. State Department has a **Visa Waiver Program (VWP)** allowing citizens of the following countries to enter the United States without a visa for stays of up to 90 days: Andorra, Australia, Austria, Belgium, Brunei, Czech Republic, Denmark, Estonia, Finland, France, Germany, Greece, Hungary, Iceland, Ireland, Italy, Japan, Latvia, Liechtenstein, Lithuania, Luxembourg, Malta, Monaco, the Netherlands, New Zealand, Norway, Portugal, San Marino, Singapore, Slovakia, Slovenia, South Korea, Spain, Sweden, Switzerland, and the United Kingdom. (**Note:** This list was accurate at press time; for the most up-to-date list of countries in the VWP, consult http://travel.state.gov/visa.) Even though a visa isn't necessary, in an effort to help U.S. officials check travelers against terror watch lists before they arrive at U.S. borders, visitors from VWP countries must register online through the Electronic System for Travel Authorization (ESTA) before boarding a plane or a boat to the U.S. Travelers must complete an electronic application providing basic personal and travel eligibility information. The Department of Homeland Security recommends filling out the form at least 3 days before traveling. Authorizations will be valid for up to 2 years or until the traveler's passport expires, whichever comes first. Currently, there is a US$14 fee for the online application. Existing ESTA registrations remain valid through their expiration dates. **Note:** Any passport issued on or after October 26, 2006, by a VWP country must be an **e-Passport** for VWP travelers to be eligible to enter the U.S. without a visa. Citizens of these nations also need to present a round-trip air or cruise ticket upon arrival. E-Passports contain computer chips capable of storing biometric information, such as the required digital photograph of the holder. If your passport doesn't have this feature, you can still travel without a visa if the valid passport was issued before October 26, 2005, and includes a machine-readable zone; or if the valid passport was issued between October 26, 2005, and October 25, 2006, and includes a digital photograph. For more information, go to http://travel.state.gov/visa. Canadian citizens may enter the United States without visas, but will need to show passports and proof of residence.

Citizens of all other countries must have (1) a valid passport that expires at least 6 months later than the scheduled end of their visit to the U.S.; and (2) a tourist visa.

For information about U.S. Visas go to **http://travel.state.gov** and click on "Visas." Or go to one of the following websites:

Australian citizens can obtain up-to-date visa information from the **U.S. Embassy Canberra,** Moonah Place, Yarralumla, ACT 2600 (© **02/6214-5600**), or by checking the U.S. Diplomatic Mission's website at **http://canberra.usembassy.gov/visas.html**.

British subjects can obtain up-to-date visa information by calling the **U.S. Embassy Visa Information Line** (© **09042-450-100** from within the U.K. at £1.20 per minute; or © **866/382-3589** from within the U.S. at a flat rate of $16, payable by credit card only) or by visiting the "Visas to the U.S." section of the American Embassy London's website at **http://london.usembassy.gov/visas.html**.

Irish citizens can obtain up-to-date visa information through the **U.S. Embassy Dublin,** 42 Elgin Rd., Ballsbridge, Dublin 4 (© **1580-47-VISA** [8472] from within the Republic of Ireland at €2.40 per minute; **http://dublin.usembassy.gov**).

Citizens of **New Zealand** can obtain up-to-date visa information by contacting the **U.S. Embassy New Zealand,** 29 Fitzherbert Terrace, Thorndon, Wellington (© **644/462-6000; http://newzealand.usembassy.gov**).

Visitor Information **Nashville:** On the baggage-claim level of Nashville International Airport, you'll find the **Airport Welcome Center** (© **615/275-1675;** open daily 6:30am–midnight), where you can pick up brochures, maps, and bus information, and get answers to any questions you may have about touring the city. In downtown Nashville, you'll find the **Nashville Convention & Visitors Bureau Visitors Center,** Fifth Avenue and Broadway (© **800/657-6910** or 615/780-9401), the main source of information on the city and surrounding areas. The information center (open daily during daylight hours) offers free Wi-Fi service and is located at the base of the radio tower of the Bridgestone Arena. Signs on interstate highways around the downtown area will direct you to the arena. Information is also available from the main office of the **Chamber of Commerce/Nashville Convention & Visitors Bureau,** in the lower level of the US Bank building at the corner of Fourth Avenue North and Commerce (© **615/259-4730;** open Mon–Fri 8am–5pm).

Memphis: At the airport, you'll find information boards with telephone numbers for contacting hotels and numbers for other helpful services. The city's main visitor information center, located downtown at the base of Jefferson Street, is the **Tennessee State Welcome Center,** 119 N. Riverside Dr. (© **901/543-6757**). It's open daily 24 hours but staffed only between 8am and 7pm (until 8pm in the summer months).

Other visitor centers are located off I-40, just east of the Memphis city limits, and at Elvis Presley Boulevard just north of Graceland.

Regional Information: For information on the state of Tennessee, contact the **Tennessee Department of Tourism Development,** P.O. Box 23170, Nashville, TN 37202 (© **615/741-2158**).

For European travelers planning a visit to Tennessee, the following countries have region-specific information available: **United Kingdom** (© **011 44-1462440007;** www.deep-south-usa.com); for **Germany, Austria, and Switzerland** (© **011 49 521-9860415;** www.tennesseetourism.de; and www.deep-south-usa.de).

For customized tours for visitors from overseas, contact **Germania Travel Tour Guide** (© **901/794-0347;** www.germaniatraveltourguide.com).

Index

See also Accommodations and Restaurant indexes, below.

General Index

A

Restaurants— Memphis & Environs

NOTES